The True Book of Sam Clear Water
Wisdom from Walden-San

By Jeff Glauner, PhD

The True Book of Sam Clear Water: Wisdom from Walden-San
Copyright © 2009 by Jeff Glauner
Manufactured and published in the United States of America
March 2009
Distributed by Amazon.com
ISBN: 144210788X

Author Web Site: http://captain.park.edu/jglauner/
Author Email: jeff.glauner@park.edu
Comments, critiques, and questions are welcome.

Dedication

Authors of original works generally thank others; but I have been hermitic, sharing little except a few passages I recited to my wife Carol because I trust only her with them. This book is dedicated first to her, my second self, and then to dear old Mom, a message in a bottle which never reaches a sandy shore but which, from across the wave, lights the horizon with its glow.

JG

Foreword

This is *my* book. Its contents seemed gloriously true when I wrote them but, later, might prove profoundly false; and I embrace both evaluations because that is the stately nature of the age-old march toward philosophical accuracy. Some who read what I have written will call me heretic, an iconoclast bursting cherished old wine skins with my "new wine" of Imagination. But I am no vintner; I am a thresher. I spread ripened wheat on the threshing floor and summon ox and ass to tread it. Then, with joyful exuberance, I toss it into the air, inviting the wind to carry it away. The chaff accepts my invitation. The threshed wheat falls back to the floor where I read it like wisdom, but all I have done is what seekers of truth have done forever. I am, in Emerson's words, "a man thinking" occupying the philosopher's chair because I refuse to resist the temptation to pass on whatever seeming truth I separate from its chaff to anyone who listens; and, sometimes, when no one listens but ox and ass, I speak to ox and ass.

My book is neither fact nor fiction but contains substantial portions of each. Characters portrayed other than my kin and a few politically and socially recognizable figures are the products of my imagination. I have tried to treat real persons who enter my book with whatever dignity and respect the truth will tolerate. Politicians and others who make themselves public figures through their words and their deeds are fair game for my discussion. Those who enter my book because they are family are good people who I would never offend on purpose and I love them dearly. I omit their names to save them any embarrassment my portrayals might cause.

Sometimes, I repeat clever lines from other texts without citing their sources. Writers of *primary* works of philosophy often do so. In general, these lines are so well known that it would insult most readers' intelligence for me to cite the sources. I make it a habit to mark such passages with quotation marks to indicate that they are not original to me.

Sam Clear Water

To the Reader

The year for the writing of my book was 2007. I completed the first draft on December 31st of that year and immediately fell ill. 2008 was a year of frustration and pain during which I found it impossible to do much more than exist, let alone face the ordeals of editing and publication. Finally, 2009 dawned like resurrection day, and I am well while the world is sicker than I was before. The world in its illness and I in wellness are, however, brimming with hope.

I was surprised when I read my book again this January that it still seemed fresh as if it were written, not for 2007, but for whatever future is beyond today. Much has changed. Senator Obama is President Obama and Senator Clinton is Secretary of State Clinton and Senator Biden is Vice President Biden. And now the hot issue is not the Iraq war, but world-wide recession sliding toward depression which seems to be the most acute problem but by no means the most dangerous.

I assure you with fingers crossed behind my back like a kindly grandfather that all of this will pass and will be supplanted by the next generation of evils which we will dismantle in their turn. The book you are reading is the beginning of that reassurance.

The True Book of Sam Clear Water
Wisdom from Walden-San
Volume 1: *The New Moon*

Advice from Yasmin Clear Water's Hawaiian Auntie on How to Read this Book:

Tinka dis book like Japanee rice ball. Firs' bite jus' white sticky rice. Hawaii bruddah say it so good it break da mouph. Udda guy need take mo' bites and get to da ume. Den he like it, too! Yeah! No?!

January 1 (*A Note from the Scribe*): Who is Sam Clear Water?
        Sam Clear Water has been my friend and mentor for most of my adult life; and, yet, he is more. He is a scholar, a philosopher, a doubter, a father, a benevolent host, a rootless pilgrim. He is everyman and he is "Nobody." He understands, before I do, everything that I learn to understand. When I tell him my dreams, he interprets them. Then he gives me new dreams. When I forget, he remembers. He waits to tell me what I want to know until I have forgotten that I wanted to know it. When I am sad, he is happy—a born laugher at tragedy and comedy alike. When I am happy, he smiles a little—that is all.
        I don't have any idea where he came from. I first met him at a Kansas City Chiefs preseason football game right after I was doused with beer by a drunken fan. Sam was sitting nearby and stopped my good right fist from getting me thrown into jail. Then he laughed as I sulked. I met him often after that. Mostly, I ignored him. I seldom invited him, but he followed me through midlife and my delayed higher education, through years of teaching high school, then college, then high school again, then college again. Now, finally, I have reached retirement, having accomplished little, having gained from Sam a vast reservoir of potential. "Potential for what?" you might ask. In answer, I can point to this book. Sam suggested it. I declined because I am not wise enough. What small wisdom I have is borrowed from books and from life and from a fortunate nativity. I own none of it; and, when I die, it should be returned to its rightful owners or, simply, molder in the grave with my body. But Sam suggested that I write this book over and over throughout my busy life of teaching and exhorting and, largely, wasting away my years. Until now! Weary of his entreaties, I turned and I said, "Sam, you are unbearable! If you want such a book written, write it yourself!"
        With a self-satisfied "Harrumph!" I turned to leave him. I thought, surely, I had heard the last of it, but he stopped me at the door with a new mandate.
        The book you are reading is not my book; it is Sam's book. He calls me his "Scribe." As such, I intervene at times. As wise as Sam is, he's no editor. He can't spell and never organizes anything coherently. Thus, I'm left with the impossible task of sluicing up his slaughtered text, left bloody and fly-specked and

all fishy smelling on the cutting board. At least, my mundane task makes me *feel* useful.

I truly love that old sprite!

January 2: *Ego Sum, Ergo . . . ?!*

I am Sam Clear Water. Oddly enough, on this second day of the new year, I am well pleased. Indeed, I am overjoyed. Totally unjustified, my joy has nothing to do with the well-being of the planet. *It*, as usual, is in a battle with humanity for its very survival. Nor have I gained any particular political power, and my bank account is still wanting.

My happiness is about (of all things!) football—perhaps, the most degenerate game invented by humanity. Unless it be war itself, I can think of no pastime more futile. However, as an unrepentant gridiron addict, I am happy because, yesterday in the Fiesta Bowl, a team belonging to a small university from my mountains beat up on a national power-house team belonging to a big university from someone else's mountains. Somehow, violence doesn't seem like such a bad thing when one has ties to the winning side.

But happiness is happiness! I'm not ashamed of any form of happiness, especially, at the beginning of a new year when we are forced by the media, family, friends, colleagues, the IRS, to look back over the previous year. What a sad custom! Indeed, I recant! Thinking back is far more futile than football. More destructive! In fact, football is not futile at all. It is a game of "I will!" Thinking back is a game of "I was." Opposites: "I will!" and "I was."

Oh, ye with minds to think, think only, "I will!" In nothing else do you have choice, only chance. In "I will!" you shake a defiant fist at a stubborn cosmos and create a new world—manifold, born out of simple. And yet a fist having four fingers and an opposable thumb is no "simple." It, along with the mind of a thinking person, is manifold.

January 3: Death Certain.

I've heard bells tolling the death knell. A year has died, but that's of little importance. I've been ready for it since July, and we have a new year that is far more promising. Two noteworthy deaths have recently been announced. First is a beloved (though I don't remember him being as beloved before as he is now) former President of a free and democratic land. He lived to 93 and died of natural causes. Second is a brutal dictator. He was hanged by a tribunal of the people he oppressed and murdered. The first ended a war that killed hundreds of thousands. The second was the excuse for a war that is killing hundreds of thousands. Why am I happy with the first and sad about the second? Is it because a dark cloud loomed over the hanging?

January 4: Native Generosity.

My 3-year-old grandson (grandchild #7) gave me a gift today. It was a kindness I had not expected. As I rose from lunch and started to stack my dishes in the sink, I picked up the little boy's plate with which I thought he was finished. He was, after all, away from the table playing with his toy firehouse. I made the comment that I might eat some of his unconsumed Vienna sausages. He looked up and informed me that he was not finished eating. I put the plate back down, finished stacking the dishes (except for his), put on my coat and hat, and headed out the door bound for my afternoon's work at the office. Right behind me, I heard the slap, slap, slap, of small feet and, "Papa, Papa!" There he was, holding up toward me in his tiny hand, one of his links of sausage, slightly squashed. I took a bite. He smiled happily and returned, eating the rest of the link, to his plate. It was nice of him.

January 5: The Oxymoron of "Imagined Faith."

Wittgenstein would call it nonsense, and it is if it is to be stated as part of a logical proposition. There is nothing logical about faith—nothing even reasonable. Faith is, as Paul says, "the evidence of things hoped for . . ." but not experienced. Nothing empirical! Nothing rational! However, intelligence can be applied both to the empirical and the metaphysical. Indeed, intelligence can be the glue between them.

I say glue, because they can never be one, only two working together: logic and faith: there-in is infinity. Infinity demands infinite power as an engine.

Intelligence denies Jehovah and Allah and all other such immortals because there is no empirical or rational evidence for such beings. Also, in our more cogent moments, we intuit that such anthropomorphic monstrosities would not be a good idea (e.g., an all-wise god who creates evil, creates man knowing that he will succumb to evil, and punishes him for doing so. Jehovah, himself, needs a course in logic).

But an infinite power? A prime mover? Because a physics of our bounded existence doesn't account for a lack of boundaries (even astronomers speak of "the" cosmos as if it has walls), we can posit another physics which applies to infinity (we see it darkly with Einstein and relativity and 25,000 deaths after two atomic blasts in WWII Japan). We cannot assume logically or empirically that the infinite power of the cosmos is a god, certainly not that such a god would be benevolent; but something must fill the void, and why not God? Why not benevolent? This is faith. If my life experience is one from which I can draw at least the hint of infinite benevolence (and mine contains a bounty of such hints), I can use that as a catalyst for a type of "faith" in regard to a benevolent god. If fact, my nature requires that I construct some kind of filler-of-infinite-space-and-time to account for an infinite prime mover, simple (nonmanifold), from which all else springs; and my experience implies, illogically of course, that space and time are filled with my own *imagined* and benevolent God.

For Wittgenstein, total nonsense! But when I brush up against infinity, it brushes back; and, in its unbridled nature, it nudges me; it feels loving, not frightening like cancer or looming cliffs or a crashing ocean. These, while they exist as part of infinity, are, themselves, finite. It is more like the feeling I get on a summer evening after a long, hard day and a big glass of port wine. I put my feet up, and I smile because they (my feet) seem too big for the ottoman—and that is good. This is the beginning of faith, the end of the absurdity of despair.

January 6: Heaven, Hell, Reincarnation?

Sam Clear Water and Siebert Wilson are sitting on stumps on a sunny hillside on the university campus:

Siebert: I heard someone (I forget who at the moment) saying that you don't believe in Heaven and Hell. Now, I have a great respect for your opinions, but this shaves pretty close to the jugular. I've spent four score and some odd years working my tail off, counting pennies, not cussing, loving my damned old alcoholic Momma, etc., etc., etc., on the promise that when I die, all this will get me into Heaven. Now you say there ain't no such?

Sam laughed, then composed himself, wiping his perspiring forehead and wildly uncombed white beard on his shirtsleeve. He continued whittling on a stick with his jackknife for a moment, then asked:

Who told you about Heaven and Hell?

Siebert: The preacher.

Sam: Who pays the preacher?

Siebert: Well, I guess I do, me and all the other folks that put money in the collection plate. But we don't pay him much. His wife adds some to it by cashiering down at the U-Totem.

Sam: And who pays you?

Siebert: I've got my Social Security now, but I used to stock shelves down at the Seed and Feed store and Norbert Grimes paid me for that.

Sam: And did you stock the shelves just any old way?

Siebert: Nope! I stocked them how Norbert told me.

Sam: And the preacher preaches just the way you and the rest of his paying customers told him to. If he didn't, you'd fire him. Siebert, you folks told that preacher to paint you a pretty picture of Heaven so you would have something to look forward to.

Siebert had some doubts about this. He had never told the preacher to do anything in all the years he had been going to church and didn't intend to start. That might, after all, be offensive to God. At least, that's what he understood from what the preacher preached. But he remained mum because he could see that Sam was puffing himself up to offer one of his philosophic lectures.

Sam continued:

Heaven is a pipe-dream. Over the centuries, good church-going folks with slave mentalities stacked up all the ideas they could think of about the ideal ways to spend eternity and came up with Heaven: streets of gold, beautiful angels, fancy mansions, plenty of chocolate, living in the personal presence of God, floating around on clouds, playing harps—forever. Why, Islamic men are supposed to get 70 virgins! I'm not sure whether that would be a blessing or a curse. Yasmin is plenty for me.

To a hard-working fellow like yourself, all this sounds pretty good—until you analyze it. Can you imagine, after a century or two, how tired you would get of cloud-and-harp derbies, of that awful reflection of the sun on those golden streets, and all that bowing and stooping in front of God! One would think that God would get mighty tired of your obeisance as well. Unless he lacks self-confidence, he surely doesn't need the reassurance.

9

Unfortunately, any specific ideas about life after death are just pipedreams because we don't have one jot or tittle of evidence that there is such a thing as life after death or even a human soul to experience it. That is not to say that there is no life after death or human soul. You'll have to ask someone wiser than I am to find out about that: maybe, the preacher. He claims to know about everything. (Smart fellow, that preacher! I wouldn't buy a used car from him, though.) All I can tell you is that the possibilities of both the soul and eternal life have been explored endlessly, and no one has come close to any rational or empirical conclusions pro or con that are not simple nonsense.

I said that Heaven is not a particularly satisfying view of eternal life. Certainly, Hell is unacceptable, nothing but a horror story to scare small children and naïve adults. But the Hindus dreamed up another system that seems to me to be a lot more livable eternity: reincarnation. It's a system of rewards of progression for a life well-lived and penalties of regression for the opposite. (The Hindus insist that they are not rewards and penalties, but that is what they amount to.) That sounds a little like heaven and hell until you realize that all of these rewards and penalties are played out right here on earth. If you live your life right, you die and come back as a higher form of life, a better human being. If you live your life wrong, you come back in a lower form. You could regress to being a slug or even a protozoan if you are intransigent enough, I suppose. By then, you probably wouldn't care, and you could slowly make your way back up the evolutionary chart to where you could, once again, sin against your own best interests and drop back down.

But consider the impetus for the good life. Just for being a little bit good, you could go from stocking shelves to telling someone else how to stock shelves in the next life. Why, even a klutz like me could, eventually, quarterback a Super Bowl if I worked hard enough on my passing and feinting skills.

I think I have made my selection—my choice of what to believe in. I can't really believe in reincarnation or any other form of life after death until God tells or shows me or until I die and land in the middle of it, but I can "imagine" that I believe in reincarnation and envision the day when I, the star quarterback, will leap over my 350-pound offensive right tackle to score the winning TD. To imagine it is to make it true—at least, for a moment. That is better than anything else we can do with a god, if there is one, who chooses to remain incognito. But, if I wake up tomorrow with a stiff neck (cursed old age!), I might change my mind about reincarnation and wish for that soft white cloud and the harp music. Maybe we could imagine that as a guitar. I already know a few guitar chords.

January 7: Bar Sinister.

I woke up this morning thinking the whole world absurd. Nothing matters. *Nada, nada, nada, nada, nada!* The sun wasn't shining because it wasn't up yet. I saw little reason for it to rise since it would merely set again on a world where we are all born to die, where everything we do is meaningless.

I yearned for youth, that early optimism when earth shone with an attractive light.

"Take this candle of my life—

10

Make it a beacon bright beyond all measure!"

    A whiff of armpit air blew me out, and I flopped my forearm across my face—tried to go back to sleep. What a waste that would be! Waste upon waste upon waste. Sleeping through absurdity! Maturity itself—an absurdity! Why not stay a child—naïve? Knowledge is power!? Power is a drag. Knowledge is pain. I know, and it doesn't matter.

    "Silent night, holy night,"
    All is aflutter, deadly still.

    Then the sun rose! The room brightened. I padded, barefoot and naked, across the room, twisted open the Venetian blind, stood looking out in warm awe— diagonal Venetian sun streaks across my hirsute belly.

January 8: Siebert on Knowledge.

This I Know
    By Siebert Wilson

I get real sick of hearing those city-boy poets spout off
About how ignorant they are.
All the time trying to show off their cool
Because they're street-smart
And know how to cuss or have sex or smoke weed
Without feeling ashamed of themselves.

Or if they do, then they brag about
How they have a tougher time getting over it
Than anybody else ever had.
They ain't ignorant. They're just stupid.
They don't know nothing,
And they make a big embarrassing fuss bawling about it.

Us country boys, we don't engage in such foolish talk—
Not habitually, anyway.
We know a hell of a lot,
And we ain't excessively proud of that either.
We don't earn it.
It just happens
Naturally!

We've seen cows making new life, calving in a February blizzard;
And we've seen the cold suck the life
Right out of those cute little calves
And leave them froze stiff, legs sticking out of a snow drift.

11

We know about women, too.
We've had our rolls in the hay,
But we don't make no fuss about respecting anybody in the morning.
In the morning, we're both out milking cows
And slopping manure out of the barn.
"Respect" ain't much of a word to be tossing around
When you have cow manure on your boots and, probably, on your forehead
Where you stuck it into old Bessy's flank while you were milking her.

And we meet God early living in the country. Real early!
Not like those blabbing TV evangelists:
"Come up here and let me lay my hands on your head!
Get saved!"
Nah! That stuff don't appeal to no proper country boy.

I must've been about six or so when I first met up with God.
I remember it was on a rocky hilltop—back on the farm.
There was this great big orange moon coming up in the east and a big orange sun setting in the west,
And they looked square into each other for about a minute and a half—
With me standing on that hill.
Just six, I was
Or thereabouts.

Not much need for talk out in the country.
We just know
And, generally speaking,
We keep shut about it.

January 9: Sam on Priorities.

I remember a time when the most important thing was to hang up-side-down by my knees from a tree. A couple of years later, after I went to a Shrine Circus, it was tightrope-walking the barbed wire fence that surrounded the corral. That didn't last long. I still have the scars on my crotch to prove that I only went part way before the staples gave way and dropped me on the next strand of barbed wire. Then, after witnessing a rodeo, it was riding Tiny (a daughter of Old Pansy, our lead milk cow). I lit tail-bone-first on a rock and, for a minute, thought I'd never walk again. Somehow, that led to basketball, then chasing after girls, then heading off to sail the seven seas for Uncle Sam. I only got through three seas before my Navy hitch ended. After that there was religion. Yes, I got religion; and, for a long time, I declared it to be the most important thing. Yes, and somewhere in there came a desire for authority and power. I can't help observing that some consider power to be the prime objective in life, and just as many are partial to money. And a sort of extension of money and power is what sells best of anything: sex and its expensive and time consuming partner, sex appeal.

Isn't it strange that most of us can go all the way from cradle to grave being dead wrong about what's important? Last night by the fireplace, I glanced over the newspaper at Yasmin, 40 years my wife, asleep and drooling on the Japanese futon that one of our daughters sewed for her birthday. Our youngest of seven grandchildren calls it Tutu's pink bed. I chuckled as I closed my eyes and leaned back in my recliner.

January 10: Emily on Courage.
Sarah Wagner
Saul Wagner
Private Emily Wagner (Daughter of Sarah and Saul)
Willy Sutton
Sam Clear Water
　　　　At the Power Plant Café, 8:30 a.m., Monday.
Sam *(entering the café with Willy and seeing the Wagner family seated in a secluded area)*: Well, well! I didn't expect to see you out so early this morning. Who's running the shop?
Saul: Closed! We won't be selling any flowers today. Hell, maybe I won't ever sell another flower!
Sam: Hmm!?
Willy: Wow! What's got into him?!
Sarah: Oh, don't mind him. He's just in a sour mood.
Willy: Why so?
Sarah: It's really about Emily. She's going back to the army post, and we won't be seeing her for a while. We'll see her off at the airport in a couple of hours.
Sam: We won't bother you, then. You need your family time. We'll just go over to the far side for breakfast.
Sarah: Nonsense! Sit down here! You two are like part of the family. Besides, we need some of your idle chatter to cheer us up. It's more than just Emily going back to the base. She's going to Iraq to fight in the war.
Sam: Well, Emily, all grown up and going off to war! How do you feel about that?
Emily *(blushing)*: Actually, it's kind of exciting. But I have to admit that I'm a little scared.
Sam: Hmm! Is a soldier supposed to be scared?
Emily: I don't know, but I am, and I'm a soldier.
Sam: And how about you, Saul. Are you a little bit scared, too? It would seem that you have a right to be. She *is* your only child.
Saul: I'm too mad to be scared, Sam. What is the world coming to, sending off a little girl like Emily to fight in a war? It was bad enough sending our fathers off to Vietnam. I guess, in your case, you are one of our fathers.
Sam: Yes. I remember.
Willy: I remember, too. I was too young, but I remember Sam going. And I remember him coming back with a chest full of medals and one arm in a sling. There were some real stories told back then about what Sam did in the war. Great stuff!
Sam: Yes. I remember.
Sarah: Sam, I didn't know you were a war hero. You never talk about it.

Sam asked for a cup of coffee and his standard breakfast which the waitress delivered. Then he continued: Sarah, are you a little bit scared, too?

Sarah: Lord, yes. Of course, I am. Not just a little, but a lot. But I'm no soldier, just a mother, and I have a right.

Sam: Yes, indeed. You do have that right. Maybe even a responsibility.

Willy: You are sure a courageous family. I don't think I could handle this if it were my child going off to war.

Sarah: I don't feel courageous.

Sam: I don't think I quite understand what we are talking about when we say "courageous." Saul is so angry that he doesn't feel scared. Emily is a little bit scared. Sarah is a lot scared. But you are all going to the airport, and Emily is going to war and you, her parents, are not going to do anything to stop her from going. Can anyone tell me, where is the *courage* in all of this?

Willy: Isn't it courage that makes them go through with it even if they are scared or angry?

Sam: It could be cowardice or courage or something else entirely.

Willy: I don't know what you mean.

Sam: Then I will clarify. What I mean is that whether it is cowardice or courage or something else is relative to why they are doing it and under what circumstances. So, I would have to ask: "Why are you going through with this?"

Saul: Like we have a choice! She got her orders. She has to go.

Sam: Is it that simple?

Saul: It seems so.

Sam: But is it? Let's look more closely. I don't see any armed guards dragging you off to the airport. You could, indeed, get in your car and go home.

Saul: Then, they would come and get Emily and haul her off to a military prison.

Sam: That is, probably, true. But she would not be going off to war. I only say it to illustrate that there is a choice that could be made other than cooperating with the order. Also, many choices that you have made (all of you) previously, have been choices made freely on your part which led to this particular choice. For instance, Emily chose to join the army. In doing so, she tacitly agreed that she would go to war if called. You, her parents, did little to stop her from doing so, though you probably could have found a way to convince her not to join up, even if it meant bribery.

Saul: True.

Sarah: Yes, but I don't think that parents should make decisions for their 18-year-old children. We have to let them go.

Sam: Have to?

Sarah: I see your meaning.

Sam: Also, go back 20 years or so. Sam and Sarah, you had a child. Was that not an agreement that you would be subjecting that child to the conditions of the social contract to which human beings born in America are subject? That would, I presume, include the possibility of military service and fighting in wars.

Sarah: Yes, but that wasn't what we had in mind.

Sam: You needn't explain. My point, again, is that you acted freely in contributing in a myriad of ways to the contract under which Emily is now serving. Would you not agree?

14

Saul (resigned): I suppose.

Sam: So, I ask again: Is your present act of fulfilling that contract courageous, cowardly, or something else entirely?

Willy: I think it is courageous, because they are doing it even when they could get out of it.

Sam: Just one problem. Are you saying that they are fulfilling the contract because it is the right thing to do or because they are afraid of the consequences if they don't do it?

Willy: Of course, it is because they know it's the right thing to do.

Sam: If it is the right thing to do, why is Saul angry? Is there ever a reason why we should be angry to be doing the right thing? Surely, that should make us feel good.

Saul: Don't talk as if I'm not here. I'll answer that. I am angry because I might be losing my little girl. Perhaps, with a man, anger is just another word for being scared.

Sam: I think you are right. That could be a topic for discussion on another day. And I don't think we should require any of you to tell us why you are fulfilling your contract. But you need to ask yourselves. That would help you to know whether your motivation is courage or cowardice or something else entirely. I choose to believe that your motivation is courage because I know you, and I know what you have done throughout your lives. Your lives have not been cowardly.

Willy: But what of the "something else entirely"? What would that be, Sam?

Sam: I don't know, Willy. Perhaps, if you think deeply enough about it, you will come up with something about that. Let me know. I'll be interested in hearing about it. In the meantime, let me provide a possible definition of courage for us all to think about (and, maybe, debunk later): "Courage is sustaining honorable and reasonable action in the context of knowing what we know and knowing what we do not know." That is a definition that Socrates considered and, finally, seemed to reject. Perhaps, he was wrong to reject it. Perhaps, not.

Emily *(as Sam and Willy rise to leave)*: Thanks for stopping by, Sam. I feel a lot better having talked with you, even if we didn't come to any conclusions.

Sam: You're welcome, Emily. We will be looking forward to your safe return home. I salute you at the beginning of a new adventure, Private Wagner.

January 11: Caves within Caves within Caves.

I've been thinking about caves. I suppose it is because I've been in the city for too long and need to take a nice long trek to the country. Or, maybe, it's because I've been reading Plato again and thought about his allegory. Or it could be because I visited with the Scribe (as he laughingly agrees to call himself; and I'm glad he can laugh at something; he's an awful sourling) in his office which, like mine, is a cave within a cave within a cave. That's where the university put him after he retired. He raised a real stink when they tried to turn him out. They preferred, I think, that he just go home and read "Guava Bear" to his grandchildren and feed sticks to the fireplace. Old professors hanging around campuses can be a nuisance, and the Scribe had made himself a real nuisance for years anyway. It took him forty years to make tenure because he always got in trouble pounding on the president's desk or cussing out the dean. Then, he'd have to wait until another president or dean checked in before he could start the tenure process all over. Life isn't easy for misanthropes, especially when they don't teach anything that makes much money for the university or its graduates. Shortly before retirement, he managed to sneak in a successful tenure campaign and even convinced the administration that he deserved full professorship. After he retired, like I say, they might have had some second thoughts and tried to ease him gently out the door. He was just raising his fist to pound on some more desks when they found him a little office at the end of a hallway in the back of the university library which is located in a limestone cave carved out of the Missouri River bluffs (a cave within a cave within a cave). My office, by the way, is just around the next limestone pillar from his, but mine sits empty most of the time. Now he works every day and gets kicked out whenever the librarian gets ready to close the library. He still escapes, occasionally, and raises hell in a faculty meeting, just for old time's sake.

Ah, yes! Caves! Everything in philosophy seems to be about caves. Plato puts us in a cave in his *Republic* as if that's about the only place for unenlightened human beings to live. Not only that, but he lines us all up in rows (like in a theater) and puts chains, head restraints, and blinders on us so we can't see anything "the man" doesn't want us to see. All we get to see is distorted dancing shadows of unrealistic marionettes cast upon a wall and originating from behind us where we can't see the puppets or the puppet masters or the source of light. (Hmm! Sounds like our living room during *As the World Turns*.)

I have come to the conclusion that most of us spend our lives in caves with occasional moments of moving from smaller interior caves (which are, merely, exterior caves to even smaller interior caves) to larger exterior caves (which are, merely, interior caves to yet larger exterior caves) and/or back again. Like moles! In our American democracy, we call this freedom. In Cuba, we call it tyranny. But, as Shakespeare put it, "A rose by any other name . . . ." Freedom or tyranny, it adds up to the same thing. Like the moles, we have been in the dark for so long that we have evolved with no eyes (or, rather, with vestigial eyes that can see only shadows and only in almost total darkness, so light would blind us.

Ouch! I think I've been spending too much time with the Scribe.

Let's try that again. Plato, the romantic, says that, if, somehow, we get loose and go out of the outermost cave (if there is such a thing, which Kant, another romantic, says is both necessary and impossible), the sun will shine so bright that it will blind us temporarily; but, if we are patient and long-suffering, our vestigial eyes will adapt to the light, and we'll be able to see ideal reality. He says that we, then, have an obligation to go back into the cave, all the way back to the straight rows where sits the rest of humanity enjoying *The Young and the Restless*, and teach them about the ideal. Bully for us!

This is the point where I could teach Plato something. He would learn it by experience if he ever interrupted a group of fans (short for "fanatics") watching a soap opera. If they were capable of actual movement, he would be dead on the spot. All that would save him would be the fact that they are chained, but the negative psychological vibrations would send him tumbling into the next cave where he could sit on a rock and contemplate his folly.

No answers here, just observations.

January 12: The Mind Empty.

16

In the Orient, optimum spirituality calls for an empty mind. I'm not sure that is possible, certainly not in a biological sense; and, because biology seems to be all that the mind contains and all that we can sense, it is impossible to imagine an entirely empty mind. It is, however, of benefit to the thinking person to be able to empty the accumulated trash that constantly clutters the mind in order to leave space for something fresh. I sometimes do that by watching Letterman on TV; but the result, since Letterman comes on late and I am tired, is that I just go to sleep with a semi-empty mind—good for personal health, but not much help in contemplation. More often, I use the game of solitaire to carry out the trash. Solitaire, after one has played it for a while, is entirely predictable in its unpredictability and one can play it without thought. Its only value is that its structure tamps other more intrusive mental junk down so it can be easily discarded. Often, after a couple of unsuccessful hands, I switch off the game and play mental pictures. I look at a blank space on the wall and, with no intentional prompting, I see what image forms up. This morning, I was rewarded with a panorama of the snow-capped Rocky Mountains:

> *My secret place of thunder*
> *Roars upon my ears*
> *With idyllic whispering,*
> *A chant that lasts for years,*
> *While mountains moan their boulders*
> *And rivers weep their tears.*

It was only for a moment, worth only a moment's poetry. At other times, such moments have produced greater poems which echo down through the years, still providing advice as I reach a fork in the road

> *There was a time upon a hill with sunlight all around,*
> *I made a plea to heaven as I rested on the ground.*
> *You lifted up the veil for me;*
> *You opened up my eyes,*
> *And showed me for a moment*
> *What's behind the endless skies.*

> *Wonderful, loving soul*
> *Who gives me life to live,*
> *I can't remember when I've been so happy*
> *As when you've taught me the joys of creation . . .*

Ah! The mysteries! It is so good to know that I will always, no matter how much I learn or how long I live, contain infinite emptiness waiting to be filled.

> *Wonderful, loving soul!*

January 13: Vulnerability and Wisdom.

It snowed today. Actually, it iced today. Then it sleeted. It never really got around to snowing. First, about the time I got out of bed and put on my pants and went out shirtless and shoeless to get the paper, freezing rain was beginning to fall. It felt good on my back though it was shocking. I didn't stay out any longer than I had to, just long enough to realize that the paper had not come. I took time to search the entire yard and even to look under the truck to see if it was there. Then, in "the dawns early light," I remembered that we had received a note from the delivery people a couple of days ago that the paper would be late today and tomorrow. So I stood there for a second like a gerontological Zeus with freezing rain dripping from my white beard and glistening from my heroic baldness, but only for a second; then I dashed in slow motion, so I wouldn't fall on the ice and break a hip, through the kitchen door.

Warming up in my recliner with the electric heater blowing on my wet feet, I thought about the four-foot snow storm that hit Colorado, just a couple hundred miles away a week ago. I heard on CNN that it froze about 1000 head of cattle. But there must have been a million cows out there in the cold, and it seems marvelous that only 1000 died. Not marvelous in cow terms! I grew up watching the cows in their winter pasture, nothing to eat but dry alfalfa hay, ice-water to drink after my father chopped a hole in the stock tank ice a couple of times a day, no shelter but their own hides and the shade of another cow, or, if they were tough enough to push the others away, a spot in the open shed by the haystack, blasted by the worst Rocky Mountain blizzards that nature could throw at them. Except for a few calves unlucky enough to be born at night during a pitched blizzard, I don't recall any cattle actually dying from the cold. No appendages, not a single teat, ever froze and dropped off, seldom even a spot of frostbite. I know because I milked them by hand morning and night in a frigid barn, the only time they got out of the bitter cold, and that was just so we, the humans, didn't have to spend time outside. They didn't die. They didn't freeze. They didn't even shiver. They stood there in a tight herd, butts to the wind, all day and all night. Sometimes, they would lie down and go to sleep. But they never froze. They never died.

Shakespeare's "poor bare forked animal[s]," we "naked apes" as Desmond Morris called us, would freeze in an hour and drop down dead under such circumstances. All of us, not just the babies! Also, we would die if we had to live on a diet of dry alfalfa hay, or if we had to survive on the polluted irrigation water that cows thrive on all summer or the ice water from the well that keeps them hydrated after the irrigation water is turned off in the fall. Isn't it amazing that such weaklings as we survived all the tests of evolution to become masters of the planet?

I use the term "masters" with an ironical smile. Once, the dinosaurs were the masters. But they were strong with thick hides and big teeth and the ones whose teeth were not so big had long necks so they could walk out into deep water where the carnivores wouldn't go or could fly their slender bones off on long thin wings. But humans: slow of foot, poor climbers, no wings, thin skin, no fur, weak teeth, minimal muscle, hardly enough to support us in the awkward vulnerable uprightness we are so vain about! Masters of the Earth?! Yet we made it: some say on the basis of our opposable thumbs which are now quite good for hitting the "space" key on the computer and develop at least a little arthritis by the time we reach age 50.

18

Of course, the real key is our rational mind. Somehow, early on, we exchanged most of our instincts (which would hardly be enough to help me figure out how to find the "control" key, let alone to match it up with "alt" and "del" to get my computer turned on properly) for rational thinking, thinking that told us to get in out of the cold, thinking that taught us to bludgeon animals to death with clubs and, later, to stab them with spears and to strip off their hides, tan them to cover our own thin skins and that of our babies, our beds, and the entranceways to our caves.

We tend to give God the credit; and, I suppose, in an important way, God, as primeval power, deserves the credit, but God seems to have made a lot of mistakes. For instance, why, after all this evolution that God is said to have started, have his seeming favorites, the human beings, not gotten over their proclivity for killing each other in wars, a totally fruitless endeavor, a product of that same rational thinking that has been our salvation. Certainly, other animals don't range hundreds of thousands of their own species against hundreds of thousands of other members of their own species with no purpose in mind except to kill each other, not for food but for domination (more often than not, under the banner of some religion that proclaims peace as its central tenet) of some poor segment of the planet's surface, a domination that never lasts longer than a few centuries, usually, not more than a few years, or even a few months.

Mother Nature, a slightly less than primeval goddess, seems to be less prone to mistakes. She, after all, as she added more and more rational behavior to humanity, took away other powers still retained by animals: flight, muscle, hairy hides, instincts, etc. In a very real sense, she took away, too, the "peace" that humans value so highly but never achieve. The other animals, Mother Nature left with those older gifts, along with natural peace. Certainly, peace can never be wrung from a blood-soaked tribal banner.

January 14: What a Miracle!
What a miracle springs from hearts full of love:
Songs like fountains come pouring shining like fires;
Prayers, like castles, to heaven lift their tall spires.
What a miracle springs from hearts full of love!

What a miracle springs from hearts full of joy:
Songs like fountains come pouring shining like fires;
Prayers, like castles, to heaven lift their tall spires.
What a miracle springs from hearts full of joy!

What a miracle springs from hearts full of peace:
Songs like fountains come pouring shining like fires;
Prayers, like castles, to heaven, lift their tall spires.
What a miracle springs from hearts full of peace!

January 15: Encomium to MLK
Today, a lot of people have the day off from work, and I realize that many of them don't really have much of an idea why. Time flies and with it flies the past into oblivion. What, to my generation, is a part of the contemporary context is

history to the next generation, ancient history to the next, and a waste of cyberspace to the fourth. It is necessary that it be so. Otherwise, the information age would turn into an information tsunami and wipe out the exposed coasts of our minds. All but a little of the past must be banished.

Behold the struggle! What will be the little of the past that we keep in the light? I, for one, am happy that we have kept Plato and Confucius and Moses, and Abraham and Jesus and Mohammed lighted even though the candles burn dim. With the shameful babble of idiocy that passes for exegesis of their teachings, the faint hope that some society will, eventually, read them right makes it worth all the blood and spite expended to keep them alive. The same is true of political heroes such as Lincoln, Churchill, and Gandhi. And scientists: Madame Curie, Einstein. And there are so many others. Even with the list pared down to the core, it is massive. Humanity has not come from there to here without benefit of a host of Titans.

The very intellectual bulk of such persons makes it hard for a humble figure like that of Martin Luther King to lift his head above the throng. He was a simple black preacher, well-educated, articulate, but still, just a simple black preacher. At first, we didn't even know about his "dream." Nor did most of us care about it. We were too busy getting and staying wealthy to worry much about "the less fortunate" among us. Anyway, hadn't Roosevelt taken care of that with the New Deal and Social Security? The old WPA had done its work; the new highways were either built or being built. If we were to worry about anything, shouldn't it be the communist threat from behind the iron curtain in Eastern Europe, that shuffling bear of a wall that continuously dragged its foundations westward and southward, threatening to envelop the entire world. What time did we have to worry about a few black malcontents?

But King knew that Roosevelt had not finished the job. He knew that the communist threat was no more dangerous than that poisonous caldron which was boiling in the heart of America: prejudice. America was dying of heart failure, and we were too busy to notice the angina. I remember the lynching of young black men by white hooded horsemen. I remember the way people looked at me and my potato picking partner, Bobbi, who was the only black teenager in our part of the county, perhaps, the whole of Gooding County, and who had a small son out of wedlock. I chose Bobbi as my potato-picking partner because she was my next-farm neighbor and because she was a fast potato picker—I could make more money with her as my partner. It was always a mystery to me why she chose me. But the way people looked at us?! I didn't understand, but I wasn't much of one to care how people looked at me, and Bobbi didn't seem to notice.

I remember Martin's "I have a dream" speech. I always thought it was a great speech; and, by then, I understood about why people looked at Bobbi and me that way. And I hated the reason. But I didn't do much about it. I've never been much of an activist. Martin was. I didn't realize until a few days ago that the "I have a dream" speech was delivered mostly impromptu. That makes a difference to me. "Impromptu" means to me that it came from his heart, and not just from a piece of paper that he had typed up earlier. Socrates said something like that to Phaedrus in defending philosophical discussion as better than prepared speeches and poetry. He was right. Martin proved it, by moving on right down to the end of his life, living to implement big chunks of his dream, especially the part where little white children and little black children could play together and work together without anyone thinking it was out of the ordinary. Maybe, by the time Martin was shot to death, a white boy in Idaho could have picked potatoes with a somewhat older black girl with an illegitimate baby without people looking at them funny. Maybe not! Maybe, not even now, half a century later!

There is still much to be done to make Martin's dream a reality, and we had best do it impromptu. If we can't do it impromptu, no amount of formal celebration of Martin's life or of reading Plato will get it done.

January 16: Complaints Department.

It's just that kind of day—a day to complain. First, let me complain about my dream (more like a nightmare) last night. I found myself in a private preparatory academy for high school children. I don't know if I was a student or a faculty member, but I was miserable, just like I was when I taught in such an academy. I'm no painter, but I was trying my best in an art class to paint a picture. I knew that it would be a masterpiece if I could get it done; but I couldn't find the right brushes or paint; and, when I went to look for them, someone stole the canvas. I had just decided to hang up the whole failed experiment and head out on my own to get a job as a dishwasher when I woke up. Sometimes when I wake up from a particularly bad dream, I'm glad to be awake. Those are the kinds of dreams where I'm being chased by a bull or threatened by a rattlesnake or when I can't find an operational toilet. When I wake up from one of those, I'm relieved to be safe or, in the last case, just "relieved." But, for some reason, this one just wouldn't let me go. I wasn't afraid, just disgusted that I couldn't get that damnable picture painted. I wanted to prove I could do it. I still do. There is nothing more frustrated than the frustrated artist. I have fellow-feel for poor old Vincent, and understand how he could be so distraught that he would cut off his ear. I found myself sizing up my left ear in the mirror this morning for possible surgery, but that was an entirely different matter. Second, let me complain that someone lost a piece of my mail this morning, and I had to run all over the university campus tracking it down. But that was good exercise—invigorating because of the cold weather and crunchy snow. And once more, I am proud to announce that I didn't fall on the ice and break a hip. At least, I don't have that to complain about.

January 17: Divine Madness.

Del Whistler (a friend who owns 40 acres of woodland) and Sam are talking as they load Sam's truck with firewood.

Del *(sitting down on a log and lighting his pipe with a wood match)*: Siebert tells me that you claim to be a madman.

Sam *(reclining across the tailgate of the half-loaded F-150)*: That's right.

Del: And he says that you called him a madman, too. Is that a fact?

Sam: Is what a fact, that I *called* him a madman or that he *is* a madman?

Del: I intended to ask if you called him a madman, but I'd be interested in both.

Sam: I called him a madman, and he *is* a madman part of the time.

Del: We can get back to *your* madness (which I think is quite evident) shortly; first, exactly, what part of the time is Siebert mad. If I know that, I'll know when it might not be safe to cross the road in front of his truck.

Sam: I'm not sure that would ever be safe. Siebert's eyesight is not so good. He sees "through a glass darkly" at best. But I speak not the entire truth, and I am bound to tell only the truth and all of it that I know. There are times when he "sees" with absolute clarity, and that is when he is mad.

Del: Now I *am* worried. No one will be safe, ever. Perhaps, we should call the marshal into this.

Sam *(laughing heartily and wiping the perspiration from his face with a large red handkerchief)*: Never fear! Our friend, Siebert, is not that kind of mad, and when he drives, he never goes more than ten miles per hour.

Del: What kind of mad is he?

Sam: Same as I am.

Del: And what kind is that?

Sam: Socrates called it "divine madness" in *the Phaedrus.*

Del: You have now mentioned Socrates, so I'm sure that the wood-splitting will wait for quite a while, and we'll be loading late into the afternoon. Start talking now or you won't finish before dark, and I'm not sure you should be driving after dark. Your "glass" isn't entirely clear either.

Sam: You have my word that I'll finish long before dark, and I'll arrive home by 5:00 p.m.

Del: I'll hold you to that.

Sam: I'm sure you will. First, I need to define "divine madness." Socrates said that it is the madness that occurs when the poet is in the clutch of the muses. Suddenly, the poet is granted the ability to write inspired poetry. Essentially, Socrates means by "the muses" that God inspires the mind of the poet and, literally, gives the poem to the poet. The poet becomes little more than a scribe. While they are in this state of divine inspiration, poets are "not" in their right mind. Thus, by definition, they are mad. The good thing is that they are in a far better mind than their right mind. That is why I say that, when Siebert is writing one of his cowboy poems, he is mad. I'm not sure whether the world would consider his poems divinely inspired, but I enjoy them.

Del: What a relief! And that would, also, explain what you mean by saying that Siebert sees clearly when he is mad.

Sam: Right!

Del: You have raised so many questions in my mind that I don't know where to start. Let me start by going backwards—to you. You write a poem now and then, but you are not, chiefly, a poet. Rather, you are a philosopher. At least, that is what you have told me you are, and I can't for the life of me figure out how you make a living doing that. It seems a little unfair that you should become a divine madman when you write a poem and not when you talk philosophically. (I say "talk" because you have argued with me several times that it is what you say that matters most, not what you write. What you write down is merely a memento to future generations for whatever it might be worth to them to see what a less evolved philosopher in our day, their past, had to say.)

Sam: You have listened well, Del. I think your listening skills show promise.

Del: One needs little skill to understand what you say. You say it very clearly.

Sam: Perhaps, I need you to interpret what I say for me. I am not always as sure what I mean as you seem to be.

Del: What I was about to ask is this: are you, also, mad when you speak philosophically?

Sam: Even madder if I agree with Socrates. That is because poetry is not as close to truth as philosophy is.

Del: How is that? Are there levels of divine? Is poetry somewhat divine and philosophy a lot divine?

Sam: What is divine, according to Socrates, is God, not the poem or the philosophical statement. However, the poem is a human-made copy of the divinely inspired poem which God gives the poet. The poet, unless he is, also, a philosopher, probably did not write the poem as "truth," but as an artistic creation presented in the form of language—or as Cleanth Brooks puts it: "A Well-Wrought Urn." This "urn" is a copy of the ideal "urn" which exists only in the mind of God. In that context, the ideal copy, but not the poet's copy, represents perfect art. The philosopher, on the other hand, has no purpose except to present truth or, rather, what is the closest thing to truth that an inspired human, a madman, can present, and this is a long way from (perhaps even the opposite of) truth. Thus, since the poet's task is to present art and the philosopher's task is to present what is as near as possible to truth, we can assume that the poet in a state of divine madness will produce the near perfect art work and the philosopher in a state of divine madness will produce the near perfect work of truth. I say "near perfect" because the philosopher, too, can only produce an imperfect copy of the perfect (or ideal) truth that exists only in the mind of God. If we get right down to cases, both the poet and the philosopher could be so far from the ideal truth that what they produce is downright seditious of God's truth.

Del: Wonderful explanation! Now I understand that neither you nor Siebert will be much of a threat to pedestrians except that both of you have fading eyesight, especially after dark, and your friends will do everything they can to keep you off the roads after sunset.

Sam: I'll set you in charge of that task. It won't be easy for you.

Del: One more question before we break for lunch, although we already seem to have broken. You have told me several times that the existence of God cannot be proven—that the nearest thing to this is that it can be proven that there is a primal and continuing infinite force in the cosmos which we might or might not interpret as God—that you, personally, find it convenient to believe that a benevolent personal God does, indeed, exist. However, in neither a rational nor empirical sense, is this enough to support the argument that you seem to have borrowed from Socrates that poets and philosophers are rendered mad by the inspiration of God in the production of their artistic or philosophical works.

Sam: Right! It is not enough.

Del: Then, of what value is everything we have said?

Sam: None, if we are trying to prove the existence of God or the truth of Socrates' theory of divine madness. On the other hand, I can attest to the fact that, not only poets and philosophers, but other humans experience the phenomenon of what might be called "divine madness." I feel it when I philosophize. Eliot was either a

23

madman or a poetic god or brilliant beyond imagining when he wrote *The Wasteland.*" The same had to be true of the blind Milton as he wrote *Paradise Lost.* Or when deaf Beethoven wrote the 9th. When Einstein did the math on relativity before substantial empirical evidence could prove it. The idiot savant concert pianist. The prophet on Patmos. Confucius. Blind and illiterate Homer. Divine madness (or the same thing without God's involvement) is far more provable than the existence of God, though the evidence is not sufficient for either given the limited inductive or even the absolute deductive proof.

I choose to accept divine madness as fact and thank God for it. I might be wrong, but this choice has, in the mad poet Frost's words, "made all the difference."

January 18: Guns and Fisticuffs.

I am trying to make sense of something. That is not unusual for me because I seldom seem to understand what goes on in the world as well as others claim to. My confusion is over two battles that I recently witnessed via television and the news coverage each is receiving.

The first is a story of a battering administered by three 14-year-old girls upon a 13-year-old girl on a semidark street near an urban playground. It was reported that it was over a difference of opinion as to which girl had earned the right to the affections of a certain unidentified boy. There was a great deal of hair pulling, flinging of fists, and a few kicks to the head and body of the younger girl. She was on the ground in a fetal position, giving herself up like a smaller dog against a pack of larger dogs during the entire fight. Finally, a car stopped at a nearby corner and the younger girl scrambled to her feet and retreated to its opening door with the older girls hanging back, apparently fearing whatever unknown adult authority was in the car. The real oddity is that someone was recording the fight, and the video was posted later on an internet site. That seemed to me to be the only part of the whole affair that was newsworthy. I recall that this kind of fight was a frequent occurrence in my junior high school days. Usually, it was among boys, but the occasional girl fight drew a bigger crowd. I think it was the hair-pulling that was most interesting. This particular fight drew national news coverage.

At first, I think, the news coverage drew interest in the oddity that it appeared on the internet; but, quickly, it became something of a sociological piece bemoaning the declining morality among American children. It has been national headlines for three days. I'm not sure how much staying power it has, but it might go on for several more days, and we don't even get to see the girls' faces since they are blotted out to protect their juvenile identities.

The other fight has been occurring in Iraq over the last three years and several months and shows no evidence of dying out. In this fight, about a million soldiers have been involved over the three years, around three-hundred-thousand at a time. Each soldier on either side (many of the Americans as young as 18—four years older than the street-fighting girls), armed to the teeth with the most efficient weaponry available and backed up with as much heavy artillery, aircraft, etc., as can be shipped into the country, is instructed to kill and/or maim as many persons as necessary to win the war against the opposing side. In addition, the battle is being fought largely in major cities where millions of Iraqi civilians live and work and play and study in the midst of the fighting. Many of them are dying, too. It seems a shame that the warriors could not take their games outside of town where only a few jack asses and camels would get into the line of fire. A limited number of prisoners are taken because there is little room in the jails to store them. Both sides insist that they are fighting a war for God. God seems embarrassedly mum about the whole affair.

We get to see pictures of the dead and/or bloody faces day and night on the television news. The rest of the war news is just as unsurprising: the streets littered with dead bodies and the hospitals filled with maimed soldiers and civilians.

My confusion is not over the battles themselves, but over the news coverage. It seems to me that news should be more about unexpected outcomes. When outcomes are exactly as expected, the only news would look like a stock market page, with lists of casualties and other costs of the war in place of stock prices. In both of the above battles, the outcomes are exactly as expected. For the fighting girls, the aggressors get into trouble with adult authorities, they get suspended from school, and the school board decides how long they will be out. The attackee gets a few bruises and is said to need psychological counseling. In Iraq, lots of people are dying or getting maimed. Not much *news* in either battle.

It would seem to me that the real news would be, in the girls' case, if we find out which girl was stupid enough to post the fight on the web so that all of them except the videographer could be identified for the authorities; and, in the Iraq case, if we have a day where nobody gets killed or maimed. Now that would be real news! That will be news I continue to hope for. I won't pray for it because God, apparently, has chosen neither to take sides nor to interfere. I respect but, often, don't understand or agree with God's choices—if God exists.

January 19: Hobgoblins.

Ralph Waldo Emerson said "A foolish consistency is the hobgoblin of small minds." He went on to explain that each day of our lives should teach us something that changes our minds about something, perhaps about everything, to a small or even a large degree. James Joyce called the learning experiences on big-change days *epiphanies*. I suppose, since he borrowed a catholic word for this, he was implying that they were, somehow, akin to the idea of revelation from God. I won't go that far, at least, not today, but our daily growth can be quite amazing. Even more amazing can be our lack of daily growth, or, to use another term that is employed to whip up on religion, our attachment to dogma. Again, dogma doesn't have to be applied to religion only. For instance, dogma is what I call received political opinions which people, especially politicians, find it so hard to adjust in their own political platforms.

Although this little discussion I am having with myself today is probably one of the most boring I can remember, it might be one of the most important for folks to listen in on. That is because it deals with a problem in society which is threatening to undermine the whole fragile and flawed (but extremely precious) framework of democracy. Very simply, we have Emerson's idea exactly backwards. Instead of, "a foolish consistency is the hobgoblin of small minds," we have adopted the opposite: a wise inconsistency is the characteristic of large minds which alienates us from them. We reject our wisest leaders because they change their minds about issues when they learn something new about those issues—or

25

when they revisit such issues using a new analytical approach to them. Or when they listen to all sides of an argument, consider each side carefully, and decide that they had, previously, reached erroneous conclusions. I can't count how many times during the last Presidential election cycle I watched political ads on TV that showed pancakes flipping or some other image that accused a candidate of flip-flopping. And for this reason, everyone should vote against such an inconsistent boob?!

With this attitude toward learning, we would not have a cure for polio. With this attitude toward learning, our fastest mode of transportation would be the train. No, the train would not exist. With this attitude, the only reaper would be the Grim Reaper and we would still be using a scythe to harvest our wheat. No, we wouldn't have a scythe. We would be using our hands and our teeth to reap grain. No, we wouldn't be reaping grain. Instead, we would be killing rats with a stone and eating them raw. No, again! We wouldn't *be* at all because we would, long since, have been eaten alive by saber tooth tigers, and there would be no humanity.

And, in the future, we can be sure that we will have no democratic humanity if this negative attitude toward learning becomes dominant and semi-permanent (nothing is permanent except permanency itself). The environment which it creates is precisely that which spawns tyranny. Next time you are tempted to change your mind because you learned something new, do it, and be proud. You are in excellent company. But don't be surprised if you lose elections. Not everyone can become the leader of the free world. Certainly, not a "flip-flopper"! Consider the comedy of errors that would happen if a person like Socrates, who *seemed* to change his mind a dozen times in every dialogue, were elected president or prime minister. The rest of us might have to do some serious thinking ourselves. Then we would be in trouble, not having any practice at it.

January 20: The Human Soul.
Kant speaks of the human soul as a "simple." A simple is an object with no parts. It is "I," "*ego.*" It is aware of itself and of sensory phenomena representing physical objects to it. Also, according to Kant, it contains *a priori* transcendental insights which require no phenomenal representation. It thinks and renders judgments regarding all of this. Because of the soul, we are able to interpret the physical world and adapt ourselves to it physically and psychologically. Kant contends that we cannot absolutely *know* whether the soul lives before it joins with a human body or whether it lives on after the death of the human body.

This doesn't sound much like the Christian soul. Kant's "soul" is useful. The Christian soul is baggage to haul with us through life. Of course, the Christian would argue that her soul is much more than this. It is the connection between the spiritual and the material world. It is the underweight portion of "body and soul." It is not a "simple," but we must not analyze it or its relationship to the body. If we do, we discover that this dualism demeans the body at the same time it places the soul in an absurd fantasy world.

Because the Christian soul, after death, is swept off to heaven, and because the body is such a smelly, heavy, painful prison, it is hard to understand why Christians would not yearn for death every step of their miserable lives. How light, how agile, "how beautiful on the mountain," the Christian soul. Yet, I see 100-year-old Christian women and men struggling to retain the sour breath they exhale to live just another day or another hour or another minute. Is it that they do not, really, believe the myth of the soul? What else could explain it? That would put it in the same category as "turn the other cheek," that largely ignored camel stuck in the eye of the needle, "love your enemy," "Do unto others . . . ," etc.

But I can really get to know and appreciate my Kantian soul. I relish scratching my itches because I don't know for sure whether I will have any itches or places to scratch after I am dead—indeed, "our Father in heaven" has not deigned to tell me, personally, whether I will exist beyond death. I haven't seen a scrap of empirical evidence for or against, and don't really care to. I have my hands full just managing the difficulties and satisfactions of this life to waste time fancying another. Here's my advice. Develop, as soon as possible, a unity between your body and soul—make them one. You can't experience your body except as its phenomenal representation to your soul. Your soul's only function is to think, and it is very good at it if you don't allow absurdity to clutter up the process. Your body is a reasonably good vehicle for whisking you from place to place and time to time to where and when the best phenomena are available for the "feeding" of your soul. Sometimes, it is a marvelous experience to just curl up as your soul within your body on a shady hillside and think until your body goes to sleep and your soul dreams about coffee-flavored ice cream bars.

Next, study what it takes to be happy as much of the time as possible. My guess is that you will find that the most reliable happiness is in turning the other cheek, avoiding being the camel stuck in the eye of the needle by selling your excess and giving the proceeds to the poor, loving your enemy, doing good to others . . . . The advice of Jesus is dandy. It is not, as most Christians seem to believe, merely, the way to get to heaven. It is a formula for happiness. Socrates taught Plato, and Plato taught Aristotle, and all three agreed that the wise person knows the straightest path to happiness is through being good. In fact, says Socrates, there would be very little unhappiness in the world if people didn't have the mistaken notion that happiness can emerge from doing ill (e.g., stealing other people's jewelry or virginity). The plainness of truth appeals to me: "Love your enemy," do good to those who abuse you, and dump the burden of your lifetime of acquisition at the nearest thrift store or the charity of your choice. Never participate in hate. "Free at last!" You might want to keep a change of clothes, your toothbrush, and a bar of soap if you enjoy social interaction. Happiness might reduce body odor, but doesn't prevent it.

January 21: On Depression and Piety.

Natural sorrow is akin to natural joy just as roots are to branches—and it is as much needed. I am convinced that depression is inevitable in the person of excellence and, though horrid, a source of piety. In the ordinary person, depression and anxiety are states to be despised and avoided and medicated. The person of excellence uses them as stones in a great open grave, stacking them one upon another as a stairway to the free air. Once reaching there, asking no more than that and being thankful for it. The stairway stones are the reasons for living. The free air is life. So is the great grave. So are the roots. So are the branches.

And what is piety beyond a glimmer of truth. That is all we, as humans, can require of eternity. More would be obliteration of the impenetrably deep and endless wall which separates us from the rest of infinity which lies within it—not beyond it because (for humans) there is no "beyond the wall"—only impenetrable depth. We cannot obliterate it, but we can walk freely into it and experience its immolation a global view at a time. In it, we think we see eternity, eternity bounded. Piety is a momentary recognition of the newly immolated segment of wall-become-exposed eternity as cousin to the walls-become-exposed eternity we have experienced since the moment of our first coherent thought. Lack of piety is the assumption that what we see is all eternity or that what we see is none of eternity. In piety, we recognize that we see both: All because it is emblematic; None because it is bounded. And each of us is All and None. Being All and None is a key to understanding. Without this key, piety is impossible.

Like any human, I curse the depressed state and call it hard names. To defeat it, I step out of me and, from the lip of the great grave, shout encouragements down to the anxious souls trapped in the hole. I shine what little light I have on building-stones.

January 22: Taking Offense.

It has come to my attention that not everyone is entirely happy with everyone else. It seems that, even though everyone in the world is out to do what is right, not everyone is making the right choices about what is, actually, right; and others are noticing and taking offense at such choices. These are, of course, among that vast hoard who believe they are right in their choices between right and wrong, certainly, not those who are mistaken. Those who are mistaken are too busy being offensive to *take* offense.

Because of this untenable situation, it is important for us to consider the most appropriate means of taking offense so that, in our righteous indignation, we do not make mistakes between right and wrong and join the congregation of wrong-doers. So "let me count the ways."

1) Kill the bloody infidel!

2) Exile the bloody infidel!

3) Knock down (with a clean right hook) and step over or go around the prone body of the poor stinking wretch.

4) Hold your nose, pass the prone wretch the latest published copy of *Notes on Becoming a Better Human Being*, and move on with your perfect life.

5) Spend the better part of a week reading the latest published copy of *Notes on Becoming a Better Human Being* to the wretch before giving up on him/her and getting on with your near-perfect life.

6) Commit yourself to changing the world one wretch at a time and spend the rest of your life reading the latest published copy of *Notes on Becoming a Better Human Being* over public address systems at mass meetings at crowded hockey and football stadia or over the airwaves on specially chartered radio and television stations.

7) Admit to yourself that a new edition of *Notes on Becoming a Better Human Being* needs to be written in light of all the wretches who don't seem to understand the current edition.

8) Admit to yourself that the next edition of *Notes on Becoming a Better Human Being* might be better if it includes some of the thoughts of the people formerly known as wretches.

9) Admit that we should include bloody infidels in the same discussion.

10) Serve wine (Concord grape juice for nondrinkers) and cheese at such discussions.

11) Accept yourself as a wretch and a bloody infidel along with all of the other wretches and bloody infidels who made such a big deal out of differing opinions.

12) Learn to love wretches and bloody infidels including yourself.

13) Seek wisdom to know what is right and what is not right wherever such wisdom might be found. Perhaps, you will learn that wisdom and love are synonymous. Perhaps, not!

Thirteen is such an unlucky number, but I have run out of "ways." Perhaps, the idea of thirteen being an unlucky number is just another of those *mistaken* ideas held so vainly by bloody infidels. If such proves to be the case, return to Way #1.

January 23: Conversation about *Phaedo* and the Death Penalty.
Michael Swelton (the W pronounced like a V)
Michelle Swelton (wife of Michael Swelton)
Sam Clear Water

Sam is walking beside White Aloe (a small clear stream in the university's nature preserve). It is a crisp winter day, two days after a 6-inch snowfall. Largely, he is there to hear the crunch of snow under his boots and to see the crystal clear water flowing in the stream beside the melting snow. Michael and Michelle (a young couple taking a romantic walk) approach.

Michael speaks first: Sam, it's good to see you. I have been waiting to ask you about something you said a year ago.

Sam: It's good to see you as well, but I can't remember what I said yesterday, let alone a year ago. You'll have to refresh my memory.

Michael: It was about *Phaedo*. I was upset about a fellow who had received a sentence of capital punishment and asked you to tell me whether capital punishment is just or unjust and you told me to go read *Phaedo*. It was unfair of you to refuse to tell me where I might find *Phaedo*; but, after a week or two, I finally found out that you meant the Platonic dialogue about what was said and what happened during the hour leading up to and including Socrates' death. By the time I discovered that by talking to Miss Apple down at the middle school, I was busy with everything else and had lost interest in the death penalty and didn't get around to reading *Phaedo* until just a couple of weeks ago.

Michelle *(holding onto Michael's arm to prevent slipping into the stream)*: I read it, too. It was really interesting—and emotional. I cried like a baby.

Sam: I did, too. I just read it a few days ago. I've read it probably a hundred times and I still end up blubbering on the last page. My copy looks like it got hit by Niagara Falls on that page. I'm not sad about it. It's just so damned beautiful.

Michelle: Well, it made me sad. I didn't want him to die, and I kept thinking that, in the end, someone would come in and say that they had changed their minds and wanted him to live.

Sam: So you were crying because you were sad?

Michelle: Yes!

Sam: Even though Socrates proved that you should not be sad?

Michelle: Yes!

Sam: Then you were not satisfied with his proof?

Michelle: Yes and no—mostly no. I was satisfied in my mind, but not in my heart.

Sam: Were you satisfied that his punishment was just?

Michelle: No!

Sam: Were you satisfied that Socrates was happy to be dying?

Michelle: Yes!

Sam: You learned one thing from reading Platonic dialogues.

Michelle: What was that?

Sam: The short answer.

Michael: You two are going on and on and leading nowhere. I have a question I want to ask.

Sam: Ask it.

Michael: Is the death penalty just or unjust?

Sam: You asked that question a year ago, and I told you to read *Phaedo.* Did you not find your answer there?

Michael: Perhaps, but I am not very sure of it.

Sam: What is it that you think you might have found?

Michael: I can rehearse what Socrates said?

Sam: Do so.

Michael: He said that he was not sad to be dying because he considered it to be the will of God that it was time for him to die and join others who had gone before him. He thought the company he would keep in Hades would be excellent.

He said that it was proper that he should accept the death sentence because it was carried out according to Athenian law which he had contracted to follow by accepting his Athenian citizenship and all of the rights, privileges, and even disadvantages entailed by it.

He said that his followers should not be sad about his death because all that was happening was that an old man would not be forced to live through the decline and pain of even older age—that he would go to his reward early with less pain involved in the process.

Sam: But how did he know that there was such a thing as life after death and all the benefits he ascribed to it?

Michael: At first, he indicated that he did not, but that if there were no life after death, then nothing is to be feared because his spirit will simply be swept away by the Athenian wind and will be dissipated into nothing. He will not experience anything, no pain, no sensation, nothing. But then, he "proves" (although I am not entirely convinced by his proof) that there is life after death based upon the twin concepts that death is a product of life and that life is a product of death— essentially, that if the soul does not continue on after death the accumulation of death essence would simply pile up until there is no room to store it. Thus, death must produce life and the soul will live again. He goes on to describe an incredibly complex and detailed existence after death which I cannot account for except in the realm of fantasy.

Sam: Nor can I, but is such a fantasy possible?

Michael: I suppose.

Sam: And wouldn't you rather have that than many alternatives?

Michael: Of course!

Sam: Then, take it for the interim. You will find out soon enough what the reality is—or, perhaps, you won't find out.

Michael: I know what you mean. I remember your argument that there is no empirical evidence to support life after death and no rational argument which raises its possibility above that of any other scenario. That we know very little *a priori*. We have a concept of space and a concept of time. We have a few essential mathematical concepts and forms that are not dependent for their existence upon time and space. Also, we know that there is infinite power in the cosmos. These are called "simples." Everything else is conditioned either as rational assumptions made *a posteriori* to our *a priori* knowledge or empirical sensory evidence— phenomena which are called manifold. Through a huge inductive leap, we can call the infinite power "God"; and through an even larger inductive leap, we can posit a benevolent and personal God. However, when it comes to life after death, we have a very small platform of evidence from which to take our inductive leap. It is, merely, a possibility of something being possible. Continuation of our lives after death might be nothing more than, as Whitman puts it, the grass under our boot-soles.

Sam: Then what of the death penalty? Is it just or unjust?

Michael: Just!

Michelle: Unjust!

Sam: And neither of you can tell me why you think so?

Michael: I can tell you. It is because some crimes can only be paid for by death. Nothing else is sufficient. Perhaps, torture, but we don't do that.

Sam: Indeed! And you, Michelle?

Michelle: I just don't think we have a right to kill human beings, no matter how bad they are. A life sentence without parole is, probably, worse anyway.

Sam: And neither of you was able to infer your conclusions from Socrates?

Michelle: No! If he had an opinion, he seems to have kept it to himself. On the other hand, his lack of objection might be interpreted to mean that he approves of the death penalty. I have the feeling, though, that he just didn't consider the justice or injustice of the death penalty in general to be the topic of the discussion.

Sam: That does seem reasonable, but I fear we cannot make such an assumption without Socrates' consent. We can, however, decide for ourselves if we narrow the discussion to that which actually happens in the United States now. First, let me ask who delivers a verdict in capital cases?

Michael: A jury (usually 12) of the accused person's peers.

Sam: And are these persons all philosophers or ethicists?

Michelle: Decidedly not. If they were, they would not be the peers of the accused unless the accused happened to be a philosopher or ethicist.

Sam: Is it possible for a jury to be a jury of the accused person's "peers."

Michelle: I'm not sure what you mean by a peer.

Sam: I'm not sure that I know either.

Michael: Nor I.

Sam: Nor anyone. A jury of peers means, according to American legal practice, that each of the jurors must be an adult American citizen who is of sound mind and not a convicted felon. Common legal practice, also, permits each side (defense and

31

prosecution) in the case to eliminate some potential jurors because they don't consider them to be acceptable peers for this particular defendant. But there are limits as to how many can be eliminated. Thus, at the end of the jury selection, the term "peer" is a very loose consideration.

We have two problems. First, it is impossible to construct a jury of the defendant's peers in a restricted sense that I, for instance, might insist that my peers must be male and old and well-read and talkative to qualify. Would that be fair?

Michael: That would seem fair to me. Those would qualify in several ways as your peers.

Sam: And the second problem is that a decision on a death penalty is very complicated and requires a great deal of wisdom and a lot of knowledge of several fields of inquiry. The only jury which would be qualified to judge whether a death sentence would be just would be a jury of philosophers or ethicists (who are a type of philosopher). Also, they would need to be experts in the particular field (or several fields) with which my alleged crime is involved. For instance, they would all need to be experts in forensics. Finally, they would have to be experts in the law. In state cases, every one of them would have to have a license to practice law in the particular state where the trial takes place. Will such a jury be selected?

Michelle: Of course not. That would not only be impossible to arrange, but against all of the principles of jury selection in the American system of jurisprudence.

Sam: Yet, a jury who is not, in a very real sense, a jury of the defendant's peers and whose members have no credentials declaring them experts in the areas of law and forensics which would make them academically or technically qualified to judge in the particular case and who have no claim to wisdom will make the decision of life or death regarding the alleged offender.

Michael and Michelle: Right!

Sam: Hmm! I suppose, then, that one who doesn't have special means to shape his jury (money, power, influence) should learn to be as pleased as Socrates was with a death sentence.

January 24: A Long Season of Rhetoric Shortened.

Let me recommend at this juncture a careful reading of *Gorgias*—the Socratic dialogue which the Jowett translation places after *Phaedo*. *Phaedo* is a tough act to follow. That is, probably, why so few readers of Plato ever read *Gorgias*. Too bad! It is interesting, and, though it is long, it is relatively easy to read. More important, it contains a particular lesson that is as valuable, if not more valuable, than anything you will find in *Phaedo;* and *that* does not demean *Phaedo* a bit.

I'll summarize for the sake of rhetorical brevity. Gorgias (a leading Sophist) and his disciples in the art of rhetoric try to convince the resurrected (a figure of speech; Socrates is no Jesus) Socrates that they are in charge of the world because, with their fine turning of language, they can convince anyone of anything, and, thus, are the masters of legislation and jurisprudence. Socrates turns the tables on them and, with his brevity along with patches of ironic verbosity, proves that they are not only the masters of an empty bucket (rhetoric is an art without a medium of its own) but that their only task is to be purveyors of injustice. That is, their work is to twist language to prove that the unjust is just. That which is just requires no special rhetoric, only truth. Only the unjust needs twisted falsity to support it.

Thus, your assignment for today is to read *Gorgias* or *The Gorgias* if you prefer esoteric mimicking of Greek grammar in English translation. I would not ask you to do anything which I am not willing to do myself. I read it today. On the other hand, you could believe that my summation is sufficient, and that you can take it to the bank. On the other hand, if there were another hand, which there is not because this is not pinochle, I am quite the rhetorician, myself.

By the way, the reason I am recommending this reading at this moment is that we are just entering a long season of political rhetoric (almost two years of Presidential campaigning) during which time you can be assured that you will hear almost nothing from politicians or their advocates which is true, and it will all be couched in language which, if you are an idiot or have been drinking heavily, might seem to smack of the truth. Be assured that it contains precious little if any truth.

Fellow Americans, I greet you on the eve of a tortuous misadventure. If you choose to enter here, and you have little choice about it unless you take the Socratic route (corrupt the youth, introduce them to strange gods, get condemned to death by the council of 500, drink hemlock—go buy yourself a toga—you can be a [dead] philosopher, too), you may emerge in November 2008 sadder but wiser. Perhaps, not!

January 25: A Worldwide Social Contract.

The world has shrunk since Plato, Aristotle, Hobbes, Locke, Hume, and Rousseau separately, but with a great deal of unanimity, established models for social contract. In much of the Western world, we still follow the general outlines of contract gleaned mainly from the last four, and, particularly, Rousseau. We owe these philosophers a great debt of gratitude for clarifying our politics and establishing benchmarks for our sociological success.

But the world shrank, or *The World Is Flat* as Thomas Friedman claims in his recent book of that title. If I might, in my economic and political ignorance (for I am neither a politician nor an international economist), venture an attempt to summarize Friedman's thesis, I believe he is saying that differences in cultures, politics, religions, races, philosophy, gender, etc. are being steamrolled worldwide by economics. All of these are being, literally and figuratively, run over and flattened like road-kill by the gargantuan tires of the monster truck, World Commerce. For those of you who have not read Friedman's book, bother to do so if you will, but it gets a little boring to those of us who are not into the details of international economics or the close ties between the computer revolution and international economics. You can take it from me that the book is convincing if you haven't already been convinced by the facts on the ground regarding NAFTA and CAFTA and downsizing of American corporations and exportation of American jobs and leaky Mexican/American borders allowing millions of hungry job-seeking Mexicans to cross while a few unfortunate Americans are stuck on the south side of the border because they forgot to pack their passports. It's something of a mess, but change is always a mess at first. Get used to it! It's not a passing fancy. The world is, indeed, "flat."

And that is meaningful. It is revolutionary. It is, most importantly, confusing. As if everything were not confusing enough as we enter the new millennium, we are faced with the issue of not even knowing who is in charge. Is it the governments of the earth led by the United Nations which is controlled by a few of the greatest political powers, each of which has veto power over who gets to use the hairdryer next? Or is it the CEOs of the major corporations of the world, each of whom commands salary and benefits large enough to buy Texas with Northern Mexico and New Mexico thrown in duty-free.

Rousseau's social contract required inviolable national boundaries. Indeed, the most important function of the national government was to protect the nation from invasion by foreign powers. Now the nations of the world are "boundary challenged" from both the outside and the inside. Consider, for instance, Kurdistan, a country which doesn't officially exist because part of it is claimed by Turkey and another part by Iraq. Even significant chunks of Iran and Syria are in that legendary country. But in the minds of many Kurds, Kurdistan stands and lives by the ancient social contract that was, at one time, real and enforced. No more! Turkey jealously guards its part of Kurdistan under the Turkish social contract. Iraq doesn't know what social contract it is living under, and the Kurds are pleased about that. The last coherent government of Iraq under a newly-hanged dictator tried to exterminate them all. Iran, I think, has forgotten all about Kurdistan. They are busy with developing atomic energy and despising Israel whom they might take an interest in "flattening" with their first atomic bomb. Not much commerce between those two nations! Not yet, anyway. But who knows? The Israelis, according to rumor, might be close to signing an agreement with Syria, a sizeable part of whose population would, also, be pleased if someone bombed Israel flat. And so it goes.

Perhaps, what we need is a newly styled social contract, one that changes the nature and purposes of international borders—not erases them—heavens, no! We need those nations. We need Kurdistan. We need Turkey, even if part of it is, historically, Kurdistan. We need Israel, and we should leave her bumps in place. And we need Iran and Iraq, if for no other reason, their names fit neatly together like Yin and Yang, almost poetic. It is, however, virtually impossible for us to continue defending ourselves from each other with massive war machines, including atomic bombs, while more and more countries develop more and more potential for atomic bombs and other massive war machines and don't hesitate to use, at least, the other war machines on each other, and while non-national entities like Al-Qaeda form their own social contracts without benefit of national boundaries. "The world has moved on" as Stephen King says in *The Gunslinger*. National boundaries can no longer be the deciding factor in world politics or in world economics or in world philosophies or in world cultures or in our two genders (along with those who live between the genders) or in our world religions. The Mexican/American border is not working as well as it was when it tried to prevent Santa Anna from shooting Davy Crockett. The Canadian/American border doesn't even prevent Canadians from showing up for *American Idol* auditions. Israel and Palestine seem incapable of coming to any reasonable conclusion about the locations of their boundaries and the Palestinians think the boundary should be the Mediterranean Sea with the Israelis 12 miles wet. They don't want Israel flat. They want it returned to them with its original topography.

We are a long way from any agreement on a new world social contract, but there is hope. America now allows China to sell its cars in America, and we hope we will not die from exposure to the lead in their paint. Hugo Chavez sells (and/or donates) Venezuelan oil to Americans even though he describes George Bush as the devil incarnate, commenting recently that he (Chavez) could still smell burning sulphur around the U.N. podium where Bush had spoken the day before. Indians spend more time emailing and phoning Americans and people all over the world than they do stepping over sacred cow pies in their own streets. And they make a lot of money doing it, phoning and emailing that is. I've heard that people from developed nations are emigrating to India to get those creampuff telemarketing jobs. The catch is that they must learn to speak English with an Indian accent to qualify.

How can we prepare for the worldwide social contract? It is simple: Ya just gotta love 'em!

January 26: Warning! Organized Religion could be Harmful to your Spiritual Health!

Just like warnings on cigarette packages, this warning should be posted on the front door of every church, synagogue, mosque, temple, hall—any meeting place for organized religion: "WARNING! ORGANIZED RELIGION COULD BE HARMFUL TO YOUR SPIRITUAL HEALTH!"

In no way am I trying to discourage people from becoming active in religious organizations. Such organizations have provided much benefit to their members. I would be far less just, far less kind, far less of a scholar had I not been actively engaged in organized religion during my childhood and much of my adulthood. Children's stories about Jesus and Moses and Buddha and Mohammad are priceless treasures that go with us all our lives. No child should be denied them. For young adults, what better environment for learning the art of personal sacrifice, sharing, forgiving, loving, praying, meditating? And for the aged, what better place to spend declining hours and years than wrapped in the peace and beauty of a well-upholstered house of worship. I find myself so-wrapped frequently, even in houses where I am not familiar with the dogma, as long as the inhabitants don't bother me with their damnable evangelizing.

Yet every member and potential member or participant in a religious organization should be exposed to this warning at least once a week and, perhaps, again on Wednesday evening. Maybe even daily for sects that meet more often. Suffice it to say that everyone should see the warning often.

Why? Because it is true! I have yet to find a religion which does not expose adherents to dangerous and unneeded pitfalls for spiritual health. Here are the three most common.

1) Dogma. Every religious organization has dogma that can be proven neither empirically nor rationally (this is a practical definition of faith). Adherents to the organization are expected and are under varying degrees of pressure to accept the entire package without question. Questions are the cup and bowl of spiritual health, and answers to these questions are spiritual health food. To be safe for spiritual health, religions must encourage members to question dogma. But they won't!

35

2) Boundaries. Every religious organization works hard to prove that it is different and, therefore, separated from every other religious organization. Such separation denies reasonable discussion among faiths which is necessary to spiritual health. To be safe for spiritual health, religions must give up boundaries and accept the concept of manifold continua of ideas: that is, every idea extends infinitely fore and aft, up and down, side to side both in time and in space. Any foreshortening of those infinite continua makes the entire idea a lie. Lies are poisonous to spiritual health. But religions will not give up boundaries!

3) Rules against change. Every religious organization resists change. That which does not change is either a nonmaterial simple (short for god in religion; short for the metaphysical according to Kant) or is dead in more than just an organic way—or both according to Nietzsche. Religions, although they claim to be perfect, are not pure and perfect simples. Thus, they must change or die. To be spiritually healthy, humans must not be denied adjustments toward perfection. Religions must abandon foolish prejudices against change. But they will not!

SINNERS, BE WARNED!

January 27: Images and Portraits.

After reading what I wrote the last couple of days, I decided that something gentle was called for:

Juniper
Sprouting from a jagged rock,
One dwarfed juniper
Survives with sagging shoulders.

Forest Sounds
A woodsman's rhythm:
Swing and chop,
Swing and chop,
'Til the sun sets,
Beckoning him home.

First step
A new-born calf
Rises on narrow legs,
Collapses,
Wobbles up again—
Toasting success
With warm cow's milk.

Frost
On her transparent window-slate
The warm room
Writes a love note to winter
In icy script.

Women's Work and Creationism
Soggy diapers
Are a direct result
Of Eve's appetite.

Black High School Girl
The Afro-Queen
Reigns at her locker door;
Her loyal attendants
Obey an impish smile.

Miss Oshima
Not merely small,
A heart large
Beneath the burnished slate of ancient Asia,
Below a *dulciana* of smiles,
Behind mellow mystery.

In Memoriam: Obachan
An orchid blooms
On Obachan's grave
Blossoming purple fragrance
From a heart that loved.

January 28: Vermillion.
Jagged sheets of black
Slash—sharp against rest;
Molten yellow suns
Strafe dull eyeballs;
Death-white winter
Ices slow blood;

Vermillion—Rich
For fatty veins—
Will kill you!

O gentle Humanity,
Look to your soft colors!
Your beiges, your grays,
Your passionless pinks:
They will not chafe tender spirits—
Won't kill you
While you are dead.

January 29: On the Human Soul.

Good, then! After that lovely poetic interlude, we can get back to some high seriousness.

The human soul must be one of the following three:

1) a nonmaterial simple (which means it has no parts) which is *a priori* to everything we are, what we do, and what we think—born parentless out of the metaphysical unconditioned womb of cosmic existence;

2) a material entity created out of our physical manifold clay, part and parcel of the central nervous system and brain, influenced by our entire bodies through the five senses;

3) some combination of the above two.

This triad of possibilities is simplistic, I know. However, such simplicity helps us to understand a highly complex situation.

Option #1 requires that we hold not only a concept of the existence of God, which is not proven and has never been proven satisfactorily without an inductive leap, but resides in the deductive world of the metaphysical; but it is a concept of eternal life, which is even more inductive in a deductive environment which requires absolute proof with no leaps. Of course, we could refer to all of this, simply, as logical analysis of traditional faith.

Option #2 reverses the situation of option #1, having no necessary concept of the existence of God and, further, offering no credence whatsoever of eternal life in the spiritual sense. This option includes no requirement of faith. Mere agreement with biological science will suffice.

Option #3 is impossible. How can there be an entity which is both simple and manifold, both finite and infinite. Yet, as illogical as it seems, if we examine human understandings over the centuries, this combined concept is the one that most religions ascribe to. How many times have we gone through the scientific process of trying to discover whether the human soul has weight? Of course, it has no weight if it is "simple." And we speak of improving the condition of our souls. Again, impossible for a simple. A simple cannot, while remaining simple, change in any way. That would make it manifold which cannot happen to a simple. A simple is a simple and nothing else. Kant, of course, takes us through hundreds of pages of "proof" that such a soul exists, especially, in removing us one step from the material world with the idea of sensory phenomena. But, in the end, we still encounter the impossible which I outlined above in this paragraph.

Thus, we have the faith-based infinite #1 or the empirically based limited soul of #2. Indeed, #2 could be said to be not a "soul" at all, but just the collection of images of trillions of sensations based upon phenomena detected by our sense organs and delivered to our central nervous systems from the moment (or somewhat thereafter) of our conception. And, of course, it can be destroyed partially by any accident to the brain or nervous system and is, presumably, destroyed entirely by death. The only thing that is eternal about such a conception is the scientific claim that matter cannot be created or destroyed, just transformed. In other words, we end up as the grass beneath some poet's boot-soles and ink for his pen. In the Far East, this might be considered to be one Hell of a reincarnational regression. But, still, it is a way to eternal existence. Not exactly popular with the Jesus crowd, but something of a boon for the atheist.

My favorite is #1. And why not? It is wonderful! Too good to be true! And there is the proverbial rub. What seems to be too good to be true is probably false. This is a hard worm to swallow even for a big fish; but what seems to the evangelical Christian or the fundamentalist Muslim, or the devout Jew or Hindu or Buddhist as a slam-dunk gimmee, has no proof beyond "The Bible, Quran, etc. told me so . . . ." Some of us, myself included, think we have additional support in the realm of "experience" with the infinite, omniscient, omnipotent, omnipresent Simple of the cosmos—God, for short. I hope I haven't imagined these experiences that I have, seemingly, experienced (the dying have risen from their death beds, evil influences have fled, the sad have found joy, the ignorant have discovered enlightenment, the lost have been found, and love has covered me like a warm blanket). But, please, don't tell me about your experiences with God. Or, if you do tell me, don't expect me to believe in them. I will not believe in them because they are not mine, and they are far-fetched, and, in many ways, impossible. I can believe only my own experiences whether mystical or imaginary, and I would be a fool if I did not doubt them as well. But I will only doubt them when I don't need them. When I need them, they are there for me, like the simple, that small essence of God, which might be my soul—or a passing angel whose wing barely brushed my cheek.

January 30: Hoeing One's Own Garden.
I think I have spring fever. Only January 30th and spring fever already. Too early! I had better mind my mind. It isn't healthful to have spring fever this early. But here it was at daybreak, furnace roaring, temperature outside 15 degrees, and I was humming the tune of "Inch by inch, row by row, Gonna make this garden grow." I guess I was trying to influence God. That would really be hoeing someone else's garden.

Voltaire put Candide through living Hell before Candide decided that his job was to hoe his own garden. I'm not sure, yet, whether it was a good decision, but it was thought-provoking. It seems to be, largely, the message of Lao Tsu's *Tao Te Ching*. And I can't help liking the *Tao*. It simplifies everything. Essentially, you mind your own business, do good things when they are convenient, go with the flow, do *nothing* whenever possible or when to do *something* could cause you or other people trouble. Indeed, according to the legend, Lao Tsu was setting out on his ox for the mountains for the purpose of doing as little as possible for the rest of his life when he was way-laid by the city's gate guard and begged to write down his philosophy before he left. I guess that we will never know whether the *Tao* is the product of Lao Tsu's writing or if the gate guard just wrote it himself, knowing that no one would be able to check up on him. Perhaps, he salted away quite a fortune with his subterfuge. But I am being cynical! Forget what I just said about the poor gate guard. He took the freshly written *Tao* of Lao and gave it free to the people, and he lived happily ever after in joyous poverty.

The *Tao* has a little of the drab flavor of the last line of the Hippocratic Oath: "At the very least, do no harm." Not particularly bold, and it doesn't seem to fit with the bold, literally vain size of the bills that are coming from the medical doctors of the 21st century. But that is, truly, another story. At this moment, it is hoeing our own little garden we are concerned about—that little garden where we grow a few tomatoes and a few radishes, and lettuce, perhaps, an onion, cucumbers. But to what end? With even a very small patch, one cannot eat all the produce. Does the excess just rot back into the soil or do you give it away? And who do you give it to. It's hard to find anyone who wants zucchini after July 15. I, usually, end up making the cows happy by cutting it up for their half-toothed mouths. But the tomatoes and cucumbers are legal tender. Everybody likes getting them for free.

I had a friend who quit gardening because his neighbors kept looking hungrily over his fence at his extra produce. He said that, since they all had lawns of their own where they could grow their own damned gardens, or, at least, they could help him hoe his garden, they didn't deserve any produce. Thus, to avoid watching their dripping tongues hang out, he quit gardening altogether and now gets his produce at the grocery store, "inch by inch, row by row," with a grocery cart. A few years back, when I was filling in as pastor at the local church, I found a lady selling her garden produce in the foyer one Sunday morning. She was quite a wealthy lady—she didn't need the money—so I risked offending her by suggesting that she either give the produce away to the parishioners or find a farmer's market for her business. I think she has forgiven me. She now gives her excess veggies away in the foyer.

But the whole combined concept: hoe your own garden; at the very least, do no harm; keep your eyes on the ground ahead of you! I find it all depressing. Very sensible, I suppose, but is it wise? We could ask Socrates. He would say emphatically, "No!" The reason: it is not a path to happiness. People who only hoe their own gardens for their own benefit, who only do "no harm," who keep their eyes only on the ground around their own hoe, their own scalpel, their own path, eventually, are not happy. They are like the second sled dog: uncomplicated work, but the view is terrible.

January 31: "Most True!"

> *Let thus much be said; and further let us affirm what seems to be the truth, that, whether "one" is or is not, "one" and "the others" in relation to themselves and one another, all of them, in every way, are and are not, and appear to be and appear not to be.*

> Conclusion of *the Parmenides* of Plato

Do you really think that I would try to explicate that? I'll let you think about it, and there is plenty to think about. I just want to focus on a couple of things: "one" and "the others."

I cannot explain what Parmenides meant or did not mean by "one" or "the others." I cannot explain exactly why Plato chose to recite (or claimed to recite) the entire dialectic of Parmenides, a pre-Socratic philosopher with whom Plato had significant philosophical differences. However, I, unlike Plato or Parmenides, have had the opportunity to read Kant's *Critique of Pure Reason* wherein he might have provided insights as to "one" and "the others."

40

You have seen me use the terms "simple" and "manifold" in previous entries. I will use them here, essentially, in place of the terms "one" and "the others." Whenever Kant is spoken of, the term phenomenon is necessary as well.

Definitions:
1) Simple: A noun. An *a priori* construct of the metaphysical which has no dimension, no weight, does not exist in time or space, but only in the human soul/intelligence one click beyond faith/imagination. Faith/imagination helps us to sense simples, but is not akin to them because both faith and imagination (whether these are two or just different versions of the same thing) require *a posteriori* sensory experience for their existence. Their help in experiencing simples is in their clothing of simples in sensory wardrobes. Of course, this is impossible. Simples are not manifold because they cannot be divided. They have no parts. They are "one." Kant finds the concept of the simple to be both philosophically necessary and logically impossible.
2) Manifold: A noun or an adjective depending upon usage. Describes anything that is not a simple. The difference: a manifold has parts. To become a manifold, a simple must be conditioned (which means that it becomes an entity which has parts) which entirely erases its role as a simple and makes it an object in space/time, available to the human intelligence through sensory phenomena. In terms of Kant's theory, a simple stands at the head of every chain of manifolds. This, too, he says, is both necessary and impossible.
3) Phenomenon: A noun. The sensory experience of a thing in itself by the human soul/intelligence. The human intelligence cannot experience anything empirically except as phenomena transmitted by the five human senses to the brain. Simples are not transmitted as phenomena. They are *a priori*. That is, they never arrived in the brain. They were always there (since they do not exist in time or space) as metaphysical entities or concepts which are, indeed, both necessary and impossible.

Parmenides' "One" is a simple. In many religions, the "One" Parmenides introduces is closely akin to God: contained by neither time nor space, indivisible, unlimited. Plato expands upon such simples as the perfect "ideas" which exist only in the mind of God (metaphorically) for all things as they are in everyday life. "The Others" are the material things as they are (things like a bed that you can actually sleep in if your bed-partner doesn't snore too loudly).

What I want to point out is the infinite chasm between "One" and "The Others." The gap is unbridgeable in our human existence. Most philosophers and scientists in the 21st century have denied the "One" because it is not available to the human senses, while exploring "The Others" with an ever-increasing technology for applying the five senses to them. This is unfortunate. They have rejected the "necessary" in obedience to the "impossible." It makes sense, "sensory" sense. But the cosmos is infinite wherein the "One" makes another sort of sense. Notice that even my words fail me, because the word "sort" implies manifoldness which cannot apply to the "One."

So what will we do? What *will* we do?! I like the way Whitman put it: "I . . . am not contain'd between my hat and boots." Don't most of us have an *a priori* impulse that supports Whitman's contention?

February 1: A Winter Walk.

Siebert and Sam are walking together down a graveled country lane muffled by an inch of fluffy snow which glitters in the morning sun. Each wooden post in the roadside fence is decked with its scoop of pure white snow. The trees are unbowed by the wintry weight on their stiff February limbs. Quite a beautiful scene; but, obviously, winter is not over yet.

Siebert: You've been at it a month now. How is it going?

Sam: I don't know what you are talking about. What have I been at for a month?

Siebert: That confounded book that you so generously included me in. I'm a little worried that I might come out looking like a jack ass.

Sam: So you've been reading it!? Maybe, you are better equipped to say how it's going than I am. I haven't read any of it since I started. So, what do you think of "Miss January"?

Siebert: Who? I don't read *Playboy*. What do you mean, what do I think of Miss January? I have trouble enough keeping up with Mrs. Wilson, let alone getting involved with any "Miss January." I go to church, ya know!

Sam: Me thinks the gentleman protest too much! I'm not talking about *Playboy*. I'm talking about my January collection of philosophical essays. Of course, you have a poem in there as well. You don't have to comment on that if it embarrasses you to talk about your own writing.

Siebert: It was good to see it all typed up. I thought, when you asked for it, that it was too hillybilly for your philosophy book, but it looked pretty good beside some of your boring stuff. At least, mine had some bounce to it.

Sam: I agree. And I am learning from you. You, after all, are my philosopher.

Siebert: Now I know you've been drinking too much of that cheap Sangria. I don't know nuthin'! But if you are serious about what I think about your book, I'll be happy to tell you.

Sam: I thought so. Tell away!

Siebert: Well, you have a way with words. That's for sure. I can read through a whole page or even five or six pages and get a certain rising of the hair in my ears from it because the words fit together so well, but when I stop reading, I suddenly realize that I have no idea what in the world you are talking about, especially, when you talk about Plato and Kant and Widgetstein or whatever his name is. If you just left them out of it, I'd like it better.

Sam (*Laughing heartily and wiping his breath-dampened beard with a white handkerchief*): I'll take that into consideration, but it's hard to leave out the greatest philosophical minds in the history of civilization when I'm talking philosophy. I'm a little like you. I don't feel smart enough to stand on my own in a philosophical diatribe. You have your Bible. And I read it, too. But I, also, have all these other bearded guys (and some unbearded women) whom I turn to for help when I can't think my way through a particular problem. What else do you think about Miss January?

Siebert: Well, she ain't no Virgin Mary.

(Sam laughed again.)

Siebert continued: There is one thing in particular that I was curious about. I've always heard you talk about coherence. You have said that everything has a beginning, a middle, and an end. (You give Aristotle a lot of credit for that line, but it seems to be pretty much what you subscribe to all by yourself.) Also, you say that one thing needs to follow another in an orderly and logical fashion. For the life of me, I can't find that in your "Miss January." She just seems to hop from one idea to the next like there was no need for coherence.

Sam: I see what you mean. But let me ask you something. When you first walk into a new town that you haven't been in before, what do you see?

Siebert: Streets, stores, people I don't know, signs I haven't seen before. You know, just the general stuff that's in every town.

Sam: And, if you were describing what you see as you walk down the street, how would you do this? Would you try to make it an orderly photographic arrangement of what you see, or would you talk first about what draws your attention first, and then add what you see as you go along, then maybe look back over your shoulder at something that makes a noise and talk about that. Remember that you don't understand any of this stuff yet. You are just getting exposure to it.

Siebert: I suppose I would take the latter approach, but I would feel a little guilty, because I would remember that you and our high school English teacher, Eleanor M___, told me I should do it the first way with everything in order.

Sam: Mrs. M___ was right in a scholarly way, but your instincts are better than her scholarship in this case. You've heard her talk about exposition in a book, haven't you?

Siebert: Yes, indeed! She gave that to us over and over.

Sam: That's what Miss January is, exposition. Chaos is the heartbeat of exposition because we go in knowing nothing and come out knowing something superficially, but not yet understanding it in depth. So chaos, in exposition, is coherence. It is the coherence of ignorance. And, Friend Siebert, do you know what philosophers would call the discussion we just had today?

Siebert: Nope! But I'm quite sure you are getting ready to tell me.

Sam: Aesthetics, my dear Siebert.

Siebert: Thank you for this tenderloin of enlightenment! I'll eat it for lunch.

Sam: You are welcome. And, please, as the year progresses, see if you can detect the type of coherence that fits the rest of the year in our book. Remember that each moment has its coherence. Each hour has its coherence. Each day has its coherence. Each week, each month, each year. We, often, even mark our calendars for this daily or weekly or monthly or yearly coherence. For instance, Sunday, in America, has multiple coherence as the Christian Sabbath and as the first day of the week and as a day when most people don't go to work.

Siebert: I see what you mean. Coherence isn't just an orderly presentation like one of Mrs. M's five-paragraph essays. It's the order of our selves, of our families, of our towns, our countries, our world, our galaxy, the cosmos.

Sam: Now you're talking. I think you could write the rest of the book for me if you only had the confidence. You, certainly, have the heart of the matter. I would only add, "and onward into infinity." That would cover the territory of coherence and the territory of aesthetics. Look over there at that snow-frosted locust limb hanging over the big black rock. That's another chunk of aesthetics.

February 2: Marmot Day.

Ahh, Candlemas! A favorite day of mine! Not exactly a holiday, but it should be. After all, there is about a one in ten chance that it will mark the end of winter. According to my recollection, that's about how often Punxsutawney Phil, the marmot/groundhog/woodchuck/rock chuck, fails to see his shadow as he emerges from winter hibernation, and stays out, thus ending winter. Phil, by the way, is not, technically a rock chuck. Rock chucks are yellow-bellied western U.S. and Canada marmots. Phil is of the braver gray-bellied clan which has emigrated throughout a greater territory. (Perhaps, members of these gray-bellied tribes have less scruple about infringing upon the territory of others, or, perhaps, because of their superior gray bellies, they feel they have a god-given right, even a manifest destiny, to "litter" the entire world. However, since they are not Caucasian Europeans, this is unlikely.) But I digress.

Groundhog Day is a product of the mixing of the European Candlemas (which occurs halfway between winter solstice and the spring equinox) with the reverence given by the Pennsylvania Native Americans to the woodchuck or *wojak* as it was originally named by the Indians. The woodchuck often emerged from its burrow about the same time, so it was a natural thing to connect it with Candlemas Day. Europeans have done it time after time. For instance, the Scandinavian *Ostra* (celebrating a pagan goddess of spring and fertility) and the resurrection of Jesus mate up to give birth to the first egg-laying bunny—truly, a fantastic reproductive feat, but one of those strange outcomes of the human need for coherence in religious celebrations leaning too hard on season and not much on reason.

I encourage everyone to celebrate Groundhog Day with a vengeance. Either Easter or Candlemas got its timing mixed up. It's a lead-pipe cinch that we'll have spring before Easter; at least south of the Great Lakes, we will. It doesn't need our help. But a February 2nd end to winter is not such a sure thing. Let's encourage it with a foamy mug or *twa*. But, if you have *twa*, don't drive. Walk, as I do. The snow sounds good crunching under your boots, especially after *twa*. Maybe, six weeks more of winter isn't so bad.

February 3: "Work, for the Night is Coming."

The words to that old Christian hymn came to mind today as I was splitting wood, and, simultaneously, smashing my right thumb between the log-splitter and a log. I didn't stop splitting when it happened, but the air turned blue from the expletives. I didn't stop because I needed at least half a dozen more split 16-inch logs to make it through another week of keeping the lower half of the house warm in the daytime with the wood-burning fireplace insert. I use the fireplace in the daytime for several reasons. Here are some of them.

1) It lowers our natural gas bill (I ain't made of money, ya know!).

2) It, supposedly, is good for the environment, but I doubt this since I fill the air with wood smoke every day which might carry quite a few harmful contaminants to my generous spirited neighbors who say they like the smell of wood smoke.

3) It saves my ancient hot water furnace which threatens every time it clicks on to expire, and which would cost me a cool $6,000 to replace, maybe, $8,000 with inflation since January, 2000,

when a repairman said it wouldn't survive until spring; but I purged it with vinegar; its bowels loosened along with its lungs, and it stopped wheezing and has been faithfully pumping hot water through its pipes for the last seven years.

4) And, finally and most importantly, because splitting wood is good for my health.

My father justified splitting wood until, at 76, he died of a heart embolism (not while splitting wood, but in the summer while irrigating his 80-acre farm with a shovel) on the basis that wood warmed him twice: first when he split it and, second, when he burned it. The first warming was one of the best things in the world for him because it added to his already excellent physical conditioning. His wood-splitting and the operation of his primitive farm were responsible for those hard-as-the-rock-under-his-boots muscles that covered his body until his untimely death. I saw that robust body along with a fierce glower scare hell out of a ditch rider who happened to be Mormon and Dad wasn't, who was, allegedly, shorting him on irrigation water in order to give it to other Mormons during a low-water year. And more than one unwanted door-to-door salesman thought better of trying to sell him a brush or a book shortly after they met him at the front door. He was built like an NFL lineman and had a frown that would make Satan cringe. And I expect, if there really is a Satan, Dad made him cringe a few times, because he, as pastor of a local church, preached sermons that sometimes included that same demeanor. But he was, really, a pussycat. But, once again, I digress.

"Work, for the night is coming." Yes, indeed. One of the few good doctrines the American Puritan colonists of the 17th century preached in New England was that every person should spend part of every day doing manual labor. Even the governors of the colonies had gardens which they worked on a daily basis (allegedly). And I believe! I do believe! I'm not as good about working as I should be, especially, in the winter when it is much more comforting to sit quietly by the fire and, gradually, morph into a huge nasty pile of fatty tissue. But I still split wood; and, after I recover from smashed thumbs, and sore muscles, and angina, I feel much better for it. And I am smarter. For the same reason, I walk up and down hills to my office at least a mile every day during the winter. And that doesn't hurt at all, and I enjoy it, rain, snow, sleet, or hail; and I feel smarter and better as I read and write in my office and respond more wisely when students or faculty members or librarians visit me there—that is, when they don't catch me napping. Then I just look like the foolish old fart that I really am.

We are, after all, what we are. One day, I will die and join my father on the worm's table. Perhaps, they can put an apple in my mouth to make me more festive. Until then, I want to maintain my energetic stride "over hill over dale . . . ."

February 4: The Gentleman of Rocky Acres.

Another of Siebert's poems, this one in honor of my father. I had a poem of my own, but I liked Siebert's better. Siebert and Dad are, after all, kindred spirits. Dad and I were only related by blood. Dad and Siebert were related in their gentle but tough-as-nails souls.

It's a long row to hoe, but I'm hoeing;

It's a long hard climb but I'm climbing;
It's a hard way to go but I'm going;
It's a weary road ahead, but I'm heading.

Old Jasper was a farmer
As he'd been near all his life;
He raised a flock of younguns
And kept a happy wife.

In all those years of trying,
He never had a dime
That didn't have a lien on it
To take up all his time.

Jasper, often, wasn't happy;
And, when he was stuck for sure,
Although he was a preacher,
He'd holler, "Horse manure!"

He used to fret and moan a lot;
His mouth ends pointed down;
He'd sit and mope about his debts,
And kids, and rocky ground.

He wasn't sure he'd make it
Through all those painful years,
And dark brown hair turned silver
Around his sun burnt ears.

He'd cuss a little daily,
And eat his beans and bread,
And sent his kids to college
Where he should have gone instead

Of landing on this eighty
Of rocks and cockleburs,
Spending all of his best years
Serving this dirty curse.

Then, suddenly, the scene changed:
He looked across the board,
And there was sweet gray Judy,
His wife, for a reward.

His eyes began to twinkle:
"Judy," he said, "old kid,"
I've done a lot of cussing;

Sometimes, I blew my lid.

Sometimes, I thought we'd lose it,
Though we hadn't much to lose;
And the kids grew up to work at jobs
I surely didn't choose."

But Judy smiled at her Old Man;
She saw a different cast:
The smile he'd hid for all those years
Was coming on at last.

He tried to hold it back, but lost
The battle to the song—
A cheery grin came bursting through
The frown he'd worn so long.

He didn't fret so anymore;
He knew he'd won the race,
But, sometimes, just for old times' sake,
He'd put on his saddest face—
And say:

"I *am* smiling!"

The epitaph on his grave stone:
"I preached the gospel of Jesus Christ."

February 5: To Do or Not to Do!

I just finish saying that everyone should do something physical each day ("let me hear your body talk!") like working in your garden or splitting fire wood, and now I say, do nothing at all?! Talk about being inconsistent! How can it get worse? So I won't tell you that. What I will tell you is that Lao Tzu said it about 2500 years ago. And he was right, or, maybe, somewhat right and somewhat wrong. Or, maybe, he was just plain wrong, but he had a point. It was in the *Tao Te Ching* (or *The Book of the Path*) that he said it. And it wasn't just a problem of interpretation. It comes out pretty much the same in several translations and in several places in the book. But you have to expand the context. He goes on to say in several other places that there are things which need to be done. An example is a point where he gives instructions on how to cross a river. Of course, one will not have a boat because carrying a boat along on a trip would be to do "something"— which Lao Tzu forbids. Instead, one must swim the river, a necessary task which trumps the "do nothing" rule. You've all heard this before, haven't you? If you want to reach a spot on the other bank just across from you, walk upstream far enough to offset the river current. Then swim across at a leisurely pace and the current will carry you to just the right place on the other bank. I can add further advice for the truly lazy: instead of walking up the bank, use the eddies near the bank to carry you up the river for a hundred yards or so. Then, if you don't sink and drown with all this floating and paddling, you'll get to the other side at the right spot while hardly increasing your heart rate.

Perhaps, the counsel to do nothing applies less to physical activity than it does to political and ethical activity. I disagree with Lao Tzu to a degree. I believe in activism. After all, I grew up before the activist 60s and was at least a little belligerent. I can't throw that overboard entirely, but I have to admit that the ones who stopped traffic by lying in the street (doing nothing) accomplished a lot more good than the ones who stopped traffic by shooting car tires.

Still, if we hadn't built all of these bridges across our rivers, Lao Tzu's advice for river crossing would continue to be useful. Also, we can still consider the advice of Lao Tzu as it comes to us through Jesus. If someone takes your outerwear, give him your underwear, too. If someone smacks you in the chops, give him your Big Mac and fries. You won't be able to eat them, anyway, with your mouth all swollen and bleeding.

This can be carried too far, though. Everything I know about people tells me that someone who would steal my outerwear and accept my underwear as a parting gift wouldn't think twice about kicking me out of the house buck naked into a snow bank—a place and circumstance into which I do not want to go. And you would not be doing anyone a favor giving them your Big Mac and fries. Consider the cholesterol! No! We must use judgment. There is a time for self defense. Let us just be certain that it is, truly, self defense—not revenge. There is no place in justice for revenge. Not "a good offense is the best defense" either—that's rationalization for someone who has itchy fists or a recipe for a successful football team, not the way to handle disputes.

So!—what do you say: "Come, let us reason together. The shirt and Levis and even the Nikes, you can have. The long-handles are mine! Keep your hands off if you know what's good for you!" Or like the old ballad goes, "'Take off, take off my gown,' said she, 'but let my petticoat be'."

And what if he takes your petticoat anyway? *Que Sera Sera!* Perhaps, a Louisville Slugger to his knees the next time you catch him napping! But as education, not revenge!

February 6: Knowledge and Wisdom—Ebony and Ivory.

On the top shelf of the hutch that comprises the top of my writing desk are 15 of my heaviest books, mainly literary anthologies and research guides along with a couple of Old English language and literature books and my 420-page doctoral dissertation. These books loosely symbolize the power of knowledge. The symbolism becomes more poignant in that at either end of the stack is an antique hand-carved ebony bookend in the shape of an elephant with ivory tusks and eye sclera holding the books in a line.

It has been said that knowledge is power, and I tend to live by this maxim in the deepest and least mercantile sense. I take it to that depth with the help of the ballast of a maxim of my own: power is wisdom—again in the least mercantile sense, for with my particular brand of power, I buy nothing and with wisdom I sell less. Indeed, true wisdom is a shrinking rather than a growing. True power makes us lighter; ultimately, if we become truly powerful, we might have no weight at all.

Henry David Thoreau advised, as his first principle, simplification. He presented the image of a man who was unfortunate enough to inherit a farm trudging with it and all of its animals and implements strapped upon his stooping back down an endless dusty road. It doesn't have to be a farm. I saw Payton Manning, the quarterback of the Indianapolis Colts football team on Sunday after winning the Super Bowl. He was named most valuable player and was given a bright red Cadillac and a trophy. I've been thinking ever since that this was no gift. It was a curse. How can he drive that car publicly without expressing an unseemly vanity which I, simply, cannot imagine in Payton Manning? How can he sell it without offending the givers? How can he give it to the poor without it becoming a tax burden to the receivers? Just as we hear in the old song, he has retrieved a mysterious "great big box" from the bay and can't get rid of it.

That is why I say that my wisdom insists upon being nonmercantile. Wisdom is power because it tells us to examine the contents of the mysterious box but to leave it in the bay. Wisdom instructs us to sell the inherited farm and distribute the money, except for seed money and a small house and garden plot for a simple living, to the poor. Wisdom warns us not to buy the lottery ticket for fear that we will win, and the winnings will disempower us. Wisdom tells us that to truly own the land is to look at it from the distance of a high hill, leaning against a friendly borrowed tree and enjoying its shade, all of which, also, belong to us—tree and shade for the moment, the experience for life.

Socrates would tell us that, if knowledge is power and power is wisdom, then knowledge is wisdom. My antique ebony and ivory elephants tell me something about that. My wife claims ownership of these elephants. They were, after all, a gift from her brother purchased in a far-off land for an exorbitant price while he was traveling for the Air Force many years ago. I lean back from my computer (which the university bought for my use) and smile. For the moment, the elephants are mine. Forever (or at least my part of forever), what they represent is mine.

February 7: Montana Dust Bowl "Okies."

Continuing with yesterday's diatribe on simplicity and wisdom, I have about the best example of a simple man anyone has ever known, and he is one of the best kept secrets in the world. Probably, he had only limited choice in his simplicity. Claude Lauftus Butts, Senior, my maternal grandfather, was legally blind through most of his adult life. Along with his blindness, he was stricken with severe chronic emphysema as a young man. He bought a farm and settled with his wife and children in rural Montana shortly before the great depression and the "dust bowl" era hit Montana. Grandma Thelma was a really fine teacher, but she could not get a contract because she was epileptic. Epilepsy was categorized as feeblemindedness then. Of course, she did spend several years during that time giving cooking and canning lessons to most of the residents of Roy, Montana, in return for a small "New Deal" stipend and whatever food was left over.

Granddad and Grandma Butts and their three young children were economically star-crossed, it seemed. It was unjust, but Granddad turned injustice into justice with a wry grin and a one-liner: "Man, these beans are salty—but that's just the way I like 'em!" The only sin they ever committed was to reuse Granddad's awful name for their elder son who finally switched to "Bud" after his school mates metamorphosized the name "Claude Butts" into "Doug Bottoms." But Granddad never seemed to mind being poor. During the early part of the depression, with no formal training, he developed a wind-powered electric generating system for the farm which operated lights, radio, and other small appliances and pumped water for the livestock. He, also, became the leading mechanic in the area for Model T Fords. Of course, no one could afford to pay him so he worked for personal satisfaction and occasional nonmonetary material favors. He mined his own coal from a hillside on the back of the farm and gave most of the coal to the neighbors. He even engineered a canal from a small spring at the other end of the farm and a water tower to provide drinking and washing water with enough left over to irrigate a garden during those drought years of the dust bowl. He was, also, the lead fiddler for the Saturday night hoedown band in Roy, which, also, paid in satisfaction.

But it wasn't enough. Finally, failed dustbowl crops and starving farm animals forced him and his family to abandon the farm. They packed everything they owned into a small trailer hitched behind a Model T and headed for Idaho which seemed to him to be a land of promise. He drove while Grandma (who couldn't drive because of her epilepsy) navigated with her voice by telling him how close to the edge of the road he was and when there was an oncoming car. In Hagerman, Idaho, after working various construction jobs where his near blindness wasn't too much of a problem, he finally, landed a job as the school janitor, which he kept until emphysema forced his retirement in his mid 50s.

The little old house where the Buttses lived in Hagerman and the swampy lot it occupied were magic. His workshop was an ancient green plywood 15-foot trailer house on the back of the lot. It was filled with rusty tools, nails, screws, wire scraps, tin scraps, Prince Albert tobacco cans, and a variety of other "useful" items, all arranged neatly so he could find them with his fingers. Every corner of the house and property had its "invention." I doubt that he ever bought anything that it was possible to fabricate. And the more unusual his designs, the better he liked them. For instance, he carved a hole high up on the wall between the living room and the bathroom and set a small electric fan there blowing into the bathroom to carry heat into the bathroom from the living-room stove, smells and humid air out of the bathroom, the first exhaust fan I had ever seen because, at that time, I had never experienced indoor plumbing in a house before. There was no reasonable likelihood of an exhaust fan for our outdoor farm privy. Of course, Granddad had a major hand in seeing to it that we got an indoor privy shortly after that and a shower as well. My first bicycle was, also, a Granddad rebuilt model from an old frame he found in a junkyard. I called it the Green Hornet (not very original), and I rode it from the time I got it in 4th grade until I bought a car in high school. Granddad, also, showed us how to create our own irrigation ditch steamships with a piece of wood and thread spool and dried horse manure. Dad wasn't too happy with that because our smoking steamships went right by the tinder-dry haystack. We never burnt down a haystack though we came awfully close once or twice.

And Granddad had a great sense of humor. One of my favorites of his one-liners was about a talkative member of Grandma's ladies' club: "If you put a cork in her mouth she'd explode." And, one Independence Day, for the purpose of protecting his shooting marble (his "taw") in a game of chase tag, he invented "hillsies."

He was all smiles and laughter when he wasn't coughing and trying to catch his breath. He loved the life he had, and he helped everyone around him to love the lives they had. When he and grandma died, there was little but trinkets to inherit and nothing to sell. He never wrote a book. He never sold an invention. He never fought in a war (though he spent a year during WWI as an army cook). He never considered himself an invalid. And he wasn't. He was able-minded, and he taught me to be able-minded—creative, to be persistent, to be quiet, to be kind, to be patient, to be able to see infinity, even though he couldn't see his own shoes—to breathe in the pure fresh air that surrounded him when he could hardly breathe at all.

February 8: Let's Take Another Look at this Wisdom/Simplicity Thing.

Bill Smith, a wealthy man and prominent donor to the university, and Sam are talking in Sam's university office while they try out a new tea-brewing pot which Sam has acquired.

Sam: Do you want milk and sugar? I understand you wealthy folk like to act like the Brits and have milk and sugar in your tea. Don't be bashful about it if you do. I keep some powdered milk and some sugar packets in the file cabinet just for such visitors as your distinguished self. My mother used to feed us kids coffee that was mostly sugar and cream and white tea can't be much worse than that.

Bill: Don't be snide, Sam. You know damn well that I like my tea with nothing in it, just like you drink it.

Sam: Oh, I put a little creamer and sweetener in it occasionally when I happen to be reading something light like *Harry Potter*.

Bill (*laughing and sipping his plain green tea*): You are relentless.

Sam: It is good to know that I am relent*less* and have *less* of something than you—other than money.

Bill: I think that you are, also, jealous of my money.

Sam: Maybe, just a little. I admit that I'd like to have more money—if I could get it without putting in any effort. But I wouldn't work my behind off for it like you do.

Bill: Now, Sam, I don't suppose that I work a bit harder for my money than you work for yours. Besides, I enjoy my work. I put in a lot of hours at the store, but I like the people who work for me, and the time goes fast when I'm busy. If I were home, I'd just be in Susan's hair. She'd have me kicked out by noon.

Sam: I know what you mean, Yasmin insists that she misses me, but I notice she's quick to hold the door open for me when I leave for the office. The house is *her* kingdom.

Bill: Ain't it the truth?!

Sam: I had ulterior motives in kidnapping you this morning, Bill. I need your view about something. I've been thinking about the concept of wealth lately. It seems that most of the philosophers and religionists insist that wealth brings nothing but misery, and modest poverty (not grinding poverty) brings happiness. Now in my family, there seems to be a lot to that. For instance, I just finished an essay about

Granddad Butts who you and I both know was a happy man, and he wouldn't have had a pot to piss in if the pot didn't come from the junk yard.

Bill: I didn't know him well. He lived in Idaho, and I only lived there through my high school years and moved away. I saw him a lot when I was in grade school. He was the janitor, of course. He always seemed happy for the shape he was in. He was so damned skinny that he would have to stand twice to make a shadow. And his shirt was always out at the elbows.

Sam: Yes! He was happy, but my question is whether he was happy because he was poor or simply because he was born to be happy no matter what. I'm having second thoughts about the bad rap money gets. Jesus is especially bad about giving money the bum's rush. "It would be harder for a rich man to go to Heaven than for a camel to go through the eye of a needle." "Sell all you have and give to the poor and take up your cross and follow me." (I notice that Jesus was, also, bad about stringing together compound command sentences. Our high school English teacher, Eleanor M___, might have some hard words to say about that.) But I've been looking around and seeing some counter-examples. It is hard to fault someone like Oprah who spends millions of dollars for a school for poor girls in Africa. Bill and Melinda Gates seem to be paying for the biggest part of the fight against AIDS on that same continent. This list of generous rich people who seem very satisfied with life and do a lot of good (a lot more than I could ever do) is a long one.

Bill: I go to church every Sunday and claim to be a Christian, but I have to admit that I don't believe what Jesus says about money. If I did, I couldn't live the way I do. I have a really nice house with a swimming pool and a dandy car, and my wife has a big SUV to haul the kids around to their expensive sporting events. And, I don't think that I'll go to Hell for it. Of course, I try to buy my way into Heaven by giving to a lot of charities. But I have to say that, if I got a little short on money, if we had some down years, those charitable contributions would be the first things to dry up. I fully intend to keep up the good (meaning rich) life. And I'm happy.

Sam: Really happy?

Bill: Yup!

Sam: But the question I want answered is whether it is the money that makes you happy or is it something else that has nothing to do with the money?

Bill: I guess I must *think* it's the money, at least partly, or I wouldn't hold onto it so tight.

Sam: But is it? Socrates says that what really makes us happy is knowing what is the right thing to do and doing it. He wasn't exactly a poor man. Apparently, he lived modestly. He said he didn't have money enough to attend the expensive Sophist lecture, so he had to attend the cheap one. But from the descriptions of his body shape, I don't think he missed many meals. So, if Socrates followed his own advice about happiness, it must have included, at least, a little surplus cash.

Bill: I agree.

Sam: And I have to admit that I like a little surplus myself. For instance, I keep my primitive campground in Idaho for my summers and our nice little house on the corner by the university here so my wife has a place for all of her stuff. Driving back and forth to Idaho isn't cheap, even if I do stay in Motel 6. Their light is always in the window, but their prices keep going up.

Bill: I know what you mean even though I never stay in Motel 6. My wife wouldn't put up with that.

Sam: And I hardly ever give anything to charity. Well, I suppose that cup of tea could be considered a charitable contribution.

Bill: Hardly! But thanks, anyway. I have to get to the store. The auditor is coming in today to check up on me. He wants to make sure I'm paying my taxes.

Sam: I guess we haven't solved anything. You and I are both happy.

Bill: Right!

Sam: You keep making lots of money; and I keep trying to hold onto, at least, two dimes so I can rub them together to keep warm.

Bill: Right!

Sam: So we can be rich and happy or moderately poor and happy.

Bill: Right!

Sam: I guess we did decide something.

Bill: What was that?

Sam: That it is not, necessarily, the money that makes us happy or the lack of it that makes us sad or vice versa because both rich people and poor people can be happy—or sad. There must be something else involved. It must be the knowing and doing what is right!

Bill: Right!

Sam: Well, well! See ya later! But get rid of that big SUV. It's destroying the planet!

Bill: Right! First thing tomorrow!

February 9: EUREKA! I'VE FOUND IT!

Yesterday, I provided a Socratic definition of wisdom: knowing what is right and doing it. Socrates seems to soften the last half of the definition because he believes that any sane human being would automatically do what is right if he or she knew what was right. The proof of his thesis is long and complicated and quite convincing in many ways; but, for skeptics who are convinced that the human will is capable of being evil by choice, I will leave the latter half of the definition in place. Indeed, Socrates throws cold water on the first part of the definition, "knowing what is right," by saying that we all know what is right *a priori* and all the teacher does is make us aware of what we already know. But that, also, is a matter for long philosophical conjecture and the outcomes do not concern us here.

What does concern us is the answer to the question of what makes us happier: wealth or wisdom. I was confused (as is evident from the previous two entries), but in reading Plato's *Philebus*, the light began to come on. *The Philebus* poses the question of which is the greater good: wisdom or pleasure? Socrates maintains that wisdom is the greater good while Protarchus maintains that pleasure is the greater good. It is obvious that both philosophers consider the other quality a great good, and it is largely a contest of intellectual dialectic to argue which is the greater. Still, in my mind, there emerges an important difference between the good of the two qualities: wisdom and pleasure.

To be sure that we are on the same page, note that I am willing to substitute the quality "pleasure" for our earlier discussion of wealth. In actuality, this is not a pure substitution because wealth is the more specific, pleasure the more generic quality. That is, the major purpose of wealth is the production of pleasure (or, conversely, the avoidance of pain). Thus, we are talking about wealth as a member of a large family of pleasure producers.

Here, let us begin the argument of *the Philebus* wherein Socrates breaks down all things that exist into four categories: 1) the finite, 2) the infinite, 3) that which is a compound of the finite and the infinite, and 4) the causes of such compounds. His essential conclusion, to make a long story short, is that perfect wisdom is an infinite and essential component of the mind of God, which is the cause of all causes. Pleasure, according to Socrates, is, also, a member of the infinite class because there is no greatest or least pleasure (an argument which is flawed). Wisdom is, however, a higher good than pleasure since it is not only closer to but is, indeed, the essence of the mind of God.

This, of course, is nonsensical to the empirical philosopher of the 21st century because it requires a leap of faith that ignores empirical reality and assumes the existence of an omniscient, omnipotent, omnipresent, not to mention, *nice* God. But we need not go as far as Socrates goes. We can stay with physical reality to a great extent and show that one or the other, either pleasure or wisdom, is the highest good while they are, indeed, in different classes of entities.

We can start with Socrates' four classes and make some adjustments. Let's make them just two. 1) Material realities along with the finite compounds of metaphysical ideas and material realities. Note that, if you cannot tolerate intellectually the metaphysical ideas, all compounds can be considered mere conditioned physical entities. By "conditioned" we mean that they have causes which puts them on a lower plain of existence than entities without causes. This class would incorporate Socrates' classes 1 and 3. 2) My second class, the same as Socrates' second class, the infinite, is that of pure and unconditioned *a priori* nonmaterial entities/ideas which do not have causes but of which we become aware when they come into proximity with class number one things. Socrates class #4 is abandoned since causes may be either material or nonmaterial. The first class would include pleasure, the second, wisdom. In miniature, then, pleasure is caused; wisdom is not caused. I justify this separation because we simply have no way to measure wisdom. It is an *a priori* quality which we become aware of as we interact with the physical cosmos. It is not produced by the physical cosmos, but is prior to it. Pleasure, on the other hand, is an *a posteriori product* (that is, it is conditioned) of our interaction with the entities of the physical cosmos. Another way of putting it is that wisdom simply "is" while pleasure is "produced." Essentially, my conclusion is that wealth (a conditioned entity because it is caused), a cause of pleasure and a member of its family, is a physical "good," indeed one of the greatest of physical goods, but limited by space and/or time. In other words, it is subject to increase or decay in itself; whereas, wisdom is unconditioned and nonmaterial, not limited by space or time, not subject to increase or decay, but only to being brought more or less to our awareness. Pleasure is, by definition, pleasant, just as pain is by definition painful. Wisdom, on the other hand, does not, necessarily, produce pleasure. Indeed, it can be a harbinger of pain as any of us know who struggle daily with the concept of the absurd in existence. But, as we also know, whether it is producing pleasure or pain at any particular moment of conjunction with the human mind, it is a pure "good." As "goods" both wealth and wisdom can give us happiness, wealth for a particular time in a particular space, wisdom, permanently in both time and space, as long as we respect it—whether that be until we die or through eternity. Wisdom, then, is clearly a greater good than pleasure or wealth.

Note: Keep in mind that, as I argue elsewhere, I do not equate happiness with pleasure. My definition of happiness would be closer to the definition of satisfaction than to that of pleasure. Consider in this regard the ultimate spiritual goal achieved by the Buddha which includes a *satisfying* and absolute balance between pleasure and pain.

February 10: Reasons to Fight.
I'm especially fond of unsubstantiated lists. Here is a list of reasons to fight whether that fight be a kindergarten scuffle or a world war.

1) He touched me.
2) He hasn't touched me for a week.
3) She stole my wallet.
4) He attacked us with weapons of mass destruction.
5) He stole my virginity.
6) She got up on the wrong side of the bed.
7) He didn't get out of bed until noon.
8) He threatened to attack us with weapons of mass destruction.
9) She stepped on my toe.
10) He is ugly.
11) She is black.
12) He has weapons of mass destruction.
13) He is white.
14) He is yellow.
15) He is Jewish.
16) He might have weapons of mass destruction.
17) He is Muslim.
18) He is Christian.
19) He is Buddhist.
20) He said he wanted to have weapons of mass destruction.
21) He stinks.
22) She says that I stink.
23) She looks Jewish.
24) She looks Muslim.
25) She looks Christian.
26) He performed an abortion.
27) He killed Jesus.
28) He drew a picture of me with buck teeth.
29) He drew a picture of the prophet with buck teeth.
30) She killed my goldfish.
31) She spilled my French fries.
32) He likes Tom.
33) He holds hands with Tom.

34) He might have wanted to have weapons of mass destruction.

35) He talked on the phone with someone who, I think, knows someone who might have weapons of mass destruction.

36) He is trying to break my toys.

37) He is trying to break my weapons of mass destruction.

38) She is Catholic.

39) He is protestant.

40) She and Susan adopted a baby.

41) She and Susan got married.

42) He said congratulations to her and Susan and to him and Tom.

43) He didn't say congratulations to her and Susan or to Him and Tom.

44) He insulted my stuff.

45) She insulted my fantasies.

46) He said, "Bring it on!"

47) They brought it on.

48) Nobody could figure out an *honorable* way to stop fighting.

49) We all have to have a job.

50) I just wanted to try out my dandy new weapons of mass destruction.

Disclaimer: This list is incomplete; but it is lunchtime, and Yasmin is ready to fight when 51) she doesn't get her lunch on time.

February 11: Reasons not to fight.
Hmm? Nothing comes to mind at the moment.

February 12: What We Don't Talk About in Third Grade Classrooms.
Place: The local grade school, Mrs. McGagen's third grade classroom.

Mrs. McGagen, a true patriot and a devout Republican, leads a discussion about Abraham Lincoln on the occasion of said President's birthday.

Mrs. M: Who can tell me whose birthday it is?

John *(waving his right arm wildly)*: I know, I know!

Mrs. M: Wait until you are called upon, John. O.K., whose birthday is it?

John: Today is Mike's birthday.

Mrs. M: And who is Mike?

John: My dog. We got her a whole big bag of pig's ears for her birthday. She just about went wild.

Mrs. M *(with a smile)*: Hmm. That's nice, John. But I meant, what person's birthday is it. I am referring to an American President.

Cindy *(timidly)*: George Bush?

Mrs. M *(with a kindly smile)*: No, Cindy. It isn't President Bush's birthday, but that was a good guess. President Bush is our current President.

Michael *(who seems to know everything)*: Abraham Lincoln's. Today is Abraham Lincoln's birthday.

Mrs. M: Right! Abraham Lincoln was our 16th President.

(Mrs. M writes "16th President of the United States, Abraham Lincoln" on the smart board. All of the students except John copy it down on their tablets.)

Mrs. M continues: And who can tell me something about President Lincoln.

John *(waving his right hand wildly)*: I have Lincoln Logs. I can make a whole house out of them.

Mrs. M: That's nice, John. Lincoln Logs can tell us something about the house where Abraham Lincoln grew up. Students, did you know that Abraham Lincoln grew up in a log cabin?

(Several students nod in assent. John smiles proudly.)

Linda *(the female equivalent of Michael)*: Lincoln freed the slaves.

Mrs. M: Right, Linda. He did that. The slaves were people from Africa who had been captured and brought to America and sold to the plantation owners of the South as slaves. They and their children and their grandchildren had been kept in slavery for over 200 years.

Bill: Wow! I didn't know people lived that long.

Linda *(stage whisper to Bill)*: Not the same people, dope! When the old ones died, the young ones took their places as slaves.

Bill *(stage whisper back to Linda)*: I know, Twit! I was just joking!

Mrs. M: Quiet, Bill. Remember to raise your hand if you want to say something. Now, class, what war was fought during President Lincoln's administration?

Linda: The Civil War. My dad said that it killed an awful lot of people, more than any other war, and that it was brother against brother and father against son. How terrible!

Mrs. M: Yes, it was terrible, Linda. And why was it fought.

Linda: To free the slaves.

Mrs. M: That was one outcome. During the Civil War, the Emancipation Proclamation did free the slaves and ended slavery in the United States. That was a very good thing. But there was another principle involved. Does anyone know what that was?

Michael: The southern states wanted to succeed from the union.

Mrs. M: That's secede, Michael. Do you know what that means?

Michael: That means they wanted to get out of the United States.

Mrs. M: Right! But Lincoln didn't believe they had the right to secede, and that is really why the Civil War was fought. And who won the war?

Linda: The North. And the southern states had to stay in the United States.

Ann: My dad says that George Bush is like Abraham Lincoln.

Mrs. M *(her Republican heart racing)*: Yes, I've heard that. Some people say that George Bush is like Abraham Lincoln because both Presidents supported unpopular wars. Many people in Lincoln's time didn't think that it was right to make the southern states stay in the union, and, many didn't think it was right to make slave owners give up their slaves; and, now, many people don't think we should have gone to war in Iraq.

Asa: I don't think so, either. My cousin is there, and I want her to come home. I'm afraid she is going to get killed. *(Asa began to pucker up but quickly wiped away the offending tear and regained his composure.)*

Mrs. M *(with a furtive glance at Michael whose father is the Democratic Central Committeeman. Michael's hand is about half raised)*: Today, since it is Abraham Lincoln's birthday, we are all going to make him a birthday card. Everyone get out your crayons. Susan, you are monitor today, it is your turn to pass out the scissors. Jack, you can pass out green and yellow construction paper.

(Michael lowers his hand and gets out his crayons. He is one of the best colorers in third grade.)

February 13: The Big Bang.

Last night, I watched a documentary on PBS about the Big Bang theory of the origin of the cosmos. It seems that, in astrological circles, it is now accepted as being as nearly factual as it can be. Briefly, the theory states that many billions of years ago (I've forgotten just how many billions) a pebble much smaller than a peanut exploded "creating" (their word, not mine) all of the physical matter and all of the energy in the entire cosmos and sending it on its way to becoming everything that exists and all the power that moves it.

Be aware that I object to the term "creating" because, if the theory is, indeed, truth, then all of the energy and all of the matter was already contained as either matter or energy in the minipeanut. It was already created. That it all came out of such a small object should not surprise us. What should surprise us is that it was *that* large considering that we are, just before the big bang, moving back in infinity to the very dawn of existence wherein the first granule, in a traditional philosophical sense, should be that initial unconditioned granule which would be a simple (indivisible) whole. What we have come upon here is the impossible necessity. That which is the original indivisible simple explodes instantly into an infinity of parts. I fear that the impossible has happened, also, in my mind. I have become even more ignorant about the creation of the universe than I was before. It is magical how learning always brings us closer to total ignorance—and wonderful!

The important change in understanding here is that, instead of dealing with the infinite, science has placed the creation of the physical cosmos except for unorganized space and time totally in the finite. They say that the cosmos contains a finite quantity of matter including a finite quantity of energy. That is different from the earlier theory of a static (in terms of space, time, and matter) cosmos which, while constantly evolving in form, was infinite in every way. In this new view, the cosmos is infinite in terms of time and space, but the material content in terms of matter and energy are finite. Science is making a statement that there is no other matter or energy in the cosmos except for that which exploded from the initial mini-peanut. This requires a whole new look.

Science can make this claim on the basis that if there were other pre- or post-mini-peanut scenarios in the cosmos they would be influencing the segment of the cosmos in which our mini-peanut exploded—and there is no evidence of that. Thus, the only matter and energy is that which came from our peanut. This is an inductive leap too far since our data collection thus far is much too small for us to claim understanding of the forces of the cosmos that lie infinitely far from our little segment. Two counter claims can be quickly presented. First, the other peanuts might be too far away to present any disturbance in our neighborhood. It is possible that the pieces of debris from explosions penetrate only a certain distance into space before they are gathered back by gravity (or forces yet unknown to science) to their mother's waiting black-hole arms. Second, it is possible that when matter and energy from one explosion come near to the matter and energy of another explosion they are drawn from one to the other where they join with the other in an orderly fashion rather than at cross purposes which might otherwise be expected. Thus, we would never notice the intrusion, especially, since it would occur so far from where we are, not quite at the edge of our galaxy and, certainly, not at any extreme edge of the cosmos created by the Big Bang. In any case, I am not convinced by the big bang theory that quantities of matter or energy are finite except in the finite context of one particular Big Bang.

On the other hand, the Big Bang theory raises the *possibility* of the finiteness of matter and energy which cannot be entirely denied empirically. But such empirical ideas are at odds with, at least, one brand of philosophical logic which tells us that, given infinite time and space, whatever can happen does happen and that whatever does happen happens infinitely. Thus, if the Big Bang happened once, that is proof that it can happen, and, thus, given infinite time and space, it will happen infinitely. This logic, however, cannot be confirmed empirically; and it is questioned even by serious philosophers. The big bang theory, for instance, poses the question, why could the coming-into-existence of matter *not* happen only once? Except to repeat my previous rational assertion ("Anything that can happen . . . "), I have no unassailable answer to that question.

The larger question, however, remains: even if it is the only peanut, what caused (created?) the peanut? Or, if that is not a sufficiently probing question: who made the stuff that the peanut is made of? With this question, we are right back at infinity—no possible beginning—yet there must be a beginning—an unconditioned simple—yet it cannot be. Religious *dogma* comes in handy at times like this.

February 14: Eros.
This is the Scribe filling in. Sam seems quite occupied today. When I last saw him, he was sitting in a remote corner booth at the Power Plant Café staring at one of those little cards from a boxed inspirational calendar. The bartender told me he had been sitting there for two hours and showed no sign of moving. My best guess is that we won't see much of him today. That's fine, because I had something I wanted to say today anyway, and he usually has more than enough to say. Thus, I'll be your guest philosopher today. Just kidding! I'm no philosopher, just a threadbare retired teacher who still likes to keep busy with scholarly stuff. Sam's the only philosopher around here. He jokes that there "ain't room for more than one philosopher in this here town, Padna." We share retirement space at the university, but he doesn't spend a lot of time here. He likes to do his thinking in less public places. He's in the back booth of the Power Plant Café today because its 10 below zero and he'd freeze to death if he occupied his usual bench down by White Aloe. But I have an essay to write before students start showing up.

It isn't really an essay. It's more like an encomium to my wife on the occasion of Valentine's Day. It isn't phony like most such encomia. I already gave her a bouquet of red roses. This is just truth about her.

I met her 40 years ago shortly after I got out of the Navy. I was a sad sight. I came into my sister's home in Missouri in the middle of a frigid December night mostly pushing my ailing Austin Healey Sprite which I had purchased overseas in one of many irrational moments when I thought I had more money than Rockefeller on my E-4 Navy salary. I was, literally, running away from creditors in order to get a new start after a bad one in New York City.

And my hitch in the Navy had been no better. I had been too sensitive to deal with the military in war time. I came out with post-traumatic stress disorder (they didn't know to call it by that name then) which left me with frayed nerves, nightmares, and temper flare-ups that still haunt me and have kept me from leading a fully normal life ever since. I still can't sit in a movie theater unless it is nearly empty without my internal organs tying themselves in knots.

I met my wife the very next morning after I arrived in Missouri. It was Christmas morning about 10 a.m. when I emerged from my sister and brother-in-law's basement where I had slept—and saw a vision of beauty. She is a small woman of Japanese ancestry. She had on a bright red velvet jumper and the most beautiful smile I had ever seen on a human face. I, instantly, got out my Sears Roebuck guitar which I had carried since I was twelve years old and throughout the four years I was in the Navy and sang her a love song. She was from Hawaii so I sang "Blue Hawaii" to her and then, because I was something of an Elvis fan, I sang her a rendition of "I Can't Help Falling in Love with You." It worked! We were married in April. (Her elder brother suspected pregnancy, but that was not the case.) We have now been married for 40 years. We have three daughters and eight grandchildren and live in a fantasy which has become truth.

I suppose what I like best about my wife is that she loves me unconditionally. She never asks me about the extremely foolish ways I ran into debt in New York. She doesn't ask me to tell her the painful stories of what went wrong with me in the Navy. (There is nothing about those four years and two months that I am proud of and less that I want to talk about.) She has become accustomed to sitting in empty theaters at 10:30 Sunday morning and celebrating holiday meals in our living room because I can't stand to eat in crowded restaurants. She kisses me every time she sees me, and I kiss her back. The only arguments we have are over her tendency to collect so much stuff that it gets in the way of walking through the house and my tendency to talk too much about wanting to live in the country. She's a city girl and makes no bones about it, and she doesn't want to spend one more day than necessary away from our grandchildren. For 40 years, we have been in love. Our love has not grown because it started out "absolute" and has continued "absolute" to this day. I suspect that when one of us dies, the other will die within the week—like the clock that "stopped, never to go again."

In a sense, my love story makes me a philosopher because I have a knowledge born of that love story which only those with such stories can have. It is the knowledge that in our sort of "absolute" love, each lover gives all of himself or herself to the other and receives back, not just all of the lover, but all of himself or herself as well. That sounds a lot like Rousseau's Social Contract, doesn't it? Except that Rousseau's contractors don't get to sleep together. I woke up this morning with my arms wrapped around my wife, and she kissed me, and I kissed her back. So it has been! So it is! So it will be!

The Scribe

February 15: Attachment.

Following the experience of disharmony in Western thought, it is good to return to the intentional mystery of Eastern thought:

61

Wherever there is attachment, association with it brings endless misery.

—Gampopa

I got this Gampopa saying from one of those little inspirational calendars in a box that Yasmin orders from catalogues. I made a half-hearted attempt to find the original source of it, but didn't find it. I did, however, find a lot of evidence that the above quote agrees with Gampopa's philosophy in general, and Gampopa, obviously, agrees with the Buddha on this issue (see his "Four Noble Truths").

That said, when Yasmin read the quote to me while I was drowsing in my recliner and trying to stay awake during a particularly tedious Lakers/Bulls game, it (the quote) woke me up enough to allow me to say to her, "Could you loan me that card? I think I can make something of it." Then I went back to sleep.

I was taken by the word, "attachment." I didn't really want to find out what Gampopa meant by "attachment," although I did a little research and have a vague idea of it. I think I have enough of my own idea about attachment to do some real damage to you here if you have managed to read this far or if the book just happened to fall open to this page and you consider it a miracle and feel compelled to read it to avoid heavenly punishment. In either case, I hope you get some sweetness and light from what I have to say.

As is usually the case with Eastern philosophical pronouncements, Lord Gampopa was, at least, half right. The other half soars off into space where it could well collide with a mini-peanut and cause another Big Bang. We won't go into that half. It is too messy and too "Eastern" for our present exploration. He was right in his assumption that attachments are a source of misery—and, if misery is always bad, this is not a good thing. By attachments, I mean any thing or idea or belief or assumption which we hold forcefully. By definition, force, is an ingredient in pain (a synonym for misery). Force, is, however, also, a necessary ingredient in any kind of success we may expect. This, I fear, disagrees with Gampopa. I am quite sure that he would say that the "good" does not come from force, but in a balance of forces wherein one's spirit settles into an absolutely peaceful homeostasis; but homeostasis is the outcome of the balance of at least two and, arguably, infinite forces. Thus, force is, if not the only factor, at least, a key factor in the successful achievement of spiritual balance.

And, in the above short paragraph, I have shown how, although we may differ somewhat in semantics, Gampopa and I are in partial agreement in principle. This agreement includes the idea that attachment is the parent of misery. I do not include the term "eternal" in our agreement because I have no idea what impact an attachment of this moment will have on my pleasure/pain status throughout eternity. Gampopa, like so many religious philosophers, is trapped in dogma which he thinks he believes upon good authority but which is, largely, fantasy. In his case, the central tenet of that dogma is reincarnation which I have earlier suggested is my favorite life-after-death fantasy, a half mile or so ahead of the Christians' fantasies, and a much greater stretch ahead of the rest of the pack. But still fantasy! Perhaps, to be courteous, I should call it faith, but I define faith in a different way, requiring more than "the Bible (or Gampopa or Cousin Leroy) told me so." Faith means to me that I *imagined* God; and then, by extension, I *imagined* that God made something known to me. Whether he actually did this is beyond my imagination and even further beyond my empirically informed understanding.

Another addition is necessary in order to express my understanding of the impact of attachment. We must add (as I did in a previous entry) pleasure, because pleasure is the alternative (along with a balance between pain and pleasure which is neither discernable pain nor discernable pleasure). Thus, my version of the pronouncement would be that association with attachment brings both pleasure and pain. In addition, I would have to say that the balance of pleasure and pain in regard to an attachment brings that neutral condition which is neither pain nor pleasure. Perhaps, this is what is intended by the spiritual balance that so permeates Eastern thought. I find it despicable! Seeking that sort of balance means seeking to be meaningless. God (according to John the Revelator) did a good job of repudiating this idea with his "Be hot or cold. If you are lukewarm, I will spit you out."

Finally, we can state this whole argument. Attachments bring pain or pleasure when their forces are not in balance. Forces are, often, out of balance when we are attempting to accomplish a task (which, by definition, entails attachment) whether that task be good or evil. The fact that a task is good or evil does not, initially, mean that it will be painful or pleasant. A "good" task can entail pain or pleasure. An "evil" task can, also, entail pain or pleasure. Of course, the outcome of a good task should entail pleasure and the outcome of an evil task should entail pain. However, unlike Socrates, I am not entirely sure that this is always the case. What should be is not always what is. I suppose the important lesson here is that both pain and pleasure are ingredients in a useful life. If you are feeling excessive neutrality, you are, at this point in your life, a waste of human essence. Watching the rest of that Lakers/Bulls game might be useful as a sedative; but you, probably, will not need a sedative if you have made yourself useful during your waking day. On the other hand, I've seen some dandy games between the Lakers and the Bulls. I wouldn't miss one of those to ring bells for the Salvation Army.

February 16: On Good and Evil.

I opened a can of worms, didn't I? Evil isn't something I like to spend a lot of time talking about, especially, since I know so little about it—and I like it even less than I know about it.

The question is, does it really exist? My wife tells me that it does. She is convinced that she ran smack into the devil himself, and that it was the most frightening experience of her life. I don't disbelieve her because I can't deny the possibility of such an existence, but I don't have (or, at least, I don't think I have) any experience such as that. If Old Scratch is really out there, he's been playing hide and seek with me without letting me in on the game.

But let's step down a rung on the ladder to what the devil represents: pure evil. There are many stances taken and more stances are taken as we move forward into the modern world. One is that evil is an extant thing in itself and that it stands in opposition to good which is, also, a thing in itself. In this regard, if they are both things in themselves and they are the opposites of each other, they must have essential forms of pure good and pure evil standing at opposite ends of the continuum. This stance is common in western religions. One chooses pure good to go to Heaven. The choice of pure evil buys a ticket to Hell. That giant missing middle is what causes much of the contention among religious sects. Of course, there are some specific pieces of dogma in each religion which must be followed: Christians must accept Christ as the only begotten son of God and as their Savior. Muslims must honor and worship Allah and pay no homage to any other deity in accordance with the teachings of the Quran. The Jews would rather not think much about Heaven and Hell, but there is certainly good and evil to consider in Judaism. Blatant disobedience to one or more of the Ten Commandments can get you shunned by parents, siblings, and congregation. But, let us face reality. Most Christians don't show by their daily lives that they truly believe in the teachings of Jesus (e.g., few of them give away all of their excess cash and baggage as Christ instructs). And Muslims don't always honor Allah, and Jews do not always honor their fathers and their mothers, and they are seldom tossed from the fellowship of family or congregation for it. Apparently, the dogma of "forgiveness," especially of friends and family, is often stronger than devotion to God or his son. At any rate, the dogma persists that evil and good exist even if not many believers indicate by their actions that they believe.

My guess would be that most moderns have a less absolute take on good and evil. Many, for instance, consider evil to be the lack of good, a void. This works well because then we can consider the ill consequences of evil to be just the loss of happiness because we have not pursued the good—very Socratic. And quite practical! By dumping Satan, we save half of our religious capital by reducing the number of spiritual beings we must love or hate; and, since hating is not a productive posture for our emotional health, it might even keep us from winding up in psychological counseling. This is the middle ground, a rung on Jacob's ladder which is neither near the ground nor in the clouds.

Nietzsche seems to be the founder of the most modern movement wherein there is neither a thing which is good nor a thing which is evil. Both are, merely, constructs to keep lesser humans in line while the true leaders lead from the privileged locus of their sphere of existence which lies "Beyond Good and Evil." It might come as a shock to realize what a large segment of the population has bought into this kind of thinking. By another name, cultural relativism, it seems to have become the gospel of everyone who does not specifically buy into one or another of the various religious dogmas—and many who do, since several major cultural groups have adopted the cultural relativist stance as part of their dogma and are commanded to respect other dogmas. Cultural relativism allows each social group, culture, nation, state, religion, cult, etc., to adopt its own positions on good and evil, the only restriction being that their positions must not interfere significantly with the positions of other proximate groups. Sounds good until you try to apply it in real human situations. Then war is inevitable.

My advice? Follow the middle trail. Whether or not Old Scratch exists, don't think about evil as a "thing" to be avoided. This is to be good out of fear. Rather, think of good as a flavor to be relished. You can even keep a little money as long as it doesn't wear your pockets out and fall through the holes. Honor your father and your mother if they behave themselves. If they behave badly on a regular basis, love them anyway, but only honor what is honorable. It would be dishonest to do otherwise. Certainly, love God! Or love whatever you choose to call that infinite power which dreamed the cosmos and you into existence. It's a nice dream. Be thankful for it. And love your neighbors including the ones who keep riding their bicycles over your tulips. Even if your life turns out to be short and painful, just an occasional glimpse of physical beauty makes the trip worth its while.

A Few Days on Forms of Government

February 17: Part 1: Three Forms of Government.

I'm not going to bore you with all of the details of all of the different philosophical ideas that have occurred over the centuries about the best forms of government. Just be aware that I am winnowing down the thoughts of five philosophers into *soft* conclusions which you may wish to accept or reject or partly reject and partly accept. To winnow these ideas down is like turning gold into feathers and flinging them into a whirlwind, but I'll give it my best effort.

The favored five are Plato (speaking for Socrates), Aristotle, Hobbes, Locke, and Rousseau. This is not to say that these five say it all. Many other important philosophers have spoken about government, but each of these five has put together a coherent essay about the best forms of government. Also, it is almost shocking that they all seem to agree as closely as they do in their conclusions.

First, the three forms that constitute the trinity of government forms are 1) monarchy, 2) oligarchy, and 3) democracy. Monarchy is rule by a single person (usually a *man* according to the favored five philosophers). Oligarchy is rule by a limited group of people. Historically, the limit has had more to do with hereditary nobility than any other single factor, but more recently, land-ownership and/or financial wealth have played a greater and greater role in oligarchic membership. Democracy is rule by the many, never, by all. Enfranchisement is, usually, a matter of citizenship, but often requires a variety of other tests including such matters as land ownership. Indeed, citizenship, itself, is often far more complicated than it would seem. Many democracies have had fewer than 25% of the populace voting. The first two slices cut out of the voting pie were almost always women and children. That, in itself, reduced the voters to far less than half of the populace. If you then cut out slaves, resident aliens, those who own no land, those who have criminal records, and those who are illiterate you have a fairly accurate picture of the modest voting register of early democracies, even the early 19th century in the United States. Those percentages have increased (note that increase in percentage would not be a positive thing in the eyes of most of the philosophers) in more recent days.

Another important factor is the way the "social contract" is enacted. In one sense, it might never be enacted at all. There is seldom an election, not necessarily a revolution, no single moment at which we can say that the people of a society have chosen the form of government which is chosen. Somehow, in the midst of all this ambiguity, a decision is made and becomes law.

Also, it is widely assumed that the social contract is agreed upon by 100% of the citizenry (with the limitations mentioned above). There are no dissenting votes except through exile or death. And, by the way, voluntary exile is widely considered to be an absolute right, at least, at the time of the enactment of the social contract. Voluntary exile after the contract is in force might require legislation for its acceptance or rejection. Furthermore, no individual citizen or group of citizens less than the entire citizenry may overthrow the social contract (although the government itself can enact legislation which allows some percentage of the citizenry to overthrow the government through legal means such as petition or election) once it is in force. It can only be overthrown by a legitimate act of the government itself, by the government itself declaring itself at an end, or by an illegal revolution. An important note: it is relatively easy to tell whether a legitimate social contract is in place in a society. It is, often, impossible to tell when and exactly how that social contract came into being. In some societies (e.g., the United States) the process and the timing are quite well marked. But the American Revolution itself might be questioned as an illegal usurpation. However, it could be argued that the British had already broken the contract by disallowing rights provided to the colonists by their British citizenship, thus making the revolution legitimate. In other societies (e.g., England) the process was spread over a period of hundreds of years. In still other societies (e.g., France in the late 18th century), what began as an illegal usurpation of the government (although, as in the American colonies, revolutionaries could argue that the government had already broken the contract through its atrocities) evolved (haltingly!) into a legitimate social contract.

One more matter is important here. That is the fact that there are good and evil manifestations of each of the three forms of government. Thus, even though the philosophers are largely in agreement as to which form is best, which is second best, and which is worst, they all recognize that an evil manifestation of any of the governments might be the worst government of all.

Finally, unless all of the above is in place, there can be no legitimate social contract, no legitimate government. Immediately, you can see that many (perhaps, most) of the governments in existence now and those that have existed in the past are illegitimate. If no legitimate social contract exists in a society, it is legitimate for any resident or group of residents without regard to citizenship to lobby for a social contract of their choice and work toward its legitimate enactment.

The above forms an essential basis for the establishment of a social contract (i.e., a legitimate government).

February 18:   Forms of Government, Part 2: The Best of Show!
And the winner is . . . monarchy! Is anyone surprised? It is true, but it doesn't come without conditions, and these conditions rule it out immediately for any large society. Monarchy is the best form of government if and only if it can be shown that a particular person is, indeed, the person best suited to be the absolute monarch of the society and that the entire society agrees with this conclusion. Then the social contract would have to end upon the death of the king or the inability of that king to rule. The only way around this conclusion is to have the monarch name his/her own successor or to have some means whereby the successor is automatically crowned upon the death or incapacity of the monarch. Often, in earlier days, that successor was assigned by primogeniture wherein the oldest son of the king became the king. Lacking a son, the oldest daughter might inherit the

throne. England still abides, essentially, by primogeniture. However, the English monarch has not been absolute since the Magna Carta of the 13th century.

Such were the original contracts of small societies made up exclusively of family members or of small villages and tribes. If we think of the contemporary family, and even the extended family to a certain extent, such contracts continue to exist within larger contract societies. The Mafia families of southern Europe with their "Godfathers" are, probably, the best examples; but we can see smaller and less formal societies (families including, perhaps, some hired help and close friends; also, churches, etc.) which turn upon the ruling hand of a single individual for life. The death or mental disability of that person is nearly always cause for a revolution that brings about the crowning of a new monarch or the dissolution of the society. However, in this series of essays, I am speaking, mainly, of governments of larger societies such as countries, not small group social contracts within social contracts.

Just what is it that makes monarchy (in its ideal form) the best form? Efficiency! One person makes all final decisions. If, indeed, this one person, the monarch, has all of the characteristics of an ideal monarch (character, strength, intelligence, loyalty to the people, honesty, integrity, etc.), his decisions will be as good or better than any decision by a group of persons, only one of whom could possibly be the "best," and he would be able to implement them immediately. What a difference that could make in response time in a war or other national emergency. It seems there can be no doubt about the superiority of such a system. Indeed, most corporations continue to abide by it in the sense that the boards of such corporations nearly always choose a CEO with absolute *immediate* powers within the *mediated* framework of laws under which the corporation is organized. It would seem ridiculous to do otherwise. Of course, there is a difference. Most corporations are governed, first, by an oligarchy in the form of a board (in office, largely, by virtue of their stock holdings) which, in turn, hires a CEO who they can fire if he/she does not follow the will of the board. Such a system allows for the ideal person for the job to be a limited monarch who is on a short leash held by an oligarchic board—a hybrid. This limited monarchy is considered by several of the above philosophers in one form or another.

Should every country consider having an absolute monarchy? Heavens, no! None should. Even if all goes beautifully through the reign of King/Queen Senior, King/Queen Junior will probably be a loser; and, even if the throne is not inherited by primogeniture, no tyrant could be lucky enough or smart enough to select the right successor on a regular basis. Keep in mind that bad choices are the norm in politics.

February 19: Forms of Government, Part 3: The Worst of Show (In Honor of American Presidents' Day)!
The loser: dear old democracy!   It is unanimous, and for good reason! Democracy, though nearly always, in modern times, defined in glowing terms, is, at base, the inmates running the asylum. And that can be, truly, base. Despite Thomas Jefferson's faith in the people, popular elections wherein nearly everyone over 18 has the right to vote cannot be expected to elect the ideal candidates on a regular basis. Elected officials' chief goals will be to please the people while filling their own pockets. (Note that we have not considered economic systems, but capitalism

and democracy flock together like blackbirds and make just as much mess of statues and other national treasures.) Of course, the goal of pleasing people will be, largely for the twin purposes of reelection and pocket filling. Indeed, that is the reason why democracy is so successful. A voter will seldom vote for the candidate who is less likely to line that voter's pockets. Thus, the candidates, usually, must have a tempered will to riches which includes allowing as many others as possible to benefit financially from the elected official's money-grubbing. The more financially satisfied voters, the more likely the official's re-election. Also, financially satisfied voters are good for the mood of a country and, also, drive down crime and reduce the incidence of social movements opposed to the government. This, in general, means a longer-lasting and happier country—thus, a successful social contract.

But am I being cynical? Indeed, there are many idealistic persons in each democratic society who, occasionally, make it into the halls of congress/parliament and even into the presidency/prime ministry. It happens. Usually, it is not a tremendously successful tenure for either the people or the elected idealist. Consider, for instance, the election of Jimmy Carter as American President. The system is simply not made for them. More commonly and more successfully, such idealists stand in the background as advisors and/or adversaries to the elected officials like voices "crying in the wilderness." (Note, again, the post-presidential Jimmy Carter.) Theirs is a critically important role. Most persons, as selfish as they are, prefer the good. Socrates was right—to an extent. If right or wrong is to be chosen, and a person is capable of differentiating between right and wrong, and if choosing the right will not diminish the person's purse or comfort, that person will choose the right. In other words, people are, basically, good. However, it takes but a breeze of stimulus toward evil to make them sway in that direction; but, without that "ill wind," they are good. Thus, the idealist serves as a wind break against the "ill wind." Of course, at the same time the "ill wind" is being blocked from the general populace, it is busily blowing through the halls of congress/parliament and through the presidential mansion infecting the elected officials who then bend toward the evils. Sometimes they lose their offices because, while they are bending toward evil, the voters are bending toward good and throw the bums out. Sometimes the bending is going the other way and the voters go out of their way to find bums to put into office. All in all, democracy becomes and stays a fat, sloppy, rich, comfortable mediocrity. Democracies seldom start wars (current American administration excluded). They are too indolent for that. They would rather eat and sleep than fight whether the fight is for good or evil. Perhaps, this is good. With a world full of democracies, there would be more eating and snoring noises than there would be cannon noises.

February 20: Forms of Government, Part 4: The *De Facto* Winner!
Oligarchy takes the prize of the system most likely to win out in the end and most likely to achieve societal success. Oligarchy is defined as government by the few. The few sometimes becomes a numerous few, and the qualifications for membership in the ruling class vary dramatically. The basic requirement, however, is individual social power. Societies which are intentionally oligarchic usually set up specific requirements. Some make it easy by establishing a hereditary noble

class. Often, this class is a remnant of the ancient feudal system wherein the nobility ranked below the royal family and above the commoners who formed up the vast majority of residents in the society. Of course, the insertion of the merchant class upset the system by adding a social group whose power lay in wealth rather than blood. Since the merchants were politically equal to the peasants, theirs became a joint venture, creating the middle class and the lower class divided by wealth and lack thereof. The merchants were joined in the middle class by successful lower class persons who beat the system to become wealthy. Merchants whose shops were robbed once too often by wealth-gathering peasant employees or whose ships sank joined the lower class. The hereditary nobility remained noble and "better" than the rest of society whether rich or poor and, generally, in their declining political power, established a somewhat pitiful (because it was mainly bluster) House of Lords. The commoners, in their own defense, formed a more powerful (because of their wealth and numbers) House of Commons. The royal family was, often, kept on as a treat for everyone else on special holidays when they were trotted out in all of their splendor to be unamused by the masses.

Pardon me! I seem to have described Great Britain in the 21st century. This dear old empire is an example wherein all three forms of government still exist. They are, technically, a democratic socialism [wherein socialism has accepted being seated in the back of the bus while capitalism grumbles in the front, but democracy (the House of Commons) is quite viable and noisy]; wherein oligarchy (the House of Lords) carries a political voice which is largely ignored; and wherein the royal family still does its share of emblematic trotting out with the paparazzi trotting along behind. England is one of the oldest representative governments. It could be said to date back to the Magna Carta in the 13th century. In most of those early days, it was oligarchic, with an hereditary nobility with its military, political, and economic force overshadowing the monarchy. Eventually, with the emergence of the middle class, it became democratic and, largely, capitalistic and has remained so to this day. It is questionable, however, whether it would have been such a stable government had the House of Lords not continuously exerted its immodest but feeble power long enough for socialist powers to redistribute wealth and human rights during and after the industrial revolution at the urging of Charles Dickens, etc., in the 19th century.

Philosophers insist that it takes an oligarchy to raise a society. And, perhaps, they are right. Although America's democracy seems, on the surface, to be a glittering exception to that rule, a closer look shows us that our democracy has constantly utilized unofficial oligarchic assistance to develop and maintain itself. Usually, this shadow oligarchy is carefully cloistered in the kitchens of government, invisible; but, from time to time, we see it peeking around corners seeking its supper.

One of those times when it got caught in full dinner attire was during the Nixon years. It became clear that President Nixon (surrounded by a brigade of wealthy and influential oligarchs), while pretending to accept the democratic triumvirate of a bicameral legislature, executive branch, and judiciary, was attempting to run the entire enterprise from the White House. I'm sure he felt this was justified since we were engaged in a major war which required a great deal of command from the commander in chief; and, perhaps, it was. However, when it became public how much lack of respect President Nixon had for the other branches of our democracy, the house cut off his money supply and the shadow government went back to its law offices and arms factories.

That was a bad moment for us, but it highlights the fact that, without some factors of oligarchy, it is difficult to accomplish the necessities of operating a large and complex society. The halls of congress are littered with representatives of industry delivering their message of corporate financial power to our democratically elected representatives. Our elections require the expenditure of many millions of dollars which an individual from the general populace cannot acquire without the help of powerful financial interests. Thus, most members of congress and senate, the administration, and, by extension, the Supreme Court, are rich and powerful citizens, many of whom have been educated at such exclusive universities as Harvard and Yale (which, by the way, give special access to members of families which have previously sent students to Harvard and Yale and to people who donate large sums of money to those institutions). All of this smacks of oligarchy. A very large (dangerously large, some would say) part of the population is allowed to vote. Large segments of that population are easily manipulated by oligarchic forces. For instance, we can see such sinister political connections as the religious right with the fiscal right. The religious right is comprised largely of conservative Christians who insist that they diligently follow the teachings of Jesus, among which is the commandment to eschew wealth. The fiscal right is made up, largely, of wealthy oligarchs whose eleventh commandment (or is it their first) is to become as rich as possible. One way they have discovered to become and stay wealthy is to enlarge their political clout by taking up arms with the religious right against gay marriage and abortion in order to align the vote of the religious right with the fiscal right. And the left does it, too. Notice how close the intellectual left became with the deadbeats, drug addicts, and other degenerates of the beat generation when it meant that they could get help from them in ending the Vietnam War. A noble cause, I am sure, but it meant that oligarchs (this time with intellectual power) used their power to ensure political gains. It will not end. As long as there is successful democracy, opportunistic oligarchy will be lurking in the shadows manipulating political outcomes.

But that is not all bad. If oligarchy simply folded its tent and went away, the asylum would, indeed, be in the hands of the inmates. It would not be long before many of us would be seeking a better asylum in Canada to escape the chaos that would ensue. For examples, see Central and South America over the last couple of centuries. See pre-WWII Germany. Democracy must be conscientiously managed or it will be disastrously mismanaged. That, often, means secret management. But does that mean we should, simply, let oligarchy have an unimpeded shot at democratic ideals? Certainly, not! We must continue with all our might to fight against the emergence of the oligarchic state. It must be contained. It has its own kind, a much more subtle kind of evil than democracy. Unmanaged democracy breeds revolution and eventual tyranny. Unchained oligarchy breeds the type of oppression and cruelty which was dealt to black Americans for hundreds of years, Japanese Americans during WWII, Chinese and Balkan immigrants during the industrial revolution, to those Americans and immigrants unfortunate enough to have Middle Eastern physical features in the

70

current era of international terror, to all those who lack the power to protect themselves. It is evident that what the ancient Buddhists and Hindus taught about balance is an important ingredient in the management of a political society. Carefully managed democracy seems, at present, to be the best form for most developed nations of the 21st century world. But we must never reject the good offices of the oligarchs who seek to make us a better nation and a better world: those brilliant thinkers who have spent their lives learning; those genius CEOs who know the path to wealth; those who know best how to repel an invading military or terrorist force. We must, merely, limit them to the fringes of politics. And our kings and queens, princes and princesses, dukes and earls—I say trot them out every holiday so we can enjoy their silly anachronisms. For those of us in countries which have done away with such frippery, we can turn to the clergy for similar entertainment. Some of them will even dress up for us in funny hats and robes. We should, however, keep our hands on our wallets and our eyes on our children while the clerical royalty performs its "sacraments." Some of them have worse than oligarchy in their souls.

February 21: Fat Tuesday and Ash Wednesday.

It all has a loose connection with the eventual death and resurrection of Jesus: Fat Tuesday and Ash Wednesday. But, in the minds of most of us, we forget Ash Wednesday, except for seeing occasional Catholics navigating through the day with ashes on their foreheads. You might be tempted to judge their devoutness by how long it takes them to, finally, wipe them off. It takes a real commitment to keep them on all day. One must respect such commitment. Of course, it isn't much along side of dying on a cross, but it is commitment. Most of us just think of Fat Tuesday not as Fat Tuesday but as the *Mardi Gras*. It is a day in New Orleans ("all my sorrows, Lord . . .!) when many folks forget their morals and do whatever they can get away with. Most commonly, a few women flap their bare bosoms in the open air and other people walk around in ridiculous costumes, advocates of every type of social cause take noisily to the streets, all but the strict Mormons and conservative Muslims get drunk, and, in general, everyone makes Merry and themselves into fools. The next day, they all have hangovers, so it is a good day to engage in quiet meditation. Suddenly, all the Tom-foolery stops and, while the rest of us sleep in, the devout Catholics go to mass and get ash crosses smeared on their foreheads.

Friends and neighbors, there is nothing at all wrong with this, so long as no small children get run over by parade floats and no one dies of alcohol poisoning. We need to celebrate something even if it is overly chunky breasts being flapped in a New Orleans breeze. If ya got 'em, flaunt 'em! That is Dionysus coming out in us. The God of wine and the feast! The guy who keeps us joyously insane in an insane, ridiculous, meaningless, painful world where nothing at all makes the least bit of sense. But Dionysus must be hog-tied and locked back in his closet before his craziness gets even crazier than the rest of the world's craziness. Then, out comes Apollo, with his lyre and his wise contemplation which, itself, can only be wise for special holy days, funerals, weddings and other solemn rites. Of course, some of us who consider ourselves philosophers tend to get all wrapped up in "Apollonianism" so much that we can't think of anything else until lunch time rolls around. Ash

Wednesday is essential Apollo time—a sort of time out for those of us who are too old for time outs. Lent has arrived. Everyone, even folks who aren't Catholics, are apt to give something up for Lent. Some of the Catholics even keep giving it up all the way through Lent. One of my grandsons (not a Catholic) gave up wasting his money because he is out of money anyway. I might slip him a fiver just to see how fast he will break his fiscal fast.

But, again, there is nothing wrong with all of this as long as we don't do something that will cause us or someone else undue pain and suffering. We tend to get far too hung up on "the good" when "the good" is far simpler than most of us ever consider it to be. Jesus wrapped it up in a few words when someone asked him what the greatest commandments were. He said: "The first one is to love God." We might speculate that he had to say that because, he was, after all, Jesus, and his alleged father (God) could be imagined as standing right there with him, listening in. It was only courteous and respectful of Jesus to say something nice like that. Then he said that the second commandment is like the first. In fact, I might add, it was exactly the same as the first: "Love your neighbor just like you love yourself." Of course, your closest neighbor, no matter how you shake it out, is God. If, like me, you don't analyze God too much, just buy psychologically into the existence, not many of the details, there is that infinite force not just beside you but inside you. As with Jonah's situation, there is no escape. If you are more traditional and make God into a gray-beard, there he is, too. Only more silly because it is quite silly to give God a gray beard. Maybe, we could, also, give him gout and age spots. Anyway, after those two commandments, which are actually only one, Jesus said something like "If you tend to these two, the rest will tend to themselves." Simple, huh?!

So enjoy your *Mardi Gras*! Then wake up with a headache the next morning and go back to sleep or go to mass and get an ash cross fingered on your forehead. Heaven (whatever god or spirit or entity represents it) won't mind. My guess would be that, with the tall sense of humor God displayed when he made my body, he would be right there at the *Mardi Gras* celebration tipping his hat and a glass of Ambrosia. But I refuse to imagine God with big bare bosoms flapping in the New Orleans wind—that is just too silly!

February 22: The Father of Our Country (if you happen to be from the United States).
Once again, in Mrs. McGagen's third grade classroom:
Mrs. M: Who can tell me, class, whose birthday it is today.
John: *(waving his right arm wildly)*: Ooo! Ooo! Ooo!
Mrs. M: *(trying to ignore John)*: Anyone?
John: *(waving both arms wildly)*: Ooo! Ooo! Ooo!
Mr. P: Alright, John. Whose birthday is it?
John: George Washington's!
Mrs. M *(noticeably relieved)*: Good! And who was George Washington.
John: George Washington is the father of our County.
Mrs. M: You mean "country."

John: No. I think he was borned in the City, not the country. I think he was borned in Washington, D.C. At least, it has the same name as what he has, except for the D.C. I don't know what that is.

Mrs. M: That stands for District of Columbia, John. Someone help us out here. What do we mean when we say that George Washington is the father of our country?

Linda: He was our first President . . . and he was our first general in the army, too. He won the revolutionary war.

Mrs. M: Right! At least, he was an important leader in winning the war. And when was the Revolutionary War?

Susan: 1776.

Mrs. M: Good! That's when it started. But it lasted for several years before it was finally over. Who were we fighting against, William?

William *(taken by surprise as he was handing a note to Phil)*: Uh!

Mrs. M: Pay attention, William. Someone tell William what the question was.

Tom: Who are we fighting?

William: Iraq!

Mrs. M: That's who we are fighting now. Who were we fighting in 1776 in the Revolutionary War?

William: Oh! England. And we won and became America instead of the Colonies.

Linda *(stage whisper)*: We became the United States, William.

William: Right! The United States.

Mrs. M: And George Washington, after being the commanding general of the Continental Army and helping to win the war, was elected our first President.

Michael: They wanted him to be king.

William: We don't have kings in the United States!

Mrs. M: That's right, William, but Michael is right, too. Some of the citizens wanted Washington to be crowned king. But we don't have kings. Why do you suppose that is?

William: Because they were sick of kings. The English king had been really bad to them. And you can't have any freedom with a king.

Mrs. M. *(who, obviously, hadn't spent a lot of time talking with Sam Clear Water)*: Right!

> *Michael, who had spoken with Sam Clear Water just a day or two earlier raised his hand with a small but seditious smile on his face (a little like Mona Lisa's). An excessively informed third grader was about to make a well-meaning but minimally prepared third grade teacher squirm. He considered that to be one of his duties in life. Sam had told him about Socrates and the gadfly.*

February 23: A Quotation from the Dalai Lama.

I found the following quotation from the Dalai Lama, and I was thinking to myself, I wonder which Dalai Lama said this (because I didn't find any date with it or a specific source). Then I remembered that there is, according to the Tibetan Buddhist dogma, only one Dalai Lama who keeps coming back, sort of like the unwanted cat or the bad penny or the great big box a-floatin' in the bay. The only difference is that none of us except the Chinese communist leadership *wants* to get rid of that delightful fellow, the current reincarnation of the Dalai Lama. What a wonderful, gentle, soul! And smart! Here's the quotation:

"True peace cannot exist in the environment of ignorance."

I told Yasmin that it was one of the most intelligent statements I had ever heard, read, or seen, after I had stared at it for half an hour or so in respect to certain Eastern philosophers and an old dog I once knew who sat for a very long time in an uncomfortable position in order to attain enlightenment. Not the dog! He was sitting on a thorn and was just too damned lazy to stand up. So he sat there and howled pitifully. Come to think of it, that is a lot like what a philosopher does. Yasmin, unimpressed, just told me to pipe down so she could concentrate on her soap opera.

The Dalai Lama, with this statement, has asserted the heart of philosophical ethics. Wisdom cannot exist in an environment of ignorance. This might be arguable, but I will explain below. One necessary law under Kant's categorical imperative which is a necessary condition for wisdom (e.g., one must do only what should undeniably be done under every conceivable similar circumstance) is that "There must be no war." The opposite of war is peace. The choices are 1) war, or 2) peace, or 3) some condition between war and peace. Logic tells us that there can be no condition between war and peace since it would be ridiculous to claim that peace can exist in a state of war. War may be more or less intense, but peace is, merely, peace unconditioned. In fact, it could be argued that peace is an original unconditioned *simple* which is unchanged and unchanging in infinite time and space—a pure and perfect gift of God which is infinitely resident in our nature. However, unless we are ruled by wisdom (beside which peace resides) peace cannot be experienced. Thus, if we desire peace, and it is hard to imagine a person who does not desire peace, we must, first, seek wisdom. Wisdom, too, we will find unconditioned in the environs of God.

Then what is it we experience when we are not ruled by wisdom but when we are not at war? Have we not felt like this many times in a quiet meadow beside a flowing stream? In response I say, consider the herd of cattle in a pasture, grazing, drinking, sleeping, waking and doing it over again until they are released by a stroke of the butcher's hammer. It seems like a state of peace, but it cannot be. Peace goes beyond the mind of a cow or a small child or an ignorant adult human. They cannot *learn* about war even if they experience it firsthand. They can only experience it. Only after one learns about war (that is, only after one has gained pure understanding of war), can one attain true peace. Only after one has totally rejected war as behavior inappropriate to human societies can one acquire peace. Only in the company of wisdom can one discover peace.

February 24: An Old-Fashioned Scrivener.
I'm an old-fashioned scrivener. I dip my sharpened quill into the ink-well of existence and hurriedly scribble down the words that adhere to the nib. Then, I blow them dry—as if they could converse with the wind.

February 25: Freedom.

Before you do a thing, always ask, "Why?" After that question is answered satisfactorily, decide whether you still wish to do the thing and whether you *should* do it. Realize that, if you do not wish to do a thing, even if it is a good thing—even if it is a necessary thing—and even if you *should* do it, you need not do it. If you *choose*, after all of this, to do the thing—or not to do it—you remain free.

February 26: A Little Exercise in Metaphysical Logic (an Oxymoronic Concept).

Given the infinite cosmos and given that, in an infinite cosmos, what can occur, will occur, we can assume that it is possible that intelligent beings can occur since there is at least one intelligent being. It can, also, be deduced from the above that there are infinite numbers of intelligent beings since what occurs in an infinite cosmos occurs infinitely. Intelligence is conditioned by infinite factors; and, thus, there are degrees of intelligence.

Since there are degrees of intelligence, and there are infinite numbers of intelligent beings, it can be deduced that there are beings with ranges of intelligence from infinitely limited to infinitely expansive.

The above arguments can be made for not only intelligence but for degrees of physical strength, size, mass, length of life, and all other qualities which are ascribed to extant beings. These qualities at the infinitely high end of the eternal continuum, including intelligence, could be summarized as omniscience, omnipotence, and omnipresence in space and time.

It has been proven by the above that at least one perfect being exists. That is, for each of the qualities listed above, the above arguments will prove that at least one being exists which expresses that quality infinitely. A description of God is that of a being who is omniscient, omnipotent, and omnipresent in space and time. Such a description would define the unconditioned being which (if there were a genesis of space and time) would stand at the head of space and time as the ideal of that being. Thus, although the name, God, is a mere whim of our time-and-space-limited human existence, the existence of a nameless god stands proven—with one condition: such an existence is impossible since a genesis of space and time is, itself, impossible in an infinite cosmos. Thus, God, as Kant has said in *The Critique of Pure Reason* is both necessary and impossible. Hmmm?!

February 27: The Achievers.

Eleven faded men slouch on the stools
Of an elegantly lighted, air-conditioned,
Red velvet tapestried bar
With heavy curtains drawn against the street,
With rounded shoulders and many-faceted talent,
Muttering dusty anecdotes and shaking heads
Against the ignorance of the world;
While the "city of light" hustles and whines and rumbles
Outside heavy curtains closed against the streets.

The eleven gray men do not see
The candy-apple-red-painted hot-rod car,

The blue-coat cop waving white gloves,
The wrinkled octogenarian leering at girls,
The high sky scraper,
The black dung-beetle racing toward the safety of a man-hole,
The harlot's smile.

The contented Eleven do not hear
The rumble of a thousand engines,
The scream of the subway train,
The crying of a baby,
The chirrup of a cricket that fell from a farmer's cuff.

They cannot smell hot grease on the train's axles.

They cannot feel the sticky heat of a summer's evening.

The cherished Eleven drink,
Order another round,
Eat peanuts,
Consider themselves good sports
For knowing the baseball averages and the players names,
Know they are wise
In the wisdom of their dusty anecdotes
On a summer's evening
Behind heavy curtains
Drawn against gaudy streets.

February 28:   Multitasking.

I am a multitasker. How, you say, can an oldster, a retired professor whose greatest virtue is concentrating on one thing at a time until the focus catches the paper on fire, acquire the teenage virtue of multitasking?

It just happened! I've been blogging online, and spending a lot of side time surfing the web for the information I need for blogging, getting side-tracked so I can order something for the truck, listening to a symphony on the media player, checking my email, taking phone calls, writing a book, reading hard-copy philosophical treatises, poetry, news articles, etc., etc., etc. Best of all, I don't think my productivity has suffered severely. In fact, I believe I'm getting a Hell of a lot more done than I ever did before.

This morning, I was multitasking and read an email from the National Council of Teachers of English that contained a link for a story in the *Washington Post* about multitasking by teenagers and how it might hurt the teenagers' ability to learn. So I read the story. It said the usual: nobody knows, but everyone is worried about it. It did one thing that I appreciated because my brain clicked into gear and began analyzing. It followed the multitasking activities of a high school girl (an honor student) as she went through an evening of activity in her room. I realized why she was successful and why I am successful in my multitasking and why so many others are not successful. She and I are not, really, multitasking at all. We are doing one thing at a time, but not for very long at a time. The failures are trying to split their minds up into several different directions at the same time. The Post story didn't seem to notice this differentiation at all; but, inadvertently, they exposed a major reason for why the second class of multitaskers, the failures, fails. It has to do with brain function. Concentrating on two tasks at a time switches the locus of brain activity from the hippocampus (mainly a center for recollection) to the striatum (which works on mastering repetitive tasks). Being repetitive, I know, is an important function of teaching, because students seldom listen the first time anything is said. They only remember it when they get sick of hearing it over and over again. But repetitive task mastery is not something that is particularly valuable for the scholar. On the other hand, recollection (a.k.a. "memory") is, along with critical thinking, which is heavily involved with memory, a monumentally important brain function to the scholar.

I said before that the honor student and I are not really multitasking. Partly, I deduced this from my own experience; and, partly I deduced it from the description of her activity. Both of us concentrate for a short time (5 minutes to 25 minutes) on one task while all the other hubbub is going on around us and we don't even hear it. We are insulated from everything else by the task at hand. Then, since both she and I have short attention spans and begin to lose track of task #1, task #2 intrudes and we move to it for a short time, and so on until we have dealt with all of the tasks, some of them just for a moment (e.g., a phone call), others for half an hour (e.g., a Socratic dialogue or a symphony). The important thing is that each activity receives full attention while we are willing and able to give that full attention. Then the next task receives full attention during its due time. All the other tasks queue up in noisy profusion—white noise, unheard, undetected, unimportant, until their turns arrive.

Wittgenstein tells us that our greatest philosophical errors (and all philosophical statements are errors according to W., but I notice that such a problem didn't deter him from making philosophical statements by the barrelful) are made because we cannot think what we have no logical language to say. This, I think, entails another proposition: to a mind filled with one task, the language of another task is foreign and, thus, meaningless (i.e., white noise). White noise is valuable in concentration upon a task. I use it every night when I select the electronic "tide" sound on my alarm clock to help me with the task of going to sleep.

March 1: Welcome to March!

Welcome to March which came in like a lion in Kansas and Missouri. We had it all: tornadoes, snow storms, torrential rain, flash floods, high winds, meteorologists, and a visible invisibility of defeated Kansas City mayoral candidates. Welcome to the windy month! Welcome to spring (in vernal prematurity, not to be officially birthed until the 21st)! Welcome to T.S. Eliot's mistake (i.e., giving to April the characteristics which should have gone to March, at least, around St. Louis where he grew up and should, as a budding poet, have been more aware of nature's early spring budding).

But my real celebration is that I finally finished reading Plato's *Philebus*. I had planned to finish it weeks ago, but I kept running into obstacles—laziness, for instance. My real celebration: finding out the inevitable truth that Socrates was right and Philebus was wrong, that wisdom is, indeed, a higher good than pleasure. But there was a delightful twist in that Socrates proved that wisdom is not the highest good. Thus, today, what I am truly celebrating are the two goods that Socrates claims (which claim I withhold judgment upon) are higher than wisdom: measure (the eternal nature) and symmetry (perfection).

There is a more central celebration. I admit it. A new window of understanding opened in my own mind. Such old fellows as I have to celebrate when, occasionally, the intellectual clouds are whisked aside and the sun shines through for a moment. It feels go-o-o-o-o-d! So here is the Socratic enlightenment.

Measure and symmetry, Socrates says, are the highest goods because all else emerges from them. Socrates, according to Plato, said it in *Philebus*, but because Plato buried *Philebus* deep under a dusty pile of dialectics, and because all of the other philosophers seemed to be so taken up with other ideas, especially the profundity of wisdom, it didn't emerge in clarity until Immanuel Kant displayed it again in his *Critique of Pure Reason*. That was in the 18th century—"the Age of Reason." Unfortunately, Kant could not resist the temptation to say everything over and over again ten thousand times; and, thus, he managed, again, to bury light in a stoppered bottle, to hide his candle under a bushel, to fart in the forest where no one heard (or smelled) it except a passing chipmunk who twitched his nose but was more interested in looking for pine nuts than enlightenment.

Let me tell you about measure and symmetry and why they are so damnably good.

Measure and symmetry are the *a priori* forms of the cosmos. They exist as space and time before and after existence itself. When the architect of existence (whoever or whatever that was) imagined creation, that architect consulted measure so that creation would be filled appropriately (no two objects occupying the same space, gravity to draw matter together, centrifugal force to keep it apart, energy to keep it moving). Once all was measured, it had to be chiseled and polished into order and shape. Neither a teardrop nor a wheel could be square, but curves and straight lines are necessities wherever we look—and the golden mean is not just a principle of geometry. It, along with all the other principles of measure and symmetry, guides our every thought.

Ahh! Thought! Thou fount of wisdom! Ahh! Wisdom! Thou freshet of measure and symmetry! Ahh! Pleasure! Thou divine gift!

Now, here is my formerly withheld judgment. Measure and symmetry are neither superior to nor prior to wisdom. Rather, they are coequal and coexistent with it as the forms necessary to any material (i.e., conditioned) expression of wisdom. In other words, the coalition of wisdom guiding measure and symmetry is *a priori*. In differentiating them, we could call wisdom the mind or soul behind creation while measure and symmetry are the mathematics for its expression. Pure mathematics remains for us *a priori*, a rare connection between the material world and that which Plato called the ideal—in the domain of the ideal, wisdom, measure, and symmetry coevally work their primeval magic.

March 2: Elegy.
A cave,
small, hidden beyond the bends of rock-walled tunnels,
where I could be found
(if you, too, were dead).
Buried,
with only the hum of the universe,
fine-tuned forks of space and time droning *basso*.

A cave within a cave,
papered with wisdom and folly of past ages
and mere yesterdays
and ages expressed in deep-wrinkled faces
of smiling cave ladies:
my contemporaries.
(I could have smooched them at the drive-in theater
in my straw-hat days had I been from here-abouts.)

Caves within caves within caves;
Plato speaks of benches and fire,
marionette shows
shadowed on walls:
Lies
beneath fancy, imagination,
truth, wisdom;
Buried
in caves within caves within caves.

The sun will shine again
and I will feel it warming my bare shoulders,
and I will let dead shadows of dead marionettes
be dead,
but not until it rises
and I walk out squinting,
Living,
wiping my wet mouth on my shirt-sleeve,
brim-full of the wisdom and folly

of dead and mere yesterdays.

March 3: Magha Puja.

Shortly before Gautama the Buddha died, a large crowd of his most devoted disciples gathered together; and he delivered a sermon, his most important, during which he introduced the Four Noble Truths and the Eight-Fold Path which are at the heart of Buddhist philosophy.

Shortly before Jesus died, his disciples gathered together on a hillside; and Jesus delivered a Sermon, his most important, called the Sermon on the Mount. Interestingly enough, the two sermons have a lot in common that all of us, not just Buddhists and Christians, should pay attention to.

Four Noble Truths.
    1) Life means suffering.
    2) The source of suffering is attachment.
    3) Suffering can be ended.
    4) The path to the end of suffering is eight-fold.

The Eight-Fold Path.
    A) Wisdom:
        1) Right View.
        2) Right Intention.
    B) Ethics.
        3) Right Speech.
        4) Right Action.
        5) Right Livelihood.
    C) Discipline.
        6) Right Effort.
        7) Right Mindfulness.
        8) Right Concentration.

The Beatitudes.
    1) Blessed are the poor in spirit.
    2) Blessed are they that mourn.
    3) Blessed are the meek.
    4) Blessed are they who seek righteousness.
    5) Blessed are the merciful.
    6) Blessed are the pure in heart.
    7) Blessed are the peacemakers.
    8) Blessed are the persecuted and reviled for righteousness' sake.

Other signs.
    1) You who are righteous are the salt of the earth.
    2) You who are righteous are the light of the world.
    3) Blessed are the forgiving.
    4) Love your enemy.
    5) Communicate simply and honestly.

6) Live simply and cleanly.

7) Consider, first, the needs of the soul.

8) Don't fret about tomorrow. Sufficient to the day is the evil thereof.

Is it any wonder that Christianity has found a comfortable home among much of the Buddhist population of the earth. Keep in mind, however, that this comfort is in the *purity* of the Sermon on the Mount and in the *purity* of the Four Noble Truths and the Eight-Fold Path. We can be sure that, immediately after this purity has been received, politicians, merchants, priests, kings, lawyers, teachers, housewives, farmers, and Madame Defarge will support lopping off heads, and mobs will crucify or poison with hemlock in its name—in the besooted name of *Purity*.

But let not all that is burned down to evil falsely in the *name* of Purity oxidize the *essence* of Purity rising from the pyre:

"Mother, behold your son. Son, behold your mother."

March 4: Einstein and I.

Many people are pleased (or, perhaps, displeased) to measure their intelligence against that of Albert Einstein. From what I have read, he didn't make a fuss about being the smartest person in the world although he could have claimed with some legitimacy that title for himself. I don't claim it for myself either, and I have a lot of evidence to prove that mine is a wise decision. However, today, I have trapped a moment of equality between Einstein and me.

I discovered that he said the following: "Possessions, outward success, publicity, luxury—to me these have always been contemptible. I believe that a simple and unassuming manner of life is best for everyone, best for both the body and the mind."

Isn't it ironic that the moment I can claim equality with one of the smartest persons to ever walk the earth is the moment when he is declaring himself "simple"? Unfortunately for me, there is a major difference. Einstein *adopted* a "simple and unassuming manner" *by choice* while it is the best I can do without making an ass of myself. But I take comfort in the fact that we are both right.

March 5: The Warrior and the Saint.

Sam and his twelve-year-old grandson, grandchild #1, are sharing some sunshine in the park.

Sam: I heard you walloped a kid yesterday.

#1: Oh, that Mom; she just can't keep her mouth shut.

Sam: I think she was a little bit proud of you. Tutu explained to her why it happened. I enjoyed hearing about your spunk. I was glad, though, that you didn't do the kid any real harm.

#1: I should have broken his neck instead of just punching him in the gut.

Sam: Why? What did he do?

#1: He called me a "stupid Injun."

Sam: Wow! That's harsh!

#1: I didn't think about it. Before I knew what was happening, I just punched him in the gut, and he sort of laid down on the ground and gasped for breath for a few minutes. But his mom was watching, and she came up and chewed me out for hitting her precious little boy. I wanted to give her a punch in the gut, too, but I didn't. I didn't know Tutu saw it. That must be why I didn't get in trouble.

Sam: Yeah! She was watching, and she was really excited about it. She doesn't get a chance to witness much violence anymore. I think you did her a favor.

(Sam laughed at the thought.)

#1: Papa, why is it that when I get mad at someone, I just have to hit 'em? I remember that you used to get mad, too. Your ears would turn red, and then you would just chew the dickens out of some poor store clerk. You even got thrown out of Toys are Us once according to Tutu. Is that true?

Sam: *(laughing again):* Yep!

#1: What happened to you? Now when someone does something mean to you, you just laugh.

Sam: I got old. I can't take credit for it. It's a natural consequence of age. Have you heard what happens to a dominant male lion when he gets old, and one of his sons or grandsons gets big enough to whip him?

#1: I've heard that he either leaves the pride entirely or becomes very docile and hangs around the edges of it.

Sam: Well, that's what happened to me. I got old and suddenly realized that I was no longer the alpha male; and, since I didn't want to wander off into the forest, I learned how to laugh it off.

#1: It's hard to believe you can do that.

Sam: It just happens. When you are young and full of vinegar, you fight and scrap and, win or lose, you feel kind of good about the fight. But when you get old, the scrap drops right out of you, and you don't feel the least bit good about fighting. We men are made that way.

That's why we have to send young people like you off to fight wars. Young folks get out there and fight to the death against people they don't even know. If they sent old codgers like me to war, we'd just get together with the old duffers from the other side and tell stories about the old days when we would have given each other a real tumble. We wouldn't even arm wrestle because it hurts our arthritic joints too much. Why fight when you can sit around and drink beer and reminisce about the past. The war would never get off the ground.

That's why all the saints are old timers and all the warriors are young folks full of piss and vinegar. You go ahead and be a warrior for now. Just don't do anything that will get you thrown in jail and you'll be fine. Do something worth while in between fights. When you get to be my age, you'll find it much easier to be a saint.

#1: O.K. I'll see you, Papa. I have to meet some guys at the gym.

Sam: Yeah! Have fun.

March 6: In My Mind.

In my mind
I see nature blue, green, and brown
and hear the rush of rivers,

taste spray from waters crashing over
round and polished stones
slick with green moss
drowning under icy spring runoff

in my mind
snow-topped mountains,
grinning saw-teeth
taunt me,
knowing I can't climb
except in my mind
where I can climb
if I want to
and I do
and I am There

in my mind
until April
when, weary of indoors and of dark tunnels,
of heavy books with loose covers
streaked with shelf moss;
dying from thirst,
I rub my dry mouth with my shirt sleeve,
the sleeve of my old blue denim shirt
that I wear every day through winter
reminding me of outdoors
with my truck-camper by a rushing river
waiting for me with rainbow trout darting madly
around slick watermelon rocks
below snow-topped Mountains—
waiting for me,
shadowing fish.

March 7: Who are the Slaves? Who are the Free?

Occasionally, I am a freedman. Usually, I am a slave. This is unfortunate, because I am sure I have it within me to reverse it so that, usually, I would be a freedman and, occasionally, I would be a slave. I doubt that anyone can make a valid claim to pure freedom. Maybe in death but only if we are wrong about our attachment to life after death.

I use the word "attachment" on purpose because that is the usual translation of it in Buddhist thought. In my mind, it is the greatest problem with, not just Buddhism, but Eastern metaphysical thought in general. In Lao Tsu's Taoism it is at its worst. When he insists that the best course is to do nothing, he seems to advocate the entire abandonment of personal responsibility to others for the sake of freedom from attachment. I find that offensive. Do we not owe something of ourselves to those whose lot it is to depend upon us, and if we do so little that no one depends upon us for anything, then what has been the good of our existing? Even a cow is more valuable because we can drink her milk, eat her flesh, and wear her leather hide. A do-nothing human is nothing but a pointless burden upon Mother Earth. Of course, even the most holy of the advocates of Eastern thought reject this philosophy *de facto*. In Buddhism, rejection of attachment only reaches its fulfillment after many reincarnations wherein the holy one realizes the value of the life which has a spiritual impact upon others but is not connected individually to those others: no marriage, no offspring, no physical production or reproduction. Indeed, individuality disappears entirely. And, of course, then it is off to nirvana for them—no more attachments at all because they are ultimately attached by being merely a particle in the ether of eternal essence, not even a particle but mere essence—a great deal of peace there, but one could not feel it.

I'm not satisfied with all of this, so I turn back to Jesus who seems to be teaching us to honor our attachments; that is, until he tells us to turn our backs on our families and loved ones, sell all we have and give it to the poor and take up our crosses and follow him. I want to say "and . . .?!" I have the image of a train of people, each lugging a cross, marching like ants across the desert to find that elusive lump of sugar some rich guy dropped. Jesus, of course, was a teacher; that was what he did; but can we all be teachers? Who would change the baby? Who would make the bread? Who would entertain us with slam dunks at Pepsi Center? The world would be a mess.

Lest I lose my train of thought entirely in this train of ant-like penniless humans following a penniless Jesus, let us return to the topic of slavery. Be it known that, since we cannot by any means give up our attachments, a certain degree of slavery is inevitable. Even the most frail and senile old crone owes it to her great-grand-children to live a few moments more and say something memorable to them. All of us who have any honor at all are slaves to a myriad of such obligations.

But set those aside and limit what we call slavery to the involuntary servitude which prevents us from living our lives in a virtual freedom which includes a number of pleasant and voluntary obligations such as kissing unwilling grandchildren leaving us wet with disgusting drool. The most well-known slavery? Working for a living! Ideally, all of us should do something for a living that we would do whether we were paid for it or not. I have had a little of that as a teacher when the students are apt and willing. But I can't stop teaching just because students are stupid and recalcitrant. Thus, slavery!

And how about the slavery of being forced to care for our bodies? That might be the worst of all. Daily, we have to find means for feeding and watering the body; and, daily, we must empty the waste and clean the body. If that were the extent of it, we would be lucky, but the body is subject to a host of diseases and dangers. If we do not protect it carefully and make sure the stuff we pour into it is wholesome and clean, not too much, not too little, not too spicy or it will make us miserable throughout our lives, making us wish devoutly for death if the body doesn't burst or rot early without our help. Thus, slavery!

And what of death? The knowledge of death seems to be the ultimate slavery. We know from our youth that we will die, that nothing we do between birth and death will change the outcome. Thus, slavery!

You can see, now, why I said that I am, partly, a slave. But remember that I also said I have the power to become, usually, a freedman. This is true because, atop that infernal bag of bones and flesh and blood which is my body sits a rational mind. Some would go so far as to say it contains an immortal soul. That might be a stretch, but my rational mind on its flesh-and-boney throne can rule this bag of frailties to the extent that I imagine I am enjoying myself immensely. The five senses can be convinced to enjoy cold or hot weather, to love squinting into a sunny day, to consider the taste of vinegar a delight, the smell of cow manure rich and mealy, the roar of a river relaxing, the pain of childbirth a blessing. All the while, the mind acts as a sixth sense, a master sense which lifts us higher than sensory experience through imagination to the metaphysical realm, fueled by the physical but propelled beyond it toward wisdom and ultimate truth. That is why I say that I can be, usually, a freedman.

March 8: Who are the Slaves? Who are the Free? (Part 2).

Siebert meets Sam coming out of the Power Plant Restaurant.

Siebert: Where the Hell have you been? I ain't seen you for half the winter.

Sam: Right here! If you weren't so blind, you would have noticed me sooner.

Siebert *(ignoring the insult)*: What you been up to?

Sam: Up to my ears in work and at least one grandchild every day to keep me from it.

Siebert: Nice! Nice! That's the way to be happy. Except for the work! I'm glad, when I retired, I didn't keep working like you did. You're a damned fool to keep it up every day.

Sam: Yeah! Yeah! I guess so; but, somehow, I can't seem to break the habit. Too many years of it, I guess. Anyway, I never really thought of it as work except when the administrators got to be a nuisance or when the students were no count. Hmm! I guess it *was* work most of the time. *(Sam laughed uproariously at his own joke and wiped his bald head with a handkerchief.)* But, anymore, since I don't teach any classes and I don't have to do what the administrators want, I spend most of my days doing "not-work" just piddling around with books and writing a few words and enjoying myself.

Siebert: I suppose.

Sam: I'm glad I ran into you, because I wanted to ask you something.

Siebert: What?

Sam: I've been writing about slavery and freedom and I came up against it when I started thinking about what money has to do with it.

Siebert: Well, slaves don't get paid, do they?

Sam: I think I'm defining "slaves" in a different way than you would expect.

Siebert: I might have known!

Sam: To me, slavery is a circumstance where you do not have the freedom to say "no" to the demands of someone else or something else. My question is, do we always have the freedom to say "no" to the demands of money?

Siebert: And the answer is, "no." So I guess we are slaves to money.

Sam: You are very quick to answer.

Siebert: It don't take a genius to answer that question. Just somebody a little bit hungry. Or a guy who smokes and ain't had a cigarette for a couple of hours. They can't say "no" to buying some food or cigarettes.

Sam: But, perhaps, they could say "no" to the money part. For instance, they could steal the food or cigarettes. Or they could rummage through trash cans. Or they could grow their own.

Siebert: You have a point, but who has the time to do any of that when you need it right now?

Sam: There's the rub! The reason a person is a slave to money is that the person has not planned a way not to be a slave to money. For instance, a person who anticipates needing cigarettes could steal a whole truckload of them and hide them in the garage. Then he wouldn't need cigarettes for a very long time.

Siebert: Probably not for 5 to 10 years, at least!

Sam: Good point! In fact, remember Red Skelton's Freddy the Free-Loader always arranged (by breaking into a store) to spend the winter in jail so he wouldn't have to find a heated place to live. They didn't call him the *free*-loader for nothing.

Siebert: Not a bad plan if you don't mind being locked up. But that's another kind of slavery, ain't it.

Sam: Right! He exchanged one kind of slavery for another. There must be a better way.

Siebert: Plan ahead!

Sam: Huh?

Siebert: Plan ahead! I think that's a Boy Scout motto or something. Freddy was doing it by getting sent to jail every winter. But if he had planned ahead further, he could have done it a better way, without becoming a different kind of slave.

Sam: Like what?

Siebert: He could have been a farmer.

Sam: Bad plan. Remember what I quoted from Thoreau about the farmer carrying his farm and tools and livestock on his back for the rest of his miserable life. Slavery, again!

Siebert: I guess we're back where we started. We just trade one form of slavery for another.

Sam: Yes. That is true, but isn't it possible that we could reduce our slavery significantly, especially the slavery we have to money.

Siebert: How would we do that?

Sam: You are doing it, already. That is one reason why I asked you this question in the first place. You seem to have become quite apt at reducing your slavery to money. For instance, how long have you been wearing that pair of overalls?

Siebert: Three days now. This is Wednesday. I always wear this pair from Monday through Thursday. The other pair, I wear Friday through Sunday. I, generally, get a little dirtier on weekends—fishing and fixing the grandkids' bikes and stuff.

Sam: That wasn't exactly what I was asking, but it is *telling*. You only have two pairs of overalls. What I meant is, how long have you owned them?

Siebert: I really can't remember. I know I got 'em used down at the thrift store for a couple of bucks and that was a long time ago. I always get my overalls there. Somebody's always *dying* to get rid of 'em. *(Siebert had a good snorting chortle out of that one. Sam joined him with a laugh and wiped his head again.)* In fact, I have a couple more pairs stored up for when these finally give out and ain't good for nothing but patches.

Sam: And how often do you get a haircut?

Siebert: Shoot! I ain't been to the barber shop since Jimmy Moore died. That must be 20 years now. I just cut my own hair.

Sam: I can tell. And when did you buy your last new truck?

Siebert: Let's see! Never! I always buy used. They ain't properly broke in until they're at least 10 years old.

Sam: I agree with you. They don't smell right until they smell like their owner. What does all of this tell you about your own slavery to money?

Siebert: Well, I can't throw away what money I get. I suppose, I'd like to get more.

Sam: Why? Would you buy new overalls?

Siebert: Not likely. I like the ones I have well enough.

Sam: Would you buy a new house?

Siebert: The one we have was good enough for Grandpa. I suppose it's good enough for me. I might put a new wood stove in it, though. I saw a good one at a farm sale that went for $20.

Sam: Right! A new one?

Siebert: Well, not exactly new.

Sam: Are you happy.

Siebert: I'm doing O.K. How about you?

Sam: I'm asking the questions here!

(Sam laughed. Siebert chuckled.)

March 9: The War on Terrorism.

Yesterday, I heard the War on Terrorism referred to as "our children's children's war." There can be no end to it—unless . . . unless What? That is the problem. A war with no specific political entity cannot end because there is no specific political entity to defeat. We say Al Qaeda. But what is Al Qaeda? Certainly, not a country. More like Emerson's "lengthened shadow" of one man. And that one man exists only as a voice and a two-dimensional figure on a video screen. And if he were dead another voice and a new two-dimensional figure would replace him.

We say that it is a battle between radical Islam and the rest of the world. Yet radical Islam, like Al Qaeda has no home, no government, no political existence. How can we fight against an enemy which cannot be defined by space and time?

It is not a war.

It is a death knell. "Ask not for whom the bell tolls. It tolls for thee."

There can be no end to it—unless . . .

Is this Armageddon? It has an eternal smell to it—a little like brimstone. For each soldier dead, two more rise from the dust. For each child killed as "collateral damage," two more teenagers don the *unholy* vestments of suicide bombers and kill more children who are replaced by more teenagers who don . . .

There can be no end to it—unless . . .

87

John the Baptist was not the only voice crying in the wilderness. So was Jesus: "I am the way, the truth, and the light." What way? What truth? What light?

The Way: "Love your enemies. Do good to those who harm you." I have not heard that recently in reference to suicide bombers.

The Truth: "Take up your cross and follow me." The cross is not a weapon; rather, it represents self-sacrifice.

The Light: "A city on a hill cannot be hid. Let your light so shine that it gives light to all . . . ." Is it a light if it emits darkness—and death? And who is *all*, just your own kind ("stick to your own kind, one of your own kind!") just your friend, your church-mate, your temple-partner, your bowling team?

There can be no end to it—unless . . . unless . . . unless . . .

Why an army and no Peace Corps?

Why guns and no food?

Why shooting and no talking?

Why no listening?

When I last taught high school, I was told that I could no longer touch a student—no arm around the shoulder—no pat on the cheek—certainly, no hugging . . .

No more touching.

No more teaching.

No more listening.

No more talking.

Just a dreadful silence followed by an awful noise—perhaps, the last noise anyone will hear.

There can be no *other* end to it unless . . . .

March 10: Ten Thou-Shalt-Not Commandments.

I can, from my own experience, vouch for the validity of the following prohibitions. Note: Because I am a man, most of these are for boys and young men. However, if the pain fits . . .

1) Thou shalt not make a ring out of bailing wire and a plastic bead and present it to your third-grade girl friend as a going-steady love token.

2) Thou shalt not call your 6th grade teacher a cheater in front of the classroom and challenge him to a fight.

3) Thou shalt not threaten to change the facial features of a long-time friend if he so much as glances at the girl you have just met and like the looks of.

4) Thou shalt not steal watermelons from the farm of a guy who loads his shotgun shells with rock salt.

5) Thou shalt not have sex with a stranger on a Greyhound bus.

6) Thou shalt not, in the act of resigning from a military preparatory academy, tell the commanding officer that you are doing so to avoid becoming a prick like him.

7) Thou shalt not as a member of a university faculty, pound on the deans desk and shout for all to hear that she is the enemy of the university.

8) Thou shalt not do unto others anything that you would not want them to do to you, unless you are a proctologist in the commission of your professional duties.

9) Thou shalt not become a proctologist unless you are sure you will hate your job.

10) Even if you do so with a smile on your face, thou shalt not ask a short person who is already standing to stand up.

(One more, for good measure, 11) Thou shalt not tell a slightly heavy girlfriend that she looks "wholesome."

March 11: Ten Thou-Shalt Commandments.

1) Thou shalt do to others only what you wish they would do for you.

2) Thou shalt smile and laugh.

3) Thou shalt weep.

4) Thou shalt arise at daybreak.

5) Thou shalt go to bed early enough to arise refreshed at daybreak.

6) Thou shalt do only enough work to make you tired enough to sleep.

7) Thou shalt find different work if your work troubles you so that you cannot sleep.

8) Thou shalt do what is necessary to support your physical needs as long as what you do supports your spiritual needs even more.

9) Thou shalt seek diligently to know what is right.

10) Thou shalt do what is right.

Note: Each of these commandments is variable in relation to commandments 9 and 10.

March 12: *All You Own* (a Brief Drama).

Jasper Willis, MD, sat in the last cloth upholstery and chrome chair on the right in the back row of the waiting room of the Human Services Office of Cosmic Service Corporation. He preferred some degree of anonymity. He pretended to be reading a tattered copy of Field and Stream. *He never fished or hunted. When, as a child, he had fished, he seldom caught anything even in the best stream where his older brother regularly pulled out his limit of rainbow trout. When his younger brother began to do the same, he quit and hadn't fished since. He didn't like the smell of fish anyway.*

Marge Southpaw entered the nearly empty waiting room briskly, looked around, then sat down in the chair beside Jasper. She leaned over and spoke in a stage whisper.

Marge: Wow! I never expected to see you here. Isn't it all *really* exciting? I've been looking forward to something like this all of my life. Oh, I guess you are here about the medical opportunities. When I saw the ad in the paper this morning, I just couldn't wait a moment. I just had to get down here and apply. Are you going to apply, too? I wouldn't have expected it. You are so successful here, and what will all of your patients do without you?

Jasper *(having laid* Field and Stream *on the coffee table in front of them)*: I suppose they would live. But I really haven't decided whether I would take the job if it were offered. After all, we don't know much about it. Mainly, I was curious.

M: Oh, but it sounds so exciting: "Wanted, qualified and responsible persons to work in the fields of medicine, dentistry, education, civil engineering, and other professions. Humanitarian assignments around the world. Remuneration exceptional." I always wanted to be in a job where I was really needed. Now I will have it.

J: You're a school teacher aren't you?

M: Yes! And it has been so-o-o-o good to me. But this year is the end of my 20th year of grade school teaching. I'm ready to retire and move on to something new. Ooh! It's just *so* exciting.

J: Yes.

Just then, the door to the human services office opened and a disappointed-looking middle-aged fellow with sallow complexion and slightly stooped shoulders came out. Without a word, he scowled at the two seated applicants, walked to the exit door of the waiting room, opened it, walked out, and slammed it behind him.

J: Hmm! Not a happy customer.

M: No! He didn't look it.

The receptionist in a cheery voice, seemingly unaware of the man's less-than-positive departure: Next!

J: You go first. I can wait.

M *(giggling)*: Oh, thank you! I'm not sure I *could* wait.

Marge sprang from her chair and almost ran through the door marked "Human Services Office." Jasper went back to his Field and Stream. *Five minutes later, Marge reemerged from the office carrying what looked to be an airline ticket.*

M *(stage whisper)*: North Korea! Leaving tomorrow. Wow!

And she left the building.

Receptionist: Next!

Jasper rose and entered the office from which Marge had emerged. Inside, he discovered a weathered Asiatic man of about 70 years sitting behind a large mahogany desk with a stack of airline tickets and a gold nameplate inscribed Adam Ichi. He rose, leaned across the desk and extended his hand to Jasper.

Adam: Dr. Willis! I've been expecting you. Have a seat. I presume you are here about the job.

J *(returning the handshake and taking the proferred seat)*: Yes! I thought I'd like to look into it.

A. We need people like you. I'm ready to offer a position to you right now. We need a medical doctor with your specialty in Jakarta immediately. Are you ready to go?

J: Uh, I would like to know a little more about it. How long does the assignment last? What does it pay? What sort of benefits? You know: the usual stuff.

Mr. Ichi smiled.

A: Rest assured, Dr. Willis, all your physical needs will be met, at least for now. You'll have housing as good as all of those around you. You won't be paid, but you'll receive what you need for your work and what you need to keep you healthy and as comfortable as conditions permit. As to how long the assignment will last, I can't assure you that it will ever end, except, of course when you die or are no longer able to fulfill your duties.

Jasper, taken aback, said nothing, which Mr. Ichi accepted as consent and handed Jasper a ticket to Jakarta.

A: You'll need to pack quickly. The plane leaves at ten o'clock tonight. Don't take much with you. You'll be given everything you need when you arrive in Jakarta.

Jasper mechanically took the ticket, rose, shook Adam's extended hand, and walked woodenly out of the office—where, as the door closed behind him, he stopped, holding the ticket to Jakarta in front of him with both hands. He stood there very still for almost a minute staring at the ticket.

Receptionist *(smiling)*: Welcome to Cosmic! Don't forget your hat, Dr. Willis.

As if awakening from a dream, Jasper Willis retrieved his hat from the chair where he had left it, walked toward the exit, let the ticket slide from his hand into the waste basket by the door, smiled a wistful smile, dabbed a tear from the corner of his eye with a white handkerchief, and left.

March 13: Aesthetics, the Queen of Philosophical Topics.

I have been delinquent. Nearly 75 entries in this book, and I have not adequately discussed aesthetics, the queen of philosophical topics. I will repair that oversight quickly before someone steps into it like an open manhole and sustains serious injury.

Why do I call aesthetics the queen of philosophical topics? That will take a lot of explaining and, even then, many will disagree. To begin, I must divide aesthetics in two: natural aesthetics and artistic aesthetics. I will save natural aesthetics, as has been my plan from the start, until I make my annual pilgrimage to Idaho for the warmer half of the year. There, in the midst of the high desert plains and the Rocky Mountains, I am surrounded by the best that natural aesthetics has to offer. I am sure to be mightily inspired. The fishing is, also, good. Artistic aesthetics, I will broach now.

I say "broach" because I cannot possibly cover artistic aesthetics in a single entry. Not in a week or a month or a year of entries. Not in a lifetime. Not ever! I can cut a small wound in its soft underbelly today and, perhaps, suck a little nectar before the wound heals.

Artistic aesthetics is more than the product of transferring images of natural aesthetics to an artistic form. Indeed, artistic aesthetics is not a slave of nature. Plato was wrong. He was far too intent upon the "ideal" form. He saw artistic aesthetics as copies of copies. First, there was the "ideal" form from which, second, the artisan created the "actual" thing as it is. Third, there is the artistic rendering of the actual into a painting, a sculpture, a poem, etc. He went so far as to call it a lie since no artist can reproduce either the thing as it is or the ideal form, but pretends to do both. Indeed, he is right that the artistic rendering is not a reproduction of a thing whether ideal or actual. We, in fact, must go even further in following Plato's trail into artistic subservience. Kant would say that, the actual thing as it is, also, is unavailable to us. Only the sensual phenomena which make us aware of the existence of the thing as it is can be experienced. That would make artistic rendition, if my poor math skills are not failing me, four steps away from the ideal, if the ideal exists.

But both Kant and Plato are on the wrong track in leaning so heavily upon the ideal. Hegel gives us a small beam of light on this dark problem. Of course, we must not lean on Hegel too heavily either or we might find ourselves laughing on the ground. But the small beam of light can help. Hegel says that, in a dialectic, nothing actually disappears and nothing is really created. If we approach artistic aesthetics dialectically, we can see that its parents are phenomena, its grandparents are things as they are, and its great-grandparents are in the ideal. None of them are dead, not even aging. Each is equal as a part of the ever-evolving dialectal stream of existence. Thus, one is not superior to the other, not even prior. Infinity, in its very nature annihilates the concepts of superiority and priority. That which makes its appearance later is in existence as a possibility pending its birth as an actuality and all manifestations are equally existent.

Now that I have confused you entirely, let us return to the defense of artistic aesthetics as the queen of philosophical topics. Let us do so with the most ephemeral of artistic aesthetics: the dream.

Dreams are art. Indeed, they embody all art: plastic, performing, and literary. I presume that everyone dreams. If I am correct in this presumption, we all are artists. Our minds create art which is as perfect at what it does as any Picasso painting, any Puccini opera, any T.S. Eliot poem. These plastic, performing, and literary images are unflawed as they appear; yet they are so fragile that they disappear, mostly within a few seconds after we wake and entirely a short time later. They are very like nature in that nature, too, exists in our awareness for only the infinitesimal instant of our sensory experience, then moves on to its next existence the next infinitesimal instant. We think when we look at a mountain or a clear stream that we are seeing a constant thing; but it is not; nothing is. It is all like a dream, not quite as stable as a dream. A dream holds its image for us a little longer "til human voices wake us and we drown."

A natural wonder, a dream, a poem: all art. The natural: a continually rolling infinite creation and re-creation. A dream: a captured image of creation hiding itself as we wake in a wrinkle of mind. A poem: a captured image, to be held in our senses, imprinted on our minds where all art begins, never ends, merely rolls continually beyond sight, sound, touch, taste, smell—through and beyond imagining.

March 14: Musical Art.

After dreaming, music without lyrics is the art closest to pure aesthetic truth. The reason is that music has no language to carry it away from that purity. It is pure thought represented as pure expression. It is important to note that much of what passes for music is not music at all. To be music, it must be carried dynamically upon the wings of melody, harmony, rhythm, and tempo. All of these elements must be present either in the positive (where contrast is felt from note to note or measure to measure) or in the negative (where the particular element is carried from note to note, measure to measure, without contrast, without change; or wherein the element is missing for as little as a fraction of a rhythmic beat or as much as an entire composition or an entire musical genre). An example of the negative is when harmony is replaced by unison. Unison can be seen as the negative in the duality of harmony and unison. One or the other must be present, just as the other three elements must be present in either the positive or some form of the negative. It has been said that silence is as important in music as is sound. Thus, it could be said that silence is a negative form of all four of the musical elements. Of course, dynamics within a composition also play such a universal role.

Notice that I did not call music pure phenomenon. Were it so, it would not be truth at all, but truth distorted by the limitations of the senses. I call it pure thought. Thought, not phenomenon, is the center of truth. Permit me to vary a statement of Shakespeare's which was also put in other terms by Erasmus in *The Praise of Folly*: "Nothing is good or ill but thinking makes it so." This means, essentially, that thinking makes truth. Truth, in other words, is not something absolute and ideal which was created before the birth of the cosmos and continues with us and past us until the end of the cosmos. What makes the lie of it is that the cosmos, being infinite, has neither beginning nor end. No! It is the thought which is truth. A poorly contrived thought is ill truth. A well-rounded thought is the good. It takes well-rounded thought to create a great symphony. But let us look at something less complex than a symphony which is, also, truth emerging from well-rounded thought. Consider the little theme which many of us call "Twinkle, Twinkle, Little Star" (a theme loved by Mozart and a number of other great composers and by millions of small children).

This theme is unison (though it has been presented in many delightfully harmonious renditions); its most striking characteristic is melody. Its tempo, in the most welcome form, is totally regular, but it can be molded into a tempo manifold which is rich, indeed. The same is true of all of its dynamics. Its rhythm, a commonplace with a staccato or pizzicato attack, is, again, most welcome in its simplest form. That is, probably, why it is a favorite of children. But in its simplicity, it is, also, a favorite of the masters. They change it only minimally for their masterpieces. It is the oddity among humans to be one who does not know this melody. It is so central to our existence that we might, if we had no hearing-impaired members of our society, call it a necessity. Of course, it is not a necessity, but it carries, in its simplicity, the categorical imperative of Kant, or, at least, nothing about it is contrary to that imperative: what you do (teach, repeat, pass on to the children, etc.) must be what you would *always* wish, in similar circumstances, to have others do. This little theme is one of the finest of the "good" things we can pass on to our children. There is nothing ill about it; therefore, it is purity—or near purity in musical art—near purity of thought.

March 15: Epic Poetry.

Gilgamesh, the Ramayana, the Odyssey, the Iliad, the Aeneid, Beowulf, the Divine Comedy, Paradise Lost, and others. They represent human phenomena filtered through thought. They have not the artistic purity of music which needs no translation except the performance of the musician(s). They must have a language of expression. The fact that, to be understood, they must be translated into a language which can be understood by the reader is far more than is needed to remove them from the element of pure thought. Even the original language of the author is impure, being the product of centuries of cultivation in the soil of civilization, sharing the same garden plot with the lowly squash, fertilized with the manure of dead grass, human and animal waste. Yet, these epics, related to music, are the melody, rhythm, tempo, harmony, and dynamics of human existence. These epics, too, are marvelous vessels for the rearing up of new generations of humans. The only evidence we need of this is that they are still a necessary ingredient in the fertilizer of higher education as well as the ancient seed of every modern story worth its fertilizer. But they have not the purity of dreaming, nor the clear essence of music. They can withstand neither the challenge of Kantian philosophical criticism nor Wittgenstein's challenge that any philosophical statement is false by its very nature: that it is polluted by impure language. I do not regret this. I only mention it as a part of reality.

March 16: Lyric Poetry.

What I said about epic poetry also goes, in smaller dimension, for lyric poetry. But the smaller dimension is important. At times, lyric poems are more like the pure thought of a melody like "Twinkle, Twinkle Little Star." There is beauty to them without much opportunity for the impurity of language. But look out. Even in the narrowest verse, impurity can lurk. Consider another "starry" artwork for children: "Star Light, Star Bright." It seems innocuous, but notice that it is a wishing poem, perhaps even a prayer poem. Is there not inference in its language that prayers (or, at least, wishes) are heard and answered by a deity (or, at least, a metaphysical entity)? This inference is neither good nor bad, but it is an inference which takes us beyond the philosophical realm of aesthetics into that of metaphysics. And that is the problem. It cannot be pure aesthetics if it broaches metaphysics. Ideal aesthetics must be purely aesthetic. Again, that does not make a poem which is combined with metaphysics anything worse or better than a purely aesthetic work, only different. And the difference must be recognized if we are to have a fuller understanding.

Note: It could be argued that dreams, which I call pure aesthetics, contain attributes of metaphysics (monsters, gods, etc.) and even of language. But these attributes are not arguments for their existence except as imaginary products of fertile thought. "Thinking makes them so." Waking makes them not so except as a gossamer memory which is, also, mere thought, not phenomenon.

March 17: St. Patrick's Day and Various Snakes.

I'm hoping, today, that the good St. Patrick will visit (Santa-Claus-like) all of the political capitals of the world and chase out the two-legged snakes that infest them.

Whoa! On the other hand, the snakes might migrate into the countryside where the rest of us live. We don't want that. How about cages? Cages would be nice. We could even install stock tickers, maybe, one of those pneumatic tube systems that used to be in department stores so they could send "insider" information back and forth to each other. Gitmo, Cuba, might be just the place. They would be in excellent company there.

Come on, St. Patrick. You did it for Ireland. Surely, you can do it for the rest of us.

March 18: Sculpture.

An interesting entry into artistic aesthetics is the sculpture. It can, certainly, be politically charged, in which case it is, certainly, in the terms already stated above, not pure aesthetics. That would be the case for a bust of Charles de Gaulle, for instance. However, in abstract sculpture, there would seem to be the opportunity for pure aesthetics. Not the St. Louis arch! It is political and economic, a ploy to draw tourists to the city it represents. It is a gateway with all of its

94

implications. Nearly every sculpture, no matter how mundane in content or character, seems to imply some sort of competing philosophical genre.

How about great balls of twine? There seem to be three of them competing to be the largest, one in Minnesota, one in Kansas, a third now in Missouri (an import from Texas). I suppose these could be considered pure aesthetics as products of poorly-contrived thought producing ill truth. The products of pure aesthetics, like truth, are not always pleasing. But I doubt myself. These are nothing but big balls of string—phooey!

March 19: Hindu New Year.

By golly, they have done it! A few years ago, looking at India as a subservient member of the British Commonwealth of nations, essentially a slave nation, a nation determined to remain in servitude forever, I would not have believed that this nation, the birthplace of Hinduism, or, more accurately, the child of Hinduism, would emerge as one of the richest and most powerful nations on earth. But it has done just that. Mahatma Gandhi's fasts and sermons and near starvation—his activities that most of the best minds of the world looked upon with reverence, but considered quite useless—have culminated in excellent universities and hospitals, leadership in technology, nuclear bombs (?!think of that in the context of passive resistance!), all in all, one of the most advanced civilizations ever to inhabit the earth.

Does this mean that peace might, truly, be the way to success? I'm not sure that even India thinks so considering their bristly relationship with Pakistan. But we have to start somewhere and that "somewhere" seems to be with Mahatma Gandhi. I noticed today that, at least, in some Hindu communities, this is the Hindu New Year. Be that as it may, Hindu New Year is always celebrated in the spring (in the north, at least, where they have a spring) when new life is emerging; and, in India, new life has emerged.

If we look at the rest of the world, we see little evidence that anyone has learned anything from Gandhi. We (including India, I must suppose) still think we can solve all of our problems by blasting our enemies to Hell—whether our enemy is a fundamentalist Islamic state, a wealthy "Christian" nation, a Jewish state seen as an interloping colony by the previous owners of their *(dangling pronoun intended)* "god-given" land, or the Hispanic kid down the street who just called you a n____. Perhaps, we will all end up in Hell together.

About three years ago, I posted a message on a website which was discussing the best way to approach the Iraq war. I suggested that we should remove all of our military hardware and soldiers and ask for Americans (and other westerners) to volunteer to go to Iraq unarmed and offer to help with the rebuilding effort. I admitted that some of them would be killed and others maimed and have their lives destroyed, but I was quite sure that the overall killing would, eventually, be reduced, and we might develop a more wholesome relationship with the Islamic world. That was the last message I posted on the site. My life was threatened from all sides. I was called many hard names, most of which I would not feel comfortable repeating here. And it was unanimous: the only good one of my sort was a dead one of my sort. The only way to end this war would be to kill every one of those devil Arabs so that the world would be forever free of them.

I notice that, today, on the first day of the fifth year of that war, it is bigger and more deadly than ever. We have made some progress in our goal of eradicating all of the radical Islamists who wish with equal ferocity to eradicate all Christians and Jews and a large part of Islam, but progress seems to have been in reverse. For every one of the "enemy" we burn, several new ones spring up phoenix-like from the ashes. Thus, we have more to kill than we started out with. Even more by emigration since radicals from all over the globe have been moving into Iraq so they don't miss their opportunities to go to heaven as martyrs (remember the promise of seventy virgins). A missed opportunity might mean being blown to Hell with the rest if us.

Perhaps, if I were a braver, more stalwart fellow, I'd post another message this day, celebrated by some Hindus as New Year's Day, advocating positive nonviolent servility as medicine for the ills and ill tempers of the earth. It seems to have worked for India, if they don't blow it by blowing up Pakistan.

March 20: Ramayana.

This first day of spring should remind us, if we are of a world mind, of an incarnation something like that of Jesus, that of Rama, the human incarnation of Lord Vishnu, Chief among the Hindu gods.

Rama is born a prince, the son of King Dasharatha of Ayodhya and heir apparent to Dasharatha's throne. Dasharatha, however, in a rash moment, promises two unspecified favors to Kaikeyi, one of his wives, not the mother of Rama. When Dasharatha is old and nearing death, Kaikeyi names and calls in the favors: 1) to banish Rama and 2) to confer the throne upon his younger half-brother, Bharata. Dasharatha unwillingly honors his pledge but dies of the sorrow that it causes. Bharata, at first, refuses to insult his brother by taking the throne which is rightfully Rama's, but, finally, with Rama's insistence, agrees to serve as regent, placing Rama's slippers on the throne to represent him as true king in exile during his banishment.

Rama, accompanied by his wife, Sita, and another brother, Lakshmana, both of whom are, also, gods incarnate, enters his period of banishment where they live humble lives, with tree bark for raiment, and food and shelter provided by the forest and by Lakshmana who is Rama's chief servant.

The three, eventually and successfully, complete the banishment, returning gloriously to the kingdom to take up their reign, but what seems most important is the willingness, indeed the eagerness of Rama to fulfill his banishment as if it were the greatest privilege of his human life. Banishment, to Rama, is not a punishment, but a gift given to him in order to fulfill his incarnation. In addition, there is marvelous beauty in the dedication of Sita as the devoted wife willing to live her best years in exile and poverty and in the equal devotion of Lakshmana whose impulse is to take revenge upon those who mistreat his brother, but who adopts Rama's instruction to accept mistreatment as a blessing. Lakshmana has much in common with the apostle Peter who is so angered by the arrest of Jesus that he whumps off the ear of one of the Roman guards. Yet, like Peter, Lakshmana, curbs his anger in order to serve his master. I can vouch for the fact that this is no easy challenge. I've failed in it often.

In the forest, all three are tested in every way gods in human form can be tested (other than crucifixion, I suppose), and they pass every test. One of the most beautiful stories in the human library is the story of Rama, Sita, and Lakshmana, living harmoniously together in self-imposed poverty and simplicity. To my way of thinking, the excesses of the later parts of the story—the wars involving monkey kings, unbelievable giants, jet-powered chariots, super-charged arrows, the ordeal by fire which Sita undergoes at Rama's command, etc.—are distractions from the simple beauty of their life in the forest, which, to me is the beating heart of *The Ramayana*, celebrated every spring in a land, part of which is without spring, by the Hindu members of our human family.

March 21: No Ruz, a Celebration of Wisdom and Life.

Happy New Year from Iran, where No Ruz (New Year) goes back 3000 years, 1600 years before the foundation of Islam; a celebration altered to accommodate the teachings of the prophet of Islam, but still recognizable as a remnant of the ancient Zoroastrian Persian religion—a religion celebrating wisdom and life, founder of the concepts of Heaven vs. Hell, a god of wisdom (Ahura Mazda) vs. a demon of evil—good equal to earthly wisdom and life and joy; evil the embodiment of the opposites.

How could we forget that Zoroaster (a.k.a., Zarathustra) gave us so much of our modern Western religion? I will not attempt to list it all here. Suffice it to say that, without Zoroaster, Judaism, Christianity, and Islam would either not exist or would embody almost unrecognizably different belief systems. Most importantly, how could we forget so dramatically, that the belief systems we have in the Western world, beliefs adapted from those introduced by Zoroaster and those who followed him, centered upon pure wisdom. And from wisdom, peace; and from peace, supreme joy and earthly productivity! All of this opposed by a spirit of evil embodied in war and hatred and sorrow. How could three of the world's greatest religions retain so many of the *forms* of the ancient parentage of Western religion and leave out its Soul?

Shame on us, *all of us*! And continued shame upon us until we stop justifying evil through religion—or a pretense of it!

Oh, by the way: Happy No Ruz! And may Ahura Mazda bless you and yours.

March 22: Vernal Equinox, Ostara, Etc.

One might wonder why the vernal equinox is of such importance that many of the world's religions have at least one and, often, more than one celebration in relation to it. In reality, it means next to nothing in terms of the actual climate or living environment of the people of earth. Spring weather, for most of the northern temperate zone, arrived and the harsh part of winter departed weeks earlier. Only a dedicated astronomer or astrologer would be able to detect it. Indeed, the celebrations for different groups are spread over several days, indicating that they once had difficulty ascertaining exactly when it happens. This year, it was, actually, yesterday, late in the day, that the sun stood directly over the earth's equator as it does twice each year.

Ostara, a Druid holy day, celebrated at the next full moon after the vernal equinox, is sacred to Eostre, the goddess of fertility. You might guess (appropriately) that the Christian Easter is related. This moment (perhaps, more like a week) is incredibly important to the human race as a symbol of life—especially new life such as the resurrection of Jesus, the fertilizing of ova, the emergence of grass from the earth. It seems that nothing is as precious as new life. Christians celebrate it twice a year for Jesus: his birthday and his day of resurrection.

Perhaps we fixate upon life so intensely because death is so dreadful. To offset the horror of death, we lose ourselves in celebration of new life. What better time to do so than at the vernal equinox when nature reprises our human song.

March 23: Beginning, Middle, and End.

I delight in Aristotelian simplicity! When I first communed with Aristotle about "beginning, middle, and end," I considered it too elementary for such a great mind as his; but I have discovered through living that his simple analysis is more advanced than those mathematical formulae which have defied mastery throughout the centuries. (I read about one such formula which would cover the entire island of Manhattan with small print if it were ever to be written at all.) Yet "beginning, middle, and end" still stands as both the insoluble problem and part of the answer to nearly every philosophical question.

It is a matter of the manifold nature of existence. Consider one human life—my own, for instance. First, we can limit what I mean by my life to that part of my life of which I have any awareness. We can ignore what happened in my existence before conception because I can know nothing of that if, indeed, there was such an existence. Also, we can ignore anything that occurs after my death because I, also, can know nothing of that. We are bounded by darkness on either side, but we are not simple in between. We have "beginning, middle, and end." If we simplify this, we can claim, as many religious fundamentalists do, that our beginning is conception, that the middle is all that happens until the instant of our death, and death is our end. (Of course, we would not find religious fundamentalists agreeing with this interpretation of our "end." They have all sorts of *supposed* and, mostly, nonsensical information about life after death.) But there is a serious problem with this idea of our "beginning, middle, and end." We are, certainly, not aware of our conception. Indeed, we are not aware of much of anything for quite some time after that, at least, until our brains have developed to a state wherein we have coherent thought and memory. Even then, there is serious question what memory exists of that which occurred before birth. Thus, the question of an exact moment of our beginning is, necessarily, ambiguous. And, if the beginning of the beginning is ambiguous, when does the beginning end? What has a beginning must have a middle and an end. A beginning has a beginning, one which is ambiguous. Is the middle and end of our beginning, also, ambiguous? A simple way to measure the end of the beginning and the beginning of the middle is to declare our birth to be the beginning of the middle, thus, the end of the beginning. So be it, though that birth itself can be divided ambiguously into its own beginning, middle, and end.

Let us skip over the middle because it is far too complicated to discuss here. When is the end of the middle? Death? It cannot be for the same reason that conception cannot be the beginning. As far as we know, we do not "experience" our own death. Every day we sleep. When we drift off to sleep, do we know the precise instant when this happens? Not likely. At least, not usually. The same goes for death. As far as we know, "our death is but a sleep." Thus, death, except as it is witnessed by those around us who are not dying, is not an experience for the one who dies. Thus, it cannot be the end. Remember that the "end" must, like the beginning and the middle, have a beginning, a middle, and an end. We can consider death to be the "end" of the end, but what is the beginning of the end?

We are still at the first level of "beginning, middle, and end," and we have not satisfactorily established a beginning, middle, and end for a whole life while we still have the entire manifold of a life to be analyzed. For instance, childhood. Its beginning is simple (at least, as simple as that for the entire life which we discovered is not so simple). But when does it end and what is the structure of its ending? Within that childhood, we have puberty. Certainly, it has important structure within itself and what of the structure of its parts?

Finally, we must realize that, in this infinite existence, though we have finitized it by ignoring the parts we cannot experience, each element of the manifold which is life is infinitely divisible and with each division there is additional manifold complication. Manhattan would be a mere pinpoint in the formula for a single well-lived human life from conception to death.

Beginning, middle, end! Ahh! What satisfaction this Aristotelian simplicity renders to mortals! And along with that, "we think we have eternal life."

March 24: A Dream about Psychological Truth.

A few days ago, I said that dreaming is the only purely aesthetic art form. I'm not sure that the following is proof of this, but it is interesting and instructive to say the least. Last night—all through the night—I experienced a repetitive dream. As usual with such a dream, I remember very few of the details, but there was one prevalent theme:

> *Everything which happens occurs infinitely and everything that happens has, also, not happened at all. This could, also, be stated in the negative: Anything that has not happened but is possible has, also, happened and has happened infinitely.*

This might sound like nonsense; but, with clarification, it makes a great deal more sense. First, I am speaking, not of things as they are. Doubts about their existence are largely academic, but we do not experience them directly. We only experience them as sensual phenomena. That is, we know about things as they are because our five senses (touch, sight, hearing, taste, smell) tell us of their existence. These sensual experiences are called phenomena. Our awareness of things as they are enters our consciousness as phenomena. Once they have entered our consciousness, the phenomena are replaced by thoughts. Thoughts are, then, used as premises for action and/or stored in various parts of the brain as memories. When I say, something has happened, I mean that, our understanding tells us something has happened. That is the only avenue by which such knowledge can reach us at the conscious level. If, however, we forget that *something* has happened (i.e., the stored thought is lost in the memory), it is exactly equal, for the individual who has lost the thought, to *something* not happening at all. Of course, other phenomena might prove that *something* did, indeed, happen (e.g., forgotten phenomenon: I was hit on the head. Added phenomenon: I have a bump on my head), but added phenomena are entirely different matters. Thus, when I talk about happening and not happening, in terms of the individual, I am, actually talking about our awareness of things happening. In psychological terms, if I am not aware of a happening, it did not happen. That does not mean, however, that society will not hold me responsible for being aware of happenings even if I am not aware of them. And I may, certainly, suffer the consequences of an occurrence whether or not I am aware of the occurrence.

This might all seem to be useless blather, but consider the impact. Each of our five senses is limited, not just a little, but a lot. For instance, we can see a pistol in the hand of an assailant only from a distance of less than 30 or 40 feet. To us, if an assailant is farther away than that, the gun does not exist for us until we hear the gunshot which ends our life. And sight is our best sense. If the gunman came up from behind, we would only feel the gun if the muzzle touched us. It is psychologically nonexistent until it kills us. Indeed, since a bullet travels (2500 feet per second) faster than the speed of sound (1125 feet per second), we might be dead before the event is imprinted upon our mind and, as far as we are concerned, there is no murder at all.

More than this, even that which our senses feed us through phenomena can be misinterpreted (e.g., what we thought was a log at the bottom the pond was, actually, a child drowning), or a phenomenon may be forgotten. You have, surely, read in the news of parents who forgot that their infant was strapped into an infant seat in the back seat of the car and left the child to cook in the hot sun in the office parking lot instead of delivering her to daycare. Physical things as they are, disappearing from the realm of thought and memory, can be devastating.

What if a fact of history loses its psychological existence in the mind of a political leader? For instance, what if the leader of a major political power forgets that there is no such thing as a good war—and starts one?

March 25: Nuremburg Justice.

I just had to let the Scribe do a little writing. He was so damned mad about the Iraq war that he was beside himself. He needed some purgation. This is what he came up with.

Yesterday, I watched a 1961 movie starring Spencer Tracy entitled *Judgment at Nuremburg*. It detailed the 1948 trials of Nuremberg judges for war crimes during the Nazi holocaust. The Nuremberg judges argued that they were not engaged in criminal activity because they were following the laws of their government when they sentenced innocent persons (guilty only of being Jewish or of having Jewish friends or of speaking against the policies of the Reich) to death or to be sterilized or to be imprisoned. They insisted that they did not know of the millions of people who were being exterminated. One of the accused judges admitted that he knew he should not convict innocent persons but that he did so in order to do some future good by staying in office to provide easier sentences to other accused but innocent persons.

100

Of course, in hindsight, we can see this as immoral rationalization. Spencer Tracy's character said it well when he said: "You became aware of the full horror of the Reich when you condemned the first innocent man to death."

America is now engaged in a war which did not have to happen which has probably killed over a hundred thousand persons, most of them innocents. The premises for engaging in this war contained obvious flaws. The premises for continuing it beyond the fall of the government of Saddam Hussein were extremely weak. The premises for continuing the war beyond the capture of Saddam Hussein were even more questionable. And, at present, the premises for continuing the fight in a conflict which has, obviously, become a civil war between Iraqi religious sects, is nonsense.

I fault the President and his advisors for the war. I, also, fault the Republican congress for lending nearly unanimous support to the President and his advisors for it in the face of such weak evidence for its necessity. However, I fault most those Democratic senators and congressmen who, having the same information as the entire world about the weakness of the arguments for going to war, assented with minimal resistance.

Those Democratic senators and congressmen are the Nuremberg judges. Just this once, they thought, we will go along with the idea of pre-emptive strike even though there seems to be nothing to pre-empt. "My country, right or wrong!" Those Democratic senators and congressmen knew that, with their consent, innocent people would die in an unjust war, or, even if the war proved to be just, not a good war. *There is no such thing as a good war.* They knew, after they condemned those first few innocents to die, the entire potential horror that lay beyond. *I knew*, and I am no expert in such matters. Simply being humans of normal intellect and morality should have been enough to give them such knowledge.

What will they do now with their majority which has placed in their hands the power to take us out of the conflict?

March 26: Siebert here!

Sam has a little indigestion because he ate too many strawberries yesterday. His middle daughter gave him and Yasmin a quart of fresh strawberries because Sam and Yasmin were expecting company and didn't have time to get to the store for what Yasmin calls "pupus." She's a gal from Hawaii, ya know. Sweet little darlin'! So daughter #2 dropped the strawberries by. The company called in sick. Thus, Sam, in all his wisdom, decided that it was his duty to eat all of the strawberries while watching his KU Jayhawks limp their way out of the NCAA Elite Eight. It seemed to ease his pain a little, 'til later.

Anyway, I have the keyboard this morning, and I have only one thing to say: "Good morning!" Maybe that's enough, though, considering how good it makes me feel when I walk down the street and people left and right say, "Good morning!"—even the ones who sort of grunt it. I've knowed 'em long enough to know they really mean it, even if it sounds more like throat-clearing than anything else.

March 27: The Fall of Man.

I appreciate the little break the Scribe and Siebert gave me. This poem fell "trippingly from my tongue" this morning. I think it has something to do with original sin or maybe just with my own original foolishness. I'll let you decide.

Yesterday, my right toe caught the top step of the stairs
Of the sidewalk leading to our front yard.
Redbud blossoms were just pinking the space
To the left of my left ear
And my wife's garden trinkets stood at attention
To my right.
Ahead of me, assaulting my downcast eyes:
Concrete;
Gray flat concrete, fifty years old, foot-worn,
Well-trodden.
I imagine that the old mathematics professor
The first owner of the house
Who poured the concrete walk
Was sure he had it right.
He did not *accidentally* make it ½ inch higher
Than my right toe would reach yesterday
As I was trying to find a door my wife had not locked
After I painted the bed of my Toyota truck
The wrong shade of gold and coated my hands
With clotted rust inhibitor.
Dastardly old fart of a math professor!—
Probably had it in for English professors—
Set the trap, ½ inch too high for my right toe.

The concrete lunged for my face.
I spread my arms like angel's wings.
Bared my teeth for concrete,
Left hand grabbing for redbud blossoms,
Right clutching at flower-garden trinkets
With brittle stems crackling like icicles
In my fist.
There was a wind a-whistling somewhere,
I could hear it as my right knee grated denim
From my jeans and skin from itself
Uniting denim with skin and concrete.
I could hear evil old Professor Robbins
Laughing his demonic laugh—
His trap, after half a century's silent yawning
Snared an English professor
Long after he (the math professor)
Died of a heart attack
Digging a sewer trench.
Both my arms slapped the ground
Palms down.

My forehead hit concrete.
Fortunately, I had gained a lot of weight
Through gluttony,
A Cardinal sin,
And my belly hit first,
Saving face.

I went for sympathy to my wife and second daughter.
By then I looked like an Islamic holy man
With a bruise on my forehead from much praying.
My wife, busy with grandchildren,
Told me without noticing the bruise
To go upstairs and get the laundry basket.
Daughter #2 gave me a knowing wince,
And I went for the basket
My fingers stuck together with rust inhibitor
And blood.

Damned old math professor!

March 28:   Poverty, a New Analysis.

Nearly every religion and philosophy unveiled to the world contains the commandment to stay poor. Yet it is a rare individual who honors this dictum with more than lip service. And there is no mistake about the doctrine of poverty. Monks worldwide from Christian to Buddhist are poor. Even Mother Theresa lived a life of poverty while many millions of dollars passed over her desk on the way to feed the starving, clothe the naked, medicate the sick. The Red Chinese government insists that its leaders live a financial life-style which is no richer than that of the average citizen (although, I get the feeling that there is more show than go in that claim.)

There are a few important exceptions. Neither Judaism nor Islam puts much stock in poverty. This is not to condemn either of them since they do place heroic emphasis upon taking financial care of members of their own faith. Israel has a capitalistically conditioned socialist government, and most Islamic countries have systems in place for sharing wealth with their poor citizens.

Still, in the world at large, philosophic and religious condemnation of wealth continues in the face of the obvious love of money which roots itself in the hearts of the human race. We need to take a new look at this dilemma. Is money really the root of all evil? Not exactly, but it is, certainly, one of the roots. And it seems to, also, be the root of most of the good that occurs in the world. Money is the mere symbol of wealth which is, actually, a root of both good and evil. Wealth is evil because people will do just about anything (good or evil) to lay hands upon it. Wealth is good because it lays the foundation for science. Without it, there can be no advanced research into cures for deadly ills, for the feeding of the hungry, for the clothing of the naked, for housing, for intervention in civil strife. Indeed, the lack of wealth in a nation is, often, the primary reason for such evil practices as ethnic cleansing. (Feed a man a fish and he will be hungry again tomorrow; inject a man with a carefully aimed lead bullet, and he will never hunger again.)

Yet the world can only produce wealth at a modest rate. With the growing human populace (which I might say could use a good supply of birth control pills), that modest wealth can only go around if the wealthy persons of the world share the wealth. Indeed, even with a small population, the greed of the wealthy can cause starvation among the poor. That has proven to be the case in every generation of the history of the world.

Thus, it would be fair to redefine the doctrine of poverty as a doctrine of sharing. Perhaps, we could redefine it better as a doctrine of not loving our own personal hoard and the wealthy lifestyle so much that we do not share it.

I have been fortunate in this regard. It has been unnecessary for me to do much sharing because I have never had two nickels to rub together for more than a couple of minutes before someone else laid claim to them. I was fortunate, also, in my parentage, which taught me through example what it means to be a family of modest means with little means of becoming a family of less modest means, but with just enough intelligence to know that such "means" were not important to us anyway. But my poverty is not honorable in any way. Had I been born with the financial genes to make millions, I am sure I would have made millions. It is not to my credit that I have not made millions. Rather, it is to my discredit that I have had little of financial value to share. I can say that I have shared my "wealth" of knowledge with my thousands of students over the years, but was that sharing not, largely, done to make a buck, so I could spend it on my own well-being? Nothing heroic about that! Thus, I must conclude: poverty is not a virtue. It is merely a financial condition, just as wealth is not an evil, but merely a financial condition. It is what is done with poverty or wealth which is good or evil.

I conclude that the person who attains and hoards wealth beyond the need for simple, safe, and wholesome living is committing an atrocity against humanity—against the earth and all its inhabitants. It is not the making of money that is evil. It is its hoarding.

I conclude that the person of intellectual means who hoards that intellect and does not share it in meaningful and useful ways is committing an atrocity against the earth and its inhabitants.

I conclude that the person of physical strength who does not share that physical strength in meaningful and useful ways is committing an atrocity against the earth and its inhabitants.

The greatest good is action aimed intelligently in pursuit of the greatest benefit for the earth and its inhabitants.

March 29: Mawlid an-Nabi.

March 31 is the Prophet Mohammad's birthday—Mawlid an-Nabi. I wish all of his followers a joyous and *peaceful* celebration. Mohammad's birthday will probably not come to the attention of most persons in the world unless they are Islamic or they are living in an Islamic republic or they are associated in some other way with Islamic persons. What the celebration of Jesus's birthday is to Christians, the celebration of Mohammad's birthday is to Muslims. But not quite (see below)!

A few things that all of us should consider about Mohammad:

1) He is, to Muslims, one of the great prophets of God. He stands in importance along side the other prophets, particularly, Moses, Abraham, and Jesus.

2) He is the prophet sent by God to the people of Islamic faith which is a continuation of the faith embodied in "the people of the Book" (essentially, the Jews, the Christians, and the Muslims) who share faith in the same god (the *only* god, according to the people of the Book), the god said to be responsible for creation and for the ancient faith essentially found in the Old Testament of the Bible.

3) Mohammad is not a god. He is a man and he is a prophet. As a prophet, in the eyes of Muslims, he is equal to Moses, Abraham, and Jesus, though he is the prophet sent to the Muslims and his is, thus, the ultimate word for Muslims. It is essential to the Muslims that Mohammad is a man, not a god because of the ancient commandment that there shall be no other gods before God—a commandment accepted as gospel by Jews, Christians, and Muslims.

4) Muslims are particularly critical of the deification of Jesus because this creates (according to the Muslims) a second god who is worshipped by the Christians in direct defiance of "the Book." The Christian elevation of the Holy Spirit as a third member of the trinity adds fuel to the fires of this apparent polytheism. This single "apostate" belief in the Trinity of the Christians (as a branch of the people of the Book) is sufficient, in the mind of Islam, to set the Christians apart as "unbelievers"—"infidels"—who have broken the most important commandment of God as the Muslims interpret it—to serve only God.

5) A word to the wise to Christians who would like to establish a peaceful coexistence with Islamic persons: consider whether it is more important to believe that Christ is deity or to believe Christ's central message that the most important commandments are 1) to love God, and 2) to love other persons as much as you love yourselves (thus: to love Islamic persons with the same passion as you love Christian persons). It is quite telling that Jesus, when asked which were the most important commandments, did not mention believing that he is the only begotten son of God. Have you ever thought to present what Jesus said when you are asked by an Islamic person about the most important tenet of Christianity? Instead of throwing the deity of Jesus in the face of a person who cannot possibly accept that deity, have you thought of saying that the most important tenet of Christianity is love—to love God and to love all people—including those who believe with *significant* scriptural justification that *you* are the infidel?

March 30: In All Fairness.

I am an equal opportunity grinch! I cannot leave the previous day's topic without noting that there is plenty that those among us who follow Mohammad (and the many who call themselves Muslim while breaking every Muslim rule in the Book) need to do in order to establish and maintain a peaceful coexistence with Christian persons (and the many who call themselves Christians while breaking every Christian rule in the Book). Let's turn again to listing.

1) The idea of Jihad (as holy war with guns and suicide bombers and the like) must be condemned. Those Muslims who rush to violent Jihad at the slightest provocation must be criticized by other Muslims for doing so. Neither Mohammed nor Jesus would approve of resorting to violence for simple insults (such as a less

than generous pictorial depiction of the Prophet Mohammad) or even for beliefs assumed by Islam to be heretical (such as the divinity of the Prophet Jesus). Violent responses should occur only as a last resort for the preservation of life and limb, and, with indisputable evidence, property and, even then, sparingly and as humanely as possible. The slaughtering of men, women, and children (including the child and other ignorant martyrs upon whom explosives are strapped) in an open market-place is inexcusable in any moral context. It should not be up to non-Muslims to penalize those who support this type of activity. The Islamic world should rise up in indignation against such acts of violence just as Christians and Jews should rise up in indignation against the use of war machines (and their operators and those who order them into operation) to carry out retribution against such acts by killing not only the perpetrators of acts of violence but anyone who happens to be in the general vicinity of those perpetrators. There can be no justification for such acts of violence or for acts of revenge against them. Neither has any whiff of "good" in it—only pure evil.

2) Muslims must stop condemning Christians because of the belief that Jesus is a deity. It is impossible for a Muslim to accept the concept of the trinity. Most Christians have great difficulty understanding it and accept it purely on faith. However, Muslims need to understand that Christians do not consider each of the three in the trinity to be separate "gods." They are three manifestations of the one God. Each of the three major faiths that are unified as "the people of the Book" believe in, trust in, have faith in, obey as best they can seem to manage, that one God. That God is not divided, has no "partner." Certainly, the Christian belief in Christ as the "only begotten son of God" is different from and offensive to the Islamic understanding that Jesus is a co-equal prophet of God along with Moses, Abraham, and Mohammad. But Islamic persons must remember that being at odds with the religious dogma of others is not justification for hatred or violent acts against those others. If anything, it is justification for sympathy toward the others. The Christians have suffered sorely for this belief which is so short on evidence for its truth, just as Islam has suffered for differing from it. (Consider, for instance, the Christians who faced death by sword, fang, and claw in the Roman Coliseum.)

3) Muslims must come to recognize and respond to the fact that we now live in the 21st century with all of its societal difference from other centuries. Some ancient Islamic customs which have come down through the centuries need re-evaluation. Chief among these are the civil rights of women. I do not mean by this that Islam must entirely abandon all of its system of beliefs in regard to the differing social expectations of the sexes. However, as with acts of violence condoned by radical Islamic groups, suppressive and violent treatment of women such as that exercised by the Taliban, must, also, be *absolutely* condemned by moderate Islam. Moderate Islam must go so far as to expel such radical groups from their fellowship. Islamic persons world-wide cannot expect to be respected by Christians as long as they do not condemn such behavior in Islamic persons everywhere.

Finally, in regard to Muslims, Jews, and Christians, along with all others of the world who wish to be regarded as "good" humans, it is not enough to believe. Each of us must act or not act depending upon the circumstances, and each of our actions and inactions must be driven by wisdom. That is, our actions must reflect the most pure conditions whereby we do not do to others (men, women, or children)

106

anything which we would not wish to be done to us, and that we do for others that which we wish others would do for us—and that we do it all willingly and joyously.

March 31: Origami Cranes.

For many years now, my wife has been folding paper origami cranes as gifts for friends and others who do favors for her or me or for any of our circle of acquaintances. To the uninitiated, these little cranes are small rewards, but I have come to appreciate them as valuable symbols of greater rewards.

First, for the mercantile-minded among readers of this note, Yasmin's skills at folding paper cranes have reached and surpassed professional paper crane folders whose cranes sell for $35 and beyond, but this is said just to catch your attention, so now I go beyond such mundane materialism.

The origami crane has been, since ancient days, a Japanese cultural symbol of health and prosperity. A gift of one of these was meant to confer the giver's wish that the receiver be happy, healthy, and prosperous. In the days before penicillin and the minimum wage, health and prosperity were not as readily assumed as they are today. Later, the origami crane became a symbol of peace. This transformation or, rather, addition was accompanied by the idea that wedding preparations should include the folding of 1000 cranes (usually from gold-foil) in order to insure that the marriage would be happy, *peaceful*, healthy, and prosperous. Of course, the groom did not have to participate in all of this folding, leading me to suspect that this was but one more way to keep the bride busy and out of high-end retail shops for a few weeks before the wedding. The actual result has been a superfluity of gold-foil cranes in the greater part of the modern world. They still, occasionally, fall out of the creases of our sofa hearkening back to the marriage of daughter #1 fifteen years ago.

As to current value, I have come to see these little cranes as true aesthetic symbols and one of the finest gifts one can receive. The importance of aesthetic symbolism cannot be overstated. It is a unique and rare way to approach truth. An aesthetic symbol like a paper crane minimizes the materialistic aspect of life experience. It is small. It is nearly weightless. When suspended by a nearly invisible elastic fiber in a window, sunlight sending miniature rainbows around the room through crystals attached in glittering piles above and below the body, it seems to dance on air. It is fragile—powerlessness and omnipotence, finity and infinity blended.

Though it is both a thing as it is and a phenomenon, it *impresses* us as neither. As we consider it truly, it flutters past these to the realm of pure thought, beyond materialism, between existence and imagination—feeding and being fed by the human soul, whether that soul is a mere electrical charging and discharging of neurons, or is at the other end of the spectrum, a pure and simple, eternal gift from a loving God.

The End of Volume 1
The New Moon

The True Book of Sam Clear Water
Wisdom from Walden-San
Volume 2: *The Half Moon*

A Further Reading Tip from Yasmin's Auntie:
Bum by, while you reading volume 1, even if you no like much da firs' stuffs, you finally say to youself, "ass mo' betta!" an' even laugh or cry a little. Now you ready for mo' good stuff. Don' be sad if Sam get boring. I tink so, too. No wonda!—he spend alla time read da boring stuff. But he a little funny . . . sometime. Anyway, da book cos' lotsa money. No waste! Eh?!

April 1: Two Good Men Riding.

What a glorious day to start a new volume. First of all, it is sunny and warm, the grass is green, the flowering trees are blossoming, and the lilacs just began to bloom today reminding me of that wonderful sad poem by Whitman about Abraham Lincoln's death.

This volume could be called *The Ascent*. It is the volume during which I go into the mountains—that's not very original, is it? It seems as if every self-respecting philosopher or prophet since Moses did that. Is my ascent different? I hope not to any great extent, except that I promise it will be more fun than most; certainly, more peaceable than the ones in Moses' *Exodus*. I look forward every year to going to the mountains in order to escape the absurdity of civilized life. Of course, from civilization, I go to the absurdity of a more primitive life, so what is the difference? You will see—I promise.

A little over three weeks from now, I will depart alone for the Rocky Mountains where I will stay until October. The first part of that stay will be the soil in which this volume grows. The other three months will be its harvest in Volume Three. Volume Four will finish out the year back in civilization.

We ended Volume One with an accolade to "right action." The "right action" for today would be to take a day off from bashing politicians, evangelists, and gentlemen of the pre-owned automobile persuasion and from all other such productive work, and to, simply, put our feet up and "thank whatever gods may be" for sunshine and lilac blossoms and Abraham Lincoln or for whatever keeps your clock ticking. If it is a rainy, nasty day where you are, you have my permission to bless your local TV meteorologist with curses.

I will, however, resist the temptation to take the day off. I cannot, in good conscience, do so because today is Palm Sunday. Not that I'm going to church. I seldom attend church. I'd rather spend what free hours I have on Sunday reading and thinking and enjoying time with Yasmin and assorted family members.

Palm Sunday reminds me of asses—Jack and Jennet asses—donkeys. The reason for that is that Jesus rode into Jerusalem on an ass, one that was borrowed ceremoniously and mysteriously from an acquaintance. His ride into town on this little beast is known as his triumphal entry—which we must assume contains its share of irony.

There is another story of a "good" man riding a beast through a city. However, this was not Jerusalem. It was a city during the late Chou dynasty in China, and it was Lao Tsu doing the riding. Also, he was riding out of, not into, the city.

Whereas Jesus was beginning his final statement, the final acts of his mission on earth, including some antisocial antics at the Hebrew Temple, a last supper with his jolly band of renegades, repairing a soldier's shorn ear, going through court proceedings, and being crucified after refusing to defend himself, Lao Tsu was riding out of town because he was sick of city life and all of its absurdities and planned to spend the rest of his life as a hermit in the mountains. According to legend, the gate guard of the city saw what he was doing and prevailed upon him to write down his best philosophical advice before he left. Lao Tsu did so, and, thus, we have the *Tao Te Ching* (*The Book of the Path*). This was about 500 years before Jesus took his last ride. The two texts that came out of these two rides (the *New Testament Gospels* and the *Tao Te Ching*) stand like terminals of an ethical continuum, one demanding that we sacrifice our lives for what is right, the other demanding that we do nothing at all. Yet it can be argued that Lao Tsu's *Tao* is the same road as the "strait and narrow path" touted by Jesus. It has taken us 2000 years since Jesus rode and about 2500 years since Lao Tsu rode to reach the 20th century wherein we discovered, finally, the truth of the absurd—that everything is nothing and that nothing is everything—that truth is false and false is true. Some of us have discovered the beauty hidden in all of this while other radicals either try to stay constantly inebriated or leap from 20th floor windows to the horror and delight of less radical but bored passers-by on the sidewalks below.

You might be reading this thinking that I will, eventually, shout "April Fool!" I will not, but you may do so if you like. However, to retain my reputation of honesty, I must admit that Lao Tsu, according to legend, was riding a water ox, not an ass. On the other hand, I will not apologize for my delay of the truth because, country boy that I am, I have seen more than one ox making an ass of itself.

April 2: Pasach (Passover).

The Israelites had been enslaved by the Egyptians for hundreds of years, indeed, since the ancient time of Joseph who was sold into slavery by his brothers who, then, followed him into slavery in a time of famine for the sake of sufficient food. The Israelites, who were said by the Israelites to be the "chosen people" of God, were finally released from their slavery after a series of godly acts against the Egyptians gauged to make life so miserable for them that they would be glad to let the Israelites go free just to relieve the pain. After snakes, toads, bloody rivers, etc., the last plague was the most severe. An apparently not-quite-omniscient God had all the Israelites mark their doorposts with lamb's blood so he would know that these were Israelite homes. Then he sent a destroying angel, passing over the Israelite homes to slaughter all the firstborn of the Egyptians: persons and animals (including, I suppose, the firstborn flies, snakes, and frogs). This might have been

109

in excess of a million persons, many of them babies and toddlers. Who knows how many animals bit the dust?

My purpose here is not to be shocking, but I *would* like you to be awake. This is an example of how religion, uncritiqued, can take on grotesque elements that are indefensible. Consider that this mass slaughter is, perhaps, one sixth the size of the holocaust in World War II Germany. Hitler was, apparently, trying to wipe out all of the Jews. God was just sending a none-too-subtle message to Pharaoh in defense of the Hebrews. That could account for the difference in dead-count. It is, approximately, five times the number of Iraqi dead in the current war there. It is in the range of five times the number dead in the current genocide in and around Darfur.

Think! Think! Think! Can this mass-murderer god be the same God who, it is said, lovingly formed humanity of the clay and pure water of the earth?

Previously, I have examined the possibility of the existence of God. First, we know through the exercise of logic that there is infinite power in the cosmos. Also, by logic, we can conclude that this power in its infiniteness is capable of manifesting itself as God. Thus, God is a possibility. That is all we know for sure. However, we can extend our limited concept of the existence of God. Through the means of our rational minds and through the sensual phenomena and *a priori* concepts which reach our minds and through the medium of imagination, we can construct a benevolent and personal God. That is not to say that such a God exists. Rather, this is *faith* built upon scavenged (perhaps, even illogical, false, and misunderstood) materials natural and supernatural. I cannot prove it, but I suspect that nearly every human being carries at least a shadow of a share of this kind of faith. I carry it in abundance because it is a wonderful gossamer burden which seems to hold me up instead of weighing me down. That is, also, why I don't load much other clap-trap upon it.

Thus, when I see a passage of scripture like the one in Exodus that reports God as a mass murderer, I, simply, reject it and move on. There are many other things in the Bible that are *helps*, not stumbling blocks, in my futile but nourishing search for truth. A god that slaughters small children to make an argumentative point is not the God I talk to when I want metaphysical support in my life, or when I just want to chat about ethics or politics or aesthetics with someone who knows a lot more about all of them than I.

April 3: Mine or Yours?

I try not to have many things regarding which, if someone were to take them from me, I could not happily say, "It is as much yours as mine. Take it and use it to a good purpose." This does not always work. As a favor to a colleague, I once traded an old guitar for an antique book that I had no use for. I have been sorry about that ever since. The book sits silent and unread on my shelf, and I miss the company and the music of the old guitar. Never sell old friends!

April 4: Good Advice from a Friend.

Sam and Siebert are sitting on a bench beside White Alloe Stream, soaking up early morning sunshine. There's a bit of frost in the air.
Sam: Do you suppose the frost will hurt the rhubarb?

110

Siebert: Not likely. Hasn't sprouted yet. *(Siebert bit off a piece of his chaw, offered the plug to Sam and returned it to his vest pocket without waiting for Sam's inevitable rejection.)*

Sam: I unhooked my garden hose last night when I heard it was going to freeze.

Siebert: Wasted effort! It won't freeze hard enough overnight this time of year to split a hose.

(A long peaceful silence. A long sigh from Siebert.)

Sam: What are you sighing about? You got the lumbago again?

Siebert: Nope! I was just thinking about you leaving in a couple of weeks.

Sam: It's almost three weeks.

Siebert: It might as well be tomorrow. It's April, and when April arrives, you are gone to Idaho whether you are physically here or not. You aren't much company because your mind is *gone*.

Sam *(Guffawing)*: I suppose you're right. I was just now thinking about going over to the second daughter's house and loading the camper onto the pickup. But I can't because we need to take the pickup without the camper to stay in a hotel this weekend. I don't like driving the pickup with the camper downtown. I can't afford wide angle mirrors, so I have big blind spots. Besides which, the camper is too high to fit into most of those indoor parking lots that hotels have.

Siebert: Gmfft.

Sam: Yeah! Me, too! The daughters got us a hotel room for Saturday night so we could celebrate our 40th anniversary there. They knew that we would just waste it away watching TV if we didn't go someplace.

Siebert: So you'll go to the hotel and watch TV.

(Guffawing from both men)

Sam: That's about right. It's hard for old folks to break old habits. But, at least, we'll be surrounded by luxuriant splendor.

Siebert: And you'll be slouching there in your moth-eaten underwear with the door locked, eating tater skins.

Sam: Right! It'll be like Heaven.

Siebert: Meanwhile, back at the ranch, before you lose your mind completely to the mountains, what advice can you give me that will carry me through the summer until you return, oh, Swami!?

Sam: Get plenty of Tater Skins.

(Guffaws aplenty!)

Siebert: *(Another sigh)* I'm serious. I'm depressed that the only person in town who cares to hang out with me for more than five minutes is leaving for six months. What do you advise that I do about it?

Sam: The reason I hang out with you is that you give me such good advice. You're the smart one. You're the real philosopher.

Siebert: Sure!!!

Sam: O.K. Here's my best advice, but you don't really need it. You already live by it.

Siebert: *(Pretending with fake pen and paper to be ready to write)* O.K. Give it to me.

Sam: Don't worry!

Siebert: O.K., I won't worry. Now what's the advice?

111

Sam: That's the advice: Don't worry!

Siebert: *(Putting away his fake pen and paper and leaning back on the park bench)* Oh! I see what you mean.

Sam: What do I mean?

Siebert: You don't, really, have any advice to give me, so you just tell me not to worry.

Sam: No, I'm serious, but I do know that, eventually, you won't worry, so my advice won't be much count since you will follow it whether I give it to you or not.

Siebert: Oh!

Sam: Not to worry is probably the best advice that can be given at any time to anyone. No one ever got anything good out of worrying. You either do something about a problem or you don't. What you do either works or it doesn't work because your solution to the problem is either right or wrong.

Siebert: Then I'll give you some advice.

Sam: What's that?

Siebert: Don't worry!

(A little guffaw from both men)

Sam: O.K. You got me. Yes, I worry. For instance, at the moment, I am worried about leaving Yasmin alone all summer. She won't be going to Idaho this summer because #2 is having a baby, and she needs to be here to supervise.

Siebert: Don't worry!

Sam: Right!

Siebert: I know you won't follow that piece of advice, so I'll give you one you might follow: Use worms.

Sam: Huh?

Siebert: You said that you are going fishing this summer, and I know what a god-awful fisherman you are. Use worms! It is the universal fish-bait. Fish like 'em. Forget the flies. Forget the corn. Use worms!

Sam: O.K. Thanks.

April 5: A Tragic Story of Living Downtown in the Twenty-First Century.

It was warm inside the old bungalow,
downtown
in a neighborhood where street gangs roam
driving piston-hot cars with loaded pistols
under the front seats:
warm because the outdoor night was cold for April,
the month of rejuvenation,
and Abuelito had turned on the electric heater in the living room
between him and the tiny girl.
He was reading in his leather recliner.
The little girl, Elisa, squatting on the floor
by the front door,
cradled and caressed,
scolded and soothed her favorite doll,
a gift from Tia Gloria.

Just as the doll was shushed fast asleep,
a bullet from a gun under a seat
ripped through the two plies
of hollow-core front door,
burned like a bee-sting
across the epidermis
near the girl's right ear.
She fell forward
on the doll
on the floor
her hand reaching for her head.
Quickly, she regained herself,
sat upright on wobbly knees, rubbing her hurt head,
looked at her hand,
covered with her own warm blood,
the doll on the floor.
She flung a look of fear toward Abuelito,
half risen from the recliner,
alive with panic;

Then a second lead bullet crashed through the plywood,
through the fine black hair,
the skin, the bone,
stopped—passive,
a white spot on an X-ray film,
in the soft brain tissue of the girl.
Fear went blank in her face
as she, once again, fell forward over
her favorite doll.

At the hospital,
a physician in a white coat,
hands in pockets,
tells a distraught grandfather that his granddaughter
has no brain waves.
Waves, waves, waves
of sorrow!
"Chiquita! Mi Corazon!"
The inevitable planning
and weeping and remembering;
and the end of a tragic story of living downtown
in the twenty-first century.

April 6: Good Friday.
It is my assessment that the Christian world is wrong about the relative value of
Good Friday vs. Easter which happens a couple of days from now. Good Friday
celebrates the sacrifice of Jesus for the cause he came to accomplish. Easter

113

celebrates his rising from the dead. I think that just about any Christian will tell you that Easter is considered to be the more important of the two, the reason being that it adds evidence to the concept of Jesus's divinity. His death on Good Friday presents him as quite human. Gods don't die, do they? For 20 centuries Christianity has had its priorities exactly backwards. It has insisted that the most important thing about Jesus is that he is, in some mysterious way, synonymous with God. The fact that he is also entirely human and capable of dying just like the rest of us has been subordinated.

It is time for Christianity to reassess. I am not asking Christians to abandon their belief in Jesus as "the only begotten son of God." I will not hold that doctrine against them. After all, I believe in God, and I think that God is benevolent. If God chose to do so, he could in his omniscience incarnate himself as a human male in Judea 2000 years ago, and he could permit himself to be crucified as a symbol of devotion to his creation and to suffer just as humans suffer. Those who deny Christians the right to this imaginative belief need, themselves, to reassess their values. My purpose, here, is to encourage Christians to find a more productive center for their religious focus.

It is impossible for human beings to become "God." Thus, it seems to me that to center our worship on the divinity of Jesus is not particularly helpful to us. On the other hand, we can become "Good." That is what Christ demonstrated in the sacrifice of his human life. Rejecting all special help from God, he permitted himself to be executed in one of the most painful modes ever invented by human beings. And he did it with wise forethought for us. That is what demonstrates that Jesus is "good." He did it with wise forethought for us, not thoughtlessly or for himself.

Resurrection, on the other hand, was inevitable. The only thing odd about it was that Jesus, according to the story, was resurrected out of a tomb here on earth using his mortal body as a vehicle. He is said to be, after all, God. If he were not resurrected here, it would have been in Heaven or somewhere else or everywhere. God, if there is a God, doesn't die permanently. The only thing that could die is the "mortal coil." Jesus did nothing exceptional in coming back to life. In essence, if he is God, he never left life. He, merely, abandoned a cadaver and then returned to it. That is what Easter is about.

Good Friday, however, is about true heroism in a human being, whether or not that human being is, also, God incarnate.

I am quite sure that Jesus would be happy to share this holiday with the multitude of heroes who have willingly sacrificed their lives, often in horribly painful ways, with wise forethought for the sake of other humans.

Easter is nice—a good time to hunt for Easter eggs. Good Friday is better.

April 7: Water.

In my travels, I have rested by many waters.
I have rested beside cold subterranean water pumped from desert wells.
I have rested beside tepid reservoirs,
      channeled away in canals to irrigate fields of corn and grass.
I have rested beside still noiseless waters.
I have rested beside tumultuous rushing waters.

114

I have rested beside clear talking brooks.
I have rested by miniature rills.
I have rested by great solemn rivers.
I have rested by wide shallow rivers with beds of round rocks
      like great dark pearls.
I have rested by flowing muddy waters.
I have rested by falling waters red with plant dye.
I have rested by flat lakes choked with algae.
I have rested by bottomless mountain lakes
      colder than sky.
I have rested on ships crowning purple oceans.
I have rested while purple oceans became gray monster waves.
I have rested in amniotic water.
I think fondly upon my first water—the simple, the amniotic—
      as I rest beside other waters.

April 8: Easter Sunday and our 40th Anniversary.

Which do you suppose is more important to me, Easter Sunday or our 40th anniversary? Yasmin and I spent last night in a four-star hotel—something we would never do on our own. It was an anniversary gift from our daughters. (Our daughters do such nice things for us.) It was great, especially the part where the concierge ordered up an immediate table in a fancy restaurant, a table we would have had to wait a week for on our own. The worst part: Yasmin wouldn't let me wear my jeans and denim shirt—too gauche for the surroundings! But, all-in-all, it was a nice quiet 20 hours. The weather outside was too cold for April. The gas company had already turned off our household natural gas at our request—we always have it turned off April 1st—Call us "green" and cheap! It saves us $40 a year. So the warm hotel was a nice break from our chilly domicile.

This afternoon, all three daughters and all eight grandchildren (including the intra-uterine one) joined us at our house for Easter treats. It will, probably, be the last time I see them all together before I depart for the mountains. I don't know if they will ever know just how much I love them, all of them: all three daughters with their differing personalities, all combinations of Yasmin and myself and whatever their experiences have added; all eight grandchildren who are as precious as their mothers; and their fathers—fine fellows in their own rights—a hard-muscled Caucasian of Germanic stock, starting his own construction business, a gentle, lightweight Guatemalan with a marvelous sense of humor; and a quiet, blue-eyed American mulatto who's almost finished putting himself through college. I have been fortunate in my daughters' choices of husbands. They could have all been sodden fellows who worked themselves into wealthy comfort and agreed with me on everything, making family life a bore. None of that here! These are real men, each uniquely to my liking.

I guess I don't have to tell you whether Easter or our 40th Anniversary is more important. I have already tipped my hand. The empty tomb yielded one living but musty Jesus. I truly appreciate and do not underestimate his gift to the world. Our marriage, on the other hand, has yielded 14 interesting and energetic persons who love and are loved in return. An old farmer like me knows something about relative yield.

Happy Easter, anyway!

April 9: Yesterday was Buddha's Birthday.

Siddhartha Gautama is said to have been born on April 8, but the year of his birth is variously reported from before 1000 B.C. to around 500 B.C. (It seems odd that we know the month and the day, but we don't even know the century.) He is better known by his eventual title: the Buddha. One of the most important facts about the Buddha is that he is not a god. This fact seems to have been lost upon nearly the entire world including many Buddhists. I will not, however, go into this matter. It is far more important, just as it is in the case of Jesus, to deal with the message than the genealogy.

Jesus's message was centered upon love and right action. Although Buddha would approve in large part of the message of Jesus, his focus was different. What Buddha sought (and, apparently, found) was balance. We might put it this way: Jesus is the prince *of* peace. Buddha is the prince *at* peace, a condition Jesus was never quite able to replicate.

Since the story of the Buddha's quest is rather complicated and difficult to follow, let me direct you to a simplified and modernized version which was one of my first coherent contacts with Buddhism. It is the story as told by Hermann Hesse, called *Siddhartha*. I'll not tell you the whole story as presented in Hesse's 1922 novel; rather, I'll provide a thumbnail sketch. First, Siddhartha was born a prince in the wealthy Brahmin class of India. However, sensing that he had a higher calling which could not be achieved in the straits of his birth, he went as a teenager on a quest which took him through various choices of lifestyle from absolute self-denial to untold wealth, marriage, fatherhood, from socialism to capitalism, from follower to leader and back again, ultimately, to his final choice of occupation, that of a ferryman. Symbolically, his seat on the ferry boat was a fulcrum, a point of perfect balance among all possible life choices. His "right effort" was to transport those searching through all of the possible choices which Siddhartha had explored and rejected.

Notice that the Buddha's story contains both full instruction to the seeker and no instruction at all. Buddha has found his place of perfect balance as a teacher. But where is that perfect balance to be found for the rest of us? This is the unsolved mystery; apparently, unsolved by anyone before or since the Buddha. I think the American Singer, Walt Whitman, put it best when he said in *Leaves of Grass*: "You are also asking me questions and I hear you, I answer that I cannot answer, you must find out for yourself."

At least, five hundred years before Jesus was born, the Buddha had already solved a problem of Jesus's ministry. Jesus's message seems so simple: Love God. Love your neighbor (including your enemy). Why is it that his example is impossible to follow? The answer is so simple that once you have found it, you will wonder why it was not obvious to you before. The question: How do I love? The answer: You must find out for yourself.

No amount of following or copying Jesus or the Buddha or Mohammad, or Abraham, or Moses, or Socrates or Mother Theresa or any of the other wise persons who have lived or now live on the earth will get you there. Again from Whitman: "But each man and each woman of you I lead upon a knoll, my left hand hooking you round the waist, my right hand pointing to landscapes of continents and the public road. Not I, not any one else can travel that road for you, you must travel it for yourself." This is the easy part.

Now the hard part, the search, the recognition when you have found it, the realization when you have lost it again, and again, and again. It is little wonder that the Buddhists provide unlimited reincarnations to find it. It might take infinity. Thus, though Siddhartha, eventually, found a fulcrum upon which to sit, his "right effort" of ferrying seekers back and forth across the river, you and I have a long way to go. Or, perhaps, it lies, in Whitman's words again: "not far, it is within reach, perhaps you have been on it since you were born and did not know, perhaps it is everywhere on water and on land. Shoulder your duds . . . ." Maybe we can walk together for a while. That would be nice. But, chances are, our paths will soon diverge. You will walk one way. I will walk another. And then, perhaps, we will meet again someday where two roads cross. I'll be happy to see you there. I hope that neither of us feels quite so lost by then. That would be progress, indeed.

April 10: Humility.

I'm sick! Not much; just a cold in the head and throat and chest and my head aches, and my body hurts. I spent a restless night dreaming that I was the maintenance man at an exclusive secondary preparatory academy and, while everyone else was enjoying uplifting and entertaining activities, I was repairing gates and fences and leaky pipes—and I was sick, even in my dreams.

This morning, I did not go to the office. Instead, I stayed home, brought out my old Toshiba laptop and took it to my recliner, plugged it into the telephone circuit, and dialed up the internet so I could work from home. I don't feel much like working, but here I am. I was planning to take Yasmin to the grocery store this morning. She's out of filtered water for her meditation fountains of which she has a multitude. But I told her that, with my dizzy head, I felt the world would be a better place if I did not get behind the wheel of my pick-up today.

What has this to do with philosophical perspective? Much more than one might think. Elevated thinking is harder to achieve when one feels lousy. Indeed, feeling ill makes me want to do what many other people are doing at my age: retire. Of course, the world thinks that I retired when I stopped getting a regular paycheck. I did not. I still put in the better part of my day working (i.e., thinking). However, it is alarming just how fast "thinking" becomes less than a major priority in the face of illness. It would be so easy to, simply, sleep it off. But what could that lead to? Sleeping off a cold could lead to sleeping off a sprained ankle or a bout of gout, or tennis elbow. Eventually, I would be sleeping it all off, and come back Rip-Van-Winkle-like to find the world has passed me by and I am, truly, as insignificant as I have always assumed myself to be. At that point, my best option would be to move as quickly as possible to the grave (or the pasture since I intend that my ashes be spread over the cow pasture near where I grew up in Idaho).

Thus, although I will not say anything particularly profound or artistic today, I have spoken. Let us never underestimate those words: "I have spoken."

Indeed let us change two of them: "I am speaking." Once more let me change one of them: "I am thinking." Then I will add: "I am doing."

I will "not go gently into that good night." *That*, I promise. Making life each day through thinking and speaking and acting is too damned much fun—even when I'm sick. You know—it was kind of fun being a maintenance man at an exclusive prep school. I felt good about myself. I was fixing things while everyone else was just wearing things out.

April 11: Cast a Giant Shadow.
Someone led you up a mountain, stood there with you on a stone.
Someone climbed along beside you; you never climbed alone.
Someone showed you hills and valleys, all the roads that cross and turn.
Now, you cast a giant shadow with everything you've learned

But what about tomorrow, when storm clouds send their rain?
When children cry in hunger and old folks die in pain?
What earthly good is showing all the roads that cross and turn
When the only giant shadow is the cloud that blocks the sun?

Just lead a child up a mountain; stand a child upon a stone.
Climb the path upon on that mountain; a child should never climb alone.
Show a child green hills and valleys, all the roads that cross and turn.
Then you'll cast a giant shadow with all a child has learned.

Each tree was once a seedling; each day was once a dawn.
The greatest flood a simple raindrop drying in the sun
But for the cool of a long green river and the shelter of a storm
Clouds that cast a giant shadow on the day that it was born.

So lead a child up a mountain; stand a child upon a stone.
Climb the path upon that mountain; a child should never climb alone.
Show a child green hills and valleys, all the roads that cross and turn.
Then you'll cast a giant shadow with all a child has learned.

When the bells are sounding evening, and the light has left the day,
When they toll farewell to old times long since passed away,
Still standing tall the evergreen mountains with their summits in the air,
Your weary soul will guide your journey, and your heart will lift you there.

Then lead a child up a mountain; stand a child upon a stone.
Climb the path upon that mountain; a child should never climb alone.
Show a child green hills and valleys, all the roads that cross and turn.
Still you'll cast a giant shadow when the children cast their own.

April 12: Respect.

So often, I have heard it said that, to rise, we must tread others down. I tell you that the only height worth reaching is the one to which, once we reach it, we offer someone else a hand up. A claim stake makes a dull companion.

April 13: Mahavir Jayanti and Baisakhi.

Mahavir Jayanti is the main festival of the Jainists (a cousin sect in India of the Buddhists). They are a small sect (if we can call anything that numbers in the millions small), but worthy of our consideration. I feel it my duty to mention them as another group that discourages individual wealth. Indeed, one division of the Jainists is so ascetic that they abstain from wearing clothing. To me, this seems excessive. I'm quite sure that any of you, seeing my naked body, would agree and consider a special law prohibiting me from practicing that sort of Jainism where anyone, especially impressionable small children, might see me and suffer permanent psychological damage.

A further note: April 13th is the day usually set aside by the Sikh religion of Pakistan for the Baisakhi Festival. This is a harvest festival; but, among other things, it commemorates the day during the early 17th century that Sikh Guru Arian Dev was thrown alive into a cauldron of boiling oil by the Muslim rulers of Pakistan and Afghanistan. It is widely reported that Guru Arian Dev was, also, opposed to excessive materialism.

April 14: A Very Brief Poem.

Just before I composed this very brief poem, I critiqued a poem by a student telling her it needed polishing down until it was a perfect gem. Then I read in the news about how terrorists had blown up the parliament lunch room in Iraq in order to make a point about American and Iraqi defenses. I realized that the image need not be a gem. It can be the opposite and still reflect the aesthetic truth. Here is the poem:

After the Bomb!
A smoky room—
muffled chaos—
gurgling peace
in a dying womb.

April 15: I will Speak in Poems.

For a while,
I will speak in poems.
It is right that I do so
In times of abundant joy
or shattered hopes
or grinding sorrow
or throaty pleasure
Or now—
When the moon and planets
Stand ready to eat one another
In glittering sunshine and darting sand,

119

When laughing churns tears
Into butter.

April 16: A Soldier's Nocturnal Meditation.
Ah! Sweet reward!
And yet, how can it be
When it spoils a day, half begun and ready,
Muscled for service, smeared with shining fat
For a day's battle?

And comes the night with more reward
To stanch wounds
And pretend no morrow's war,
More wounds to stanch.

Better, perhaps, no reward earned
(Nothing earned, nothing gained—nor lost),
And yet, how can it be?

Suffer little rewards to come to me.
I'll sleep with an arm snugged around them
Until morning.

April 17: Virginia Tech.
Today at Virginia Tech, a young Korean man, a student at the university, slaughtered 32 persons and wounded 15 more before turning the gun upon himself. His was the 33rd and last death.

It is reported that he left a disturbing note in his dormitory room after shooting two persons in one building and before shooting 31 more in another building two hours later. I do not really need to read this note to know that Cho was psychologically, if not nominally, a kind of terrorist. Indeed, it would be a relief to me to find that he was connected to some terrorist organization such as Al-Qaeda. If he was not, he is a pure terrorist born and taught by the world culture of the 21st century.

This would be most disturbing because that would mean that the first class of such terrorists has now been graduated and is turning its attention to its goal, the utter destruction of whatever offends them.

We have always had our radicals. Now, since 9/11 perhaps, they have become a class of people, a nationality, with no nation, living in every nation. Such "patriots" cannot be intimidated by threats of physical violence since their ultimate personal goal is to die taking as many of the "enemy" with them as possible. And the enemy might be defined as half of the world's population. They need no secret training camps because their methods are simple: 1) buy guns, 2) enter a crowded room, 3) shoot the occupants, 4) shoot themselves. Of course, there are many other simple means to the same end.

Is this Armageddon? Not likely. Just a scuffle, so far, in a particularly chaotic moment of human history.

120

What can be done? I have said it so much that I am embarrassed by my redundancy: respond with love, not hate; with generosity, not greed; with repairing, not destroying.

Will that happen? Not likely!

April 18: The Poet Teacher

It was almost a poem—hearing her name
And her words
On TV this morning:
"I asked that he be taken out of my class
Because he was scaring the other students,"
She said.

And Yesterday,
He killed 32 of them,
Students, that is, and teachers.

The Poet
Who had been his teacher;
Or was he her teacher?
Sometimes, it is hard to tell the difference.

Her next poem might show us
Who was teaching whom.

April 19: Radical, Moderate, and Liberal Vs. True.

Irshad Manji is my inspiration for this entry. Yesterday, on public television, I watched a documentary she prepared regarding her "liberal" view of Islam. I have the greatest respect for her. She, a Canadian Muslim, is putting her life at risk by publicly challenging some of the most sacred traditions of Islam. She is called "liberal." I would not call her that.

I'll explain in connection with the three major Western religions which have emerged from the same ancient source: Judaism, Christianity, and Islam. Believers in each have recently been labeled radical (or conservative for the less radical), moderate, or liberal.

Radical conservatives believe in the absolute perfection of their scriptures and in the prophets or supposed deities (e.g., Jesus) who delivered them and, apparently, in all of those who transcribed, copied, translated, assembled, interpreted, etc. these scriptures. When push comes to shove, all that any of them have are the much-handled copies of copies of copies of scriptures none original or verifiable as identical to the originals nor even verifiable as the true words of the prophets or Jesus. Radical conservatives have an annoying habit of insisting that everyone in the world must either believe exactly as they do or be consigned to Hell. Many of them stand ready to assist the unbelievers in arriving there quickly by whatever means of transport is at hand.

Moderates, at least to some unspecified degree, believe everything that conservatives believe, but don't believe in foisting it off on others as absolute truth.

Moderates might even question some of the softer beliefs of their religions. For instance, a moderate Christian might claim that Jesus didn't really mean it when he said that one cannot be both wealthy and a Christian.

Liberals throw out all the trappings of the religion and go right to the heart, at least, the heart of their religion as they interpret it. I could best compare them to political anarchists who want no rules, just what makes them feel good. They approach religion as if it were a smorgasbord: picking and choosing among the salads, entrees, and deserts; rejecting the stuff they have no taste for, dumping much of what they choose in the waste bin after a bite or two. Some of them are thinkers. Most are not.

Notice that I am harsh with each of the above. The most dangerous, I must admit, are the radical conservatives, especially the ones who carry (or provide others with) guns, bombs, knives, explosive belts, etc. But the liberals are not far behind in their "anything goes" philosophy which often places them in the positions of mules to carry out the public relations-work for the conservatives and moderates. Moderates don't get off the hook either. They are, simply, less emphatic in their prejudices. They might, for instance, disagree with the war, but drop their buck in the collection box to support it anyway. After all, some of the money might go to pay for medical supplies instead of bullets.

You might have known that I have an alternative to any of them. I call the alternative the True Jews, the True Christians, the True Muslims. Let me introduce them through Apostle Paul's "dark" glass. Paul said that "we see through a glass darkly" in our scholarly and spiritual immaturity. He might have been referring to both the obscurity caused by dirt or coloration or irregularity in the glass and to the reflective quality of glass turning it into a mirror. Our life task, then is to clean the lens of dirt and any other obstructions to clear vision, grind and polish out any irregularities that distort images seen through the glass, bleach out the colors in the glass so that we see the entire spectrum through it, and align and shield it so that it no longer reflects our own image back at us so that we think that we are seeing God when it is only ourselves in the mirror. The result: we see truth—not really truth, but as nearly as it is possible for human senses to detect truth.

Add to this that, if we are nice to one another and admit that our individual and corporate senses are still limited by our humanness, God *might* just enlighten us a bit more so we can catch a fleeting glimpse of absolute truth—essential truth which lies beyond any glass, no matter how clear, smooth, and non-reflective it is. Of course, by then, we will know better than to brag about it, much less start a holy crusade or jihad about it.

I think that Irshad Manji fits best into the "True" category. She wants Islam to open up a scholarly debate about its beliefs. What better way to begin polishing the dark glass! I feel a little ashamed that I have not been more vociferous about the same possibility among Christians. It is not even likely that anyone would send me a death threat about it, unless, of course, I should challenge the divinity of Jesus or support gay marriage or ending the war in Iraq. I once received some death threats online from Christian radical conservatives because I suggested that America send its army to Iraq *sans* guns and with shovels, saws, hammers, etc., instead. I hope that, someday, I will get to meet and talk with Irshad. I fear, however, that it might not happen, at least, not in this life. I am old, and the chances that she will outlive me seem slender at the moment.

April 20: Solomon's Peace.
I found peace
at 6:51 this morning when I awoke
to the cooing of turtles (doves, they were)
as Yasmin,
my foxy beloved,
came back to bed,
lay down beside me,
and asked me to scratch her back.

April 21: The Pilgrimage.
Each April, I begin my journey, a sort of pilgrimage, to the mountains. It is hard to leave the family, especially Yasmin, and 3-year-old grandchild #7 who can't possibly understand why Papa has to go away for a long time. How can I explain it to him when I can't explain it to myself? Let me try to explain it to you.

I both dread and joyously anticipate the departure. I dread it because I know it means leaving Yasmin and all the others behind. I, also, dread the inconveniences of the road. This will be the last time I will have to look for WiFi connections along the way since I will not be teaching online again after May. That will be a welcome relief. Maybe, without that distraction, I will be able to concentrate on the beauties of nature that have become so familiar to me between here and Idaho.

But that is not justification. Why do I go? My answer is, simply, that I must.

I am a hermit—not your proverbial hermit hiding out in the forest with a shotgun hanging on my forearm and wearing a dirty shirt. But, still, a hermit! I need time to consider. And don't ask me what I will consider. It never works out as I planned. I go there to my small intermountain acreage in the southern Idaho irrigated agricultural desert, and I farm. At times I drive my pickup camper into the nearby mountains and camp by a river or lake and fish or just sit. Sometimes, I read. Seldom is my reading particularly fruitful, because, always, I think. And the thinking constantly interrupts my reading or my fishing or my farming or whatever else I might be attempting to do. At times, even when I am walking down the aisles of the Jerome Walmart, my thinking will get in the way of my walking, and I will stand stock-still in the middle of the aisle blocking traffic like a breakfast cereal display until some kind shopper wakes me with a greeting, and I proceed on my way to the cabbage bin.

Thinking! That is the full and unaccompanied justification for my pilgrimage. Six months of pure thinking each year make the rest of the year tolerable. Unfortunately, or perhaps fortunately, I am a hermit. Thus, most of my thinking doesn't go beyond my own head. Many hermits are monks. Being a monk is one thing a hermit can do in life. In my case, I didn't wish to become a monk: too many other monks around, and all that humming and chanting! Not for me! I became a philosopher several months before my birth if I remember right—

about the same time I became a hermit—and both occupations stuck. Being a philosopher is being a thinker. Being a hermit makes thinking possible.

Thus, my pilgrimage and my hermitage for half of each year. Sometimes my family visits me, but not for long. They are not hermits or philosophers, and my farm makes them hungry for city life; and my mountains, they think, are full of bears and lions waiting for a meal of human flesh—ticks and mosquitoes live there, too. It is no secret that they want human blood.

Thus, I find myself mostly alone in my hermitage and in my mountains. Alone with my thoughts. And that is why I go on pilgrimage. But when October arrives, I am eager to return to my city home with Yasmin and all the daughters and sons-in-law and grandchildren.

April 22: An Old Man's Prayer after Breakfast.
God!
I hope this fish-oil gel-cap stays down
And doesn't burp up to flood my mouth with
The taste of stale cod
Like the one yesterday did.

April 23: Last Day in the Office.
This is my last day in the office. Tomorrow I hit the road—next stop, Nebraska. It will be difficult doing without my convenient modern office with its high-speed equipment, but it is a thrill to be on the road. Sometimes I think my nomadic roots have enveloped my trunk and branches as well. There is nothing more exhilarating than the open roads and all the possible by-ways that go along with them. Philosophy has much to say about the social contract and civilized society. Sometimes I wish for what went before that. Of course, we can never escape society entirely and still be fully evolved human beings; but, for me, it is absolutely necessary to have momentary jailbreaks. Tomorrow night I will "Kamp" in a KOA. That is a sorry substitute for a mountain cave painted with birdlime beside a babbling brook, but it will have to do. I still have a couple of weeks of teaching online, and I will need the WiFi. Some hermit I am!

April 24: First Day on the Road.
It is amazing how cold wet weather can spoil a mood. I left the house in Parkville this morning after kissing Yasmin and daughter #2 and the youngest grandson goodbye. The sun was shining, it was warm, and, except for a certain sorrow about leaving the family for so long, all was right with the world—for the first 60 miles. Then everything changed. The clouds moved in, the rain came down, the wind met me head on so the truck had to struggle to pull the camper through it. And the temperature dropped so that even a rest stop was misery. Then, I was sure I was making a big mistake. Why didn't I just stay home and watch the NBA play-offs and do a little yard work and act like a retired old fart is supposed to act instead of this annual going-off-into-the-mountains routine. I had to struggle with all my will to keep from turning around and going home to Yasmin. I succeeded.

I am here at Gothenburg, Nebraska, and I have caught up with my online students. My feet are freezing, but I have on my winter coat, the old one my daughters would like me to throw away, and the KOA WiFi is working. But I am still depressed, tragically depressed. I know that I will be better as soon as the sun comes out. Tomorrow, I travel through Wyoming ("Big Wonderful Wyoming" according to their license plates). The weather forecast is terrible (cold, wet, windy). The only way it could get worse is if it turns into a winter blizzard. But the forecast for Thursday in Idaho is sunny and warm. I'll look forward to that. I'll shell and eat my sunflower seeds one by one by one tomorrow as I drive to Rock Springs. I'll spend the night in Motel 6 there because I don't dare challenge the Wyoming spring weather to a duel by camping out, especially, with tomorrow's frigid forecast.

I won't be taking a shower tonight. Too damned cold for that! Sometimes it is good to stink as much as the weather does. This, too, if I don't freeze to death, will pass.

April 25: My Secret Place of Thunder.

My secret place of thunder
Roars upon my ears
With idyllic whispering,
A chant that lasts for years,
While mountains moan their boulders
And rivers weep their tears.

My love we've crossed the valley;
Its floor was hot and dry;
From gentle Eden hied we
To granite walls thrice high,
To tumbling shale-stones slipping
And peaks up to the sky.

Black calluses are burned there
Upon our muscled feet;
The rosy blush of innocence
Has darkened with the heat;
We faint remember Eden,
But faint memories are sweet.

Climb high across your mountain,
And clamber up the hill;
Shake off that dread desire
To lose what's left of will;
We'll find our touch of heaven
Above the highest rill.

When we have reached the summit,
We'll turn and see the ground

Ten thousand miles below us,
And level all around;
With Eden just before us,
Our hearts now hear her sound.

My secret place of thunder
Roars upon my ears
With idyllic whispering,
A chant that lasts for years,
While mountains moan their boulders
And rivers weep their tears.

April 26: Arrival.
Excuse me! Even a philosopher needs a day off occasionally. After 1,250 miles in a small pickup with a "too-heavy" camper dragging it down to 50 MPH on every slight incline, I'm ready for a break. See you tomorrow.

April 27: Work.
I'm in the midst of a whole batch of "firsts," at least, for this year. There was the first night on the road, which was a night in Hell. Then, there was my first look this year at the Western sagebrush desert. That was about halfway between Ogallalah, Nebraska, and Cheyenne. It is such a sudden change from the geography of the Midwest that it is as if God drew a line in the sand and said, "On this side green grass; on this side gray sage." Then there was my first look at Wyoming, one of my favorite places to enter—and to get out of when I reach Utah. When I reached Utah, I was listening to conservative talk radio. I always listen to conservative talk radio as I cross Utah. Somehow it seems right there and would seem ridiculous anywhere else. Bill O'Reilly, on his "No Spin" program, was bemoaning the liberal media's spinning of stories to benefit liberal political agendas. At the same time, O'Reilly was making liberals out to be either liars or idiots; take your pick. It is, of course, the only way most recent political events could be interpreted. Right? No spin?! At the Juniper rest stop just inside Idaho, I proved that I was an idiot with my usual ritual: kissing the Idaho ground.

And here I am. Today was my first full day of work on the farm where my campground sits. I got up at 6 a.m., the first light of dawn, well, maybe the second. I set my irrigation water. Then I sorted out a few odds and ends that I had tossed around the living room when I landed yesterday. Then I ate breakfast, after which I visited dear old Mom who lives a third of a mile up my grassy road. After that, I took my grocery list to town and spent a fortune on food (all healthy red and green and yellow and purple stuff), and $82 on a nonresident fishing license (which is an outrageous price considering there are hardly any fish left in Idaho's streams), and I bought three and one-half gallons of gasoline to be used in my lawn mower this summer. That only cost me $10—what a bargain. Then I came back to camp rubbing my sore and significantly lightened wallet.

It was time to attack the foot-tall leather-tough grass, which I did with vim and vigor and a dull mower blade which I have promised I will sharpen before I continue mowing tomorrow. I managed to finish about one third of the lawn when I felt myself slipping into a coma and stopped for lunch. I'll do another third tomorrow. *And then, the online teaching!* Only three weeks more of it until I can retire. As a side-light, I chewed out one of my honor students by email because she has been shirking her duty of producing an honors project. I must maintain my reputation as a curmudgeon.

Do I ramble without philosophical purpose? No! I do not. There is an important central purpose in this—the work part. Work, not wimpy every day stuff, but real muscle-threatening, neck-wrenching, mind-twisting work is one of the most important things a philosopher can do. If life is easy, the philosopher smells sweet. Give me a good ripe arm-pit anytime as a catalyst for thought, as long as I don't overdo it so much that my brain is baked into a crusty brown mass of forgetfulness. There is always too much of a good thing. This nasty headache I have is probably a sign of "too much." I'm going to take a couple of Extra Strength Tylenols and a nap and then spend the evening watching NBA finals on my 8" TV for which I store enough solar electricity for three hours viewing.

April 28: Science.
I call my campground Walden-San: *Walden* for the pond of the philosopher, Henry David Thoreau, who made me realize that I, too, am a philosopher (which is nothing to brag about); and *San* for the Japanese tradition brought into my life by Yasmin. When I chose the ground, it was nothing but a dry, rocky knoll with a view. It is now green, has a few flowering shrubs and trees and is populated by a 26-foot travel trailer, a superannuated cab-over pickup camper, and an 8 X 12 foot cabin reincarnated from the old family farm's granary which was originally built by my maternal grandfather, Claude Lofftus Butts, Sr. It is legendary that he built the old granary in 1946 without benefit of any kind of measuring tool, using only his bare hands as guides because he was legally blind. This legend is probably true since there is not a square corner in the building, and no two boards lie exactly on the same plane. Those characteristics, however, could be due to the ravages of time and the several roll-overs that have occurred in conjunction with Idaho southwesters and at least one tornado. I retained most of the building's measured imperfections as I rebuilt it in honor of Granddad Butts. I use the granary as my study, and that is where I am sitting at present, inside the sliding glass door which cost more that the rest of the building combined.

All of the electricity I use, except for rare occasions when the sun is not shining in the Idaho summer, is produced by three 120 watt solar panels located on the roof of the porch I constructed on the front of the granary. To me that is a marvel which, before I installed it, could only be imagined. During the 20th century, British philosophers made much of the idea that science is taking over what had been philosophy before the 20th century. Indeed, several of them declared philosophy dead because of these advances. They said that, because we can now assume there is a scientific solution to all questions contained within time and space, and, because there is nothing beyond time and space, philosophical speculation is no longer legitimate. Therefore, philosophers should stick to helping scientists at counting beans and reporting their numbers accurately.

This conclusion came to me as quite a shock because I had studied philosophy from the oldest first to the newest last. Thus, I discovered the conclusion during a relatively recent phase of my study. Not just shock, but disappointment! Had I really been wasting my time? Am I, truly, as useless as teats on a boar, especially since I am not good at counting beans and don't care much whether anyone reports their numbers or not?

But then, I went back to Kant, perhaps, because his philosophy had been declared dead along with God and Plato and other such temporal wastrels. Kant, with his seriously flawed proof of the existence of God, in its very flaws, was the salvation of philosophic faith for me. (Oh, maybe not! I'd have found some other path back to truth(?)-seeking even if I had never heard of the *Critique of Pure Reason.*) What the British philosophers forgot is that, although science provides the raw material for much philosophic speculation, philosophy deals with concepts that emanate infinitely outward from science in every direction and fore and aft through time. And infinity has no bounds. They had forgotten that scientists continually speak of matters such as *the* universe and *the* cosmos: always *the*, always *limited*, never infinite. The dimensions of philosophy are always limitless; there are no absolute answers, only questions with constantly evolving conclusions receding like horizons before a moving vehicle. And here we are back at science. Every scientific advance advances philosophy. Every limited advance in science produces infinite advance in philosophy. Where did Kant go wrong? He worked too diligently at applying limited scientific theory to limitless philosophical thought. Thus, his proof of the existence of God, along with just about everything else that he seems to think he has proven, is stated as if it is contained between infinite beginning and finite present. Infinite beginning is nothing but a peering into the boundaryless mist of past. Finite present is a necessary myth of science. The only physical reality is the future and the space that it involves, and we cannot predict it with scientific accuracy except in the realm of discovered cosmos (an infinitely miniscule dot upon infinity). We have only a few of the infinitely unlimited scientific variables at our disposal for making such predictions, many more than we had in the past, but still only a few in the context of infinity.

Philosophy imagines the future and posits ideas for living it based upon our experience of the past. Philosophy is not dead. It was only just born, as it is reborn eternally so long as there are human minds to think.

Three solar panels on my porch roof-top collecting sunlight and turning it into electricity! A scientific and technological marvel indeed! A host of scientific and technological marvels all gathered together on my crooked little roof-top! And yet, such puny little miracles they are compared with what *might* be ahead, if anything is ahead for us. I wonder what will be left for us after we destroy the precious resources of the delightful world that some infinite force, knowingly or in immeasurable ignorance, provided for us. Yet something lies ahead whether or not we are there to experience it. It is the philosopher's task, since no one else will take it, to explore that beyond, peering blindly into the mist, building crooked but beautiful imaginary granaries for which scientists may, someday, provide squaring tools. God, if there is a God, and I imagine that there is, knows what lies ahead, but careful philosophers who follow the light of *good* are as right about it as anyone can be. We need that guidance. We are bad enough with it. I fear that we would be much worse, infinitely worse, without it.

April 29: The Morality of Fishing.

I just returned from three hours trout fishing at Oster Lakes which are a five minute pickup ride from Walden-San. My hands smell like fish which stands as evidence that I caught some, which I did. In general, I make a habit of not killing any animal that doesn't need killing. I have always included trout among those species that need killing since they are important to my diet and since they aren't particularly valuable members of the animal kingdom except for food. I have significantly reduced my intake of beef, and I never kill cows except in humane acts to end bovine suffering because I got to know many very personable cows and, though they make delicious meals, they are hard to part with as friends. I've met some relatively pleasant little goldfish, but I have never become firm friends with a trout. Thus, I have only passing anguish as I rip out a swallowed fish hook, along with a lot of throat, or as I decapitate one of my trout acquaintances. I recognize that this is hardly justification for murdering my fellow beings. I'm sure that some of my human acquaintances would like to murder me but refrain from it on moral grounds.

This brings up an important consideration that is one of the most dearly held tenets of most religions: the sacredness of life. Of course, this usually refers to human life, but for some (Hindus for instance) it extends much further into the animal kingdom. If I were trying to recruit you to my form of religious belief, I would hold out as bait the tenet that life is not sacred. It is good, and it is something most of us hold quite dear, especially when the life is our own or that of someone whom we love. However, it is not sacred. It is mere biology. Millions of years ago, carbon got together with other elements in just the right doses and in just the right catalytic environment and became life. Later on, just the right things happened to produce a rational mind in one of the species, in particular, human beings—and here we are!

Trout emerged in somewhat the same way, *sans* rational mind but finny and quite beautiful if you are watching them leap in a lake and not trying to kiss them on the lips. There are definite interspecies limits to our perception of beauty.

And life is beautiful, but not sacred. That is why I can kill a trout, preferably, as painlessly as possible but without regret; and that is why I can eat it for dinner and love every bite—because it is only biology, not sacred. Unfortunately, for the core of most religious doctrines, neither is human life. It, too, is only biology, not sacred. That is where justice should take over instead of religion. Religions have always found purely material reasons to kill other human beings, trumping what they would otherwise count as sacred law. Indeed, it is the rare religion that does not call itself the epitome of peace while, in the name of that religion, killing persons who are in disharmony with it. With justice, there can be none of this. With justice, the death sentence must be limited to one who has committed a crime which has been proven worthy of the death penalty in the light of wisdom which would be slow to justify a death penalty for a human being except as a matter of self defense. So much for crusades and jihads!

Meanwhile, back on the dock at Oster Lake #2 where, this morning, I killed three trout and brought them home and cut them up to supplement this week's groceries. A couple of days ago, I paid $82 for a nonresident fishing license (a horrible price), and I figure that I will need to kill and eat about 30 more trout this summer to break even. There is the justification—fiscal, not sacred obligation, not even justice, just the price of filling my belly—mere pragmatic economy and biology. Thank you, friend trout, for making the ultimate sacrifice, though you didn't seem entirely willing as you tried to flop back into the water from the dock this morning.

April 30: Now—Like the Sun.
Reveille!
Rising Eastern radiance,
Shimmering Rex!
Glistering Apex
Bloated on horizon west
Glowing cloud red,
Sinking from sight.
Taps!
a day is done in only a moment!

May 1: Becoming.
Tingling air in the church—
Precious souls
Sitting in well-worn pews of paint and wood carvings,
Feet out-stretched in dress shoes,
And cuffs of well-tailored suits
Undampened by adventure,
Sitting and watching
And hearing;
Tingling air:
Atoms built on scale
To arc and touch and become and become—
Numberless becoming,

While old men and silent women watch
And feel that "becoming"
Of which they would be part
If it were not for becoming one
With tingling air, atoms of unexorcised power,
Flinging power with a jolt with every tingling touch.
They hear of one who becomes—the anthropomorphic metaphor
Who cries out,
Writhes in death—
The holy necrophiles suck life from death
And keep their shining dress shoes safely
In the shadow of the next pew.

A basalt boulder juts
Over a rushing stream
Ten feet deep and icy clear
To the green moss and black rocks of its bed.
A child poises, dreading the cold and current
With squinting eyes and arching back,
And heart pounding—
A crouch and tensing of muscle,
Springing!
A second's suspension in infinite air,
Splash and roar!
A million ice-cold bubbles
Caress a live being:
And shrill laugher from the pool's edge--

While the dress shoes of the dead
In the tingling air of the church
Rub ancient wood from their musty coffins.

Children romp in a snow-drift;

131

An old man walks a new path;
A mother climbs a mountain where newborn air swaddles sleep;
Well-tailored suits get wet cuffs
From walking in snow—
It should be so
In becoming and becoming and becoming
With the tingling air in the church.

May 2: Why must my Art be Angry?!

Why must my art be angry?!
Bitter fluid,
Morphing from gay flower colors
To midnight?
Is it because my pockets are empty,
Or is mind a parched and barren place?

I will soak my nibs in club soda
And come back tomorrow,
Fresh as a hunchbacked saint.

May 3: Nature: Life is Hard!

I woke up this morning freezing. The weather, during the night, turned stormy. In Idaho, that means that yesterday's 85 degree sunshine and calm air turned into upper thirties, frigid, stabbing rain, and 40 mph west winds. The thin insulation of my no-travel trailer is no match for these. I pulled up my extra quilt and tied my hoodie sweatshirt around my head and stayed in bed for an extra hour. Finally, when it was full daylight, I leapt from bed, rushed to the thermostat and turned on the furnace. Then I hopped back into bed for another fifteen minutes while the trailer warmed up. I can't run the heat for long during such weather because I get my electricity from the sun and the gas furnace has to have electricity to run its circulation fan. I have a back-up gasoline generator to recharge my batteries, but I don't use it unless I must because I love my planet, and such generators pollute it. Luckily for me, the sun has come out, though the temperature is in the low 40s and the wind is howling. Thus, I will have electricity for another frigid night, one which promises to drop into freezing range. I'll have to remember to drain my drinking water hose.

A morning like I have just had reinforces my agreement with Shakespeare that I am a "poor forked animal." I am lucky. I have a no-travel trailer and a furnace to warm it up and solar panels to create a little more electricity for tonight. But what if I, like millions of human beings on this earth today, had none of these? What if I, like Shakespeare's "Poor Tom-o-Bedlam" was reduced to living in a doorless hovel with cold rain, wind, and mud as my constant companions? I cannot believe that I would live. I would die within a fortnight and rot in a ditch were I not fortunate enough to be eaten by hungry dogs, thus cheating the county out of a fee for my cremation.

Yet, I am also lucky that I have the opportunity to return, as I do, to a more primitive lifestyle than the wealthier part of humanity has come to require as an absolute standard. My older brother, this morning, came bustling into my mother's house where I had gone after breakfast to wash clothes (and, partly, to warm my feet) in his shirtsleeves, shivering from the cold, saying that he had not even realized, in the protection of his modern home, that the weather had changed.

Those of us more fortunate live like protected and pampered children, unaware that the outside world is hot or cold or blustery or sunny or might have entirely disintegrated in our absence. We would not know it and would step off the edge of existence into the abyss right after we kissed our spouses and children goodbye some morning if we didn't keep our eyes open.

But a sizeable portion of humanity is living in that abyss. Unfortunately, their abyss is fully populated. It is full of cold, rain, bullets, disease, starvation, pain, war, devastation, everything that makes their last few years, weeks, days, hours, or moments, or seconds of life miserable, "naked apes," as Desmond Morris calls them, all around us, and we are hardly aware that they exist. We see to it with triple-pane glass and multiple layers of insulation over and under and around us, and in slick cars, and high-flying fast airplanes to take us over them without seeing them, and with colored glasses and thick parkas, and "all." Too much of all!

Most of us are not living life. To live life is to share life. The first principle of shared life is to use less of "all," to make it available for "poor Tom-o-Bedlam." What I do with the warmer half of the year is emblematic. I cannot pretend that it is a great sacrifice, not even a gift for "poor Tom." It helps me to think clearly to be away from much of "all." I think I would be better off if I were away from as much of it for the rest of the year as well. Maybe, then poor Tom could wear a warm coat and sit beside a warm stove during the cold part of the year.

May 4: Happy Birthday to Me.

I will eat a beefsteak today because it is my birthday. What an honor for the cow that died to fill my belly for one day out of the year. I doubt that I will eat another beefsteak until the 4th of July. The cow who died would not feel particularly honored to fill my belly often. I am not that important a man.

May 5: *The Praise of Folly.*

I have just finished reading for the second time Erasmus's *The Praise of Folly*, and it has given me reason to hope that I could be both a fool and a wise man. Madame Folly praises herself so effectively that I begin to think that we are all fools and none of us wise, but she leaves a small window cracked open slightly, probably, for a breath of fresh air, but it offers me a possibility of escape, not from being a fool, for I have always been and will always be a fool, but from the lack of the possibility of wisdom. It is a small crack, indeed, and I am reminded of Christ's comment about the camel and the eye of a needle. Can a man carrying such a robust ego as I drag himself through that sliver of an opening?

Ah, but first the crack. What is it? Folly claims as followers those fools who think they are wise and take pride in it. And, of course, it is almost certain that those who think they are wise are naught but fools. But what if we simply want to be wise and seek that wisdom in diligent, reasonable, and just ways and never know for sure that we have found it, thus taking no pride in it. We can achieve a certain foolish satisfaction in the *hope* that we will discover wisdom and apply it to our lives and, perhaps, share our discoveries with other seekers. Thus, I think it would be possible for someone to be both foolish and wise, but one would never know for sure about the wisdom. And what do I do with my blubbery ego. How can I reduce it to a less than laughable size without reducing along with it my delightsome foolishness?

Read Erasmus's book! It is difficult to read it without becoming, at least, a little more humble, and that couldn't do most of us any harm.

May 6: A Moment of Pleasure.

I have discovered a means of achieving pleasure which I would like to share with you. Here in Southern Idaho, the weather has been absolutely miserable for the past several days. My primitive camp does not have the facilities to keep out those miseries; it has been necessary for me to suffer the cold and wind and rain with only modest protections against them. I am not complaining. I expect such discomfort here. Otherwise, I would be an even bigger fool than I am to come here each year.

And my current discovery is not so new. I have discovered it over and over again, but this is the first time I have discovered it to you, so I can act as if it is a new discovery. The discovery is this: comfort does not have to be particularly great to be exceptionally pleasing. It just has to follow an extended period of discomfort. For instance, at this very moment, it is wonderfully pleasant that, for the first time in five days (because the weather has taken a turn for the warmer), my fingers typing on the keyboard don't ache with arthritic cold. The simple lack of pain is a delightful pleasure. Had I not suffered the pain over the past five days, I would not feel this pleasure. I do not wish for the pain to return so that I can feel the pleasure again when it goes away; but, expecting that pleasure will be the eventual outcome, I am more willing to suffer pain from time to time.

May 7: A Little Noise.

Today I introduced a little noise into my environment. Up to now, I had been too busy and weather had been too unpleasant to enjoy setting up the little fountain with a chubby winged cherub on top outside my office door. Today with temperatures in the 70s, horizon to horizon sunshine, and not a whiff of wind, I did it—I set up the fountain. Now I remember the most important thing about it, the sound of falling water. What a difference the sound of a little stream of falling water can make in my office. I think that I have indicated elsewhere that I consider water not as just one of the four primeval elements (earth, air, fire, and water), but the primary one. I cannot turn back evolution and become a creature of the sea again. I must live on dry land. But, with the impetus of a small waterfall, I seem to feel the gentle *shush* of cold water sliding over my scales as I flip my slimy tail against resilient salt water.

May 8: Just for Oldsters.

I suppose I should have expected this, but I didn't, and it is not one of the most pleasant experiences of my life. I retired recently (that would be "recently" in "philosopher" years). I have noticed since then, that, although I have not been diagnosed with Alzheimer's Disease or any other condition which would cause dementia, and that I have neither been drooling excessively nor forgetting (any more than usual) where I put my hat, people have begun treating me as if I were in an advanced stage of senility. I would provide an example, but I can't remember one.

And Let's Hear it for the Ten Commandments!

Those of us reared in Western religious tradition are familiar with the Ten Commandments and, often, take them, not only for granted, but as absolute truth. Indeed, we seldom can remember them at all no matter how many times we have committed them to memory. It is a shame how quickly they can slip out or our memory once memorized. More important, however, our assumption that they are absolute truth is something that needs to be questioned. Absolutism in regard to this group of laws can be real trouble for us. In case you've forgotten them, below is an indecorous translation.

> 1) I am your god; you shall have no other gods before me.
> 2) Don't take the name of God in vain.
> 3) Keep the Sabbath holy.
> 4) Honor your parents.
> 5) Don't kill people.
> 6) Don't commit adultery.
> 7) Don't steal.
> 8) Don't lie.
> 9) Don't desire your neighbor's wife.
> 10) Don't desire your neighbor's property.

During the next ten days, I intend to inflict a little close criticism on them.

May 9: 1) I am Your God; You shall have no Other Gods before Me.

This was a commandment given to the Hebrews as they wandered in the desert after having spent hundreds of years as slaves to the Egyptians who worshipped a plethora of primitive gods. Keep in mind that God did not say that there *are* no other gods. God said that the Hebrews (including, in advance, others who follow the tradition of Jehovah worship: Jews, Muslims, Christians) must not worship any other god as if that god is better than God.

This commandment shows God as a jealous god. He (and I use the masculine pronoun because the ancient God was always assumed to have masculine genitalia, long white beard, etc.) did not take kindly to his people treating other gods better than he was treated. This could be a page right out of ancient Greek or Norse mythology. In reality, the god of the universe, the infinite power which not only creates but establishes all rules for the operation of the cosmos, is not likely to hold petty jealousies. The "jealous god" theory takes anthropomorphism to an unacceptable low for anyone who has a high regard for God. Thus, let's toss this one. Better yet, let's reword it to read something more like #4: "1) *Honor* God as creator and sustainer of everything."

This whole commandment in whatever form it takes is a serious problem for the Christians. The problem is the name of another God (called Jesus) who is

135

co-equal with the One God who has no equal. The Christians don't exactly break the commandment. Jesus is, after all, not senior to God, but no matter how hard the Christians shake this snake, it turns and bites them. The Christians claim that Jesus is not a separate god but a separate manifestation of the same god. But Jesus, himself, gives this the lie on several occasions by praying to God (the father), a separate being from himself. At one point, he even separates himself in terms of hierarchy by insisting that his followers not call him Lord because there is only one Lord and that is God. Come on Christians! This claim of deity has been the root cause of the slaughter of millions. You will never convince the Muslims or the Jews of the truth of this heresy against "The Book." Even Jesus rejects it. Common sense has always denied it. I don't insist upon your rejecting it entirely. Just put it in its place as a questionable thesis. Recognition of Jesus's love is infinitely more important than belief in his deity.

May 10: 2) Don't Take the Name of God in Vain.

Notice that I capitalized the word "God" to make it a proper name. I suppose that this is appropriate for those of us who think of God as "the one," "the simple," that heads the phenomenal chain of existence which has no beginning and leads to the phenomena of the present moment. There can't logically be more than one of those, so God becomes a proper noun in honor of that "simple." Of course, for normal discourse we still need the common noun "god" as referent for all those other *lesser* manifold gods out there. The term "God" refers to Jehovah, Allah, and God—all the same God.

But what about "in vain"? This has long been considered an admonition against using the name of God in conjunction with vulgar language and taking oaths that one does not intend to fulfill. Once again, however, the central meaning here is that we dare not offend God, the jealous God, by using his name when it is not being used in a devout and submissive manner. Nonsense! We carve out a relationship with God, each in our own way. However, none of us should be so egotistical as to think that we could in our miniscule presence offend the infinite power of the universe. Rather, our lack of regard for God prevents us from recognizing in our own small ways how we might utilize germs of that infinite power to make our lives and the lives of others more worthwhile. Let's reword this one, too: 2) Speak well and think well of God, yourself, and others."

May 11: 3) Keep the Sabbath Holy.

A reasonable means of having a holiday once a week! Keep it! Just remember that keeping the Sabbath holy does not mean spending it prostrated before God. We were not stood upon our feet by the process of evolution in order that we might spend the Sabbath lying on our faces. Lying down is for sleeping or loafing or looking at the stars. Our days are for other things: working, playing, fishing, drinking beer. A holiday gets rid of the need to work. Fishing and drinking beer (not too much beer) sound like excellent pastimes for such days, including Sabbaths. Of course, there are other pleasant things to do. Take your choice. Spend the day in church if you like. That, too, can be a pleasant diversion. The only word that is wrong is "holy." That seems to imply that awful jealous God again, for whom we must spend the greater part of a holy day building up His ego.

So let's shorten #3 to "Keep the Sabbath!" The exclamation point is intentional and part of the commandment.

May 12: 4) Honor Your Parents.

This is O.K., but, somehow, it doesn't seem to rise to the level of one of the top ten. Too often, parents are not honorable; thus, to honor them, would be dishonest. This one, we will lengthen significantly. Sometimes things cannot be said tersely: "Honor your parents if they are honorable; respect them in the legal sense, even if they are not honorable, until you attain your majority; beyond that, treat them (and everyone else) better than they deserve to be treated—that is, 'Don't do to others what you would not have others do to you.'" I guess it can be said tersely. Conclusion: #4 should be supplanted by the Golden Rule.

May 13: 5) Don't Kill People.

Let us not only keep this one but take it more seriously. Let's add some things to it for good measure: "5) Don't kill people, even in war or at the gallows, except as mercy when they are deathly ill or in horrible pain (and, then, only with their permission if they can give it); kill animals only as mercy when they are sick or in pain—or humanely and sparingly for food. Kill plants when you need to harvest crops, mow the lawn, or clear a fence-line, but appreciate them, even the ones called weeds."

You might have noticed that I haven't gotten into abortion. That's an issue far too complicated for considering in the context of the Ten Commandments. Although its discussion starts with old number 5, it doesn't end there.

May 14: 6) Don't Commit Adultery.

Hmm! This could eliminate a number of abortions.

Good idea! Also, keep it if you don't want to incur the wrath, perhaps via shotgun, of an angry spouse! This rule works well in society. We are talking here only of married persons having sexual relations with persons outside their marital boundaries. Sex between unmarried couples (simple copulation) follows a somewhat different set of rules. I fall short of outlawing it altogether. For some that is just unrealistic fantasy. For some, such a prohibition is merely silly. For instance, consensual sex among unmarried or widowed folk in the retirement center, if the participants are certified free of communicable venereal diseases, should be encouraged as excellent aerobic activity and positive psychological therapy.

May 15: 7) Don't Steal.

This seems obvious, but we often overlook, even condone, the most egregious thefts. Shakespeare's villainous Iago claimed that the theft of one's "reputation" was the grandest of thefts—one's purse, trash. Of course, he was just trying to empty Rodrigo's purse into his own. But Iago is right in claiming that there is more valuable property that can be stolen than one's material property or cash. Probably, the most valuable thing that can be stolen is peace of mind. Terrorists have managed to steal that commodity from most of the people of the world. Certainly, since the second (and last) attack on the World Trade Center, our new laws, especially, the Patriot Act, have reflected the loss of a degree of peace of mind.

It is right that a nation should make laws which protect people even by some restriction of freedom. However, it is wrong for us to allow our individual peace of mind to be stolen away. All we need do to preserve it is to recognize that it is a gift that costs us nothing and requires no particular set of external circumstances for us to keep it. Peace is within us, even when there is only lack of peace external to us. Is that not what the Buddha teaches us with his tranquility? Admit no lack of peace into our souls, and our souls will be at peace.

And yet, so many, perhaps all of us, lack the mind control necessary for this sort of perfect peace. For our sakes, please don't steal. On the other hand, those of us who have something to steal, know ye not that you are leading some poor fool to larceny!? Find the poor fool and give it to him before he takes it. You might both find peace. Or you might steal the poor fool's peace by giving him property to protect.

Everything becomes so complicated!

Please, don't steal more than you must. It will only cause you grief. Yet, if the wealthy would redistribute their extraneous wealth, there would be little left to steal except peace of mind, and peace of mind would become much more easily protected.

May 16: 8) Don't Lie.

Here is another one that is far too ambiguous to take literally. Do I tell a perfectly nice young lady who happens to have perspired a little that she stinks? Even if she asks?! What if telling the truth (or not telling a lie) in a wartime situation could get a lot of people killed. Do I still tell the truth (or refrain from telling a lie)? Do I tell a three-year-old that there is no Easter Bunny? Do I tell a 30-year-old mother of small children that her cancer will probably kill her? Even if it is the truth and she knows it already? So what do we say: "Don't lie unless it is for a good cause"? A better way to put it is: "Always do what is right." That would cover this territory as well as a lot of other important stuff. I watched an episode of *Survivor* on TV the other night where a major fuss was made about a fellow who had done a lot of dissembling throughout the episodes of the show. Such activities as reality shows and athletic contests show us just how ambiguous commandment #8 is. I don't think we can keep it. It just causes too much trouble—probably more trouble than it is worth. Just go back to "Always do what is right"—unless you are stupid. That being the case, "Don't lie unless you ask someone smarter for advice about it." And we probably should add another commandment: "Know yourself." But, if you are stupid, that might not be possible for you.

My, but this is thick pudding!

May 17: 9) Don't Desire Your Neighbor's Wife.

I suppose this one needs updating because we no longer discriminate in terms of gender regarding our sexual desire. And I suppose that we are, actually, talking about sexual desire here. First of all, I would have to wonder if the elimination of sexual desire is possible or even healthful. I suppose one should just think about something else instead, but the sex drive is powerful. Perhaps, we could curb it with chemicals. Second, the question must be asked whether, along with the particular desire, there is any concomitant action or hope of such action taking place. In other words, is there hope going along with this desire? Or, at another level, is the desire causing harm in any other way. For instance, if the desire for a neighbor's spouse becomes so intense that it degrades one's relationship with one's own spouse or with the desired spouse's spouse, that has to be a negative. On an entirely metaphysical plane, all desire might be considered negative. That would be especially true in certain Eastern philosophies where total elimination of desire is a goal—sort of like the atheistic conception of death as individual annihilation. Indeed, the only condition I can imagine entailing a complete lack of desire would be the atheistic concept of death. Hamlet said, "to die, to sleep, perhaps to dream . . ." But what is a dream but a desire. And what is death without life beyond but a cessation of desire? So what about this commandment? Perhaps, we should hope that all of our neighbors have undesirable spouses. Or, a more likely scenario, we could continue working to reduce our human tendency to want things we cannot or should not have. That would cover commandment #10 as well. Let's pitch this one as redundant. 10 covers the territory if we are not excessively hung up on sex. Perhaps, there should have been a commandment about not being excessively hung up on sex.

May 18: And, finally, 10) Don't Desire Your Neighbor's Property.
By gum! We dealt with this along with #9.

Let us summarize the new Ten Commandments:

1) Honor God as creator and sustainer of everything.
2) Speak well and think well of God, yourself, and others.
3) Keep the Sabbath! A dandy opportunity for recreation.
4) Don't do to others what you would not have others do to you. *(Note that we supplanted "honor your parents" for this more general rule).*
5) Don't kill people, even in war or at the gallows, except as mercy when they are deathly ill or in horrible pain (and, then, only with their permission if they are able to give it); kill animals only as mercy when they are sick or in pain—or humanely and sparingly for food; kill plants when you need to harvest crops, mow the lawn, or clear a fence-line, but appreciate them, even the ones called weeds.
6) Don't commit adultery.
7) Don't steal, and don't subject others to the temptation of stealing.
8) In regard to lying, refer to #4.
9) Don't get excessively hung up on sex (and see #10).
10) Practice the annihilation of desires for what you cannot or should not have.
11) Seek and follow wisdom in all things.

139

12) Practice loving.

I added the last two as necessary conditions for all the rest. Thus ends our commentary on the Ten (now Twelve) Commandments.

May 19: Advice.

That which is attained without effort usually has similar worth to the effort it took to attain it. Yet our ultimate goal in life is to live in complete peace with all good—without effort. To reach this goal, one must learn to live with such conundrums.

May 20: A Letter from Siebert Wilson and Sam's Reply.

Dear Sam,

How are you? I am fine, except that I have a question. It started when I went to church yesterday and the preacher told us that we should pray for our troops to win in Iraq. Well, I thought that was just fine until I got home and began to think about it. You see, I got to thinking that, in order for our troops to win, the other side has to lose. That, probably, means that a lot of them will have to die, the other side's troops, I mean. I hear from the preacher that all of us human beings are "God's children." If we are all God's children how is it good that one side lose (and a lot of them die) even if the other side wins and a lot of them don't die? What should I tell the preacher if I want to argue with him about this?

My granddaughter Emma is pregnant. She thinks it's a boy because it kicks a lot. I tell her that is nonsense. Your house got run over by the flood last week. No, that's a lie, but it was within a couple of blocks. Your house is too far up the bluff to get run over by the river flooding. The park is a mess though.

I hope all is well for you and you are catching lots of fish.

Siebert

. . . .

Dear Siebert,

Tell the preacher, "Always use worms."

And you know damn well you aren't going to argue with him. It would give you nightmares about fire and brimstone for a month.

Sam

May 21: The Global Transcendence of Capitalism (and here I am Leaning toward Socialism).

About a year ago, I read a book by Thomas Friedman called *The World is Flat.* The thesis of that book is that the capitalistic enterprise is becoming evenly spread across the world so that it is no longer focused in the major financial centers like New York and Tokyo. Rather world economics has made the world economically "flat." No matter where you happen to be, and with minimal financial and educational means, you can now participate in the economic enterprise, perhaps, becoming a major player. This is a movement which happened recently and suddenly. The basic message is that the economic world has made a sudden

140

shift that is changing and will continue to change drastically the way all of economics work.

As I read the book, I was not particularly surprised or alarmed. It rang true. However, over the last year, thoughts of the book have returned to me. This economic flattening is, indeed, revolutionizing the world and will continue to do so in the near future. Let us consider, for example, the impact it will have on politics world wide.

It is already evident that economics, which has always been a step-child of politics, has now become the step-parent. Corporate enterprises can no longer be reasonably called American or Japanese or Chinese or German or French or by any other national name. They are world corporations, and many of them have corporate wealth which exceeds the net worth of some of the nations in which they find themselves. This corporate wealth is no longer a commodity of a particular country but of the world. It has been said that money is power and that is not far from the truth. It seems likely to me that the average corporate CEO will soon have more power than the average head of state. Indeed, some heads of state are now as much CEOs as political leaders. Consider, for instance, the royal family of Saudi Arabia. The Saudi king (or his designee) is the CEO of the Saudi enterprises, and he (the king) is the head of state. The same might be true of persons such as the Chinese Premier who heads the communist central committee along with that vast Marxist (socialist) enterprise (purely capitalist in the world marketplace). Next to these corporate behemoths, individuals like the British prime minister and the American President (with little control over their nations' capitalistic enterprises) seem like helpless orphans in the modern flat world. Business, and even the United Nations, scoff at the American President's (shall we now spell "president with a lower case P?) claim of being the "leader of the free world."

My guess would be that, before too many years have passed, the corporate CEOs of the world will make up a vast and powerful "board of directors" for the economy of the world; and, having control of the world's economy, they will, largely, have control of its politics. Politics will be reduced to the role of handmaid. We in America will no longer have to worry about immigration reform. Workers will either migrate to the jobs of their choice or stay in their own countries while corporations move their factories or computer connections to them. Oh, and war?! Nations can have their armies and navies and air forces, but if they take on a war which the "board of directors" does not approve, such a board will have it in their power to shut down the supply line so, if nations wish to fight an unapproved war, they will, truly, do it *mano a mano*.

This flat-world economic power is already here. Read Friedman's book for details. One does not need a degree in economics to see that he is right. It is no longer a matter of whether it will happen. It is what we will do with it. Perhaps, it will lead to a new worldwide democracy, perhaps, repressive oligarchy. Maybe, we can individually or nationally make a difference in the outcomes, maybe not. It won't hurt to try.

I make no value judgments. Such changes will make the world a worse or better place. At times, I think that it can't get much worse. Then I think of the comment made by the character Lara in *Dr. Zhivago* (the movie version) that "this time [the period in Russia just after the Bolschivic Revolution] is an awful time to be alive," and I realize that our world could be much worse. It has been worse in many ways in the past and will, probably, be worse in many ways in the future. And it could be better. It would be in the interest of the economic powers to keep the workers of the world happy and well fed, housed, clothed, and entertained. After all, these workers are, also, the customers, and remember that "the customer is always right." The Baha'i faith and some other millennialist movements insist that we are heading for a marvelous world system of peace and wealth and harmony. I hope they are right. Of course, some other world religions have us heading straight for Hell—on earth or elsewhere. I hope they are wrong.

May 22:   A New Ode to the West Wind.
You are cold, West Wind, and strong,
Bending elms and tossing ladders from their places
Against haystacks and barns.
You are cold, but so is the world in which you howl.

When will your howling cease?
When will the ache in my bones
Go with you to wherever it is you are going,
Sowing your icy seeds even late in May,

When white and purple flowers should be the toast
Of the garden, and alfalfa blossoms are topping,
And children of farmers want to play in the lane,
Shirtless and wet from mud puddles,

Not hiding in bedrooms with city toys,
Not lurking in dark kitchens with scowling mothers,
Not searching through refrigerators.

You are painful to small children
And to old men
Who want to go out and play
And can't when you spoil May.

May 23: Humanism! ☹
        The fundamentalist (A.K.A. evangelical, conservative) Christian's argument against liberalism: Humanism. Humanism, in this incarnation, could be defined by the fundamentalist as the placing of the particular above the general or absolute. In simpler terms, it is considering the created above the creator—persons over God. Of course, it is an evangelical myth that the liberal is, automatically, doing this, but that is the definition they have for the liberal sin of humanism. To take the argument deeper, the fundamentalist insists that liberals have removed the meaning of life. That is, they have, by questioning the authenticity of the Bible as the pure and perfect word of God, where God introduces himself and tells us something about himself, indeed, where God claims his own existence, lost their spiritual moorings along with all hope and all happiness. They are adrift on a sea of

142

"nothing," trying to understand an absurd world without meaning or purpose. They are naught but machines walking hand-in-hand with other machines down the path of wasted (and sin-fettered) life *ad infinitum* until they lurch headlong, hooves over horns, into flaming Hell.

Those liberals who claim to believe in God, the conservatives say, do not believe in a real God, but in a God who requires them to take a "leap of faith" between their disbelief in the Bible to belief in a God who does not reveal himself. In the Bible, fundamentalists say, God reveals himself, first, as the creator of the universe, second as Jesus, and always as the Holy Spirit. All three have significant value to the Christians—though they insist that they are really only one, even as they have God talking to himself over and over again in his three manifestations—significant value which the Bible tells us about. They are "the unity" that fundamentalists rely upon to provide meaning for this life and the life hereafter (also vaguely sketched in the Bible).

The problem: the assumption that the Bible is the absolute and true word of God is every bit as absurd as assuming that the Quran is an absolutely accurate and true narration of God to Mohammad, and carries the same weight of authenticity as *Aesop's Fables*, Norse mythology, and *The Ramayana*.

"Yes! The Bible is mythology!" say the liberals.

"Nay!" Screech the fundamentalists. "It is Truth! That is all-important—for us—and for you if you know what's good for you."

Of course, they would never call the Bible mythological at all. That would insure eternity in Hell for themselves and punishment for their offspring until the end of time. I'll not get into the arguments for and against the literal truth of the Bible. The arguments for its literal truth are simply irrational—which is the whole point. The fundamentalist argument that the Bible is a solid platform of literal truth proving not just the existence of God but the virgin birth and resurrection of Jesus and the actuality of the parting of the Red Sea and all of the other miracles contained within its pages just because it says it is true and because it is the pure and perfect word of God is a house of straw. And we all know what imaginary wolves do to imaginary houses of straw. Huff! Puff!

The truth is that liberals have not *created* a world without meaning, but some of them think they have *discovered* a world without meaning, an absurd world. They are, of course, wrong. What they are right about is that we know next to nothing about our world or the cosmos; we have discovered nothing absolute about its meaning. We have experienced phenomena which seem to reflect the things as they are in the real world. We have not experienced the things as they are. Nor have the fundamentalists. They and the liberals are together competing in a great race that has been run throughout prior infinity and continues without getting closer to an imagined finish line or farther from an imagined starting gate. Fundamentalists insist that there is no happiness without the knowledge of God through the Bible so they cling desperately to it. Some liberals consider life to be a sorrowful waste of creative energy, but they cling desperately to that sorrowful life.

I do not feel their desperation. Indeed, to me, the ambiguity of life, the fact that meaning skitters away into infinity before I can lay hands on it, is the greatest source of happiness that I could ever imagine—far greater than an eternity of bowing and cringing before that demanding Biblical/Quranical Tsar God who has

143

been known to order the deaths of "every man woman and child" in a settled country in order to make way for the "people of the Book."

And I am not the least bit afraid of hellfire because I speak badly of that God, for I am convinced that such a God does not exist. That God is an illogical fantasy. My God is kind and loving and teaches me. I learn something about my God from reading great books like the Bible and the Quran. I learn more about God from nature because it is the book of my senses. I never put myself or any of the existing natural "particulars" (especially financial wealth) ahead of God. That would be silly. My God is "imagined" because that is the only way I can have a God who emerges as a grand and simple original from the wonderful infinite power and scope of the cosmos. But my God is far more real than anything I have read about in a book. David, as the shepherd boy, probably not as the king, seems to have known this God when he wrote the 23rd Psalm:

The lord is my shepherd; I shall not want.
He makes me lie down in green pastures:
He leads me beside still waters.
He restores my soul:
He leads me in the paths of righteousness for his name's sake.

Though I walk through the valley of the shadow of death,
I will fear no evil: for you are with me;
Your rod and your staff comfort me.
You prepare a table before me in the presence of my enemies;
You anoint my head with oil;
My cup runs over.

Surely goodness and mercy will follow me all the days of my life,
And I will dwell in the house of the lord forever.

I told you that I learned something about God from the Bible. When I read the psalms of the young David, I think of my own childhood on the farm, of the dark nights and the daily threats of snakes and bulls and electric fences. And I think of the peace that God's personal spirit (at least, I imagine it is God's personal spirit—I am too naïve to know for sure) gave to me and still gives to me today—and the happiness!

Oh, ye flaming fundamentalists and atheistic liberals, read this, and move away from your own great peril. Abandon despair all ye who traverse here, for in this "ye *think* ye have eternal life," and *know* you have joy unbounded!

May 24: Soda Springs.

A friend of mine wanted me to write a history of my family. I declined. The following story, based loosely on a (perhaps) true story from one branch of my family, is part of the reason for my declining.

Will Pickering rode hard toward Cheyenne. He would be safe there, no avenging angels past Rawlins, he figured. But they had fast horses, the best ones Brother Wilfred could come by. They would surely catch him before he got past

Rawlins, but he would ride hard even knowing that he would end up like Ben Ridgley last March, dead, rotting, dragged for miles behind fast horses before he was left beside the town pump in Soda Springs, Idaho, wearing only the remains of tattered holy underwear, his body marked with holy signs. He, especially, remembered the cross with a circle around it branded over his heart.

Will cursed his luck. Why could he not be like his cousin Parley who had been almost worshiped as a missionary elder? Parley had walked hundreds of miles to convert the Indians because the Book said they were the ones whose blood had to be in the church leadership, in the prophet, before the millennial reign could happen. Will believed that. He had always believed it. He wished he had Indian blood. Then, maybe, he would have been allowed to pick Sarah for his wife. His first wife—his only wife, damn it. He would not be like his father, Sam Pickering, who had four wives in three states. Of course, the only legal one was in Utah, near Granite City where he had a wife and a family of eight children. His other three wives were illegal even in the church since the U.S. government had forced them to outlaw polygamy. Since then, good elders had more than one wife, but they had to keep it secret from the government. When Sam was with Will's family at Soda Springs, anytime they saw the dust raised by horse or wagon coming up the lane to the farm, Sam headed for the root cellar out behind the wood pile, clambered into it, closed the door, and sat there in an ancient wicker chair until whatever guest it was left—unless it was a church member. In that case, one of Will's sisters would go out and tell Sam that he could come out. They had lived that way ever since Will could remember, and that was about 16 years. Will was now 20. Sam stayed with them a couple of days short of one month out of four. He didn't do any of the farm work. He had church work enough to keep him busy, so Will and his brothers didn't see much of him during his visits. Just the top of his bald pate while he said grace at the table and gobbled down meat from the "fatted" calf and potatoes and green beans that the girls had grown in the family garden. Will hated his father— that fat, egotistical, self-righteous, violent bastard—but he never mentioned it. It would not have been safe to do so.

Then Will fell in love with Sarah and she with him. Neither he nor Sarah mentioned it to anyone else for two months after they first met at the park after Wednesday night prayer service and ended up kissing and hugging and holding hands. Not even when it went farther, much farther, behind the city hall two weeks later. But when Sarah realized that she was pregnant, they had to do something. Sarah admitted to her mother what had happened. Her mother turned ghostly pale and sat down on the kitchen floor and wept uncontrollably.

"Will is dead! Will is dead!" is all that she said, over and over. And Sarah knew why. She knew that she had been promised in marriage by her father to Bishop Southern in Ogden. In fact, her trip to Ogden was planned for July, just two months away.

Will knew it, too. And, when Sarah told him that she had told her mother, he paled as well, and tears ran down his face, and Sarah cried. She didn't cry for herself. She would live, but she would never marry Will as she and Will had planned in their midnight rendezvous a couple of days earlier. Sarah's mother had told her husband, and her husband, a true believer, immediately sent word to the bishop and disowned Sarah, ordering her out of his house.

Will took the fastest horse in the corral, saddled and bridled it. Sarah gave him bread and a slab of cured bacon, part of the provisions her mother had given to her before she left her family home. Will galloped off to the east. Sarah watched him disappear over the horizon, then went to the livery station to catch the next stagecoach east with a faint hope that she and Will could be reunited in Cheyenne. She, at least, would be allowed to retain her life and that of her unborn child.

Rock Springs was behind Will when the bullet took off a piece of his right ear. He said a prayer he had learned in Sunday school and drew his horse to a stop, his head hanging dejectedly. It was over. He felt the sting of the bullwhip as it wrapped around his neck and pulled him backwards from his horse. He held his eyes tightly closed as a black cloth bag was tied around his head. He felt his clothing ripped from his body and smelled the smoke of the sagebrush fire that had been kindled. He heard the reading of the charges. He made no vocal complaint beyond groans as the branding irons were applied to his body, marking him with holy signs, especially, a circle containing a cross over his heart. The last thing he felt was his body crashing and bumping through the living sage brush of the Wyoming desert. The smell of the sage brush was good. "This day I will join Ben Ridgley in Hell," he thought.

He didn't know when they stopped dragging his body and tied him across his own saddle for the trip back to Soda Springs. He did not see Sarah's tear-stained face in the window of the stagecoach near Kemmerer. They dumped his body beside the town pump and returned his horse to its corral, unsaddled and unbridled it, and fed it a ration of oats and hay. No one dared to touch Will's corpse except the hungry coyotes that ate it during the night by the light of a full moon.

The next day, a grieving mother put the scant remainder of his bones in a gunny sack, took them home and, weeping steadily, burned them piece-by-piece in the outdoor canning stove.

May 25: Energy!!!

It would sound outrageous and certainly heretical to say, "Energy is God." However, a discussion of energy in connection with the existence and nature of God can be illuminating. Here is how that goes.

First, we consult Kant. He is the one who presents the clearest view of the "simple," though he seldom refers to simples. Instead, he talks of those entities that head series of "manifolds." Manifolds are phenomena which we experience through our five senses. They are complex in that they are changed from the original simple by "conditions." Each generation of a manifold adds something to it or takes something away as it moves farther away in time and/or space from the simple. Indeed, Kant seems to consider God, himself, a simple (the original simple of all simples). This is where Kant gets a little too complicated for his own good and his argument becomes incoherent. However, his point of the simple is important to our discussion.

As finite human beings, we are not able to experience simples—except one: energy (a.k.a. force). Energy is not a manifold because it has never been conditioned; that is, it cannot be divided, nor can it be measured. Only its *impact* in various applications can be measured. Energy in itself is, merely, energy. The same cosmic energy responsible for the "big bang" is responsible for the combustion of gasoline in the engine of my Toyota truck and the fart that just escaped into the cushion of my chair. There is only one "energy," the driving force of the cosmos, and it is infinite (unlimited in time and space) and simple (unconditioned). It, on the other hand, is a conditioning element of every manifold. Indeed, it would seem that matter, the basis of every phenomenon, is not possible without energy.

Consider Einstein's theory that if matter were to travel beyond the speed of light it would become pure energy. I am not certain that we can prove this absolutely, but atomic theory has convincingly demonstrated that high speed is responsible for incredible bursts of energy, at least, indirectly. If, indeed, matter becomes energy under certain conditions, then matter is, in actuality, made up of energy and, originally, with very little stretch of the imagination, could be said to have emerged from energy. Thus, everything which is now material was once energy.

The big bang is an example. We might speculate that the big bang was a product of the sucking of matter into a black hole (or something similar to a black hole) and compressing it into *almost* pure energy. All that remained material was an incredibly dense sphere much smaller than a peanut serving as a *locus* for all of the energy needed for the production of the material cosmos. The peanut, at the pressure-point of becoming pure energy without a locus, could not, for some reason, make that final transmutation and had no choice but to explode into trillions and more pieces thrust post-haste from the theatre only to be sucked billions of years later into other black holes in other parts of the cosmos or, perhaps, back into the black hole that formed up at the site of and in response to the original big bang (cosmic recycling?) This, of course, is an infinitely simplified account of what might actually occur in a big bang. Role switching, at least to some degree, is a principle of energy (energy to matter, matter to energy).

Now to my point! Energy, as the only simple which presents itself to the human mind (soul), becomes the point of contact among scientists, philosophers and theologians. We see a possible application for science which has no interest in God because it is only interested in that which can be measured. Infinity always extends beyond where science ventures, but science constantly measures the matter which emerges from energy and is beginning to learn how to measure the matter that returns to it. Philosophers can imagine energy as the unlimited simple which could be called God and a certain phenomenal experience of the noumenon (thing as it is) which could be, at least, the creative breath of that God. Theologians claim to experience God, not energy, but, at least, the master of energy, the prime force in the cosmos.

This falls just short of saying that God is energy; but, without doubt, energy plays a role in creation, which is said to be God's handiwork whether the creative hands are those of God or the ignorant tools of impersonal absolute force. There is, indeed, this infinite and absolute *One* in the cosmos that scientists, philosophers, and theologians experience in unity.

May 26: Infinity Lost.

I just read 20 "logical" arguments for the existence of God, none of which turned out to be logical. The list was compiled by a professor of religious philosophy with outstanding credentials, but it seems that even the best Christian apologists can't get past false premises and logical fallacies.

First, let me reiterate that I do not qualify as an atheist. I *imagine* that God exists. On the other hand, I do not qualify as a theist because I do not have sufficient evidence (rational or empirical) to prove to myself the existence of God in the sense that I imagine God to exist. I discuss my belief in God in other entries, and I will let them stand as authoritative.

Nearly all of the arguments I read suffer from the same set of shortcomings. They insist that our orderly cosmos could only have been created by an intelligent designer and that intelligent designer must be God. In a finite world, this makes sense. It is not likely that in a little world bounded by beginning and end such marvelous order would have sufficient time or space to develop. However, none of the arguments prove that the cosmos is finite. There are arguments to that effect, but all of them fail. One argument, for instance, insists that the big bang theory is evidence that the cosmos is finite (that it has a beginning). They entirely omit reference to origins and development of the less-than-peanut-sized lump of incredibly dense matter which exploded at the beginning of the big bang. Thus, their supposed beginning is nothing but a continuation of whatever went before it. In an *infinite* cosmos, there is neither beginning nor end, no outer or inner limit of either time or space, thus, no place for an infinite intelligent designer standing outside finite limits of the cosmos, no God.

Another argument insists that we could never have reached a particular point in time if the cosmos were infinite. Thus, we would never have reached the present moment. Obviously, the designer of this design doesn't have a clue about what is meant by infinity. In an infinite cosmos, infinite points would be reached moment by moment. The only difference finiteness's outer boundaries would make would be that there would be a way to measure time and space between the first event and an event at the present moment. However, even if there were no first moment, events of the present moment would occur.

In an infinite cosmos, our beautiful orderliness is not only possible, but inevitable. A powerful rule in regard to infinity is that anything that can happen does happen and anything that happens occurs infinitely. Thus, because we can see the orderliness of our cosmos, such orderliness is possible. Because it has occurred once, it occurs infinitely in the endless time-and-space reaches of infinity. The less-than-peanut-sized lump of incredibly dense matter/energy is replicated infinitely across infinity, as is the big bang (if, indeed, it did happen) that emerges from it. And infinite as well are the orderly ecosystems of life and nonlife that populate infinity, infinitely many, infinitely like and unlike our own.

Another point about orderliness in the cosmos. Everything that can happen, even that which is disorderly, happens. Consider measles, for instance. It is not a particularly valuable asset to the human race. Yet it happens. But, since we have largely overcome for the time being the possibility of human extinction by measles, it is not much of a factor for us. We tend to forget about it as a disruptive phenomenon. However, the collision between the earth and a large meteor some time ago which is, according to some scientists, the reason for the extinction of dinosaurs, is a disorderly factor which has made quite a difference in our environment.

Most disorderly elements introduced into the cosmos merely happen and disappear. That is why we don't notice them. They do not fit in with the other parts of the context which are in symbiotic relationships with each other, so they have no friendly environment in which to thrive. Only those occurrences which find a friendly place among the elements of a particular environment survive. This does not mean that highly disruptive elements will not be introduced which will disrupt the current order. We have, for instance, managed to fabricate bombs which could wipe out all life on the planet. At the moment, they fit neatly into silos and other closets, largely ignored. Should they slip out some night and do their work, our world might find itself ready for another eon of cosmological enterprise, perhaps, this time without life.

Be assured, though, that human life just like ours is progressing in innumerable worlds, all, probably, too far away from ours to notice our little mushroom-shaped clouds.

Note of disclaimer: The philosophical theory that everything that can happen does happen, and everything that happens occurs infinitely is not accepted by every philosopher or every scientist. Naysayers insist that the mere possibility of something happening does not create a necessity of its actually happening. Such thinking is short-sighted given the limitless nature of infinity. Indeed, possibilities must become actualities. However, it is necessarily true that infinite *failing* actualities blink in and out of existence so quickly and completely that the cosmos barely registers their existences.

May 27: A Question from the Audience: If a Tree falls in a Forest outside the Hearing of any Sentient Life Form, does it make a Noise?

We are not amused by silly questions, and this is a silly question! The answer is "no." The existence of noise requires a sentient mind to interpret and apply its elements in the act of creating it. Therefore, noise exists only in the mind of the hearer. Next time, prove your sentience by thinking before you speak!

May 28: Ownership.

I claim to believe that if I owned only that which is necessary for the sustaining of comfortable and useful life, I would be the richest person in the world; but, obviously, I do not really believe that because I am bent nearly double beneath the weight of ownership. We human beings are odd creatures.

May 29: Class Reunion.

During the last few days, Hagerman, Idaho, has been celebrating its annual high school class reunions and Fossil Day. Fossil Day celebrates what Hagerman thinks it is most noted for, the discovery of the fossilized bones of a small prehistoric horse which is thought to have looked much like a zebra. Hagerman's fossil horse was recently honored by a national truck rental agency which decided to put an image of that horse (looking very like a zebra) on the sides of each of its trucks. Hagerman began celebrating Fossil Day about the time the Mormons abandoned publicly celebrating Pioneer Day (July 24) because it had evolved into a two-day drunken brawl and was beginning to stretch into a three- or four-day drunken brawl. Mormons are not keen on drunken brawls, so they took their Pioneer Day and morphed it into a private Mormon party, quite a tedious affair from what I have heard—nothing like the big parade, carnival, rodeo, and dance which Pioneer Day had generated. Pioneer Day was, indeed, the best thing Hagerman had to offer. Basque Shepherd Dances came close in terms of consumption of alcohol and number of arrests, but they were not of much value to the kids since there was no carnival, or rodeo, and no parade led by the oldest cowboy riding the oldest horse (other than the fossil horse). Fossil Day with its miniaturized carnival and a few food booths in tandem with class reunion weekend was supposed to be the equal of the traditional Pioneer Day. It is not! Actually, it is a little embarrassing to those of us who remember the real thing.

However, the reunions are interesting. Most interesting is that the reunions are akin to Fossil Day in that we get to see the old fossils who used to be our teenage classmates in the old high school that used to be across the street from the Legion Hall where the reunion and accompanying dinner and dance and happy hour are held. It is difficult to recognize which fossil used to be which teenager and always a little disappointing to see how little of them is left to recognize after fifty or so years. I still am a little shocked to look in my own mirror. I think that I am seeing a stranger there, not the same fellow I looked at half a century ago and shared bicep flexes with. Now I smile and the image in the mirror smiles back, gap-toothed, wrinkled, and bald. Imagine that smile greeted by a room full of gap-toothed, white headed, wrinkled, stooping, old farts. It is a nightmare. Yet it is intriguing to think that, in a few years, the whole room full of us will be transferred to our local cemeteries, and we will be replaced in the Legion Hall by other older-than-dirt survivors of Hagerman High School. Rah! Rah! Go Pirates!

The fossil zebra horse has something on us. He/she has been dead longer and couldn't care less that his/her visage is pasted on the sides of 1000 rental trucks. We have to pretend that we matter. He/she doesn't have to pretend. He/she is just bones turned to rock, no mirrors, no wrinkles, no Legion Hall, no Legion.

May 30: Peace on Earth!

Here it is more than half a year from Christmas and I'm thinking about "peace on earth, good will to its people." I am convinced, ignoring for a moment my own theory that CEOs will take over the world and rule it peacefully, that there will never, unless everyone is dead, be a general peace accord which covers the entire earth, at least, not one that works for more than a couple of minutes. Somewhere in a small corner, someone will be offended because someone else says or does something that is not listed in someone else's catalog of stuff that should be done or said and—whop!—no more peace in that corner. I doubt that we can resist the temptation as a world of nations to offend or be offended by neighborhood nations. Mr. Rogers' neighborhood is a myth.

However, the passion the world has for taking offense need not damage our individual peace on earth. In fact, Yasmin and I are living proof that two persons can have peace in each other's company for years at a time until too much "Peace on earth!" becomes too much for us and we engage in a hearty verbal battle—mostly my words. She goes silent on me and that is the worst possible thing in a verbal battle, totally unethical. Then we get over it and live peaceably for a while.

I've even managed to live peaceably around a variety of coworkers and associates and various others for long periods of time without anger or retribution. Of course, there is always someone I wish ill upon for at least a little while. Such wishes usually lead to more discomfort for me than for the one upon whom I wish chronic diarrhea or bitter beer because I just go around wishing and seldom tell the offensive person about it. Sometimes it gets worse. I once told my academic dean that she was "the enemy" of the college. I managed to keep my job but not without a lot of phony apologies. She was, truly, one of the most miserable excuses for a human being I've ever had the misfortune of meeting. Loving "everyone" is another of those things that several religions require of us. I'll just have to accept missing the mark on that one. I'll do my best not to smack them in the chops, but I won't *love* all of them.

But back to "peace on earth!" After four years of slaughter in Iraq, we are no closer to peace in that part of the world than we were when we started, and I just heard it said by a leading American military officer that we will be there almost permanently. If it takes "peace on earth" to reach what the Christians call "the millennial reign," we can all take off our boots and relax a while. The Iraq war will fend off the millennial reign for a good while yet. In the mean time, however, I have a bit of advice for personal peace. It comes from Jughead in the old *Archie* comics. When Archie became overwrought and began losing control of his emotions, Jughead would just smile and say, "Relax, Archikins, relax!" And all would be well for the moment. Of course, Jughead was not notable for being particularly bright, but his advice seems good—almost like that of Lao Tsu in the *Tao Te Ching*. If we could all just relax and let the offenses of the world flow around us, we would be a more peaceful world. "Relax, Worldikins, relax!"

May 31: And by the Way.

While you are relaxing, get into a canoe on a sunny quiet day, row out to the middle of a clear still lake, look over the side at the reflection in the water. Not at your own reflection; you see that all the time in the mirror. Look at the reflections of clouds—not just a glance at them, but take a long learning look.

151

June 1: A Compass Point.

Start out on a day when you don't have to do anything in particular following a compass point and follow that point (any point will do), and keep following it for twenty-four hours (making whatever adjustments are necessary to go over, under, around, or through obstacles). Take along a loaf of bread and a canteen of something to drink. Twenty-four hours is a long time to walk on an empty stomach.

This is practice for following a path to the "Good." When you are on that path, you will often think that veering to another direction would be better than the path you are on; but, if you are intent upon reaching the good, you must continue in the direction of good. In fact, staying on the path to the good is the same thing as achieving it.

By the way, do some advance planning. Remember that, at the end of the 24 hours, you will be 24 hours away from home. Where will you sleep?

June 2: Eternity is Now.

Always, when I was sitting in church as a young boy, I understood eternity (and eternal life) as being something that begins later, after we die. This is a misunderstanding of infinite dimension. Eternity (another word for infinity) has no beginning and no end. Each moment of your life is part of eternity. The only questions are whether you, a mortal with mortal limits upon the life you are now living, were a living/thinking individual before you became a mortal human and whether you will be a thinking/living part of eternity after your mortal death. The fact remains that no matter how many claims to faith and knowledge and wisdom may be made by theologians and philosophers, you do not know the answers to those questions. Even if God told you personally that you had pre-existence and will have eternal life, you would not know for certain whether the message came from God or some other spirit or a corner of your own imagination; and you could not assess its truth. Thus, even in the presence of perfect knowledge, you would remain ignorant. What you do know, however, by pure logic and without me telling you is that every moment of your current existence is part of eternity. Enjoy it while you have it whether it is a short time or forever.

June 3: The Nature of Imagination.

Logic + Empirical Data + Mind = Imagination.

The formula looks simple. Of course, nothing is ever as simple as it seems except a "simple" itself (which has no formula because it has no parts). Imagination is no exception to the rule of inevitable and infinite complexity. First, it is essential to separate imagination from fantasy. Fantasy is mind without the essential benefits of logic and/or empirical data—that is, without the need for assessment of possibility. With fantasy, we can create the possible or the impossible without consideration of the difference. When fantasy has finished its work, we have nothing but the memory of a fanciful construction made from nothing into nothing—nothing but entertainment for whatever it is worth.

With imagination, we create the possible which goes beyond the scope of logic (reasonable thinking) and empirical data (phenomena) to metaphysics. The process is something like this. Let us use the love of God as an example of a metaphysical idea which cannot be established through reason and phenomena. First, we apply what we can of logic. We discover through logic that God is possible and, according to some philosophers, even necessary. Let's stick with "possible" since the "necessary" is a stretch of logic. Very briefly, the idea of the possible is supported by the concept of infinity which we can assume involves unlimited energy (or power). The proof of this is simple enough, especially if we accept the idea that power (energy) is the original simple which stands behind the manifold cosmos. We know that power is resident within the cosmos. The cosmos is unlimited, so the power within it is, also, unlimited.

Next, the unlimited power of infinity could, legitimately, be called God. We could say, in other words, that "God" is as good a name as any for the unlimited power of infinity since, by definition, both God and infinity include everything which lies within infinity (and, of course, nothing lies beyond infinity). Although God is not contained in infinity (because God *is* infinity and, like infinity, cannot be contained) God is as inclusive as infinity (i.e., fully inclusive). It must be concluded, then, that God (if God exists) is identical to infinity.

Thus, though the outline of God's *possibility* is dimly traced, we have demonstrated that such an existence is *possible*. Next, if we want something more than a dim outline of possibility, we must establish characteristics. Remember, God, if he exists, is a simple: no formula, no parts. Thus, from the start, what we are creating is a mental convenience rather than a phenomenon of something as it is. Thus, we must use imagination. Consider imagination (in this function) as a connection between phenomena and simples. Concepts contained in imagination are connected to phenomena. Thus, they are well grounded in what we assume to be things as they are. Things as they are are members of that unlimited tribe which populates infinity. We assume that some members of the tribe (e.g., humans in the physical body) are limited to a small segment of infinity while others extend farther and last longer. All of these are subject to change. The simples, not subject to change and not divisible, last forever and are neither extended nor not extended in space or time. We assume that the primary simple, God, as the infinite creative power of the cosmos, caused every nonfinite entity to exist. Thus, we further assume, using our imaginations, that his creation demonstrates something akin to him.

One profferment which we might hope that God offers is "love," especially, love for human beings. (I use the term "profferment" as an alternative to "characteristics" because God, a simple, has no characteristics.) Because many human beings, especially those closely related to each other, have the characteristic of love for one another, we recognize that such a profferment is, indeed, available in the cosmos to thinking beings. Thus, we can easily imagine that God, the ultimate thinker, proffers love to us. That is, oversimplified into finite terms, he loves us. This conclusion, although seemingly logical, is neither logically nor empirically sound because God is not reflected as a phenomenon but as a spiritual entity, a simple. Thus, we have no way of *knowing* whether he follows the logic or facts which bind finite beings. Thus, our imaginations complete the formula: God loves

153

us. Call this faith if you wish. Along with Apostle Paul, we hope for the love of God. Our imaginations can give us a loving God, and our faith can hold that love intact.

One advantage of imagination is that we are not required to imagine anything we do not wish to imagine. However, beware! Imaginations, like skittish horses, have a propensity for running away with us. For instance, read Mark Twain's *The Mysterious Stranger*.

June 4: An eMail from Siebert.

Dear Sam,

Well, you should be happy! All three of your girls and all of their husbands and all of their children were over to your place yesterday painting your window-frames that you've been so worried about. Although I don't know what you were so worried about. My window frames ain't been painted since 'Nam. And they still make their way all the way around the windows just like they always did. But I think I understand. It has something to do with that little Japanese lady called Yasmin. She likes everything in order, doesn't she? And you aim to please her. Well, you did it this time. She was just running around and around the outside of the house and they wouldn't let her do nothing and she pretended that she wanted to but I could tell she really didn't want to get into that sticky old white paint, and she had a smile like a chessy-cat on her face all day long. I stayed around, too, most of the day. #2's husband fixed burritos, and they was mighty fine—fiery fine! If your family was any more diverse, you'd be the United Nations. Is that on purpose or did it happen just by accident?

I have some bad news. Ya know that old wood chuck that hangs out around your back-yard pond. He don't hang out there no more. He got run over by a dump truck on Highway 9 last week. I guess he was just too slow to get out of the way. We held proper rites for him and then threw him into the dumpster down by the college apartments. We didn't tell the grandkids. We figured they might take it kind of hard.

I planted my garden early this year, and now I already have a few zucchinis to eat. They're delicious when you pick 'em young and eat 'em with a little mayo on 'em. By the end of July, I'll be throwing them over the fence for the wild animals. Ain't it strange how zucchini tastes so good in June and so bad in July? I guess its cause cucumbers taste so much better. Of course, I'll get sick of cucumbers by August. Then it's cantaloupe and watermelon. I don't want to think of that now, though, cause it might ruin my taste for zucchini.

Life is like that, ain't it? We learn to like what we got. Hey, Sam! Maybe we ought to start a church with the motto, "Like what you got!" That might be even better than painted window frames.

Well, I like what I got and you like what you got, so I guess I'll just go fishing.

Regards,

Siebert

June 5: An eMail from Sam to Siebert.

Go fishing, indeed, Siebert, and so will I! I will catch these fine Idaho trout, and you will catch those stinking Missouri catfish.

Thanks for watching out for Yasmin. She's good at watching out for herself, and the daughters make sure she never has to cook anything. That's good because she likes cooking about as well as she likes painting window frames. But you are a good friend for going over to see that things are alright.

I have been a bit down in the dumps the last few days. We just got over a three-day blow. It was freezing cold, down in the 30s overnight and the wind was gusting to 50 mph all day and all night. It drizzled (not really rained, it never rains here, just drizzles). My gas heating system in the trailer is adequate, but my solar electric supply is limited and the furnace has an electric fan that tends to deplete the batteries, so I can't leave the furnace on overnight. So I've been sleeping in a hooded sweatshirt so my bald head doesn't get frostbite. My office has been so cold that I couldn't type without suffering chill-blains in my fingers. Nothing is comfortable, and I still have that cough I had for so long before I left Missouri. Can't shake it! Maybe it's the dust that the wind blows up. Anyway, it's just downright depressing, and you know me when it comes to depression. It isn't a pretty sight. No, indeed!

Today, however, the sun is peeking through the clouds now and then and the temperature has risen into the high fifties. These are hopeful signs, but I'm waiting for further confirmation before I shut off the depression switch. I don't want to just get it shut down and have to wind it up again.

Hell! I wish it was that simple. I do miss Yasmin and the kids and grandkids a lot, and sometimes I wonder why a person who claims to be a straight-thinker could possibly make the decision to go away for five months. Of course, I forget that I need this sort of activity for inspiration and for clear thinking and for my health and a host of other reasons that sound like trash at the moment. Also, I forget that I wouldn't be alone except that we have a new grandchild coming in June and Yasmin can't be gone when that happens. I wouldn't have it any other way. I'll be visiting in July (after the little cherub gets his/her wrinkles ironed out a little). I'm looking forward to that and to seeing Yasmin and all the others. You, too, you old fart. Save me some catfish. I'll choke it down somehow.

By the way, there will be no "like what you got" church unless you start it. I'm retired! I "like what I got": freedom from such nonsense as clubs and churches and other disabilities.

Sam

June 6: Scribe here!

I just read what Sam wrote to Siebert. I'm happy to see that Sam is, finally, taking some little personal responsibility for his own limitations. It has always been his habit to blame me for every discomfort and inconvenience and let me do the worrying about it. I think these five months will be very good for him. He might even learn some things about himself that he didn't know, or didn't want to know. Or maybe not! He has an awfully hard head.

June 7: Sam on the Front Porch after a Three-Day Blow.

If, as Eliot says, "April is the cruelest month," and if "April showers bring May flowers," what the hell is June for!? Weddings? Unless we are making bad choices, we get only one of those. And I made an excellent choice in Yasmin. The garden should be already planted. Of course, I still have that row of green beans to plant, but it should have been planted in May. The mountains are still too chilly for camping. The streams are too cold for swimming. It is a good time to sit on a porch and look off into the distance. But that can get old quick; as soon as the sweat dries and the flies start to buzz around my ears, I am ready for some kind of action. But the action gets old, too. Now comes the repetition of everything over and over and over. Nothing new under the sun! No guarantee of sun, lots of cloudy days yet until July. But a guarantee of the same old things to do over and over again.

Yet that is the life many folks would call the ideal. Especially, when that repetition is exactly what I bargained for. I'm comfortable. I'm free to do exactly as I please. I have plenty of good Walmart food. Plenty of cheap beer. Television for the NBA playoffs. Cows in the pasture. A view to kill for.

I miss my Yasmin! Even a philosopher is weak when it comes to his one and only woman. Socrates complained about Xanthippe, but even after she dumped a pot of piss on his head, he didn't stay away. (I'll never believe those stories that say he eventually remarried. Of course, that might be the reason hemlock didn't seem like such a bad idea.) His Greek society didn't frown on his relationships with young male scholars, and he blushed at the thought of them, but Xantippe, though an awful shrew, was his anchor; philosophy was only a pastime by comparison. Oh, Xanthippe, Xanthippe! Socrates loved a shrew. Oh, Yasmin, Yasmin, Yasmin! No one is sweet like you!

June 8: "A Just War": An Oxymoron.
From *The Times:*
Local Soldier Dies in Iraq

The Department of the Army has announced the death of a local soldier, PFC Emily Wagner of Windfall Lake, Missouri. Private Wagner had been in Iraq since February. She was stationed in Baghdad. She was killed when a road-side IED exploded under the supply truck in which she was riding during a routine mission near the Green Zone. She was 19 years old. Five other American soldiers were wounded in the incident.

June 9: Happiness.

You might well ask how, following the discontent of my last few entries, I can turn so quickly and speak of happiness; and I would answer that it is the most natural direction in which to turn. The greatest frustration leads to happiness. The greatest depression leads to happiness. The greatest sorrow leads to the greatest happiness. It is a simple thing. Happiness is like looking at the broad horizon after climbing the most insurmountable mountain. What is frustration but a natural response to the craggy impasses of a forbidding mountain? What is depression but loss of strength in the middle of a long ascent? What is sorrow but shadow because the sun is hidden behind a glooming peak? Nature teaches us to appreciate the negative as harbinger of the positive—pain as the sign of emerging pleasure.

June 10: Diplomatic Victory vs. Military Victory.
Why is diplomacy a better bargain than fighting? With successful diplomacy, all parties profit to a greater or lesser extent. In military conflict there is one victor (or, perhaps, a stalemate with no victor at all) while all parties in the battle suffer loss: greater or lesser numbers of slain and dismembered soldiers and civilians and greater or lesser social and economic destruction. Indeed, it is quite possible that the army declared the victor might have suffered more losses than the defeated army.

But wait! I spoke in error. There are winners in war. Those who sell weapons or other logistic support for war become rich, indeed! If those who profit from the sale of weapons or other logistic support for war are, also, political leaders in the warring factions, they are particularly abominable. They choose war over diplomacy in order to become wealthy. Normally, I oppose the death sentence; but, in their cases, I approve of it. The world cannot afford to harbor such monsters.

While I am speaking of war, I will broach the subject of war that is not war, the "war on terrorism" which was declared six years ago after the final bombing of the World Trade Center by members of the terrorist group, Al Qaeda. I say that it is not a war because, to be a war in the political sense, it must involve two or more opposing armies from one or more geographically and politically defined nations. Al Qaeda has neither a well-defined army nor does it represent any geographical/political nation or group of nations. Thus, this "war" has only one legitimate politically based army, that of the United States (with limited support from its shaky little "coalition" of nations).

What, then, is it if it is not a war, and what difference does it make what we call it? I would call it a police action. In a police action, representatives of legitimate governments, unilaterally or in alliance, attempt to stop what they perceive to be evil actions of individuals or groups of individuals who wreak their havoc within their nation of residence or outside that nation against the population of any legitimate government. Al Qaeda certainly meets the definition for a group needing the force of a police action and did not meet the definition of a political power comprising the leadership of a legitimate nation or group of nations. Thus, America's "war" against Al Qaeda is a police action, not a war.

The difference this makes is profound. In calling this action a war, America has confused its mission of limiting or eliminating Al Qaeda with an alternative mission of regime change and nation-building. This confusion has led to America's replacing the governments of two terribly flawed but minimally legitimate governments (those of Afghanistan and Iraq) and seems to be edging toward doing so in other recognized countries (e.g., Pakistan and Iran). Nation-building might be a legitimate activity in certain extreme circumstances. Such intervention is something that might be fruitfully explored, but it was far from the goal of the so-called "war on terror." Calling it a war has appeared to legitimize nation-building without the clear mandate from the people of the United States or any mandate from the United Nations or the civilized world in general. In our misdirected adventures in nation-building, we have lost track of our original

157

purpose; and, in the process, we have allowed Al Qaeda to prosper, and we have damaged our political relationships with most of the nations of the world.

No objective person would want us to reverse our political accomplishments in Iraq and Afghanistan. However, common sense tells us to return our gaze, as quickly as possible without causing more human suffering than is necessary, to our original goal of *policing* Al Qaeda.

June 11: Sam is Daydreaming about Yasmin: "Hearts Crossing."
Let's sit here awhile
Under the shimmering trees;
For half an hour we can let our hearts dance
To the song of the leaves
Caressed by the sun and sweet breeze.
We'll cry for our sorrows,
And we'll laugh for our joys;
We'll suspend all but the sound of our two hearts,
Beating as one
With the shimmering leaves of universal Nature.

On parting, I'll heave a clumsy arm
Around your shoulders and draw you tight against me:
An embrace where two souls meet,
Mutually drinking of living nectar.
For a moment, we'll taste the divine dew of eternity
Which we gain from loving.

June 12: Patience.
Perfectly clear water is always a joy. It seems to sparkle with the life it contains and, even, with the life that it might contain at some future time. It is an emblem of the good and all that might become good. But water is seldom perfectly clear. That is not a problem for the patient person. First, one must go to a flowing stream whose headwater is perfectly clear. Then one must wait. When the source is pure and the stream flows, passing water, if unmolested, downstream will become clear. All one need do is wait. The same is true of thought (which is known to some as soul or spirit and others as rational mind).

June 13: Fishing Magic.
Yesterday, I did what everyone who is capable of moving about should do often. I went fishing in a desert reservoir. It was a temperate day with a light Idaho breeze, plenty of sunshine and plenty of perch waiting to be caught. (The perch I caught, of course, were not the lucky ones.) Other than a friendly pair of game wardens who congratulated me on my bucket of perch and checked my license, I was the only person near enough to speak to throughout the entire day. And I talked to myself (and to the perch and a couple of ornery seagulls who kept trying to steal the perch from my bucket) quite a lot.

The reservoir is called Magic. The dam which formed it is called Magic dam. I should probably check my facts, but I like my fantasy. I suspect that the

158

"magic" was in turning broad acreages from desert to green farm fields, for this is an irrigation reservoir. I've been told that it, also, houses a water-driven dynamo that produces electricity. Cold water from the melting mountain snows and springs that flow down to the reservoir as the Big Wood River are talented and multifaceted, producing electricity for lighting houses and bringing television into the most remote homes, thousands of acres of green fields, an end to the ancient floodplain that prevented settlers for a hundred years (after the forced expatriation of the native tribes) from building their homes near the Big Wood River. Now the area is in danger of becoming over-populated with rich Californians coming to Idaho to escape other rich Californians.

But for me, alone on the east bank of the reservoir with only myself and perch and seagulls to talk to, it was like waiting patiently for my soul to be perfectly clear. Of course, my soul will never be perfectly clear. It is not that kind of soul, but I can come close to a clear mind alone on the east bank of Magic Reservoir. Reclining there on big flat stones, I have the opulence of a king with none of the responsibilities. What can a king do in such surroundings but think—and, of course, catch perch or scold marauding seagulls.

I went home reluctantly when the sun was within a couple of hours of the horizon. An hour's drive and I was cleaning perch at home behind my no-travel trailer at dusk. There is no royal opulence to that. I was worn smooth and wishing I had curtailed my fishing an hour or two earlier. I had tried, but that extra Magic time was too magical. I finished the cleaning and scaling, showered off the fish smell and the fish scales that adhered to me like a second soul, and went to bed aching. I am too old for 14-hour days. But this morning, looking back at yesterday, it was all worth it. Even the fish-cleaning! I must, however, learn the wisdom of limits, especially as I get older and stiffer in the joints. A flat rock with an indentation for my *gluteus maxima* is not an easy chair.

June 14: Sewer Rat!

This is a story that had to be told. It is not, directly, a philosophical note, but it shows a little something about human nature.

Yesterday, #2 daughter, due for delivery of grandchild #8, was in our basement in Missouri with her pants down ready to sit down on the pot when she noticed something floating there. At first, she thought that Yasmin had become forgetful and failed to flush—then it moved! It swam! #2 "re-riz" from half-way down narrowly avoiding the immediate birth of #8. She determined on closer inspection that the moving target was a small rat, and she quickly closed the lid shouting for Yasmin. Yasmin came post-haste fearing that #2's water had broken and that she would be stuck driving her to the hospital (which she fears more than death because she does not drive on freeways or big-city streets). When she got there (to the toilet, not the hospital), #2 pointed to the toilet and shouted "rat!" At which announcement, Yasmin sprinted up the stairs and called across the street to the next-door neighbor, Wallace. He is the designated emergency man when I am not at home. Grandson #5 remarked: "Wow! I didn't know Tutu could run so fast!" Grandson #3 remarked: I need to go pee, but I'll do it upstairs." He was seen again only after the entire episode ended.

159

Wallace arrived quickly. He was carrying a pair of long-handled pruning shears and a black plastic trash bag. He went right to the basement. Yasmin said that he hesitated before he lifted the lid. I suppose he was trying to decide how to open the lid without allowing the beast to escape. Surely, he was not afraid. His hesitation was opportune because it allowed Yasmin time to slip into the shower stall and close the clear glass door. Wallace opened the lid, caught the little fellow in his pruning sheers dropped him in his trash bag, stomped him to death, and left the house carrying the rat in the trash bag. Several hours later, after 9 p.m., during free-minute time on my cell phone, Yasmin called me to let me know that I had missed her hour of greatest need and that Wallace was now her hero. I said that I was sorry I had missed it and told her about my successful fishing trip the previous day (36 fish—trout and perch). She said, "Wow!" She knows that I am a terrible fisherman.

All is well. Yasmin said that she doesn't know what she would have done had Wallace not been home. I remember another time a rodent accosted her in one of our previous homes. She was walking by the open door of the bedroom of #1 daughter when a mouse ran out of that room in horror upon experiencing the housekeeping failures of daughter #1. Yasmin screamed. The mouse fainted dead away, apparently having suffered a heart attack from compounded fright. Yasmin got up from where she had slipped and fallen on the floor and put a bucket upside down over the dead or dying mouse and sat there until I returned home several hours later. She suffered a bruised hip, but otherwise was simply glad I was finally home. She needed to pee and was afraid to get off the bucket for fear the mouse would turn it over and run away. The mouse, by the way, was, indeed, dead.

Yesterday, when I told her that, had Wallace not been around, she could have just as easily gone to the garage, retrieved our pruners and reached into the pot for the little rat herself. I suggested that a better plan would have been to cut him in two with the pruners in the toilet where he was and flush him down. She said that she had tried to flush him down but he just swam to the top of the water. I said that he would probably put up less resistance if he were cut in two. Most importantly, though, she said that a woman is, simply, not able to do such things as rid toilets of rats. I suspect that she is wrong about that, although I know of many women who have lived for years with *two-legged* rats, seemingly unable to get rid of them (with or without pruning shears). Could we say the same for women in conjunction with cute little four-legged-pointy-tailed rats? If this is a learned response on the part of women, we need to do some better early training of our female offspring. Wallace cannot be everywhere.

June 15:   Know Yourself! Accept Yourself!

I am on a rampage today. I am irritated with good people who refuse to self-actualize because they underestimate their own capabilities and accept that underestimate as their "karma" for life. I know it is not nice to judge, but I would prefer to judge such persons as misguided rather than stupid. In either case, however, if they are intelligent, capable human beings who have committed themselves to the good, their next step should be to evaluate themselves at the highest reasonable level and seek that level or higher in everything they do. Not to do so is to look "good" in the face and then to turn and slink away from it. I, generally, avoid the term "sin." However, I can think of no better term to name this slinking away from life's responsibilities.

But, be careful! Don't link what I have just said absolutely to social status, position, and political power. It is entirely possible to change the world as a house-maid or a soda jerk. However, it is less likely. What we generally need is the best education we can get and the kind of job that is tailored for doing good. Then, back to self evaluation. We must use that job—along with whatever we do besides work for a living—as a platform for achieving the highest good.

Know what you are capable of. Can you read well? Can you write well? Can you speak well? Can you compute well? If not these, what can you do well? If you can do nothing well now, what can you learn to do well? Invest what time and money you have and, perhaps, can borrow in learning and practicing and discovering and doing what you can possibly do. Know what you can do? Accept yourself at *that* level no matter how abysmal your performance has been thus far or how minimal others have convinced you that you are. Achieve at your best level. Guide your achievement, not to wealth, power, or fame, but to the good. (Seeking wealth, power, or fame will only get in the way of real success.)

I know a man who became convinced by a series of failures that the highest calling he could fulfill in life was that of a janitor. He found himself working nights in a grade school cleaning classrooms and restrooms.

Something happened! Four years after he had sunk to this level, he moved from being the janitor at a grade school to being the principal at a high school. The principalship lasted but a year. He then moved on to full-time secondary teaching and eventually to a university professorship.

What happened? He re-evaluated his potential. He re-established his desire to serve the good. He did what he had to do. He went to college (after working-hours) and attained a degree followed, in time, by two advanced degrees. He spent the rest of his life, nearly half a century, teaching, and guiding students (and the many others he was able to influence with his enhanced professional/social platform) toward the good.

Knowing the truth about yourself and acting upon that knowledge for the sake of the good are all that I would ask of you.

June 16: And, by the Way . . .

Annihilate all desire except the simple desire for good. Within that good, you will rediscover—in ideal form—all that you annihilated.

June 17: Faith and Father's Day.

Today is Father's Day, another day created to give Hallmark a larger bottom line. Yet it is, though not a real holiday, a holiday which has significance to me—both good and ill. First the ill. I am in Idaho while my children and their children and my children's mother are in Missouri. Thus, without further explanation, I am depressed. I feel like that bag of tired, wrinkled, rotten potatoes which I looked at and smelled and threw over the fence where even the cows turned up their noses at them. I will not have a baked potato with my Father's Day steak tonight. What else I will not have will be my wife and children and their husbands

161

and children gathered around me while I have my Father's Day steak tonight. That is what depresses me the most.

Yet for the good, each daughter and Yasmin contacted me to wish me a happy Father's day. Yasmin called on Friday to let me know about the rat in the toilet and, also, reassured me that, even though we are far apart, we are one in spirit. She still loves me even though she has to depend upon our neighbor Wallace to get a rat out of the toilet. #1 sent me email pictures of all three children along with their love and well-wishes. #2 called and let me talk to both of her boys and her delightful Guatemalan husband. They seemed truly happy to greet me. #3 sent me a card that asked whether she should thank me or just lick my face. She filled me in on what her boys are doing (competing in youth triathlons, etc.) and sent a gift certificate from Walmart which she had earned by filling out a survey. She knows that I don't like her to buy me gifts because I prefer that she spend what she has on the boys and herself, so she assured me that she didn't really have to spend anything on this gift. Nice of her to think of my feelings. She's good that way. With the certificate, I bought my Father's day steak, a few groceries (*sans* baking potatoes), and a new western belt to replace the one that was about to break. (I really must lose weight!)

What has faith to do with this? Everything—and nothing! Because that is, indeed, what faith is. Everything because in this world of sensory phenomena, "all" is little more than a shadow of a shadow of a shadow. Faith is what brings reality to sensory experience. A mountain, a mind, a beloved wife, children, grandchildren, extended family, cows in a pasture, beans sprouting in the garden—without faith, these are just random phenomena of questionable value and even questionable existence. With faith they are concrete joy in perfect harmony. Nothing?! How can all this be nothing? Yet I see wretched persons everywhere drowning in sensory phenomena and choking to death on emptiness. "Wretched" is something I will never be.

I seldom consider faith in connection with God—though that could be a faith issue if I ever had need of it. Faith for me is, ordinarily, in the ordinary: a kiss on the telephone, a card in the mail, a picture of a grandson with his violin tucked under his chin, the smell of frying onions and steak, a steer that likes me to scratch him behind the horns, a cat that curls around my ankle, love, and respect, and a setting sun and a rising moon, and even my own death.

June 18: (No) Strike Reservoir.

No strikes except by a few munchkin bass which I quickly returned to the greenish-yellow water. I, probably, would not have kept a big bass for fear of getting a disease from eating it. The Snake River, my friends, which is the source of water for Strike Reservoir near the small town of Bruneau deep in the Idaho desert, *is polluted*. If we can do it there, we can do it anywhere, and we have done it there. Wasn't it in Genesis that humanity, as the rational and intelligent being capable of moral perfection, was told to exercise dominion over the earth—*to take care of it!?* Brothers and sisters of the big brain, the thinking brain, the logical mind, what we are doing is not working.

Oh, by the way, last night listening to a news broadcast, I heard a report indicating that Idaho's bark beetle epidemic which is killing so much of the national forest is getting worse because of global warming. Now, because the climate has changed, those beetles which previously had time during the short mountain growing season for only two reproductive cycles, have time for more which means more dead trees. More dead trees mean more desert, less forest, less oxygen for the atmosphere we breathe. Hmm! Maybe the beetles will die from oxygen starvation. Shoot! Forget what I said above. NPR and I are merely alarmist liberals.

June 19: New Church Day.

I suppose that I will have to develop a new respect for Emanuel Swedenborg since I discovered that he has a contemporary following that refers to him as "The prophet." Swedenborg's "New Church" celebrates each year on its birthday Swedenborg's "divine" revelation which he received on June 19, 1770. It all goes back to the biblical book of Revelation where the prophecy is for the birth of a "New Christian Church." A woman travails. A child is born. Swedenborg is not alone in seeing this prophecy as being fulfilled. For instance, Joseph Smith, the founder of the Mormon movement, referred to the same passage in founding the Mormons in 1830. Also, the Jehovah's Witnesses, founded in the late 19th century, spend a lot of time counting heads for membership in that "new" church which they refuse to call a church.

The biggest question is just what difference this new church (generic) makes. It seems to be just one more denomination of the old church commissioned by Jesus and organized and developed by his followers after his death. The Apostle Paul had a lot to do with that. He got his Swedenborgian revelation when he was struck blind on the road to Damascus. He went and joined (instead of going on to persecute) the Christians and recovered his sight as a reward. The Mormons call the new church the "Restoration" instead of a new church or a reformation of the old one. It all seems to mean about the same thing. Nobody's new church seems to draw anyone into a new direction. I ask the same question I have asked all my life. Where is God in all this with fresh new suggestions for getting the world together for the millennial reign (also prophesied in Revelation)? All I see, even with the "new" revelations, is more of the same old failing stuff: "believe and be saved," etc. When will someone get the idea that "being" good for the sake of being saved is not being good at all? Rather, "doing" good just because it is good is *the answer* if there has been or even needs to be a question asked. Surely, we don't need to wait for a benevolent God to "reveal" this to us. It is so damnably obvious! The "Aquarians" of the 1960s probably had the right idea. Remember them? They were often called flower children or Jesus people or the like. Unfortunately, though they had the right idea in terms of being passively engaged in the "good," they drowned it (the good) in a sea of drugs and sex and petty crime and laziness that would have made Sodom and Gomorrah blush.

June 20: Summer Solstice.

The longest day of the year in the northern hemisphere! That will be tomorrow. I just thought you should be warned. Not being a climatologist, I wonder why the longest day is not the hottest. It is the day that the sun shines longer than any other day of the year. Yet I know that we have a couple of months now of weather that will get steadily hotter until, suddenly, almost overnight, early in September, the summer heat disappears. We have a great deal to think about this year and in following years as we swelter through June, July, and August. That excessive heat is from global warming partly caused by our own neglect of the planet. Whether we swelter more and more and whether global warming leads to the cataclysms that some scientists predict for the not-too-distant future might depend upon what we do about our continued pumping of excessive carbon dioxide and other gaseous contaminants into the atmosphere.

June 21: Be a Star!

Becoming a star seems to be the secret wish of a very large number of people, but most of them are thinking of the wrong kind of star. They want to be a Mozart or an Elvis, perhaps a Pascal, a Hemingway, an Einstein, a P-Diddy (or has he changed his name again by now?) These are, indeed, stars, but why would they wish such a fate upon themselves. Except for Einstein and, perhaps, Pascal (I don't know much about Pascal), these persons had or are having extremely trying and sometimes short and miserable lives. Whatever gods there be: please don't make me one of these, except an Einstein or, conditionally, a Pascal. Rather, make me just who I am only as the best that I can be at what I enjoy and what will be good for others. And, while I am at it, don't make me be just one kind of star, but give me a variety and the option of changing what kind of star I am now and then, before I get bored with the kind of star I happen to be at any given moment.

Although I am not a great fan of the first President Bush for his politics, he introduced at least one great idea. He called it "a million points of light." He was making an analogy between the stars in the sky and people who do just little good things for society. He believed that all of the cumulative light from all of these million points of light would lead to a greater environment for everyone.

The way I want to be a star is to be a number of these points of light as I go though life, each point of light representing one time when I have been the best that I can be at something that results in good for others. For instance, I spent several years being a high school English teacher. I was the best that I could be (which was not very good at all) and I managed to do some good (I think). I, also, spent a couple of years as a church youth minister. That was hard work and fun and I was about as good at that as I was as a high school English teacher. And I spent a couple of years traveling to a lot of churches delivering (with the help of Yasmin and my three daughters) sermons in song which I had written. I happen to think that was a particularly good season. I doubt that many others but Yasmin agree with me about that. She has been a fan of my singing ever since I sang "Blue Hawaii" to her on Christmas Eve 40 years ago. Speaking of Hawaii, I spent a brief tenure as pastor of a church congregation there. I felt a real calling to do that and, when it was over, I was relieved but satisfied that something good was accomplished. And I have done quite a lot of other stuff. I won't count selling tires over the phone. I doubt that I did anyone any good with that, especially, the guy I woke up to tell him that I had just noticed his front left was bald and I had just the replacement for him. He assured me that he had a full head of hair and that if he ever found out who I was he would have me flayed. He hasn't found me. I hope, by now, he has forgiven or forgotten me.

164

You get the idea. Not once have I been rich or particularly famous. Never did I wield a great deal of social or political power. Never did I stay at one task (volunteer or professional) for a long time. In every case, I have been eager to light up each new star and just as eager to move on to the next. Right now, I'm writing this book of helpful(?) philosophical notes. It will be finished with the first draft, you might guess, on December 31 of this year. What will I do next? Hmm! That will give me a great deal to think about as my excitement about writing a philosophy book wears thin over the next six months. Whatever it is, I must not let the light be extinguished for long. At my age, it's getting harder to remember where I put the box of matches; and, with my minimal financial success, I can't afford a new box.

June 22: Hegelian Dialectic.

I am full to overflowing of Hegel. I have been reading Hegel since a couple of months before I left Kansas City. That would be about three months, maybe more, of reading Hegel. I say that I am full of Hegel, but in a way, that is like having a sack full of various types of beans which have not been sorted. Now, there are not a lot of types of beans, just pintos, reds, limas, garbanzos and a couple of other common varieties, but there are a lot of beans to sort. Also, it seems that no matter how many beans I take out and sort, there are more beans than ever in the sack. Except for Hegel declaring an end to the beans by suggesting that the whole process of bean sorting would soon reach a climax (perfection?) in the Christian world, the sorting could go on infinitely. The suggestion of an end is the gravest mistake Hegel makes in his dialectic for, although there can be (and will be) an end to the human race as-it-is on this earth, the bean sorting will go on in some other world with all the high seriousness that it goes on among philosophers here and now. With the necessity of infinite reason (mind, will, spirit, soul, self-consciousness, etc.) comes the necessity of infinite bean sorting in whatever time/space context that continues to occur.

I would not, however, say that Hegel is entirely "full of beans." It is just that he, along with every other philosopher, is short of the full truth which always evades us no matter how many beans we manage to sort. An important part-truth that Hegel uncovers is the concept of process. Every philosopher knows about process, but the sense in which Hegel explores it is unique and has changed the way we view our total existence, especially as reasonable human beings.

In a nutshell, the process is that for every idea (thesis) there emerges immediately an idea (antithesis) in its opposition. This antithesis for every thesis is a necessity, and it always leads rationally to a third manifestation of the idea which emerges as a synthesis deleting both the thesis and the antithesis except as memories which, due to the nature of rationality, could be recalled at any time that it seems fitting to do so. However, they can never be recalled in the same thesis/antithesis sense because the synthesis has become a higher level of thesis which is joined by its antithesis. And so on.

This is an over-simplification of Hegel's process that does not come close to completely encapsulating the dialectic he describes or the infinitely more complex cosmic system of dialectic which he doesn't attempt to describe. What I want to note today is the importance in our everyday lives of the Hegelian process.

Essentially, what it does for us is separate us from the rest of the animal kingdom, the multitude of soulless(?) species that cannot think rationally. This separation is the source of what Hegel insists is our total freedom as individuals and, in parallel with that, our possibility of freedom within a social contract. According to Hegel, if we use this rational thinking in the way that he describes it in his dialectic, we are absolutely in charge of our decisions. Starting with the moment when we emerge as individuals by recognizing our own separate existence from all other things, we begin making decisions based upon the sensual phenomena which present themselves to us. Our minds (souls, spirits, etc.) examine these phenomena and, through the dialectical process, make reasonable decisions in regard to them, *ipso facto*, moving us to the next higher plane of being with that much more information. Thus, forces from outside our spirits may attempt to "change our minds," but the actual changing is entirely within the control of our rational spirits.

The obvious challenge to Hegel is that his thesis rests heavily upon that Atlas called religion—specifically, upon the Christian God who provides each person with an infinite soul. Hegel is not convincing when it comes to proving the immortality of this soul. The empiricists insist that the "soul" is nothing more than a collection of interacting brain cells which die when we do. As such, they are programmed to respond predictably to the phenomena to which they are exposed. A great variety of responses, but no freedom!

For those who would like a thorough examination of the possibility of existence of an eternal human soul, read Kant. Then you can, also, read a host of other "believer" philosophers' arguments for the existence of an eternal human soul; and, if you are truly objective in your reasoning, you will become less and less convinced that such existence can be proven in any satisfactory way except faith (imagination)—which is not a bad way to go. Even Hegel refers at times to the spiritual world as a product of the imagination.

June 23: Hegelian Obfuscation.

No one except a dolt like me dares to say it for fear of being classified as a dolt like me, but I feel that I must warn those who follow me into Hegelian study that he has a certain sense of humor based upon obfuscation. In other words, he sometimes seems to make his meaning unclear on purpose and, aware that the brilliant thesis behind what he says will alter the course of human thought, has fun wondering how many otherwise brilliant readers will think that his impenetrable meandering from point to point is, also, brilliant.

Brilliant! Yes, even a brilliant sense of humor. I can imagine his students becoming more and more anxious about the next exam as they become more and more confused.

It is, however, a delight to search out the essentials of his theory while getting thoroughly dizzy unwinding the Gordian knots of his discussion. Of course, much of what he says is repetitious because his theory, at its base, and exactly like all brilliant philosophical theory, is quite simple: human progress (focused upon reason) is a cycling of the same dialectic of thesis, antithesis, and synthesis. If you look carefully at his discussion, you see that it cycles through this dialectic about every thousand words. I have a feeling that it would be even more fun in German, but my German language mastery is not sound enough to bother with the attempt.

June 24: One Dead Cow.

She was the oldest cow in the herd, and she had experienced health problems for the previous two years, but she kept getting pregnant each spring, so Brother #3 didn't have a chance to sell her off for hamburger. A couple of weeks ago, she would have brought up to $500 at the sale ring as a cutter/canner. Yesterday, #3 had to pay $40 to have the Darling Dead Animal Collectors haul her off. Of course, #3 does have the calf she bore. He will be worth about $500 by fall, so #3 hasn't really lost anything but the $40. But he is a little out of sorts about that. Two years ago, when he had a dead cow hauled off, Darling charged only $20. Double the price in two years is too much of a hike. #3 says he remembers when Darling paid him for dead cows. After all, they do get a price for them at the rendering plant.

The calf is not happy. He bawled all night around the spot where his mother went down. The rest of the cows held the funeral before the old cow was dead, right after she fell down and couldn't get up. They always do that. They sound like keeners at an Irish wake except that they moo instead of keen. They all run to the spot where the dying or dead cow has fallen and set up a full chorus of moos. They will keep this up for an hour or so if they are not disturbed. In this case, after I told #3 about the funeral, he opened a gate to another pasture and wailed "Come, Boss; come, Boss." The funeral was immediately adjourned *sine die* and the whole herd, less the dying cow and the dying cow's calf and a couple of the calf's young friends, stampeded to the fresh pasture and, apparently, had not another thought about the dying cow. I herded the three calves in the direction of the retreating herd, and they, too, joined the herd immediately.

It was time, then, to deal with the dying cow. I had assumed that #3 would bring his rifle to the pasture to put her down. He didn't. Brother #1 drove his tractor around to the pasture dragging a log-chain behind and stopped near the cow. #3 secured the chain around the cow's hind legs. #1 put the tractor in gear and dragged the old heifer off to the haystack yard. I was walking behind. I could see a wild look in the cow's eye, the left eye. The right eye was dragging on the ground. I can't tell whether she was in any pain. She had not the strength to do more than waggle her front legs a little. She didn't bellow or make any sort of sound. I could hear the sliding of her hide against the bluegrass pasture and then the rumble of gravel when she reached the driveway. After that, I was too far away to hear anything but the crack of #3's hunting rifle as he put her down with a bullet between the eyes in the stack-yard. When I got there, she seemed brain-dead but with a regular pulse throbbing in her neck. I think she still had that pulse when Darling's driver winched her into the enclosed steel truck and latched the big swinging doors closed. I noticed before the doors clanged shut that there were already a few dead cattle in the truck. It stunk of rotting meat. I handed the driver the $40-dollar check that Mom had written and given to brother #4 and #4 had given to me. She writes all of #3's checks. He doesn't like checking accounts, so he just gives her cash. She puts it back in her bank account or spends it on groceries.

I wondered, briefly, why #3 had not shot the cow in the pasture to ease her suffering earlier, especially, before the long drag to the stack-yard. Then I remembered the keening. Cows can smell blood from a dear departed in a pasture for years after it is spilled and will repeat endlessly the same crazy funeral rites every time they smell it. To shoot a dying cow in a pasture is to ruin that part of the pasture for years.

Life on the farm is like that—natural. Practicality is the main issue. Humans, the reasonable life forms, are in charge. Soulless animals are commodities. #3 would have liked to euthanize the cow as soon as she was down, but it would have been foolhardy. He had to act in accord with the laws of nature or pay the consequences. I suppose that this is what God meant when he told Adam to "subdue the earth." #3 is not thinking of subduing anything except the decline in his cash. He would have preferred to dump the dead cow in a hollow on the desert south end of the farm. I objected strenuously since my summer camp is within smelling distance of that hollow. I have pretty much lost my sense of smell, but the rare visitors to my campground, catching a whiff of rotting cow, might think I am forgetting my hygiene as I age. In a sense, then, it is my fault that #3 had to lose his $40 to Darling. However, I am not sorry I objected. I had a higher purpose than money. It was that "fig," reputation, which drove me.

June 25: Vulnerability.

Maybe it was the old cow dying in the pasture that honed the edge of this morning's 2 a.m. trauma regarding a beetle the size of a straight-pin head which entered my right ear and danced a tarantella upon my eardrum. At any rate, I rediscovered just how vulnerable we humans are to the little things in nature.

I woke up suddenly from a sound sleep with a tickle in my ear. Then I felt it going deeper into the right side of my head and arriving at my eardrum where it continued walking. I don't know why it was so determined to walk upon such a limited piece of real estate as my eardrum, but there it chose to stay and to walk continually back and forth sounding more like thunder than a tiny bug. And there it continued. It was not long at all before I was out of bed looking for anything that I could poke into my ear up to the drum to attempt to remove the intruder. This was a wasted, not to mention hazardous, effort during which I use a paper clip, a wooden chopstick, and my right little finger. Then, after my ear canal was thoroughly chafed, I hatched the brilliant idea of luring the bug out with heat and light. There I stood with a huge flashlight pressed against my ear, shining down my ear canal, supposedly the flame attracting the moth, but the beetle was obviously not a moth and was probably stuck knee deep in earwax. Indeed, I did not know then that it was a beetle. I imagined it, because of its great shoes and its tarantella, to be the size of a yearling rattlesnake but, like the serpent in Eve's Garden, with a multitude of legs.

Finally, searching through the cabinet for a better solution, I discovered a nearly-new 32-ounce bottle of canola oil. Instantly, I had my logical answer. I would drown it and flush it out. I retrieved a cup-and-a-half measuring beaker from the cupboard, poured a small amount of canola oil into it, heated it slightly over the cook-stove, then, with my left ear flat on the kitchen counter, poured the oil into the portal of my right ear. I thought for a moment about Hamlet's uncle pouring acid into the ear of King Hamlet. I wasn't sure what impact canola oil would have on an eardrum. But the impact was quick and positive. The insect stopped dancing. Perhaps, it had drowned. I turned my head over and caught the dripping oil on a

168

paper towel. Nothing but oil! I repeated the pouring and the draining, and this time the wee drowned varmint came out on the paper towel along with the oil. By then my upper body was pretty well saturated with canola oil and I felt better. I wiped off the oil as best I could and returned to bed, wondering through the rest of the night whether a hoard of little beetles was waiting mischievously behind my pillow to do it all over again. I didn't sleep at all for an hour, nor did I sleep at all *well* for the rest of the night.

Had I not been able to remove the beast for myself, I'd have been forced to visit the emergency room this morning and would probably have paid a nurse or a resident MD and the emergency room several hundred dollars for the extraction. My health insurance is not valid outside the Kansas City area except in life-threatening emergencies. I doubt that United Health Care would consider a tiny beetle doing a dance on my eardrum to be life-threatening.

The cow was old, but she didn't die of old age. She died from an infection caused by a tiny barbed seed from a foxtail weed growing wild in the pasture. Such infections happen quite often on the farm. The cow eats the foxtail. The seed punctures the skin inside the cheek and enters the flesh around the jawbone. The flesh becomes infected. #3 administers antibiotics. The cow gets well—unless the cow is 14 years old and weakened already by previous illnesses. Then the cow dies.

People are the same. At 2 a.m. today, I thought it entirely possible that a tiny beetle dancing joyously on my right eardrum could be the death of me. As Eliot said, "I am old! I am old! I shall wear the bottoms of my trousers rolled." The mermaids stopped singing to me long ago. They have little interest in wrinkled, bald men. My ear canal is quite sore. No "sea-girls dressed in seaweed green and brown" for me. Just a damnable little bug! Hopefully, I won't get an ear infection. In order for me to get an insurance reimbursement, I'll have to wait until it is life-threatening to go to the emergency room. What is a life-threatening fever? 104? 105? Perhaps, I should do some research so I know when to go in.

June 26: Hegel (Cont.), Revealed Absolute Religion (e.g., Christianity).

I must continue researching Hegel's writing. I read in the criticisms about Hegel that he was a devout Christian, and that might be true; but I experience a degree of doubt about his personal commitment to Christianity when, in the culmination of his "Phenomenology of the Spirit" where he defends Christianity as the dialectic culmination of human religion, he writes in such a way as to avoid committing himself to belief in the Christian dogma. I am not denying that Hegel was a Christian, even a devout one. The question I am entertaining regards the *nature* of Hegel's attachment to Christianity.

Throughout his writing, Hegel equates reason with freedom. The freedom of rational thinking is to be able to reach ones own rational conclusions about everything. On the other hand, the advantage of Christianity, according to Hegel, is that it is revealed (absolute) religion. That is, it is the religion in which the rational god revealed himself as a real human being (verified by a bundle of phenomena) to those who would be Christians. That absolute revelation makes it possible for the human spirit (equal to self-consciousness because the individual spirit can experience itself as a phenomenon as well as a spirit) to be conscious, also, of God. Thus, God the spirit is also God the man. This is the only way God could make

169

himself truly known to the human spirit in a way that crosses the boundary between spirit and concrete existence.

This, like any analysis of Hegel's philosophy, is pitifully limited. However, it might help me to explain my question about his commitment to Christianity. The question is whether his commitment is an entirely rational decision to follow Christianity because it is the ultimate synthesis of his dialectic of religious process or whether, like most Christians would put it, God touched his soul and spurred his faith in the Christian doctrine. The latter, though it seems necessary to traditional Christian conversion, would seem to deny Hegel's belief in human freedom. To be free, his decision must be entirely rational, not a matter of emotional religious conversion. The former must be the case, in which case, I would have to say that Hegel is an admirer of Christianity, and even a participant in Christian goings-on, but not a sheep of the Christian flock. That would require sacrificing his freedom; and freedom, for Hegel, is the very essence of rational human existence. In reading his works so far, I am not sure that Hegel recognizes his own dilemma. I will continue to search for answers. I feel like Socrates whose discussions so often end without resolution of the problem.

June 27: Hegel's Dialectical Error.

Hegel errs when he says that Christianity is the ultimate culmination of the dialectic of religious belief. There can be no ultimate culmination of any dialectic. Particular forms are finite. Dialectic is an idea, not a form. Ideas emerge from the infinite. They are of use in examining forms, but they continue infinitely in every dimension of time and space. Thus, for example, Christianity is, merely, a form (a synthesis in this case) which emerges from theses and antitheses. Immediately, upon emergence of a form, it produced antitheses (not just one) which, in conjunction with Christianity as thesis, produce new syntheses (again, not just one). Indeed, Hegel oversimplifies dialectic by making it appear as if it happens in chunks called thesis, antithesis, and synthesis. In actuality, these three are happening and overlapping with other theses, antitheses, and syntheses at infinite speed and number to the extent that no particular form upon which they are based can be identified precisely at any given instant. If, somehow, time could be stopped for a moment, and spatial expansion/contraction could be held in check for that same moment, perhaps we could experience through phenomena certain things as they are (at that moment). Since such stoppage is impossible, we can not experience anything as it is because, by the time we experience it through phenomena, it has changed its form.

It is not difficult to see that while a form of an idea (such as a particular manifestation of Christianity) might seem readily explainable, definable, describable, it is far more complex than it seems. In fact, it seems ludicrous on the face of it, to try to explain, define, or describe it. However, our rational minds have the habit, the need even, to keep working at it. One rule of evolution seems clear: everything which evolves into successful continuing existence does so because it is compatible with its context. That which is incompatible evolves out of existence.

June 28: Marx's Error in Believing Hegel.

170

Marx, with his political dialectic contained in the Communist Manifesto, made the same mistake Hegel made with his dialectic. Actually, the mistake is manifold. First, no dialectic, in an infinite cosmos begins or culminates. Dialectic is a never beginning, never-ending process. In contradiction of this infinite reality, he assumed that the final victory of the proletariat would be truly final. Instead, it is, merely, another possible synthesis, one which would evolve into the past like all the others even if it were to arrive in its full fruition. Second, dialectical outcomes are far too complex to be predicted by mere humans. What proponents of dialectic forget is that millions (perhaps billions or trillions, perhaps infinite) dialectical situations are progressing and overlapping at any given moment. How all this overlapping will impact a particular dialectic is a material complex so extensive that no mathematics, not even quantum physics, could possibly untangle it in advance. Indeed, not even after it occurs. All we need do is recognize how near to impossible it is to follow Hegel's journey through just a small sampling of dialectics to see that multiplying those dialectics and placing all in competition with each other would make accurate prediction of outcomes a ludicrous goal.

Yes! I see the Marxian dialectical political hypothesis as a possibility. Red China's outcome might, eventually, be a distant cousin to the Marx-predicted outcome. But, even now, it is obvious that capitalism is making too much of a difference in that country to see it emerging with the socialistic outcomes Marx envisioned. Vietnam might be moving vaguely in a direction of a Manifesto outcome. Time will tell. Cuba? Not even close!

June 29: An Old Friend.

Yesterday I had the chance to visit with an old friend, my very best friend from my early teens. When we were post-pubescent boys, we seemed to have little in common except for our friendship and the fact that we were both members of the same odd little church. Although we remained friends through our high school years, the friendship grew a bit more distant as our obvious differences in personality and individual life choices manifested themselves.

Yesterday, however, we discovered together just how much the same we are. Of our little graduating class of about 20 (give or take a migrant worker or two), we are the only two who ended up with strong liberal leanings, went (late) to university, came out with PhDs, and spent our later professional years as liberal arts professors. Beyond that, there are still some differences. He, for instance, still looks no older than 45. I look 80. He still plays basketball regularly. I gave that up 20 years ago when my signature spin move spun me to the floor. He chose to teach at a major public university while I chose a small private university. I retired early from my professorship a couple of years ago to conduct my scholarship and what remains of my life in a private way. He intends to keep working for a paycheck in academia forever.

Yet we spent the two hours we had together discussing Hegel and Marx and other philosophers and theologians and asking each other about our thoughts on a variety of contemporary topics; and I came away convinced that there was providence in that simple and innocent relationship that flourished over a half century ago when I remember that we would sit side-by-side at a calm river bend or in a room in his house or on a hillside near his father's sheep pen pondering ideas that we were not then aware were too big for us and which we have both since realized we will never in this life be big enough for, but continue to ponder.

It was a good conversation.

June 30: That's the end of the first half of *the True Book of Sam Clear Water.*

I hope you enjoyed it and that you'll stick around for the second half. I've just started re-reading René Descartes, so I can be Cartesian ("I think; therefore, I am: *cogito ergo sum).* In its own way, *cogito ergo sum* is the most profound statement of existence in all of philosophy even though it seems simplistic. But simple is often the path to profundity.

I'll see you on the other side.

End of Volume 2
The Half Moon

The True Book of Sam Clear Water
Wisdom from Walden-San
Volume 3: *The Harvest Moon*

Yasmin's Hawaiian Auntie is Back with a Piquant Suggestion:
At my house, I don' want nobody come in an' take my bes' jewels, like my gold Hawaii cha'm bracelet or my little chain necklace. So I hide 'em all ova da place, una da bed, in da attic. Dat's da way you hafta look for Sam's bes' stuff, hiding here and dere like da kine mouse in dark corners eating Spam crumbs da keikies drop. Read slow so you don' miss any or step on 'em!

July 1: The Sun Looks Into the Eye of the Moon; the Moon Blushes Back.
    It seems prophetic that this first day of the last half of the year and the first day of the last half of this philosophic treatise happen on the very day in Idaho (which I look forward to during every cycle of the moon) when the full moon rises a moment before the sun sets. It is a beautiful sight from the rocky desert knoll south of my camp. The moon seems ten times as big and ten times as bright as at any other moment of the month. The sun dims itself and turns orange like the moon. They are twins for just that moment before the sun dips below the horizon. Brother Phoebus retains his machismo at his opposite pole to Sister Phoebe. Bright as she is this night, she cedes her brother his due as the light of day; and soon she rules the night with a softer light. Masculine and Feminine, brother light and sister light across Mother Earth. It is done! It is good! Sweet grass smoke stirred by an eagle's feather.

July 2: Descartes' Most Important Rule.
    The following is Descartes' most important rule for solving problems. In working toward solving a problem, start with the *a priori* matters (number, line, color, extension, duration—as ideas, not as particulars) which are involved. They are received whole and complete by the mind. Apply them to the least complex manifold (thing divisible) which is related to the problem being approached. Do not go beyond examination of this manifold until you have proven conclusively its exact and complete relationship (in regard to the problem you are trying to solve) to the simple (the indivisible *a priori* which stands as the central idea). To move ahead without such proof breaks the chain which is necessary to solve the problem and destroys the validity of any solution which eventually emerges. Once you have the needed proof, you may move on to the next least complicated manifold involved in the problem. The same rule applies, but now you must prove the relationship of this manifold to the first manifold without breaking any of the rules of relationship between the first manifold and the simple. Continue this chain of analysis until you reach the problem itself and show how it is related to the entire chain including all

of its manifolds and the simple that heads them. Precise and complete thinking takes a great deal of time, but it is the only thinking that is worth the effort.

Do I agree with Descartes about this? No! There is a serious problem in identifying simples when they go beyond basic mathematical or scientific concepts. Some philosophers insist, for instance, that the immortal human soul is a simple. Such assumptions are deadly to the discovery of truth. It is justifiable to accept one or more of the various arguments for the immortality of the soul. Some of them seem quite convincing, but such arguments are, merely, arguments, not facts. Even an argument as powerful as a child of Kant's categorical imperative (e.g., There must be no war.) does not produce a simple. It is, after all, conditioned offspring. Descartes' problem-solving record stands as evidence. His only bona fide problem solution was *cogito ergo sum*.

By the way, although Decartes' formula seems complicated, it is not. In plain English, it is, merely, this. When examining a problem, begin with the whole and move, a rational step at a time, down through the parts to the problem. (For a model, see in *the Poetics* Aristotle's "beginning, middle, and end" as the initial division for analysis of dramatic tragedy.) The formula is simple, but when the problem deals with metaphysics, the central idea (the simple) always seems to be *necessary* but *impossible*. It isn't easy to get past that initial roadblock to the parts.

July 3: Wonderful, Understandable Descartes.

Now I remember why it is that I love Descartes. It is not because he is right about everything. It is because he is clear about everything. This has a great deal to do with his method. I mentioned that above. You can get it all in his 1637 *Discourse on Method*. Besides a clear delineation of his method of approaching philosophical problems, he introduces some of his most important "truths." A truth to Descartes is almost, but not quite, equal to what Kant would call a categorical imperative. It is something that, by the time Descartes' entire "method" has been applied, he is almost absolutely sure that it cannot be denied as the truth. Of course, as I say above, I disagree at times with his conclusions about truth, but I enjoy his arguments because they are clear and simple. Would that Hegel had taken lessons from him! Perhaps, not! Hegel in his obfuscation carries his analyses much further and remains upon firmer ground than Descartes ever can—except for *cogito ergo sum*.

July 4: Global Warming, Ice Cream, and Independence.

Freedom has got us where we are in America today. Of course, it is not freedom which has got China to nearly the same spot. The spot I am referring to is global warming due, at least in part, to increased world-wide dumping of carbon dioxide into the atmosphere. Probably, the world is on a warming track without our help. It does such things. But we are urging it along. In America, we do the urging because we believe that it would infringe upon the rights of our "free" people to do anything about it. In China, they urge it on because they want to prove that they are right to enslave a huge part of the world's population in a political system which has proven to be disastrously flawed for an even larger part of the world's population. It would seem that, no matter what our politics are, we are intent upon making the world unfit for human habitation. During the cold war, we stockpiled nuclear

174

weapons in case we got a chance to blow up the entire world. Now, we have decided that it will be cheaper to heat up the atmosphere and boil our brains out—or to drown our coastal neighbors with melted glacier.

That is why, this 4th of July at the family compound in Idaho, we will not be barbequing chicken and pork chops and steaks and hamburgers on a grill. Not because I am a vegetarian. It is just too damned hot—105 degrees in the shade. Brother #1 is making ice cream in a freezer which looks much like the one we, as small children, used to take turns sitting on while someone stronger turned the handle. But there is no handle on this one, just an electric cord and no one need sit on the bucket. It loses something in romance but the ice cream is still good. We will all eat it after we have separately eaten whatever else we can find in our various refrigerators or neighborhood restaurants. I will stay home and eat a fat-free cheese sandwich with celebratory peanuts.

July 5: An Important Discussion Regarding U.S. Citizenship.

I had a discussion with Brothers #1 and #4 this morning. It revolved, as our most animated discussions often do, around illegal immigration into the United States, especially, from Mexico. My brothers and I disagree sharply regarding what should be done about this immigration. They say deportation should be the rule. I argue that this would be inhumane as well as impractical. It would cause terrible hardship for illegal immigrant families who have been in the United States for long periods of time, some of them nearly all their lives. In addition, it would cause financial tragedies both in the United States and in Mexico.

One aspect of our discussion today was whether the children of illegal immigrants born in the United States have the birth-right of U.S. citizenship. There was disagreement as to whether this supposed birth-right is nothing more than a tradition, or if there are laws to support it. I went, just now, to the law, the constitution, and the records of the U.S. Supreme Court. Here are the facts.

The Civil Rights Act of 1866 declared that anyone born in the U.S. is a citizen of the United States. Added to that, the 14th Amendment to the U.S. Constitution begins with the sentence, "All persons born or naturalized in the United States, and subject to the jurisdiction thereof, are citizens of the United States and of the State wherein they reside." Fairly clear-cut, I think. But, to make it a home run, the U.S. Supreme Court in 1898 in the Case of the U.S. v. Wong Kim Ark reaffirmed that first line of Amendment 14 as meaning exactly what it says: Anyone born in the U.S. is a U.S. citizen except (as the court wisely affirmed) the children of diplomats from foreign countries. As far as I can discover, this ruling and the 14th amendment still stand.

Is the law equal to "justice"? I suppose that depends upon your point of view. When a pregnant woman rushes across the national border to give birth to her child in the United States so that it will have U.S. citizenship, some would say that is not justice. On the other hand, consider the person born 21 years ago in the United States of illegal immigrant parents who were knowingly (by government officials) permitted to stay in the country unmolested, to buy a home, to raise a family, to work for U.S. business/agricultural concerns, etc. What if, now, the United States decides to deport the family to Mexico? I would argue that even the parents and the children born in Mexico before the immigration deserve better than deportation. But the person, now adult, having been born in the United States, educated here, working here, has a just *and* legal case for claiming citizenship.

Indeed, the birth-right of citizenship in the country of birth is widespread and ancient. The rule in the United States is a direct descendent of the British common law. The British common law emerges from common law that goes back to the Roman Empire, perhaps, earlier.

Finally, do we really want to deport a U.S. citizen by birth to a country she has never seen, about which she knows almost nothing, and where she would have no way of making a living? That would seem to be the greatest injustice. Where one justice and another justice conflict, we must decide which justice might lead to the greatest harm, which to the greater good—avoid the harm and promote the good.

July 6: We shall See?!

Can I write at a public computer in a public library? That is a question that will now be answered. Yesterday, my number one laptop computer, the one that belongs to the university, crashed. It was 103 degrees in my office and I was reading the dissenting opinions in the 1898 Supreme Court case I discussed yesterday. The computer was running behind me. I think the heat got to it. It said not a word aloud; but, silently, the Windows program stalled and, the screen turned blue with white block lettering. Before I looked around at it, it was posting a note that obviously meant, "Aaargh! I'm choking!" The note said, "STARTING TO DUMP MEMORY." Somehow, I knew I was too late. I was right. I had to pull the electric cord and the battery to turn off the computer. When I started it up again, all I could get was that plain blue screen with white block lettering saying: "NO HARD DRIVE FOUND. REPLACE HARD DRIVE AND TRY AGAIN."

Death must be something like that. We turn blue. We feel like we are choking. We try to tell someone, but no one will listen. We dump memory. We die. But are our souls immortal? In the case of my laptop computer, I doubt it. I think that crashed hard drive was all the soul it had. Are we different, then, from a computer? Is that collection of cells we call a brain just a vehicle for an immortal spirit which lives on after the collection of cells strangles for want of oxygen when the hearts stops beating? Does the immortal soul float up to a comfortable vantage point in the upper south-east corner of our hospital room and watch the fun while our dead bodies get jolted with Code Blue electricity? If the jolting works and the heart beats and the neurons revive, does the soul slide back into the carcass and resume its duties? If we die, does it see a light and move toward it, toward Grandma with her small round glasses who is smiling and waving from the center of the light? Does Grandma still have beautiful white hair and yellow false teeth? Can we have extra rare chuck steak in Heaven? It all seems so complicated that I think I prefer that my immortal soul would just pass away with the rest of me. No problems! At any rate, I am not certain that I *want* to live with myself eternally.

July 7: Self-Centered Human Beings.

In reading Descartes' *Meditations 1-6* yesterday, I came to a new realization of just how self-centered we humans are required to be in our sensory world. Our minds (souls?) constantly receive flawed sensory information in the form of phenomena. These phenomena provide information as to the extensions, colors, sounds, tastes, feel, and smells of things as they are. Of course, we are, otherwise, entirely separated from things as they are. Also, in keeping with Kantian philosophy, we are receiving from the metaphysical world *a priori* data regarding the absolutes (simples) of the cosmos and beyond (if there is such a thing as beyond). Kant would admit, and Descartes would disagree, that we know even less about such simples than we know about material things as they are. In either case, Descartes indicates that, in the initial stage of searching for things with absolute existence, things as they are must always be considered as in doubt (but don't hold Descartes' feet too close to the fire about this lest he wiggle free), and our *a priori* knowledge, though absolute, is limited to a very few matters. In terms of my present topic, our minds have no direct contact with material things as they are and contact with simples is—well—"simple." What can you really know about something that has no parts or extension or temporal progression, something that merely *is*? Added to this, we have the accumulated attic storage of all of our sensual and spiritual data since the moment of our conception—a jumble in attic splendor. From all of this, our minds recreate, unaided from anything outside, the images (notice the relationship of this word to "imagination") which we depend upon 100% in order to respond to our existence in the cosmos.

For instance, last evening I was lying in my hammock and saw birds flying overhead. With brightly colored clouds influenced by the sunset and the smell of new-mown hay coming from the neighboring field and the feel of a soft wind across my perspiring body, the taste of cold beer in my mouth, I was pleased with my environment. Then I thought: "What difference would it make if I had a severe headache? Would my environment be as lovely as it is now? What if my brain, as it often does, momentarily produced a little less of this fluid or that. Would the world be as beautiful as it is now? I realized that not only is the total image of anything I experience false; it becomes a new falsehood with every minor adjustment in my physical or mental context. Yet the entire image is created, not by the world, but by my own mind. If I were accompanied in my yard by a dozen hammocked persons, each would have a different and unique image of the context we are all sharing, each as profoundly false as the other. Each of us would assume that what we were creating for ourselves was the perfect image of the material world. All of us would be wrong. None of us would have any reason to think that the others were not sharing all the details of a single unified image—except for brother #1 who has a neurological problem with his dominant eye which makes him see everything strangely, and I have noticed that, at times, even *he* seems to think that everyone else is seeing things as he does. We are, indeed, each in a world of our own. No wonder I have a constant sense of loneliness! It would be interesting to, actually, meet one or two of these people who I thought that I knew all of my life—meet them, that is, as things as they are.

July 8: Faith and the Existence of God.

Descartes' proof (the first one) of the existence of God is as follows. There is infinite power in the cosmos. That power is self creating. Since I exist, and since I could not possibly have created myself, I must have been created by that infinite power (a being) in the cosmos (a power which contains everything required

177

for my creation). That superior being, because it was self-creating, must have created itself as a perfect being (infinite, omnipotent, omniscient, omnipresent). And, of course, since God is perfect and deceitfulness is a character flaw, this superior being is not a deceiver who would falsely trick me into believing that he exists. I, because I was created below him in the cosmic order, am an inferior copy of that perfect being. That necessary creator being is God.

I am not convinced of the validity of this proof. The inductive leap from the necessity of infinite power in the cosmos to that power being manifested as a benevolent and fully honest God is a broad jump indeed. I am, however, convinced to the point of considering it absolute knowledge, as I have said previously, that there is infinite power in the cosmos. I am convinced by the imaginative cogitations of my mind (i.e., I have faith) that this power is God—a loving and honest God. Why do I have faith that the infinite power of the cosmos is a loving God? I am convinced by what I *imagine* to be a personal relationship between God and me. I will not go into detail as to the relationship because it is, after all, personal and nontransferable. However, I will say that it involves what some would call divine revelation, others (e.g., Socrates) divine madness. In other words, I believe that God, from time to time, has taken personal interest and action in the affairs of my life and my mind. I suspect that he has done so in the lives of many other persons. Some of them make such claims in great detail. Most, I suspect, who make such claims are great liars or are greatly deceived about their relationships with God. Others are probably entirely truthful; they—and I—might be wrong. We might all be the victims of our own active, falsehood-producing, imaginations. Since there is no way that we can verify *a priori* experience (i.e., experience which has no sensory connection, no extension in time or space), we cannot prove that it actually occurs; and, indeed, I congratulate those who reject it. Such persons might be intelligent, coherent, and rational. I will never try to convert another person to belief in God on the basis of my own *a priori* experience combined with servings of logic and sensory experience. Those who want such experience will have to seek their own. Prayer and/or meditation have often been suggested as avenues to such experience. Timothy Leary, a few decades ago, suggested LSD. I reject that suggestion. I suggest a simpler route: initiate the conversation. If there is an infinite, kind, honest God, he can hear what you say or think. It is just possible that he might respond. Such response might be an audible voice or an image on a TV screen, or a burning in your heart, but I suspect that God is, ordinarily, much more subtle than that. It seems obvious to me that, if there is such a God, he remains largely anonymous on purpose. If this were not the case, it would be with great ease that he could become everyone's closest and most intrusive neighbor. I fear that, if this were the case, some of us would begin to lose our fondness for him.

But I digress. Belief in God (not knowledge of God, for that is impossible in our human existence because our *knowledge* is limited to material matters and even the preponderance of that is questionable), must be the result of a personal relationship with God, not a relationship conditioned by a church or a minister or a doctrine or a Bible or a Quran or a Torah or any other material entity. If someone tells you that they know that God exists, you have my permission to consider that person a liar or a person tragically deceived. Even if that person claims direct revelation from God, the person cannot know that it has not come from some other source. If someone tells you that they have a personal relationship with God, thank them for their testimony and tell them that you can gain nothing more than encouragement from their relationship with God. More than that must be gained from the relationship that *you* have established. If you have not established a relationship with God, let me be the first to make such a suggestion. My relationship with God, though it is without doubt at least partially false, is rewarding.

The other day, I suggested to a couple of travelling evangelists who told me they know God personally, that they were either liars or were deceived. That, by the way, was after I told them that their god is a tragic failure if he can save only 144 thousand souls (their claim) out of the billions who have inhabited the earth. I would be considered a terrible teacher if only one in a million students gained valuable insights from my teaching—and I didn't have the advantage of *creating* my students. My God, by the way, is a great success story.

July 9: Falling into Error.
Descartes says that I cannot fall into error if I do not pass judgment regarding things I do not fully understand. Yet, it is important according to his method that I doubt nearly everything, at least, initially. But it is necessary, in order for me to fulfill my human responsibilities, to act upon things which I do not fully understand. Action, positive or negative, would seem to require some sort of judgment. Thus, action is necessary even in the environment of ignorance, and in the long run, error is inevitable since the less complete my understanding is of a particular matter in regard to which I must act, the more likely is the possibility of error. If I act upon something about which I know absolutely nothing, my chance of error would seem to be at least 50% if there were only two possible choices, and there are always more choices than that. If I know something, but not all, about something, then my possibility of error might be less than 50% given the same two possible choices. If I take no action at all, my possibility of accomplishing a desired end is zero unless that desired end occurs without my action (which is a possibility of unknown likelihood). Whether I choose to run the risk of error in a case where the likelihood of error is high depends upon the nature of the consequences of failure. For instance, if I were to expose myself to a disease about which I know that many persons survive the disease but a few die, and the end I sought by exposing myself was of great importance, I might take a chance on error. Indeed, we take such risks daily as a part of ordinary life. On the other hand, if many die from the disease and few survive, I would be less inclined to take the chance unless the potential positive value of my action were high indeed.

Simply put, Descartes' method leaves a lot to be desired in the world wherein we must be constantly making judgments. It is a good method for discovering absolute truth (if, indeed, we limited humans can ever discover any detail of absolute truth—which I seriously doubt to the point of *that* being one of the absolute truths among all the rest which cannot be discovered), but my message to Descartes, who seems to be afraid of decisions nearly as much as he is of church authorities, would be to take pride in his one seemingly absolute grain of understanding (*cogito ergo sum*). In that, he has proven Socrates wrong: "This I know, that I know nothing." Beyond that, neither he nor anyone else, including the empiricists who put so much stock in sensory data, has proven anything definitively. I like Kant's theories in this regard best. He, while recognizing empirical data as questionable in its relationship to things as they are, and *a priori* metaphysical understandings as nonmalleable, recognized these two types of understanding as the essence of both our material and our spiritual existence. Both the noumena of metaphysics and material things as they are behind phenomena are out of our reach. Not a problem! We can live with our flawed understanding as it is. Indeed, it is the understanding which God(?) has given us. And it is such a delight. We have complete freedom (according to Hegel) and adequate capacity of imagination to make of it what we will.

July 10: Worry plus Incomplete Understanding.
One of the most troubling aspects of acting upon incomplete understanding is worry. Worry is much maligned as a waste of valuable thinking time, yet what is worry but the mind's attempt to complete incomplete understanding of some topic which might or might not be soluble by an incomplete being like myself. Only God and a few mathematical facts are complete. Math facts in isolation don't solve problems at all, and God seems to delight in leaving us short on information for solving problems for ourselves. The problem seems to be in discovering when worry can be useful and when it is a waste of time, or worse, a destructive activity.

Simple rules (since I am, at present, reading Descartes who calls for rules of thinking to be simple):

1) Never worry over and over about the same problem unless new data is added. The new data, however, can take various forms. It can be material data (e.g., addition of a new phenomenological ingredient, previously unknown, to the possible solution). But it can, also, be as simple as being a different part of the day. Some of us think better in the morning. Or it could be that we just feel particularly inspired to solve the problem on a particularly glorious day. What item #1 mainly means is that you cannot solve a problem on your own schedule. You must be patient. Sometimes, ironically, the answer occurs to us just after the catastrophe (e.g., the patient dies just before the EMT discovers the chunk of raw liver lodged in the patient's trachea). Outcomes are not always (in fact, are seldom) ideal.

2) Stop worrying about so many things. Concentrate on one problem at a time and leave the rest alone. Perhaps, many problems will solve themselves.

3) If you begin having anxiety attacks, you have worried too much. "Consider the lilies of the field which neither spin nor reap" nor worry. Of course, they die with the first killing frost of the fall. But, Hey! "Ya wanna live forever?!"

4) If all else fails, make your worrying a matter of personal pride. People will laugh at you if you worry too much. Thus, your worry has made people happy if only for a moment. For some of us, that is a greater accomplishment than we should have expected during the entirety of our lives.

July 11: Postscript on Descartes.

I thought it best to save this clinker until we were leaving our discussion of Descartes since he saved it for the last pages of his *Meditations* after misleading us up to that point. Remember all of those material bodies which he insists are necessary to doubt? And I do mean "all" of them. In the end of the *Meditations*, Descartes does a 180 degree about-face and declares how silly it was of him to even consider doubting such obvious stuff. After all, God is no deceiver and would never place all of those objects in our minds so clearly if they did not truly exist; and as to the idea that he (Descartes) might be dreaming, he can, certainly, tell the difference between sleep and wake. He, at that point, revises his doubt of the existence of corporeal things to doubt that our minds see them exactly as they are. But what does that really matter if we have an eternal soul which is helped in arriving at proper conclusions by an infinite, honest, and benevolent God.

Unfortunately, this last *seems* (but only seems) to put Descartes in a league as a philosopher with Mammy Yokum ("Good is better than evil because it's nicer.") Descartes' flabby ending to a solid philosophical work for its day, which a careful reader sees coming much earlier in the text, should not destroy the whole work for you. It should, however, remind you that even the best bananas go soft if left out in the sun too long.

July 12: What my *Soul* did on a hot Day instead of Seeking Truth.
Still Sea-Sentimental after 40 Years
That's Chanty, mates,
When the sea whispers in my ear
And leaves it wet
With the spray of a thousand storm curses
And cold with the malty breath
Of a thousand drowned mariners
Raking my wind-froze cheeks with beard bristles—
Rosing them with lies, laughter—
Lechery washed pure by crystalline crests of purple
Beneath the prows of flying clippers:
That's Chanty, mates;
And I eat it hearty
With salty beans and leathern biscuits.

July 13: The 20ᵗʰ Century.

Today is Friday the 13ᵗʰ. What better day to talk about the 20ᵗʰ century? It was, without doubt, the century during which human achievement was more rapid and profound than at any time since humans rose above the rest of the animal kingdom with the power of rational thinking. Yet there must have been some sort of bad luck operating because it was the most disastrous century of all time as well. Since we have spent so much time exploring philosophy of the past, I think it would be well for us to visit our own time and the time which went just before our present day.

181

The 20th century was, to begin with, disastrous for philosophy, especially, if one were a follower of the British. It was the century in which many British philosophers (followed closely by a vast number of philosophers world-wide) declared philosophy dead, to be used in the future as nothing more than a linguistic handmaiden to scientific disciplines. This declaration followed, first, the 19th century declaration of Nietzsche and others that "*Gott ist tot!*" It took a century for this message to settle in with philosophers who had been studying Descartes and Kant and Hegel with their endless and fruitless search for proof of the existence of God and the immortal human soul and their just as endless and disastrously false declarations of having found such proof. Nietzsche simply stated the obvious. If, indeed, God ever lived, the state of human existence and everything which surrounds it proves beyond doubt that he is now dead. Although hardly anyone likes Nietzsche, and, perhaps, even fewer love him, his declaration had far-reaching and long-lasting impact. First, it linked almost immediately with the Darwinian world of evolution and existence by chance, not design. Next, it was carried on the muscular shoulders of realism out of romanticism into the quagmire of determinism crying "You can't go home again!" to all of humanity. And we didn't. We emigrated from the comfort of Victorian pretence to the savage recognition, first, of the futility of existence and, finally, to its total absurdity.

By then, we had endured two world wars divided by an economic depression which had America's best and brightest flinging themselves from the balconies of sky-scrapers. And then came the atom bomb, child of the beneficent thinking of Einstein, but not a grandbaby he could love. And more wars, first in Korea and then in Vietnam. And scandal and more scandal and . . . loss of faith.

I am not speaking here, in particular, of religious faith. I am speaking of faith in life. By the time we had reached the end of Richard Nixon's presidency, we trusted no one, not even ourselves, certainly not God, although the religious right, with its odd twists on faith in God based largely on a couple or three specific but minor doctrines and its contempt for everyone who was not an evangelical Christian believing exactly as they did, became a major political force forging unholy alliances with fiscal conservatives whose faith lay entirely in money and its entirely material power. Keep in mind the absolute condemnation of the love of money expressed in the New Testament of the Bible and you cannot help wondering at this alliance. But while the fiscal conservatives swore to the social conservatives (evangelicals) that they would back them politically in regard to gay marriage, abortion, and stem cell research, the social conservatives vowed not to notice that obese fiscal camels could not possibly crawl, with or without packs, through the low slender eyes of needles.

And here we are in the 21st century—fearing everything, trusting nothing, watching the world marketplace swallow American dominance, fighting a futile war in Iraq, another hopelessly tangled one in Afghanistan which is spilling more and more into Pakistan where we cannot go without destabilizing that government which is already about as unstable as it can get—watching, with Tao-like passivity, the genocide in Darfur.

And where is philosophy? Many of our philosophers are busy pretending to be happy with merely creating the perfect language for scientific analysis. They have, of course, been struggling with this for most of a century now and three things become obvious:

1) no progress is possible toward such a goal,

2) none of the sciences care about such a goal,

and 3) no one could possibly understand anything that those linguistic philosophers have said during the last 50 years because of the philosophers' complete inability to communicate anything at all with their excessively specialized philosophical language.

So much for linguistic philosophy! Score one for absurdity!

Yet there is hope for philosophy. Even though metaphysics has been declared dead, there are many who experience life as being more than a collection of differentiated cells.

Although the existence of God cannot be proven, nor can the immortality of the human soul be demonstrated, neither can these be disproven. The argument, in other words, is alive. The brighter lights among philosophers have stopped trying to prove the unprovable in order to seek the path to harmonious, just, and useful living of this life—the life that we have—coming full circle in the process back to the most common topics of such early philosophers as Socrates.

Standing above the crowd are the true philosophers of the 21st century, still fools on their hills, wise persons who recognize wisdom and (sometimes) follow it, offering its fruit freely to world citizens quite busy with their own concerns but who pluck and eat ripe and tasty nuggets of it as they happen to pass close by the trees. Global warming might get us, but my guess is that science will find a way to deal with it and the many other problems we face, at least for the 21st century.

And if humanity loses the battle, who will know? Perhaps, God? Perhaps.

July 14: To Us a Child is Born.

Two weeks ago, daughter #2 gave birth to Mayte (pronounced *"my tay"*) Nozomi Borrayo, our eighth and, probably, final grandchild. Mayte is a Spanish name, apparently picked up in Guatemala, the home country of #2's husband. Nozomi is Japanese (honoring Japanese Tutu Yasmin), and means "Hope." I thought that this would be a good day, in light of the darkness of my Friday the 13th entry yesterday, to introduce "Hope" to a troubled world. She is a real beauty. I don't normally say that about newborns. Indeed, I told Yasmin that I didn't want to see the baby until it was two weeks old so that some of the wrinkles would be flattened out.

Hwat! Mayte was a smooth baby from the day of her birth. She reminds me a little of my *Tia Maria la Gloria del Rosario Rodriquez Velasquez Butts* from Seville, Spain. Mayte has the same sort of regal loveliness that Aunt Gloria displayed in her wedding photos a half a century ago. Of course, Gloria was in her twenties and the pictures I saw of Mayte showed her in her first couple of hours of life.

Jesus was referred to as "a child of hope." That is because he, supposedly, was God incarnate so that he could die as a human to save all human souls who would believe that he was God incarnated as a human being so that he could die in order to save all human souls who would believe . . . . Whoa! I have no such hope for Mayte. Perhaps, she will do something to save the world from its own nonsense, but probably not. More likely, she will take what we as a family and a society can give her and carry it a bit further for the next generation.

I have come to expect that of the next generation of our family because I have come to think of our family as on the rise. My great-grandparents were all (as far as I know) pioneers of sorts, probably more like fugitives running from poverty to anywhere that they could find hope for a better life. That was shortly after the American Civil War. In the case of my father's family, some of them from America's South, were trying to get started again outside the South after the Civil War. My mother's ancestors were (at least in part) Acadians from Nova Scotia who had been exiled, first from France, then from Nova Scotia toward New Orleans. But my ancestors never arrived there. Instead, they got off the boat somewhere in the region of the convergence of the Ohio and Mississippi Rivers and headed west on foot, learning English as they traveled. My mother's parents, talented and industrious but unlucky, ended up in Montana during the height of the great depression and the dust bowl and, again, were exiled, this time toward Idaho where my grandfather, an excellent mechanic but nearly blind, served out most of his remaining years as a school janitor before chronic emphysema forced his retirement. My father's parents, several years earlier left a farm which could not make them a living in Soda Springs, Idaho, and ended up in Hagerman, Idaho, where my grandfather managed with only a high school education to become an Idaho state senator and the unremunerated pastor of a church while making a bare living raising watermelons and other fruits on a rocky cliff-side farm.

Their children, my father and mother and a tenth of a hundred others, rode out the depression in various trades, and emerged mostly as poor farmers and construction workers.

This is where I sense the beginning of the rise of my family. Suddenly, the children of my grandparents' children caught a break. Many of us went to college. I can count at least three doctorates and a number of other advanced degrees, probably the first college degrees ever in either family. Others became successful in business, military, and the trades. It must have been some kind of whiplash impact from the depression that sent us toward success. I can't explain it any other way. We are an economically and intellectually successful generation. And the next generation is following suit. Daughter #2, for instance, is working toward being the first member of the family with both PhD and MD degrees. The family has, also, diversified, as I have said elsewhere. What was an all-northern-European family with a pleasant little infusion of Native American, suddenly became a family representing every race and a large variety of cultures. Indeed, my own little three-generation branch of the family represents all of these. We could benefit from translation services around the dinner table.

Mayte is, probably, the last member of that new generation which represents our new "great hope." I am far too prejudiced to be objective about it, but I am convinced that every one of the eight is beautiful, talented, wise, just, and brilliant. Indeed, for them, this book is being written.

July 15: Another Kind of War.

There is a kind of war which does not come under the prohibition of war in terms of Kant's categorical imperative (make no rule which should not be applied universally for all persons in all circumstances). I experienced a volley in that war about 4 a.m. today. It came in the form of the smell of skunk wafting through my bedroom, strong enough that it tainted my dreams and then woke me from a sound sleep in a state of psychological disarray.

A skunk's smell is obviously intended by nature to be a weapon of self-defense. The skunk, whenever it feels itself to be in danger, emits a cloud of stink so powerful that bird nor beast nor human will remain in the vicinity. Other than this, the skunk has little with which to defend itself and less to employ offensively.

However, today at 4 a.m., a skunk turned its defensive weapon into an offensive weapon wafting across my bedroom and entering my sleep. It became a psychological weapon which shook my very being. I love my summer campground. But, in a moment, I considered abandoning it entirely; then, realizing that I would be leaving tomorrow for two weeks in Missouri with Yasmin and all the kids, I was both relieved and frustrated—relieved because I would not have to worry about the skunk for a couple of weeks, frustrated because I wouldn't be here to prevent the possible attempt of the skunk to move into permanent quarters under my granary remodeled as an office.

I am sure the skunk had no intention of going to war with me. Perhaps, it was warning off a coyote which had wandered too close. Or, more likely, the emission was the result of the skunk being smashed by a car on the highway a half mile away. Skunk smell travels a long way. But, unknowingly, it took the offensive at that moment in a war between rational humanity and the nonrational animal kingdom. And it won the opening salvo. It turned me into a weakling. I found that I have no weapons to combat it. The crawlspace under my office is large enough to provide comfortable housing for a skunk and its immediate family while it is far to narrow for my body. If I should try to poison it, I would, undoubtedly, poison my favorite cat in the process. To take any violent means against it would lead to a second salvo of stink-artillery which would not clear the area for weeks. If I tried to ignore it, I couldn't because skunks carry that smell in modest but unpleasant quantities wherever they live. One cannot live harboring a skunk under the porch for long. At the moment, it is a cold war. No one is setting off atomic bombs or even IEDs. But what makes a cold war horrid is the fear that at any moment, it can turn into a shooting war, one which no one can win. In nature, the skunk's smell is not nice, but it is only a threat to would-be predators. It is, indeed, the evolutionary factor which has made those pretty striped kitties competitive for space on the planet. When nature conflicts with reason (with humanity), everything goes out of balance. I build a perfect skunk den and declare that no skunk may live there. If skunks come near, I am tempted to go skunk hunting to remove the threat. If I lose the battle, the final standoff can be ugly. My sister still remembers the humiliation caused to her (at 12 years old, I think) by the skunk which moved in under our outdoor privy, just two-hundred yards from my present office. We, her brothers, gave her hell when she smelled like skunk after using the privy. She has not liked Idaho much since then.

July 16: On the Road.

It was a long 18 hours from Twin Falls to Denver—1:00 p.m. to 7 a.m. I have found that I'm not as young and flexible as I used to be, but I have proven that

I can still take it on the chin (perhaps, more to the point, on the butt upon which I have been sitting for 18 hours) and come back smiling.

Greyhound used to be the luxury line of highway transportation. It has, now, gone through "the worst of times" and seems to be trying to make a come-back. This is not easy when the whole world has changed and Greyhound buses are the same as they always were. People have grown accustomed to beginning their descent into the destination city within a couple of hours after take-off. On the bus, you go on and on and on—with no cabin attendants, no drink and peanut service, no in-flight movies, just chatter, often obnoxious, from people you don't know but whom you know far better than you ever wanted to by the end of a few hours.

It is an experiment in human relations, riding the bus. An example: in Ogden, we picked up about 20 passengers—Standing Room Only! This isn't supposed to happen, but suddenly Greyhound was not prepared for a rush of passengers and had no spare bus or driver to deliver them to Salt Lake. Therefore, "All aboard!" A 90-year-old lady, fragile, timid, sophisticated, was among them. I was near the rear in a window seat. She walked gingerly all the way to the back looking side to side while a score of young bucks wriggled nervously in their seats and pretended not to see her. It came my turn. I rose.

"Here, take my seat."

"No, I couldn't do that," she replied with Victorian coyness.

"You must," I declared. "I will sit here no longer. If you stand, I'll stand beside you."

"Well—alright; thank-you," and she accepted my seat.

It was something of a comedy of manners staged more than a century after Oscar Wilde was dead and gone. Of course, as soon as the play was over and I, an old geezer with baggy eyes and pants to match, was standing in the aisle, half a dozen youngsters became obsessed with offering me their seats. I refused with aplomb. Actually, I had an aching shoulder from carrying my computer around Lowe's home improvement store in Twin Falls while I waited for my delinquent bus to arrive, so it was a relief to stand up and stretch my muscles—less than an hour of standing between Ogden and Salt Lake, and it is good to appear to be self-sacrificing in Mormon country.

Just time enough for me to watch the final unfolding of another drama. Two young men had an abundance of some sort of illicit drug and were making regular trips to the bus toilet to imbibe. Both had, also, been taking opportunities at rest stops to buy and consume alcoholic beverages. They were totally snockered by Ogden. One of them sat in a near-catatonic state mumbling. The other talked loudly on a borrowed cell phone, first to his wife begging her to take him back and swearing that he had always been faithful to her—then to his physician's office, describing just as loudly the symptoms of his sexually transmitted disease. All of this, he did with an arm slung around the shoulders of a young blonde woman he had met on the bus. I have no clue about her, and I'm sure she had none about herself. I think her name was Mary.

I'm becoming convinced that riding the bus could be fodder for stories—who would believe?! But it would take a lot of riding to move from fiction to philosophy. It would be worth the study for philosophical purposes, lots of ethics and politics involved with the human interactions here, but one emerges with a skewed vision. The worst of bottom-feeders speak their minds loudly and obnoxiously while the modest number of the intellectually gifted, the honorable, the just, remain cautiously incognito. Such research would need to be guarded carefully against bias.

July 17: Denver to Kansas City.

The Denver to Kansas City bus departed an hour late, so Yasmin will be waiting for quite some time at the depot in K.C. I'd call her, but I don't have a cell phone, and I'd rather eat rat droppings and brush my teeth with lye than ask to borrow someone's cell phone. (Footnote: Some nice Alabamans later offered me their cell phone without my asking, so I tried to call Yasmin. She was out and has no voice mail on her phone, so it was a wasted effort.)

It's quiet on this bus. I got near the head of the line hoping for a seat to myself so I could rest my painful shoulder strain in a larger space, but a family of Alabaman catfish farmers (they smelled fine and were quite refined as Greyhound patrons go), father, mother, and teenage daughter, surrounded me—nice people, quite talkative.

My shoulder aches like Hell!

I discovered a wee psychological ploy on this trip. If I want to change the tenor of the conversation, all I have to do is let it slip that I am (or was) a college English professor. I've done it three times and it has worked each time. The only problem is that it cannot be predicted what change will occur in the conversation. With the drunks, I was suddenly left out of the society. With the teenaged boy going to Norfolk, Virginia, to explore joining the navy after high school next year, he first sought out my advice and counsel about such enlistment. I told him that since he is afraid of water and can't swim and because he hates taking orders, he might want to consider other occupations. After that, he bent my ear for hours about the high intellectual levels of his plans as soon as he manages to overcome his five-credit deficit in high school where he had nearly flunked out the previous year, a deficit he intends to make up this year by attending night school as well as day school even though he has a reading disability and has a terrible time with math. I was delighted when he drifted off to sleep in mid-sentence and left me writhing in the pain of my shoulder.

A note on our stop in Salina, Kansas. We got a new driver there. The previous driver stopped at a fast-food restaurant and informed us that we had 30 minutes to eat lunch and that the bus would be gone for most of that time. Everyone would have to get off. He would leave and pick up the next driver at his home and that driver would return with the bus. Twenty minutes later, a restaurant employee shouted out that the bus would be leaving immediately. We made a mad dash for the door. I was in the bathroom with my pants down, so it took me a moment to get reassembled and back to the bus. By the time I got on the bus, our new driver was counting heads. When he returned to the front of the bus, he turned to the rest of us and said calmly into his microphone, "Ten people are still missing but the bus will go faster without them."

He strapped himself into the driver's seat and started out of the parking lot as the unfortunate ten were streaming out of the doors of the restaurant toward the bus dragging their children and infants behind them, screaming for the driver to

187

wait. He didn't. He kept driving until he reached the end of the parking lot with the crowd weeping and shouting behind him. Then he turned around and drove past them, laughing gleefully, heading for the exit to the street. At the street, he stopped, opened the door, let the sweating passengers (it was near 100 degrees in Salina) catch up and board. When they were all aboard, he announced on the P.A. system, "That will teach you that when I say the bus is leaving, it is leaving."

Then he headed down the road. At the next meal stop, he issued the warning that, if passengers were not in their seats at the exact minute prescribed, he would leave them behind. At that stop, the passengers were in their seats ahead of time. The bus driver was ten minutes late in arriving. Methinks I detect a Hitler wannabe.

The Alabama family, upon learning of my occupation: the father went immediately to sleep. Mother and daughter talked endlessly to each other about shopping. I got out my steno pad to pen this entry. I will now writhe in pain and try to sleep. Last night I advised a fellow traveler who was having trouble sleeping to "not try to sleep"—rather to think about other things. It worked. She went to sleep almost instantly. I wanted to kill her. I had a terrible time sleeping. Thus, when I see Yasmin tonight, I will be quite groggy.

July 18: Arrival at the Manger.

For Jesus, it was a bunch of shepherds and three kings (Zoroastrian wise men?) I'm not sure how wise the wise men were—smart enough to avoid excessive contact with Herod. The shepherds are ironic figures. They are just what a newly delivered mother stuck in a livery stable needs, a passel of unwashed strangers from the hills stopping in for a visit. I'm sure she was thrilled! Mary was having her taste of "the bad life." She had just got off a donkey in labor (Mary, not the donkey) in a town where there was no place to stay but a stable. The town was crowded since it was tax time in Bethlehem, and everyone who owed paternity to Bethlehem also owed taxes and had to go there (no online submissions, please) to pay them. They were lucky to have a piece of manger. It could have been much worse. The manure pile was, probably, only a few feet away. Its decaying manure would have been warm, but not exactly the place for the newborn king-of-kings. Somehow, Joseph was able to round up some swaddling clothes. Maybe they had brought them along on the journey, just in case. Messy! The whole episode, if you think about it too much.

But Mayte Nozomi Borrayo was born in a hospital, an excellent one. Her mother, daughter #2, has full health insurance and a guarantee of a room, bed, a delivery room, a qualified physician, attendants, even a pair of tan cloth slippers with no-slip bottoms. Two days later, a quick trip via automobile to her air-conditioned home and loving family with Guatemalans enough to get past most any crisis. But then, Mayte didn't have to impress anyone with her poverty. Nor her wealth! She was lucky to be born an unknown in the great American middle class without the albatross of divinity about her neck. She is absolutely beautiful and shows undeniable signs of being an eventual Nobel laureate. For now, however, she is at peace. She has learned a lot. I noticed yesterday that she had discovered the connection between defecation and eating. Each time she crapped her diaper and was changed, she went immediately for #2's left breast. Smart kid! Both for

188

choosing a family of lesser note and for making that important physiological connection so early in life. May she go on in life always finding a clean, comfortable place to relieve herself, and the equivalent of a well-stocked breast! With those things and someone's loving arm around her, she can put up with almost anything, even smelly shepherds looking for an excuse to get in out of the cold and well-intentioned but quite lost (they were lucky they didn't stumble into the Black Sea following that low-hanging star by night) wise men.

July 19: They *Like* Me! They Still *Like* Me!

I just talked to my friend, the administrative assistant to the university provost. He (the provost) is a friend of mine, too, from my point of view, but it seems presumptuous of me to refer to him as such. She, the administrative assistant, says that they will not kick me out of my office this year and that they will look for a replacement for the computer that crashed a couple of weeks ago in Idaho. Why should I be so fortunate in my old age being revered as a retired professor to the extent that they will put up with me even in my uselessness? I must work on doing more to make myself worth keeping. I think that the most important thing in life is to feel that I am worth more alive than dead. That means, in essence, that I have to be more valuable than that manure pile that Jesus didn't have to be born on because he arrived in Bethlehem just before the manger would have been taken. It's probably a matter of luck, but I like to think that there was divine providence working.

July 20: Family Ecology.

I will nab this opportunity while I am in the midst of the family in the middle of summer with none of them deployed in schools, etc., to explore the impact of that mythological encounter between Yasmin and me forty years (and counting) ago. It was wonderful, as such encounters tend to be—"Some Enchanted Evening," etc., etc., etc. It was my sister's house. I had been released from the U.S. Navy in July, went to New York City to seek my fortune, didn't find it, and six months later drove, pushed, pulled, kicked my ill-starred Austin Healey Sprite from New York City to Kansas City where I rolled into my sister's family driveway on the morning of Christmas Eve. I slept that night on a comfortable guest bed in her basement and, next morning, I emerged much rested. "But what to my wondering eyes did appear"—not Santa and his tiny reindeer, but Yasmin dressed in a bright red jumper, fixing breakfast in my sister's kitchen, a vision lovelier than I could have possibly imagined. She was single and available. I was single and available. I sang "Blue Hawaii" accompanied on my old Sears guitar. She fell for the ploy. Zap! "Love, Never Ending!" 40 years of happiness, near poverty, children, grandchildren.

That's my story, but what of the outcomes. To what harm or good has this led in a troubled world? I herewith summarize.

From us two came three: daughters, each beautiful, talented, spiritually rich, wise (within reason). I am not sorry that we, being only two, brought three into the world, thus crowding it by one. The positives of these three in regard to the well-being of the world far outweigh the negatives.

#1 is a teacher. So much a teacher that she can never conceal her excitement at every new teaching dragon she slays. She is, probably, the most positive person I have ever met. Of course, she is a lousy housekeeper, but what is new about that? When she lived with us, we had to keep her bedroom door closed to keep her stuff from tumbling into the rest of the house Fibber-McGee's-closet style. She has a husband and three children.

Her husband is a pleasant and industrious fellow. Loves his family. Loves his dog. Loves going to the country to pick mushrooms and mowing lawns.

It is little wonder, I think, that their oldest son (grandchild #2) is known as "Nature Boy." Grandson #1 tagged him with that name when he (#1) tagged himself "Computer Boy" a couple of years ago. #2 is outdoors most of the time. He is much more comfortable with a snake wrapped around his arm than with a pencil in his hand.

Their second child (granddaughter #1; grandchild #3) reminds me of "the disciple that Jesus loved." At the last supper, he is pictured with his head resting upon Jesus' shoulder. She, as Poe puts it, loves "with a love that is more than love." It is the center of her existence, and it is catching.

Their second daughter and third child (Grandchild #6) has learned her place in the world from her father and older brother. She is an independent soul who hears what she wants to hear and does what she wants to do, but I trust her to do, largely, what is right even at six years old. And who could resist loving the girl behind that beautiful smile.

Three wonderful children!

#2 daughter is, also, a teacher, but of a different ilk. She got her first doctorate, a PhD, from Berkeley as a research scientist. She is now working on her second (an MD) from University of Kansas after spending time on the research faculty of that medical school. Her final act before moving from faculty to student was to garner a grant which will financially support her replacement on the research faculty while she is in medical school. The school likes that. She, also, teaches preparatory classes for students-at-risk who have been accepted into the medical school. Some of her classmates find it interesting that she is both teacher and student in the medical school.

Her husband is a delightful Guatemalan whom she met while she completed a year-long social mission there after Berkeley. During that year of counseling indigenous Guatemalans attempting to work their way into society after the revolution, she mastered Spanish, met her husband and married him. He's a fine mechanic. I haven't lost a daughter; I've gained free oil changes.

Now they have three, children that is, the older two, boys, the youngest a girl.

The oldest (grandchild #5) seems to be all intellect and serious thought. He smiles at me, and loves deeply, but his first challenge in life is, obviously, to learn everything. I wonder which mother he got that from.

The second (grandchild #7) is a dilemma for his mother. For his Tutu Yasmin, who cares for him every weekday, and for me he is a perfect loving little gentleman. For his Mama, he is something of a wild child. Yasmin and I just enjoy the fact that we get the best side of him. He is bound to be a winner.

The youngest (granddaughter #3, Grandchild #8) is a beautiful princess. She was born a couple of weeks ago and is the reason I am visiting Kansas City in the middle of the growing season in Idaho. She talked to me on the phone when she was only a few days old. I swear she did. I spoke to her. She babbled back and waited. I spoke again. She babbled again. And again and again. Ridiculous, you say?! Not to a doting grandfather. She is an absolute genius bound for glorious social leadership. Probably, not the first female President of the United States. Maybe the third or fourth. She is Mayte!

Daughter #3, our songbird, spent a great part of her preschool years traveling with us as a family singing group. She was the lead child soloist. She was a hit at churches across the Midwest. She still sings but mostly in the shower. She is, also, the least socially assuming of the three. She didn't want to go to college. She attended classes for two days, I think. Instead, she has become one of the most successful credit card collectors on earth. They had to promote her out of the general collectors' ranks because she was winning all of their incentives and ruining the purpose of incentives for all the other collectors. I am very proud of her, not just for that, but because she is one of the finest, most interesting persons I know.

Her husband, the quiet one in our family, puts up with her heroically. I'm proud of him, too. After dropping out of college on the same second day as #3, he has come back now to being within a term or two of finishing a bachelor's degree, all this while working a full-time job. I did that, too. I know how hard it can be.

They have two fine sons.

The first (grandchild #1) spent his first year living with us along with his mother. I witnessed his birth because I happened to be the only family around at that moment. I remember the raucous trip to the hospital when we were not entirely sure that she was in labor, but he was born within about an hour, curly-haired and beautiful. I was the first member of the family to hold him (other than his mother), and the bond is still secure. He mows our lawn and takes good care of his Tutu Yasmin when I am out of town. He is truly a gem. He displays his genetic heritage proudly with his tall afro, his high caramel coloring, his ambiguously hewed eyes. He is, at the same time, the gentlest of gentlemen and the fiercest of competitors. He is a winner.

The younger (#4) is a real treat. He loves hard, plays hard, works hard, studies hard. And he is in trouble much of the time because he does everything hard. But a sweeter, kinder, gentler, more wonderful child you could never find on this earth. And beautiful.

This is the tribe. Three daughters, eight grandchildren. Eleven souls we've added to the earth. (Of course, we won't underrate the participation of the sons-in-law and the other grandparents.) We have not caused a burden upon the world with these offspring. They have made the earth lighter by buoying it up with their laughter, their kindness, their honor, their young and burgeoning wisdom. I am proud to say that if Yasmin and I were to die tomorrow, we will have left the cosmos in better condition than we found it. Will that get us into Heaven, God?

July 21: My Own Personal Vanity.

How could I say that with a straight face? Well, I didn't! But in case you thought I was serious about leaving the cosmos in better condition than we found it, please realize that I was making an ironical statement. Just as we, as finite humans can neither create nor destroy matter, we can neither add nor detract from the ultimate condition of the cosmos. For a moment, it might appear that we have done something that improved some small aspect of the cosmos for the blink of an eye, but it will not last. It is like wiping condensation from a cold window. It is not a permanent condition. Nothing we can do is permanent. That is the nature of our finite existence. We are formed out of the substance of the world. We hold that substance together in the form of a creature for as long as we can. Then it returns to the world. If you want me later, look to the earth. I will be there somewhere in some form. At least, my body will be there. As to my spirit, there is question as to whether it even exists apart from the cells of my body. Indeed, it is one of those things (not a thing at all but an imagined noumenon, not represented by phenomena) which might be impossible since there is no sensual evidence or defensible *a priori* evidence for its existence. Thus, as far as I know, all matter which makes up what I am could, upon thorough investigation, be found scattered upon, above, or under the surface of the earth after I am dead and rotted away.

Yet I continue to believe in my significance? Why? Is it, merely, a defense mechanism, a form of denial attached to rational thinking; or is there, indeed, something infinite about me which I will only discover beyond death? The former seems to be reality. The latter, romance. Yet, I choose the latter though such a romantic scenario seems to promise infinite pain along with whatever pleasures may be attached to eternal life.

And what might I improve with my life on earth? The earth itself and the lives of its inhabitants. Even though the earth is a finite thing which will someday be no more, I can make it a better place for those who live on it while I live and for those who live a little longer. For what more could I strive? And it would be a fine bonus should some stranger living a hundred years hence open this book and gain an hour's happiness from what is printed on its crumbling yellowed pages.

July 22: A Stranger in the Mirror.
Each morning I meet a stranger in my mirror.
I do not want to look there
Because I am a hermit
And prefer to recognize myself from yesterday
And the day before and the day before.

I hide my contempt and smile at the stranger in the mirror
Knowing that he will not know
What to do with this new day,
Just as I would not have known,
Had I been allowed a second day.

But I am gone;
Naught but a memory which will fade with another day or two
Or three;
And I will not be back.
I am like my Great-Great-Grandfather Isaac,

Not the Isaac (Yitzhaq) who would have been roasted by his father
If not for a convenient Goat;
Just a black-and-white photo
From a charred album saved from the fire
That burned my mother and her mother
And all mothers
Who thought they were infinite.

I look away.
It is time for breakfast.
Even a newborn knows that.

July 23: Fifth Wheels.

A "fifth wheel" in this discussion is a politician who doesn't fit the mold of any particular political party or group. It is clear from the moment these individuals enter political races that they will not win. This might seem appropriate because what we are trying to achieve in electing representatives in a democracy is consensus. Consensus, on the other hand, is often synonymous with compromise which can be good in some cases and bad in others. If compromise manages to get a gridlocked congress out of gridlock and back on a productive course, that is good even if the compromise doesn't please everyone, as long as it does not work in severe opposition to anything which should be placed under the umbrella of the categorical imperative.

But let us reconsider the fifth wheel. Consider the fact that nearly any intellectual will be categorized as a fifth wheel because that person will not affirm common beliefs with a particular party or group. In demonstration, notice that whenever a group of intellectuals gathers for conversation, they seem to delight in disagreeing. It seems to be their credo that wherever there is a crack in an ideology, that crack must be exposed and patched; and all ideologies have cracks. Consider, for instance, Wittgenstein who maintained that every supposed philosophical statement is nonsense. Now, it would seem that such a perfectionist would be just the person to represent us. After all, do we not want to fix the imperfections of our political system? But consider what would happen in the U.S. House of Representatives, for instance, if 435 intellectuals were elected to serve there. This would result in incredible gridlock, 435 competing doctrines on every issue, each defended deftly by one representative and condemned as deftly by each of the other 434. Perhaps, we are right in rejecting them early in the process. Perhaps, they should be limited to roles as advisors to the less intellectual but more politically adept politicians.

Fifth wheels who have not been eliminated quickly have presented themselves over the years. At times, they have, actually, been elected. It is possible, for instance, to place Thomas Jefferson in such a role—and Abraham Lincoln and John Kennedy. These three, however, seemed to be more than fifth wheels. They were capable of negotiation when pressed for it by necessity. We must consider, also, that two of the three were assassinated before they finished their tenures.

One or two degrees more on the turn of the wheel would have eliminated them before election. Hubert Humphrey was an intellectual, but most people didn't notice that very much. What they noticed was that he was a funny looking little fellow; and that, when added to a fine mind, is enough to have him counted out of the race. Dennis Kucinich, also, has the appearance problem along with his fifth-wheel characteristics. He espouses odd political positions, but they make a lot of sense when he explains them. However, because he is such an odd looker, he seldom gets a hearing for them. I have listened to them and they seem to me to represent the careful thinking of a true intellectual. That is unfortunate because it means that he will not be president: intellectual + funny looking = unelectable. Remember how handsome and suave John Kennedy was?! Marilyn Monroe was especially taken with him. His good looks and sex appeal got him a pass on his intellect. Al Gore has fallen into the fifth-wheel trap by exposing himself (after he very nearly made it to the White House in an earlier campaign) as an eco-intellectual at the same time he had gained 50 pounds. Deadly combination for a political aspirant! Fifth wheel + fat = retirement from politics.

What does this mean to the current Presidential race in America? It means that neither Ron Paul nor Dennis Kucinich need spend any further money on the campaign and Al Gore should continue working on ecology. Paul and Kucinich would be well-advised to return to the business of their House seats where they were lucky enough to have the support of their home districts. Home districts sometime elect fifth wheels because such individuals often support cherished ideas of those home districts. Such persons should, also, be honored to be in the company of such intellectuals as Socrates who, as you might remember, was required by law to develop a taste for hemlock because he was a fifth wheel.

July 24: Mormon Pioneer Day.

Now, here is a religious(?) celebration I really know about. I grew up in Mormon country (Southern Idaho) second only to the Mormon country south of the border (Utah). And, in Hagerman, we had the biggest Pioneer Day celebration in the region. It lasted two full days (July 24-25) plus a few hours of early start if the carneys got the rides set up on the 23rd. We saved our money for months ahead of time. This was when I was a teenager (and even younger) and employment was limited for kids. So we couldn't save a lot. I, usually, managed to garner 10-15 bucks which didn't go far against the slick carneys who could separate you from your money almost instantly. We steered clear of the booths that promised big rewards. We knew what that amounted to. All the bowling pins you were supposed to knock over with a softball were locked solid to the shelf (probably with magnets) except when one of the carneys (posing as a customer) came by to show everyone how easy it was. This fellow would toss the ball softly in the general direction of the pins, all the pins would fall to the ground and the carney running the booth would present him with a prize of the biggest stuffed animal with which he would instantly and joyously depart returning later to the back of the booth to exchange it for a small gratuity.

The official opening was on the morning of the 24th (unless the 24th was on a Sunday—I can't remember what we did about that) with the parade. This was a real parade with literally hundreds of horses and floats of all descriptions. Of course, even then, all the politicians were out in force. (I have yet to understand what function politicians waving from shiny new cars have in a parade. But there they were, and there they still are. In fact, in the parades that now go through Parkville, Missouri, the politicians are, by far, the largest contingent.) The Hagerman parade floats didn't have to toss out any candy to lure kids to watch. The parade was enough all by itself. It was fantastic. What I liked best were the horses, the cowboys, and the cowgirls. I always wanted to ride in the parade, but I knew I would be a laughing stock riding old Bessie, my retired workhorse, pot-bellied and swaybacked, and the slick little sorrel, Babe, would buck me off and run away. So I stayed on the sidelines.

The carnival (rides and test-of-skill booths) and all of the food booths were open for two days. We all rode the Ferris wheel and whatever new and thrilling rides the carnival had invented since the year before. We didn't waste our money on most of the old rides. And we always bought a few food and drink treats; but, since we were close to home, we found it economically reasonable to bring our lunches in a bag. Lunch was pretty hot since the July 24 temperatures usually reach over 100 degrees in the Southern Idaho desert. Lettuce and mayo were a bad idea.

What we were all anxious for was the two-day rodeo featuring, along with local cowboys and events like calf-riding for the kids, professional rodeo cowboys from across the country. Southern Idaho, being big cowboy country, provided some of these professionals, so we sometimes got to root for the winner as a homegrown star.

Calf roping, calf riding, steer wrestling, bareback riding, saddle broncs, wild cow milking, cow cutting, and, finally, the big event, bull riding. We lined up to pay our money two days in a row, and it would have been a bargain at twice the price. I, honestly, have not witnessed as good a rodeo as these were anywhere anytime in the world. And I have seen a lot of rodeos. Of course, part of the allure was that I knew some of the cowboys personally. One of the best, for instance, was my church youth leader. He managed to break so many bones that he had to retire in his mid twenties; but, up to then, he seemed to be on his way to national ranking.

The rodeo was the biggest event, but the most famous event was the rodeo queen's dance on the second night. Everyone in Gooding County attended. It was in the Legion Hall which could not hold more than a tithe of the attenders at once, so the celebration spilled constantly out onto Main Street (U.S. Highway 30). Added to the drinking inside the Legion Hall during the dance was ten times as much drinking in the streets. Our city marshal ("blind in one eye and can't see out of the other"—his own words) was incapable of even beginning to control the crowds, so the county and state police were always called in to help. Even then, little could be done. Before the night was over, every telephone pole on Main Street had one or two drunks handcuffed to it to dry out. Not much jail space in Hagerman either.

At any rate, some years after I left Hagerman to join the Navy, the Mormons got together and said enough is enough and cancelled the whole shebang. As I said earlier, it has been replaced by a sorry little mostly-Mormon celebration on somebody's ranch. I've heard that it is a waste of time to attend it.

Oddly, Hagerman's 60-hour party was the ultimate outcome of what the Mormons considered a holy day. They were celebrating the day when, leading

195

thousands of Mormons from the Midwest to Utah in July 1847, Brigham Young looked down on the Great Salt Lake Valley and said: "This is the place!" If you've seen the Great Salt Lake Valley recently, you will realize that Brother Brigham was right in his assessment. It is, truly, a brilliantly developed piece of real estate. What God or divine providence had to do with it is a question which will, probably, never be answered. Most people, unless they are Mormons, would say, "Nothing whatsoever!" Conservative Evangelicals might even say that it is the work of the devil. I'm neutral on the issue. I've never been much impressed with big cities built into pristine mountain valleys. I like nature in its natural state. But I appreciate the effort it took to do all of that (supposed) up-hill irrigation. Any idiot knows the seagulls-eating-the-locusts story is bogus because every time the locusts happen to come through the Great Salt Lake Valley, the seagulls are not far behind. That's just the food chain working at its best. Maybe, that's the nature of divine providence. By the way, if you are hungry enough, seagulls make a reasonably good lunch. I felt like having a seagull lunch a couple of months ago when a flock of seagulls tried to steal my stringer of perch at Magic Reservoir. But divine providence came through for the gulls. I didn't have a shotgun with me.

July 25: Humane Benchmarks.

Most often we are complaining about our humanity. And we deserve our own self-criticism. However, on the way to the office this morning, I had the thought, largely because I watched the YouTube/CNN Democratic Presidential Campaign Debate a couple of days ago, that we have, in the United States, managed to surmount some important benchmarks of human progress. Mainly, these have to do with our toleration of diversity.

The ones that came to mind because of the debate (if it could be called such) are threefold:

1) We are in a position, because of the recent self-destruction of the Republican establishment, to elect not just a Democrat, but a female Democrat, and not just a female, but a particularly controversial one. Hillary Clinton now leads the pack, not just of Democrats but of all declared and undeclared candidates. And her lead is not small.

2) Behind Hillary is the first African American candidate for President, Barack Obama, to show signs that he might actually achieve the dream of becoming the first African American President. The word on the street is that, if he doesn't get it this time, he will get it in eight years (if he doesn't self-destruct along the way, and if Hillary doesn't somehow cause the self-destruction of the Democrat establishment).

3) More distant in the poles, but in contention is a Latino candidate, Bill Richardson, one the first of his culture to make it so far. It is not likely that he will make it, but he has a foot in the door for Vice President in 2009 or the future. It is obvious that few Americans are holding his ethnicity against him.

These are three benchmarks met: gender, race, and ethnicity. It has taken us a century and a half to go from slavery to the possibility of a black American President. It has taken just as long for us to go from women as property ("controlled by their fathers until they are wives, then slaves to their husbands the rest of their lives") to a woman as the leading Presidential contender. These benchmarks go much further. A large percentage of our American medical doctors are now Indians (from India). Many of our most noted scientists and musicians are Asiatic. Major media network anchors are female and/or of various minorities. Our popular novelists are just as likely to be women as men, and we seldom ask about their race or ethnicity.

Speaking of minorities, every Democratic candidate supports domestic partnerships with full marital rights for homosexual couples. Some of them even support homosexual marriage.

This list could go on and on. We have made some human progress; and I am proud to say, as a philosopher, that many of these benchmarks have been set up as challenges throughout history by philosophers.

Unfortunately, religion has not been so progressive. Religions still must be whipped into shape. The Catholics had to be sued multiply before they could be convinced to penalize their priests who sodomized small children. Jimmy Carter had to become President of the United States before he became aware that his church congregation discriminated against African Americans. And what will it take to convince Islam that suicide bombing is not condoned by Allah? And when will the Jews recognize that peaceful coexistence with Islam can come only with human love (including the ceding of a significant and fair amount of land to Palestine and the full sharing of Jerusalem and its vicinity with the Palestinians), not inhumane hatred. The same goes for those Christians among us in the United States who believe that we can shoot our way to democracy in Iraq. Even I, one who does not take the Bible as literal truth, can see the marvelous wisdom of the teaching of "the Prince of Peace." Why can't the Christian fundamentalist see it, too?

But I have returned to the negative. Let this be a day to end on a positive note. If Hillary or Barrack or Bill doesn't win the presidency, they will have, at least, proven that such persons have a chance to do so with our new attitudes about diversity. May the next hundred and fifty years bring additional progress. Perhaps, we can even establish the most important tenet under the categorical imperative: **There must be no war!**

July 26: Death.

Siebert and Sam are sitting on a bench in the nature preserve in Parkville.
Siebert: It's a fine thing to have you back in Parkville for a while, Sam. I missed you.
Sam: And I you. You are a far better conversationalist than a cow.
Siebert: Indeed! You didn't say much after you heard about Emily Wagner dying in Iraq. Why not?
Sam: What's to be said? She is dead. Her family is in mourning. The President continues to provide unconvincing justifications for the war.

Siebert: I'm thinking on a more intimate level. I have a hard time looking her folks in the eye when I pass them. There is just something about the death of a child that spooks me.

Sam: But Emily was not a child. She was a soldier.

Siebert: I never saw her as a soldier. Just as a child.

Sam: That means that you're getting old. Did you think of yourself as a child when you were 19?

Siebert: No.

Sam: And you weren't. And neither was Emily. In some ways, 19-year-olds are more adult that we are.

Siebert: How's that?

Sam: As we get older, we tend to lose our grip on reality. A 19-year-old ignores death. That is a healthy thing. Thinking about death is an inhibiting thing. When we get older, we think about death. It becomes, eventually, a good friend to us, but we always consider it the enemy of youth.

Siebert: Interesting!

Sam: Let's take a rational look at death. First, though, when a person is born, is any new material produced?

Siebert: The person changing the diapers might think so; but, no: babies are made of the material that is already part of the earth.

Sam: And when we die, is any material lost?

Siebert: Nope! In fact, if you live as long as we have, some people are glad to scrape what's left of us into the grave.

Sam (*laughing*): But even what gets scraped into the grave isn't going any place far, right?

Siebert: Right.

Sam: But there is another consideration. What about the human soul? Where does it come from and where does it go?

Siebert: From God—to God.

Sam: Good answer. If, indeed, there is some sort of detachable human soul, it arrives with the person and departs upon the death of the person. Have you ever met a human soul?

Siebert: Not that I know of. Human souls seem to stay pretty much incognito.

Sam: Perhaps, that is a good word for it. Of course, the preacher would say that the soul is spiritual and it can't be seen. The romantic philosophers would say the soul is an *a priori* noumenon which cannot be experienced sensually but which is a real entity. In both cases, the soul (some would call it "mind) is a commanding presence in a living person. It is what makes us rationally human rather than just nonrational beasts.

Siebert: Right! So something is lost when people die: the soul.

Sam: That would be a sad state of affairs, but there are other points of view. Some philosophers say the soul is nothing but the result of millions of neurons functioning as intelligence. In that case, it is born with the body and dies with the body. No interference from God. Nothing gained with birth, nothing lost with death. But we can skip over that one. If there is an independent noumenon called a soul and if it is eternal, it enters the body at conception or sometime after that and leaves it when we die. You already agreed that it comes from God and goes back to God. Even though we are finite as bodies, are we not a part of infinity?

Siebert: Yep!

Sam: And since we are part of infinity, if the human soul goes back to God, then it has not, actually, left us. It is still part of infinity with us. Is that not so?

Siebert: As always, you are right.

Sam: Thus, if the human spirit is not created except as an eternal entity by God and it does not cease to exist when we die, and since our bodies rot, but, rotting, gain further existence as elements of the earth, nothing is lost at death. Nothing new is added at our conception/birth. Nothing is lost at our death. Emily is still with us. "Why stand ye there looking up?"

Siebert: I feel better about it now, but the death of a child still spooks me. Phew!

Sam: Me, too!

Siebert spits tobacco juice into White Aloe Stream, and they both watch it as it disappears around the bend.

July 27: Social Contract in a Shrinking World.

Not long ago there was some consensus that Plato, Aristotle, Hobbes, Locke, and Rousseau had something of a lockdown on the basic philosophical theory of Social Contract. Now, it is obvious that much has changed. The most important change has been in the autonomy of individual nations. Before the 20th century, each nation was, essentially, its own keeper. Of course, many nations retained a type of autonomy by buying it through tribute from a more powerful nation in their geographic vicinity. Essentially, in this way, stronger nations established commonwealths without conquest. But, because management of commonwealth is complex and expensive, smaller nations were, generally, allowed autonomy beyond the tribute. The Roman Empire tried hard to be an exception to this, attempting to maintain direct control over all its acquisitions, but it failed in the long run to do so.

The 20th century was a time of great social progress, but, also, a time of terrible confusion. Indeed, social (along with industrial and technical) progress was responsible for much of that confusion. In 100 years, we went from a primitive agrarian world, separated from each other by expanses of wilderness and sea and, perhaps, even more by language, culture, religion, and politics to a world united instantly by the World Wide Web and all of the technology which supports and is supported by it. In first-world nations, few people must do the back- and soul-breaking labor that was the standard of the 19th century; and, now, even third-world countries are moving the bulk of their labor from sweat shops and primitive farms to air-conditioned computer kiosks—air-conditioned, not for the worker but for the machine. Certainly, the sweat shops and farms still persist, but they are no longer the spine of society; and they, too, will go extinct as profits emerge more and more from newer, more profitable business structures. Even here in America, we have made this transition. I, personally, began my life in a family farming with horses, drawing water from a 120-foot-deep well with a hand-pump, using an outdoor privy, heating the house with sage-brush cut from the Idaho desert. When I retired it was from a professorship devoted to teaching English grammar to students around the world—online. I am surprised I am not dead from culture shock. Perhaps, I am.

But enough about the 20th century. The 21st century is my topic. And the big change in politics is that every nation is now dependent as never before on every other nation. The U.S.A. is still a super power, the only one on earth, but George W. Bush has accomplished one thing with the war in Iraq if he has accomplished nothing else. He has proven that America, with all of its might, cannot, with its democratic political configuration, rule the world. Indeed, it cannot even bring a semblance of order to a minimal political entity like Iraq. What we have learned for certain during the last five years is that, without the cooperation of the nations of the world, sociopolitical progress is impossible. Thus, one of the major factors of the traditional social contract is now null and void. Nations can no longer take responsibility for their own autonomy. Even America cannot control its own borders. Through decades of sociological and political struggle, our border with Mexico has become even more porous than it was originally. Indeed, our struggle to close it more effectively has led to nothing but internal political strife in both countries. The answer to this and to nearly every other such problem is international cooperation.

This, also, means international sharing, not just of ideas, but of wealth. That is what is behind all of the exporting of American jobs. It has become possible and economically lucrative for American enterprise to export jobs. On top of this, it has become positive economics (and positive in many other ways) for American enterprise to import skilled workers from other countries. What is the result of all of this give-and-give? The economic playing field world-wide is becoming level. Pour water into a basin with impermeable dividers and the water will stay in the segments of the basin where it is poured. Pour water into a basin with no dividers and the water will flow equally to all areas of the basin. That is a picture of modern existence: a world with no dividers—or only porous dividers.

And what of language, culture, and religion? They, too, although they flow more slowly (like honey rather than water) will find their new level. Even religions resistant to change will, eventually, discover the advantage of living peacefully with other religions. All major sects have done so already in much of the world.

Religious warfare will become, in the future, a historical consideration. The pain is that it is now a very real type of armed conflict. How will that change occur? Again, economics and practicality.

In the meantime, "**there must be no war.**"

That is not to say that military intervention can always be avoided. It might be necessary around Darfur to establish a militarily controlled no-fly zone. It will, undoubtedly, in the same place be necessary to intervene militarily between human beasts and their prey. This would not have been necessary if we (the citizens of the world) had all cared enough earlier to prevent the expansion of this situation into full scale ethnic cleansing. Earlier, the solutions would have been easier: economics and practicality. But what is happening in Darfur is not war, it is genocide. Intervention to stop genocide is not war. It is police action. Police action in a human world will sometimes be necessary.

But "**there must be no war.**"

What of terrorism? Must we not have a war on terrorism?

Terrorism is the result of centuries of abuse carried out multilaterally among races, cultures, and religions. The answers, again, are economics and practicality. Open world-wide sharing of wealth will end most hostility (except among corporate executives and their ilk, and most of them should be jailed anyway—replaced by more honest folk). And it is simply practical to treat those of other races, cultures, and religions as we would be treated ourselves—practical because it spawns in-kind responses. Of course, just as in genocide and the abuse that leads to it, there must, occasionally, be police actions to intervene . . .

But . . ."**There must be no war.**"

July 28: How do We Learn Prejudice?

I have never been taught on purpose to be prejudiced. In fact, my mother always declared all human beings equal and deserving of equal treatment. So did my father. And yet, my mother's dialect of the English language has been (and is less now because I have brought it to her attention) sprinkled with prejudicial idioms. For instance (and forgive my usage in context but it is necessary for the discussion) Brazil nuts were called "nigger toes," and a favorite description of anything brightly white was "shiny as a nigger's heel." I, first, reminded her that the "n" word is now taboo. It is not just a variant on the generic word, negro; and even the latter should be avoided except for rare formalities (e.g., the American Negro College Fund). Second, I provided a brief history lesson. The idea of the shine of an African American heel comes from the reflection such a heel makes in the headlights of a pickup loaded with racist white people chasing the African American down a road with intent to hang him. She was aghast and vowed never to use the phrase again. Brazil nuts, also, lost their nickname in the process.

My father, a very kind and devout Christian minister/farmer, I'm sure, never had an unkind thought about any minority. Indeed, he was a great fan of the black culture. He had suffered through the depression in much the same way African Americans suffered (abject poverty) and showed in many ways his respect for the stoic dignity of the poor African Americans. However, he used the "n" word occasionally until the civil rights movement brought it to his attention that it was inappropriate at which time it disappeared suddenly from his vocabulary. He then turned to an older term which seemed to him to carry much less negativity: darky. And when he sang one of his favorite African American songs (which he, apparently, assumed were composed by African Americans but were probably composed by white persons posing as blacks for theatrical purposes) or told a hobo joke ("Ma'am! Could you please sew a shirt on this button.") He used the term "darky" to identify the extremely courteous and dignified hobo. I doubt that he ever realized the negative side of the songs and jokes. I'm not sure he ever stopped singing them or telling them.

Yesterday, I took daughter #3's boys to the swimming pool at their apartment complex. As I have said before, the boys are a quarter African American. They and I are quite proud of that heritage along with their Asiatic and Caucasian heritages. The other swimmers in the pool were black (apparently, all black). They were friends, or, at least, acquaintances of my grandsons. My grandsons joined in with them in water games (Marco Polo, Keep-away, etc.). I was troubled because I, supposedly the epitome of open-mindedness regarding race, could not avoid that

201

tribal sense of superiority to these black people who I know are equal to me. As far as I know, they might have come from families much higher on the human food chain than I come from. And their parents might be more affluent than I. Yet, that same false sense of superiority felt by the prejudiced *honkies* in a pickup chasing the black fellow down the road at night, following his flashing heels, was in me. On my part, no animosity, no hatred, no fear of blacks getting out of their social place, just ugly assumed superiority.

The question: Are those silly songs and jokes to blame? What about the unfortunate nickname of the Brazil nut? Odds and ends of prejudicial idiomatic expressions? Perhaps, it is merely hundreds (thousands?!) of years of whites feeling superior to blacks. Whatever is the cumulative cause, it gives me uncomfortable pause to think that I, who have fought such feelings throughout my entire life, still have them. What of those who have not fought them as hard as I have? We must have a long way to go in our fight against prejudice and stereotyping. It is possible that we will have to wait as long as it takes for the very forces of evolution to take us there—if a great mushroom-shaped cloud doesn't take us to absolute equality first. In that case, look for me "under your boot-soles" as Whitman puts it. I will be the grass; and you, whatever your color or the shape of your eyes, will be there with me. We will have no boot-soles. Will I still believe I am superior because I am blue-grass and you are a mere orchard variety?

July 29: Wet Missouri Day.

It's wet. I couldn't mow the grass because I have a wimpy rechargeable electric mower that gets stopped up if the grass is wet. Not so bad because I didn't want to mow the grass anyway. So, instead, I cut the excess foliage from a tree that grows in the neighbor's back yard but whose limbs hang into mine. I'm not sure why I feel like a cat burglar whenever I do this. The neighbor doesn't care about the tree. It is a seedling elm that got started in the fence ten or so years ago, and I've been pruning it back ever since. I'd cut it out entirely if I could do so without destroying the fence.

This is my last day in Missouri. Tomorrow I get back on the Greyhound headed for Idaho and Walden-San. Much has happened there since I left. The biggest thing and the only thing I'll mention here is that my 87-year-old mother fell and broke her hip. We have reason to hope that it isn't one of those end-of-the-road disasters because the surgeons have indicated that the prognosis is reasonably good, but she will be in the rehab center for at least a couple of months, probably more.

I have rediscovered the fact that Missouri and I are incompatible—at least in the summer. I started feeling ill within 24 hours of my arrival; and I have been ill (more or less) ever since, not ill enough to slow me down, just ill enough to make things less enjoyable. My bones ache, my stomach hurts, I fart incessantly. I've, also, gained five pounds, about what I managed to lose during my first three months in Idaho. Too bad! I'll have to start over.

Missouri is not an unhealthful place. I am just not adapted to it. Things I do in Idaho as a matter of course, even in 106 degree heat, I come up short on in Missouri. I don't shovel as well, I don't play dominoes as well, I don't diet as well, I don't write as well—and I am not as happy (except that I have Yasmin with me which is always a source of happiness). When I am asked to what I am not adapted,

I usually just say "Missouri." Pressed for more detail, I say that it is the humidity. I know this is trite and lame, but I think it is true. Little things (like relative humidity) can make big differences. What if Plato had spent his time feeling "under the weather" which is a good way to describe an allergy to high humidity? Would we have had *The Republic*? How about Einstein? If his bones had ached all his life, would we have the theory of relativity?

One important piece of advice to would-be geniuses: don't stay where nature doesn't like you. Find your Walden-San and move there early in life. When Frost said

> *I chose the road less traveled*
> *And that has made all the difference,*

this is exactly what he meant. It wasn't that the well-travelled road is not a good one leading to fine destinations. It may be that the humidity at those destinations gave him gout.

July 30: On the Bus.

Late again! The Greyhound bus, I mean. We just left the Kansas City terminal an hour and fifteen minutes late. The layover and bus change in Denver (about midnight tonight) is supposed to be only an hour and five minutes. That means, if we don't make up time, we won't arrive in Denver until after my connection to Salt Lake is scheduled to leave That would cause me a six-hour layover in Denver and, by extension, a twelve-hour layover in Salt Lake because the bus to Twin Falls only runs twice a day. Lucky for me that Greyhound is always behind schedule. Thus, it is almost certain that my Salt Lake connection will be late in departing, at least, enough late to allow for our late arrival.

Unluckily for me, I will, because of my foolish nature, worry about it all the way to Denver. Why should I do that? The worst possible scenario is an 18-hour delay before arriving in Twin Falls. The world will not end. I've slept in bus terminals before. Yet I will worry. "Sometimes, I wish I could turn and live with the animals." Whitman said something like that. His basic message is that cows don't sweat the small stuff and neither should I. And there really isn't any big stuff. We humans are such primitive aborigines that it is a wonder we don't lose track of our own existence. Maybe that is the answer. We worry so we won't forget that we exist. *Fatigo, ergo sum!* Perhaps, when we have evolved into beings that, actually, make a difference in the cosmos, we will be able to stop worrying.

July 31: Confirmation!

The trip on Greyhound east a couple of weeks ago was not an anomaly. The return trip to Idaho has, so far, been as miserable as its mirror image. The record still holds that no leg of the journey has begun less than half an hour late. The actual goal for departure seems to be one and one-half hours after the posted departure time. There is some good news. I have not experienced a drunk Greyhound driver during the return trip. Being drunk while driving is, apparently, not the standard for Greyhound drivers. The reason I mention this is that, during my previous trip between Twin Falls and Salt Lake, the bus was weaving all over the road between Twin Falls and Ogden. Then, at Ogden, the same driver overloaded the bus with standing room only passengers. At Salt Lake, I witnessed that driver being led off on unsteady legs by a pair of armed security men. Drunken driving, if that is what it was, is not accepted by Greyhound, but confusion at terminals is common. At each terminal, the atmosphere seems to indicate that none of the employees has done any of this before. Getting anything right is cause for rejoicing.

I suppose this final comment about "Going Greyhound" should be focused upon frugality since that was the major factor in my decision to ride the bus. Of course, frugality is, in general, a good thing; but this trip has proven that there are limits to the benefits of being frugal. Taking the bus saved me a good deal of money. I paid only $130 for the round trip. The plane would have cost around $400. Driving, about the same. But next time I will drive. I fear that this one bus trip has shortened my lifespan by at least a year. It has been devastating to my nerves. A plane trip, on the other hand would entail asking one of my brothers to take me to Boise (200 miles round trip) and pick me up there when I return. That would be two full days of their time and a lot of wear and tear on their vehicles. Such a request would not be fair to them. How can they say "no" to their brother? I could easily become *persona non grata* for seeking such favors. If I drive, I can start my trip with a leisurely breakfast, spend two days on the road, and one night in a motel (about the time it takes for the bus trip). $400 is a lot to spend on gasoline and motels, but I suppose the old adage is true in this case but not always: you get what you pay for.

August 1: The Dog Days.

Probably, every American region has a time of year designated as "the dog days," meaning that it is deplorably hot at that time. The reference is to a tired old dog, unable to perspire, dripping away its life-moisture instead from the end of its lolling tongue. It is, probably, an appropriately framed image, but it is not a very dignified reference to man's best friend. Aw, well! Dogs don't sweat the small stuff anyway. Indeed, they don't sweat at all; but I do believe that they worry, probably more than people do. Otherwise, what would make them wear that path around the circumference of their owner's yard to protect the property, especially, since, for most dogs, the only thing they would do if the property were invaded would be to either cower behind their owners or lick the hand of the intruder? Domestication has not been kind to the dignity of the canine.

Of course, one could say the same thing for people. They do a lot of cowering and hand-licking as well, and it is not becoming. On the other hand (the hand-not-licked), we have experienced cases where cowering and hand-licking among humans was in short supply, and that is not a pleasant world either.

I'm not sure I like hand-licking and cowering much better than war, but that is because I, too, am the product of evolution which has taken us away from ancient dignity and toward more and more indignities. What is better about us after all this undignified evolution? The mind! With it, we can create new dignities, better than the ancient ones, employing the newest and most humane weapons to cut out the other person's heart efficiently. But my basic instincts miss the violent old days.

August 2: Homecoming.

Mike stands like a sentinel
Atop the last hill
Below the farm house—
Waiting,
His long tan coat
Flicking and parting and streaming
In southern Idaho's sunshine wind;
Tail arching its brush toward the blue
And head held high,
Open mouthed,
Tongue lolling,
Panting from the half-mile run,

His dog-sharp eyes spy the yellow school bus—
Children dismounting.

Majestic canine dignity transformed
Becomes wriggling subservience
And his joy is completed
In ecstatic face-licking.

August 3: The Last Battle.

205

Flat fluorescence flooding Gray desktops
In the shabby aftermath of a dingy day
In a narrow office:
All that is left
Beside the neat stacks of paper and tumbled disorder.

One man, bleary from routine reading, writing, signing
Of routine papers,
Sits amazed, dull—
Ears hot from anger—
Savage Passion,
Thrust against the Gray brick,
The silent Gray
Of institutional, warm-bread-moist, flannel unconsciousness;
Savage Passion
With nothing to slash in pillow-soft society,
No enemy to kill,
No food to hunt,
No backs for striping,
Wants to scream like an eagle.

He would cry out
Against life—bred for gentleness and tender meat—
A bloated castrato—
But dissolves to dejected sloth
Burning for sleep.
Rubs his eyes, checking the clock,
Rises, departs,
Shutting down the flood of fluorescent light.

One bare incandescent,
Forgotten,
Glares ferociously in a cluttered storeroom
Through the torpid night.

August 4: Transitions.

Yesterday, I sat, alone, in the living room of my mother's house for several hours. I wasn't merely contemplating my naval. I went there to wash a load of clothes. I don't have laundry equipment more sophisticated than a washboard at my campground. Thus, in Thoreau's livery of childlike humility, I make the 200-yard trek to my mother's house for such services. Thoreau walked a bit farther than I do, but the concept is similar. I am much older than Thoreau was when he stayed by Walden Pond, but I still am fond of Mother's apron strings. It isn't maudlin stuff— just practical. With only D.C. electric power, only special (and very expensive) automatic laundry equipment would work. I'd rather not spend the money and I enjoy chatting with Mom while my clothes go round and round.

But, yesterday, I sat alone, not just while my clothes went round and round, but for a couple more hours while my mother's clothes went round. Her planning was poor. When she fell and broke her hip two weeks ago, she failed to anticipate her fall and left a full hamper of dirty clothes. I found it yesterday when I went to wash my own and washed hers first so that when she finally can put on regular clothes instead of the hospital gown she must now wear, she will have her favorites: flower-print nylon blouses and polyester slacks bought used at the Youth Ranch Thrift Store in Jerome. She takes pride in her frugality. I fear that she would ride Greyhound if she had a trip to take and could manage such a trip. She must have 20 pairs of used polyester slacks with elastic waistbands and 30 used nylon blouses, mostly with floral prints. At least, packing is easy for her. You couldn't wrinkle these numbers with a steam roller.

Then I started throwing out excessively old canned goods, fruits and vegetables which Mom put up sometime during the twentieth century.

Mom will, probably, come home again. I hope so. So often, such an accident occurring at her advanced age begins the rapid process of degeneration that leads to either permanent residency in a retirement center or death. Mom is not ready for either. She still plans to occupy her little house that two of my brothers built for her after a can of paint exploded in the trailer house she had been living in and burned it down. She barely escaped with her life and the singed bathrobe she was wearing. Her canary, adopted when *her* mother went to live in a retirement center, the same place where Mom is rehabilitating now, was burned in the fire.

I talked with Mom a couple of days ago. She might get well enough to come home. So much depends upon attitude and Mom's attitude is that she is not yet ready to cash in her chips. She has stuff to do. She will probably go to church on Sundays. She will read those awful romance novels, mostly westerns. She might make a quilt out of her box of rags torn from superannuated polyester slacks and nylon blouses. She has made hundreds of quilts. The sale of her quilts has kept the women's department at the church financially afloat for generations. Each of her children, her grandchildren, and every one of her 28 great grandchildren has at least one as a welcoming gift from Mom. Only little Mayte, #29, born a couple of weeks before Mom fell down by her bathroom door and broke her hip, is without one. I'm quite certain that Mom has one stashed away in a closet that will do the trick. If not, I am of the opinion that she will try to make a special one for Mayte.

Some people, even when they are weak, are strong. Mom is that way. Maybe she will be home in three months. When the time comes for her to pack it up for good, she will know, and she will pack her own bag. For now, she's not packing.

Song of the Mountain Maiden
A Short Story in Ten Movements

August 5: First Movement—The Mountain from Whence She Descended.
More of a ridge than a mountain from whence she emerged on June 10th, 2076, dressed in denim jeans and T-shirt, a 1-foot square leather satchel hung over her neck and right shoulder by a leather strap. Rugged high-topped leather boots to protect her from rattle-snakes, always a danger while climbing down a mountain.

That was all: just a small leather pouch which had been laced together with leather thongs by her maternal grandmother and the clothes on her back and her feet. Not much for a slight girl of 18, just 18 on May 14, the day before the village elder handed her the satchel containing a map to lead her down the mountain to the frontier. Slight but with rippling muscles beneath the tanned skin of a child of mixed races, skin darkened further by a lifetime of mountain sunshine. Long black straight hair, slender figure. This is what the Teacher-at-the-Frontier saw when she came out of the woods at the top of the ridge several hundred yards uphill from his camp.

The ridge was long and flat, and behind it was a broad, clean river, and behind it was a myriad of smaller streams leading to the river down from the high mountains hidden except for their snow-capped peaks behind the ridge, thousands of miles of them, one would suppose, though the worn school books she had read told of Alaska and of Hudson Bay and of the North Pole. Her teachers in the Village-in-the-Mountain had made very little of these places. They told her that these are places to the north where no one goes. Especially, not since the return of the ice. There would be no need for her generation of mountain children to learn about them. Perhaps, her children's children would need to know.

Her mountain was a tall one. It had a snowy peak. The permanent snow had been coming farther and farther down the mountain for the past 20 years until now, it was only a mile from the Village-in-the-Mountain at the end of July. Winters had become so severe that houses had to be re-enforced with a foot more insulation than that with which they were originally built. The people loved the village site and had been loath to move farther down the mountain to avoid the cold winters. But the village farms had moved so that, now, farmers had to either stay in tents or simple cabins at the farms during summer or walk the 3 miles each direction it took to get to the farms and back to the village. Most farmers just came home from time to time for provisions and stayed at the farms through most of the summer. They were not particularly lonely since, generally, entire families migrated in the summer to work the farms. Indeed, the village was a lonelier place. Only the halt and the lame, the artistic, and the aged, and the insane, and the lazy stayed there during the summer. No one was required to work on the farms or any place else. The village had adopted a socialist form of government when it was originally founded after the global warming and the lava eruptions and the earthquakes and the floods and the devastation which led swiftly in the early years of the century to migration toward the earth's poles. Some migrated toward the equator. It was a choice between the frigid north and the incredible heat of the Torrid Zone with average high temperatures ranging up to 130 degrees when the sun was over the equator. Some chose the Torrid Zone because it was a good way to get rich by taking over the lucrative businesses of those who had abandoned them to find more comfortable habitations and found that they could not find managers willing to stay there to manage their businesses.

Not many went so far north as the people of the Village-in-the-Mountain. The people of the village were tired of the frustrations of complicated modern society and wanted a society of their own choosing. They went far into and up the mountains until they were sure no one would want to share their place with them. In the warming high mountain valleys, they cleared small trees which were beginning to grow and planted their crops and were rewarded with rich harvests. There was plenty for everyone. The master-teachers did not fail to bring important technology with them. Thus, it was not necessary for people to work grindingly hard to grow and harvest crops. They had fine tools and effective *natural* insecticides and fertilizer and they even developed hybrid varieties which matured in half the time of the ancestor plants so that the short growing season was not a problem. Solar- and wind-generated electricity insured that their factories did not smoke. Delegations were sent to the south to barter for raw materials that could not be found in the mountains, but few such materials were needed because the people were blessed with wise master-teachers who could, seemingly, work magic with whatever raw materials were available nearby to fabricate whatever was needed. Eventually, it became obvious that such trips were unnecessary; and, finally, it had been decreed that no one was allowed to leave the settlement for the outside world unless they intended to leave permanently. In that case, they were sworn to silence about the location of the village.

The first few years were hard while the villagers were building the village and its factories and clearing fields for the farms; but, as soon as these were built, solid to last for centuries, little work was required to keep them productive. Thus, it was not necessary for those who wished to spend their time creating works of art or writing stories and poems or reading the poems and stories of others or simply sitting on a rock and thinking, to work. Because there were plenty of people who *wanted* to work on the farms and in the factories in order to stay fit and energized and to feel useful, persons who were artistically or intellectually inclined might live not a wealthy life but comfortably in the special tenements constructed for them in the village with their small private bedrooms and common lunch and hobby and library rooms. They could pick up denim jeans and T-shirts and heavy boots at the dry goods store, food from the market, medicines from the drug store—all free of charge. If they were sick, they could go to one of several physicians who were schooled by the physician who originally arrived with the settlers. The necessities of life were free. Indeed, teachers, village officials, and other respected citizens and their families were expected to live such lives.

However, those who desired a more opulent existence were encouraged to engage in local commerce. They were paid modest wages for highly skilled work on the farms or in the factories or they could establish their own businesses as long as these did not interfere with the production and distribution of those commodities which were free. Some people, for instance, lived in large houses paid for through day wages or entrepreneurialism. They were often the butt of jokes about wasted effort.

Between the green ridge where the 70-year-old Teacher-at-the-Frontier waited for Mayte to climb down to his camp and the great mountain of the village was a lush and dense forest, 150 miles of it according to Mayte's map. The trail was well marked in ways that only the holder of a map could follow, but it had taken her 14 days to make the trek. She had not hurried. She had been taught that one who hurries might starve in the mountains while one who takes her time will find the path strewn with food a-plenty. She had enjoyed plenty as she traveled down the mountains. Now, with the humid heat (which she had been warned about by her Master-Teachers), she felt uncomfortable, but strangely elated at her arrival at the frontier. The Teacher-at-the-Frontier was, after all, her great uncle. She had not seen him for four years since he was promoted from Master-Teacher to this necessary job. Mayte had learned that, no matter what teaching assignment a teacher occupies, a teacher is a teacher and must be respected unfailingly.

Thus, she crossed the small clear stream of water which separated the frontier from the mountains, and she knelt before the waiting philosopher.

"Good morning, Uncle," she said. "It is wonderful to see you."

August 6: Second Movement (Part 1)—Frontier School in Session: "Respectful Silence."

"You have grown, Mayte."

"Yes, Uncle. You have been gone from the village for four years now."

"Has it been so long? One loses track of time. I know, however, that you have been chosen to cross the frontier to learn the ways of the New World."

"Yes, Teacher, I have been chosen."

"That is a great honor, Mayte, and a great responsibility."

"It is, Teacher, a great honor and a great responsibility."

"Please stand up. I appreciate the honor with which you treat me, but you cannot walk around on your knees all day. We have work to do and it must be done now. Have you had your breakfast today?"

"Yes, Uncle," she replied, rising and dusting off the knees of her jeans. I ate three eggs from a magpie's nest. Then I ate the magpie when she complained. The magpies are laying their eggs later in the spring. Normally, I'd have expected to find chicks instead of eggs in the nest."

"The ice is moving down upon us quickly. Soon the entire village will have to be moved down the mountain and, perhaps, across the frontier. Your task will be to explore the lands and civilizations beyond the frontier so that you can come back and teach the rest of us how to live there, whether we might join together with other villages or towns, whether, indeed, we will be able to remain a village or spread out among the members of the newly developing societies. It is my task to teach you how to go into the New World and return successfully. I cannot teach you about the New World. I have not been there. No one who we have sent before you has returned. These were fine, strong young persons. It is a mystery what has become of them."

"I know. My brother, three years older than I, went two years ago. I still cry myself to sleep wondering where he is and if he is well—if he is alive."

Tears welled up in Mayte's dark brown eyes and spilled down her smooth cheeks. She wiped them away, embarrassed at her own emotions. The Teacher-at-the-Frontier put his arm around her shoulders.

"No need to weep, child. David is well. I cannot know where he is or what he is doing, but I know he is well. And, if you learn well here at the frontier and if you are diligent in your explorations, you will be reunited with him."

"Teacher, let us begin our lessons. I am anxious to finish them and move on."

"The lessons have already begun. The first lesson was crossing that little stream and coming before me upon your knees. This is humility. You have shown that you know what to do in the presence of authority. Authority, of course, takes infinite forms. My authority is that of teacher. Realize, however, that authority in the New World will take forms to which you are not accustomed. You must learn to recognize them not from the habits of the village in the mountain, but from the essential nature of authority itself. It may be a wise authority or a foolish authority. You must recognize the difference before you act. It may be a good authority or an evil authority. That too, you must recognize before you act. In any case, wise, foolish, good, evil, you must show respect. For instance, the magpie that you had for breakfast was the authority over her nest, but she was a foolish authority in thinking that she could scold you away from the nest and she paid with her life. However, I am sure that you killed her respectfully causing as little pain as possible."

"Yes, Teacher. I held her gently in my hands. Then I quickly pulled off her head."

"More than I needed to know, child! What not to say will be the substance of another lesson."

"Sorry, Teacher."

"No need for sorrow. You told the truth and truth is the ultimate good even when it reveals that which is not pleasant. It is just that the wise person limits the truth being expressed to that which is being sought at the moment. Did you cook the eggs and the magpie before you ate them?"

"Yes, Teacher."

"Good! That is, also, respectful to the nature of the eggs and the magpie. Also, it is respectful to my patience that you did not tell me how you cooked them. You are, also, learning how much of the truth to tell. You see, since I have come to live here rarely seeing other humans and always communing with the animals, I have become a vegetarian, and I never kill animals if I can avoid it. I get a little queasy hearing about other people eating them, and yet I know it is a natural thing to do. Thus, it is a part of kindness to say no more than is needed in a particular circumstance. Your best response to my question of whether you had eaten breakfast would have been, "yes." Consider, for instance, the possibility that I might have come to worship the magpie as a god. In that case, my religion might have compelled me to kill you for telling me that you had just ingested one of my gods. What seems incredibly foolish to one person makes perfect sense to another."

August 7: Second Movement (Part 2)—Frontier School in Session: "Do and Speak only Good."

"You will notice that, in these lessons, I will not teach you what I think you already know either from your lessons in school at the village or from your life experience. Thus, since you know that it is better to love than to hate and it is inappropriate to kill another human being except in self-defense, and you must never torture butterflies, I will not waste your time by teaching such stuff. You might not, however, have considered some of the major principles behind such ideas. Kant's Categorical Imperative is one of these principles. It is a lot like the Golden Rule (do not do to others what you would not want them to do to you) except that it is more restrictive. The Categorical Imperative is this: Do not take an action or make a rule unless such action or rule would be appropriate in every possible situation where it would be applicable. Some subjects of the Categorical

Imperative are expressed in the negative. For instance, an important one is that there must be no war. The Categorical Imperative leads to a short list of actions or inactions which are subject to it. Add to this that before you take an action or withhold action in any given situation, you must be sure that such an action or inaction is appropriate in that particular situation. This makes a host of actions or inactions appropriate which would not be appropriate under the Categorical Imperative. I can simplify this. Do and speak only good, and, though there are a few things that are either good or evil by nature, much of what is good changes, at least in form, in differing contexts. Remember what I said about people who worship magpies. Do you understand, Mayte?"

"Yes."

"Good! Then explain it to me. I'm never sure that I have this right."

The great uncle smiled and winked at his great niece. The great niece smiled and winked back.

August 8: Second Movement (Part 3)—Frontier School in Session: "Never Claim Knowledge Which You Don't Have."

"Are you hungry, Mayte?"

"Yes, Uncle. It is noon and I am accustomed to eating lunch about then."

"I will go and see if I can strangle a magpie for you."

Mayte, remembered from when she was a small child that her great uncle had a penchant for humor, and she smiled.

"No magpie, thanks. I'd be happy if I could have just some fruit or a piece of bread."

"Thank God! No magpie!" exclaimed the teacher with a dramatic wave of his arm. "You shall, indeed, have both fruit and a piece of bread. You shall have wine as well."

The old man proceeded to prepare meals for both himself and Mayte. When he was finished, they sat cross-legged on the grass under the liberal branches of a plum tree and ate their fresh strawberries, which were then in season, large puffy rolls made with coarsely ground grain, and a generous cup of wine made from berries that grow wild on the side of the ridge. While they ate, Mayte told her uncle the latest news from the village, that Emma, the second oldest resident had died. She was 98 and, when she became angry over what she considered a bad call by a referee, had slipped and fallen off a boulder from which she had been watching the children play a game of soccer.

"Too bad!" muttered the teacher. "Was she right about the call?"

"I wasn't there, but my cousin was playing in the game, and he said she was right. Of course, the call went against his team."

"That generally makes it a bad call," chuckled the teacher.

They finished their meal.

The teacher said, "If there are such things as sins, claiming knowledge which you don't have is one of them, and it is our most common bad habit (several steps worse than eating our animal friends). Popes, priests, emirs, ayatollahs, rabbis, and ministers of every stripe are the worst sinners in this regard, for it is the backbone of religion. Nearly all religion is based upon lies by a prophet or other founder or a follower of that prophet or founder who claims spiritual knowledge which humans cannot possess. Most often the particular false claims are in regard to special relationships between the prophet or founder and God. The irony is that no one, no prophet, no founder, no follower of a founder can tell for sure that what they believe to be divine revelation is, indeed, divine revelation. The gap between the phenomena which apparently reflect things as they are and the things as they are (including God, though God is not a thing, and whatever other physical and/or spiritual entities that might exist) is unbridgeable. We have only our five senses to detect them, and each of our five senses is limited and fallible. To claim more than our five senses can detect is questionable at best. At worst, it is an outright lie. The differences between believing that we have received divine revelation and the fact of divine revelation are irreconcilable. Thus, there is no authoritative religion. Only faith! Faith in God is not a bad thing in itself. Indeed, it is one of the best things we can have. However, it cannot be corporate. Faith in God based upon someone else's experience or upon a book, is faith in the other person or the book, not in God.

"False claims to knowledge are not limited to religion. We humans have an insatiable appetite for self-aggrandizement which we try to satisfy by claiming more knowledge than we have. I'm sure that you have studied Plato and Descartes. They are part of your curriculum in the village. Plato's philosophy is right when he reports that Socrates' claim to knowledge was limited to the knowledge that he knows nothing at all. Descartes tidied up the Socratic claim by saying that we do know one other thing. That is, we know that we exist because we think, and things that think must exist. Of course, much of what Descartes said after that is malarkey apparently stimulated by his fears of offending the church fathers as Galileo had done. Thus, Descartes ends up making claims to a great deal of knowledge which neither he nor the church fathers could have. Perhaps, I am wrong about his motives for making these claims. Perhaps, he had really convinced himself of their validity, or others had truly convinced him. In that case, it is unfortunate that his philosophy is so highly regarded.

"As to how this applies to you, I will tell you a little more about your mission. What you have learned in your life in the village from nature (human, animal, plant, and inanimate) tempered by what I teach you here serves as the means for achieving the objectives of your mission into the New World. Those young persons from the village who went before you have, apparently, failed in their missions. Their missions were to go into the New World, learn of it, and return to me and to the village so that we could prepare, using their understandings, to move either into the New World or elsewhere. They did not return. Thus, we must assume that they have failed. Your mission is slightly different for it is, in all likelihood, the last mission. Your mission is to go into the New World, find the other young people we sent there and bring them back to me. Of course, you, like your predecessors, have the mission of learning about the New World and bringing that information back with you.

"It is probable that the failure of your predecessors in their missions has to do with a failure in one or more of the principles of their learning. Either they did not follow the dictates of their learning or the dictates of their learning have been insufficient or false. I sorrow at the possibility of the former and shudder at the prospect of the latter.

213

"I, truly, believe (that is, I have faith) that you will return to me and that you will bring news about one or more of your predecessors. There have been three including your brother David. Believe me when I say that your speedy return and with what you return might make all the difference in the future of the village.

"Believe me, also, when I say that, if you do not follow the principles which you have learned as they apply to your experiences in the new world, your mission will surely fail. Finally, believe me when I say that following is not enough. You have been chosen because you have proven yourself to have a capacity for reason. Reason fills the sails of the ship within which you travel. Trim your sails with care lest the storms of your journey sink your ship."

August 9: Second Movement (Part 4)—Frontier School in Session: "Thought is Better than Thing."

The Teacher-at-the-Frontier continued, "We can never really know a thing. A thought is the spiritual realization of an imperfect phenomenal representation of a thing. Thus, thought is far more perfect than the phenomena representing a thing as it is because, though thought is based largely on phenomena, it is mixed with the spiritual which brings it closer to God (or whatever we might call the infinite force of the cosmos).

"Never depend upon the apparent truth of phenomena. Begin with thinking about phenomena and end with faith. But remember that faith must be only in the infinite force of the cosmos (God). It cannot be in other people.

"Taking one step further, however, it is necessary to have a certain degree of trust in some people. Know the people very well that you must trust so that you can better ascertain how well you can trust them. And remember that people change. Even those young persons who went before you might be more or less worthy of trust when you find them. You must depend upon reason, observation, and faith to discover what trust, if any, you might have in them. Whether you are right or wrong in your conclusions in this regard could make the difference between a successful mission and failure.

"I do not know your faith. I can only make generic recommendations about it, but I know that it is not the strength of faith that counts, but its accuracy. In other words, faith is of no use to a person who does not reason well and does not constantly seek that which is good.

"That which is good is always in the realm of right reason."

August 10: Second Movement (Part 5)—Frontier School in Session: "Know Your Duty—Fulfill It."

The teacher asked, "Mayte, do you know what your duty will be on your mission to the New World?"

Mayte replied, "I have a bare outline of it. I am to go to the New World and seek out those who have gone before me and bring them and/or news of them back to you. Also, I am to learn as much as possible about the New World, especially in regard to how the people of the village might fit into it."

"That is a good start," said the teacher. "Indeed, it is about all (along with my teachings about wisdom) that I can teach you about it. You must do your duty when you find it. You will not know it until then. Chances are, you will still not quite know what your duty is when you are called upon to fulfill it."

"But, if I don't know what my duty is, how can I fulfill it?"

"You know, even now, in part what your duty is. However, even that could change. For instance, you might discover that it is your duty to leave one or more of those who have gone before you behind in the New World. That is where reason continues to guide you—along with faith."

"Teacher, I have to admit that I do not yet know if God exists. How can I have faith in a god that might not be?"

"Have faith in the reason which tells you that God might be. Then extend that to having faith in the conclusions to which that reasoning leads. That is the best any of us can do. Perhaps, God will reward your faith with spiritual assurance—perhaps, not. Remember that doing your duty will, if you respond to it reasonably, always lead to good. That is the best outcome for which any of us can hope. Hope is closely akin to faith."

"Then, Teacher, I shall answer your question later. I will show you my duty when I return."

"When you return, I will look forward to seeing it."

August 11: Second Movement (Part 6)—Frontier School in Session: "Honor Simplicity."

Then the Teacher-at-the-Frontier continued: "Thoreau says, 'Simplicity! Simplicity! Simplicity!' Make your affairs so simple that you can count them on a hand. Yet we have just examined how complicated your duty can become. Yet I say along with Thoreau, 'Simplicity! Simplicity! Simplicity!' It is the hallmark of wisdom and the preface to good."

"And I am sure, Uncle," replied Mayte, "that you are going to tell me how this paradox can be reconciled."

"Right!" replied the Teacher-at-the-Frontier. "You are beginning to know me. That is a step toward simplicity in itself. But remember that simplicity is merely a tool for fathoming the infinitely complex cosmos. Aristotle gives us a clue to this simplicity in his *Poetics*, when he tells us that a tragedy has a beginning, a middle, and an end. 'Of course, it does,' we reply. 'Why does Aristotle tell us what is obvious?'"

"Why does Aristotle do this?" asked Mayte.

"Because it is the beginning of his analysis, and he begins it with the first and simplest part of his analysis. Using these three terms (beginning, middle, and end), he has reduced the complexity of his entire analysis into thirds. Now he only must tell us what is contained in each of the three major parts of the tragedy separately. Of course, tragedy (along with life itself) is never so simple as to be broken neatly into three parts; but if we tried to approach all of the complex overlapping of the three parts of a tragedy at the beginning we would be entirely confused and not be able to finish the entire analysis at all. Thus, though Aristotle is quite aware of the artificiality of breaking the tragedy into these three parts, he, also, is aware that he must do so in order to make the task of fully analyzing the tragedy possible. The subtle overlapping can be explained in detail after the general overview has been examined.

"That is exactly how you must go about analyzing each life situation you encounter during your journey. Think whole to parts—entire wholes to the largest possible parts first; then divide these parts into their largest possible parts; etc.; until you have examined all of the parts of the entire situation. This is basic analysis. At that point, a synthetic approach takes over. The various parts must be reconsidered to see how they work together as a whole.

"Of course, you are examining a particular situation because you must solve particular problems in regard to that situation. So it is important that you be able, in the end, to separate out the specific situation from the general situation, the part of the situation in which your problem lies. That happens after you understand the general situation. It requires the same sort of analysis as the general situation requires: Whole to parts analysis, then parts to whole synthesis. Finally, you must synthesize the whole of the specific situation to the whole of the general situation. Then you should be ready for the evaluation which leads to the solution of the problem you started out to solve.

"An important concept is that you must understand the context of a problem before you can solve a problem contained within that context.

"Do you notice that, in using this system, you never have to consider more than a few items at a time? You are not as likely to make mistakes in your evaluation if your mind must only consider a few items at a time."

"Yes. I noticed that. I will need to practice. 'Whole to parts analysis, parts to wholes synthesis, general to specific analysis, specific to general synthesis, evaluation and solution.' I think I have the idea. But, oh, I will have to practice a lot to master it."

"You'll have plenty of practice as you journey into the New World. I can assure you of that."

August 12: Second Movement (Part 7)—Frontier School in Session: "Study Nature and Philosophy. Also, Study Religion, but Beware of It."

The Teacher-at-the-Frontier continued: "As you travel, study nature and study philosophy. These two together will help you to know your duty and how to accomplish it."

Mayte replied: "You said before that faith plays an important role. Should, faith, not also be a part of my study."

"Indeed, it should be," replied the sage, "but you must distinguish between faith and religion. Faith and hope, as I have said, are close relatives. Faith, no matter what the clerics tell you, has almost nothing to do with religion. Organized Religion is a fabric of lies which can entirely destroy your faith. It is important, though, that you, also, make religion a part of your study. Religion is a possible extension of your philosophy once, through philosophy, you have found reason for faith. Once faith is in place, it is not entirely useless to develop the tenets of a religion, a religion based upon the faith which you have already established through a study of nature and philosophy. Thus, religion is a possible product of philosophy, not *vice versa*. Religion, at best, is based upon hope for the actualization of things hoped for. When the clerics tell you that it is *knowledge* of anything, including things hoped for, they are lying. Both reason and empirical study tell us this. Those who claim that God tells them anything are only assuming

216

that whatever voice they heard is truly the voice of God. It could just as easily be the voice of Satan (if there is a Satan) or the voice of the contaminated magpie meat they had for supper. They are spreading fantasy as if it were fact.

"The same is true of those who tell you to trust Bibles and Qurans and other books of so-called scripture as if they are the pure and perfect word of God. Such books can be very useful in your study of philosophy, but they cannot be verified as the pure and perfect word of God. In fact, a quick study of any of them shows them to be self-contradictory and contaminated by much "man-handling" over the centuries, as contaminated as that magpie stew that gave them such a bad dream that they thought came from God.

"I will never eat magpies again!" exclaimed Mayte.

The old man chuckled. "Don't let me spoil your appetites, my lovely huntress. It is just difficult for me to relish the eating of my pretty little feathered friends. I might, however, enjoy a nice fried trout once I get past cutting off its head, ripping out its guts, and feeding them to the magpies. Or maybe not!"

August 13: Second Movement (Part 8)—Frontier School in Session: "There is a Negative to Every Positive. Both are Valid as is the Infinite Path between Them."

The teacher continued: "When we are engaged in doing and speaking good, we stand at an infinity of fulcrum points. An important test between good and evil is that good is always balanced? The Chinese have a symbol for this. It is the circle with two figures, one black, one white, each with an eye of the opposite color. It represents Yin and Yang, the two balancing forces of the cosmos. It is said that they represent the masculine and the feminine, but it is much more than that. The major thing wrong with the Chinese conception of Yin and Yang is that they seem to make the cosmos finite and to divide it equally and with limits between these two limited forces. In actuality, Yin and Yang should represent the infinite cosmos as manifestations of every sort of force, every kind of act or speech or thought or anything else which occurs in the infinite cosmos. Thus, each moment of our existence, if we are managing our existence for the good, finds us balanced at the fulcrum of each and every force, thought, word, act, etc. involved with our existence. In actuality, it takes no effort whatsoever to retain our balance, since in an infinite world every point is a fulcrum. All we need do is stand quietly in place. This, indeed, is the central thesis of many oriental philosophies.

"In Western philosophies, however, we tend to demand action in order to make our lives worth while, that is, good for *something*. The Oriental ideal of stillness seems to make us totally useless. That is why I like the Western approach better, but it is dangerous.

"There is yet another infinite set of lines of action, the positive and the negative, which associate with the simple lines of action or inaction described above. We are, constantly, tempted to actions leading us down these positive and negative lines where our actions might lead to either good or evil. Keep in mind that the good is not always toward the positive and the evil is not always toward the negative. That is where reason enters in. We must analyze, synthesize, and evaluate (as I have described above) every circumstance in which we find ourselves and choose the course, whether positive or negative or merely neutral, which leads to good. Of course, all of this assumes that there is only one good course and all others are evil. This is not true either. Everything is flung at us in infinite varieties of choices. It is easy to see why the Orient prefers the neutral, balanced stance. It requires complete lack of reason once it has been established. If we were merely cattle in a pasture, this would be the proper course for us. We are not."

"Wow!" exclaimed Mayte.

"Wow! indeed," quoth the teacher. "Now, after you have had a night's sleep and a good breakfast, you will be ready to be on your way."

"Wow!" repeated Mayte. "I don't feel ready."

"That is as it should be," replied the sage. "You might try prayer as you go along your way. It has its benefits."

August 14: Third Movement—Mayte's Journey into the New World.

Mayte slept fitfully that night on the straw mattress that her great uncle had provided for her in the corner of his tent. She dreamed of her grandmother, the sister of the Teacher-at-the-Frontier, and of her great grandmother, now a wizened but healthy102 year old, the oldest person in the village and still serving as a medical doctor to the residents there. When she was young, she had been the only physician to accompany the tribe of survivors who had eventually become the citizens of the Village-in-the-Mountain away from the death and destruction of the eruptions and earthquakes of the American Midwest. She had many stories of how her father and mother had led the convoy of cars and trucks (ten altogether, many family members, others friends from the suburban Kansas City community of Northlake. Northlake had been lucky enough to be a distance away from the geological fault-line that had erupted so suddenly across southeast Missouri and Tennessee. Mayte remembered from her schooling that the fault-line had been called the New Madrid Rift. It had let itself be known many times through earthquakes, but no one predicted that it would erupt into volcanic action or that the volcanic action would spread through the Midwest and most of the South. It must have been something to do with the accelerating global warming, the storms, the warming oceans, the disappearing coastlines. It was not the only place to go ballistic. Fault-lines around the world, especially in both temperate zones erupted sending the surviving residents, not many people at all, in both directions, north and south.

Those who went south knew that they were heading for the Torrid Zone nearer to the equator. Average temperatures had risen 15 degrees over a 30-year period. Dry, sandy deserts had grown to cover most of Africa and South America. Antarctica had become mostly barren rock, Australia and New Zealand, all desert. The rain forests of the world had shrunk. In between was fertile and productive tropical farmland for those who could stand the 12 months a year of intensive heat.

Those trapped on the north side of the conflagration headed north toward Canada and Northwest toward the Rocky Mountains. Those few who reached the Rockies found them to be as unbearable as the plains. Although there was little seismic activity, the thinning air at the higher altitude made for frigid nights and blistering days. The very few survivors of the first winter season moved on to the northeast into Canada and were not heard from again. They, however, fared the best. Northward from the American plains to the Canadian plains, the weather cooled from the intense humid heat of the American Midwest to more temperate weather in the Canadian midlands. Unfortunately, it was already settled and the Canadian farmers who lived there, though peaceful in general, found it necessary to protect their property from the Americans, not just from the Midwest but from both coasts of the United States and Canada that had to be evacuated because of the rising tides which had wiped out every coastal city and settlement. Rural Canadians proved to be formidably armed. So everyone moved on to what had been the Northern tundra, now mostly swamps and emerging forests. They stopped there and made what living they could by farming and hunting. It was not much of a living, but it made for several decades of survival for those who did not die of malaria and a variety of swamp diseases until the climate change suddenly reversed causing a reverse rush for what would be left of U.S. soil after much of it was covered by lava. Indeed, that is what was now called by Mayte and the villagers "the New World" toward which Mayte travelled.

Mayte's great-great-grandfather, an old man at the time, had something of an epiphany when he saw that the tundra was swampy and unhealthful and convinced most of his convoy, now on foot, to continue north toward Hudson Bay and into the mountains of northern Canada where no one had lived except wildlife and widely scattered American Indians. He thought that the rising world temperatures would have changed that part of Canada into something of a Garden of Eden, and he was right. After a long walk through the mountains, quite comfortable because of the nature skills that seemed so natural to Great-Great-Grandfather and which he taught liberally to all who went with him, they came to a marvelous valley, green and cool and rich in soil and water and air. Beyond the valley, up a ravine into a majestic snow-peaked mountain, they went to establish their Village-in-the-Mountain, which never had another name because it remained the only town and a secret from the rest of the world for three generations. Until the weather began to change again.

Mayte awoke from her troubled slumber pleased that she would be starting her journey. Her great uncle had prepared her a breakfast of fruit and berries and his own home-made bread (dubbed "Papa Bread," a recipe which had come down all the way from Great-Great-Grandfather).

Mayte's great uncle smiled and asked, his voice crisp with irony, "Do you, also, want some magpie?"

"No thank you, Uncle," She replied. "This will be just fine."

After breakfast, Mayte gathered her few things together into her leather satchel, silently hugged and kissed her great uncle and headed south across the broad plain that lay before her.

August 15: Third Movement—Mayte's Journey into the New World (Cont.)

Mayte wept.

She was beyond the range of her beloved mountains for the first time in her life. She was barely a woman. She was a stranger in a strange land. The clouds were heavy. The sky was heavy. It dripped with the humidity that made her forehead drip and her clothing stick to her perspiring body.

"Water, water, everywhere, and all the boards did shrink;

Water, water, everywhere, nor any drop to drink."

She remembered the lines from Coleridge.

She remembered her grandmother who had read to her the entire *Rhyme of the Ancient Mariner*.

Mayte wept.

And she perspired.

And she walked—steadily to the south—while the temperature gradually rose as she walked into lower latitudes and altitudes. Through the swamps that Great-Grandmother had told her about. The swamps that were still marked on the old maps as "tundra." No people now lived in the swamps. The few who had lived through malaria had gone elsewhere.

The colder temperatures had not yet started changing the swamps back to tundra. She wished that they had. The mosquitoes attacked her in dark swarms. She opened her satchel and got out the small bottle of repellant that Great-Grandmother had given her. She rubbed it on the exposed parts of her body, her arms, her neck, her face. It worked. She became invisible to the mosquitoes and they sought elsewhere for blood.

She did not want to stop, yet she would have to stop before she emerged from the swamps. She knew that there were hundreds of miles of them to cross before she came to what had once been forests. She wondered what they would be now. Some of the Indians who had moved to the northern mountains during the past 50 years from places East, West, and South told of vast deserts and of lush rain forests depending upon the direction one traveled. Mayte had no way of knowing whether she was heading for a deathly dry desert where she would die of thirst or a rain forest where she might be eaten by marauding descendants of escaped zoo animals—lions, tigers, hyenas—which had, also, moved toward the northern mountains to find respite from the heat of the land farther south. Many zoo-keepers had, in the face of bankruptcy and eminent starvation of themselves and their animals, merely opened the cage doors and left. The human population which remained and that which the animals found along the way north became welcome repast. There would be, indeed, fewer humans now in that former super power, the United States of America, than there had been for a very long time.

Mayte drank sparingly the water from the canteen that her great uncle had given her. Never before had she needed a canteen. In the mountains, there was always fresh flowing water nearby. Here in the swamps, all was watery, but none of the water was fit to drink. When evening came, she sought out a sheltered spot beneath some scrubby broadleaf trees. She gathered together enough leaves, twigs, and fallen branches for a small fire and boiled swamp water in her combination sauce and frying pan. After filling her canteen with the boiled water, she boiled more water for drinking tonight and ate one of the hard rolls and some of the dried berries and fruit which her uncle had, also, given her. She would, first, eat the food in her pack before she scavenged for more, she thought. That would make the pack lighter and *her* fleeter of foot for catching whatever food was available.

She lay down under the tree and was quickly asleep. She stirred with every stirring of the weedy swamp ready to awaken at any perceived threat to her safety. Then came the thunderstorm with lightning that lit the sky in eerie black and white. It lasted for half an hour and soaked her. She was thankful for it since it washed away much of the stinking mud which had stuck to her feet and legs during the previous day. When the thunder died away, she went peacefully to sleep for the rest of the night.

She awoke refreshed the next day. And the next. And the next. All the way to twenty-eight days.

And then she found herself standing upon the edge of a wide, clear, swift river. The water of the river was shallow, rippling and tumbling loudly over a bed of stones, some as large as houses, some mere pebbles—all worn smooth and round by centuries of passing water. It was bordered by trees of many species, both broadleaf and conifer. She was about to bend down to drink when she heard the rattle of a rattlesnake. Then two! Then many!

August 16: Third Movement—Mayte's Journey into the New World (Cont.)

Within a few minutes, Mayte had captured, killed and cleaned two three-foot rattlesnakes and had them roasting over a small fire skewered on green willows cut from beside the river. She ate one of the roasted snakes for breakfast. The other she cooked until it was dry and leathery, cut it into small round pieces, and packed it away in her satchel, wrapped in a large leaf for lunch. She smiled as she wondered if her great uncle would feel the same way about her eating rattlesnake as he did about magpies. "Probably!" she answered her own question out-loud. She had become accustomed to talking to herself since she entered the swamp. It took away some of the dreariness. She would go over math problems and philosophical theories and talk about whether there is really a God and all of the flawed arguments for and against. One of her imperfections for which she criticized herself was that she held people who do not reason coherently in some contempt. Her cousin Roletto, for instance, always threw some salt over his shoulder if he spilled any on the counter while he salted his tomato. She made fun of him for doing so, and he would say, "Better safe than sorry!" and bit into his tomato, usually squirting juice on his shirtfront in the process.

"What shall we do now?" she asked herself as if she were plural. Shall we try to cross the river here or go downstream to see if there is a better crossing? These rocks look slick and, if I fall in, I might bash out my brains. It can't hurt to go downstream except that I'll have to spend more time sloshing through this swamp goop. Hmm!"

Looking across the river, she could see conifer-covered foothills backed by tall blue snow-capped mountains. That was more her kind of country.

"I'll just tread carefully," she said. "I can make it across those rocks."

And she did. The fellow who watched her do it from the other side was reminded of a young doe goat gamboling over mountain boulders in search of fresh pasture.

"Ahh! Fresh pasture!" he said aloud to himself. And he smiled.

August 17: Third Movement—Mayte's Journey into the New World (Cont.)

Mayte smiled, too. It had been four weeks since she had seen another human being and six weeks since she had seen anyone unwrinkled by gerontology. This fellow was beautiful: long blond wavy hair extending over bare broad

221

shoulders, iron jaw, piercing blue eyes, narrow waist, muscular legs, six-feet-six of manhood unimpaired. The virgin explorer met her first challenge.

"Welcome!" said the hunter (for that is what he appeared to Mayte to be). "You must have come a long way across that swamp. In fact, you are the first person I have ever seen coming from that direction."

Mayte noticed that he glanced away from her as he said this. His diverted glance might have troubled her had she not been so taken with his form.

"But you," he continued, "surely, have a story to tell. If you'll be so kind as to accept my invitation to accompany me to my cabin for dinner, I'll be thrilled to hear it, the story, that is."

Mayte grinned and wrinkled her nose.

"Tell me where it is. Then, you go first. I *must* wash off some of this mud before I go into a house. I'll find you a little later."

The man looked doubtful.

"O.K. But if I don't see you soon, I'll be back here looking for you. Don't get lost. Just go up this gulch (he pointed with his left forefinger) about a quarter mile. Then, go right on the trail by the big oak tree. I'll tie a rope around the tree. About 100 yards in, you'll see the cabin."

"O.K. See you soon. Go away now, and no looking back. By the way, what is your name?"

"Shawn Rawlins. What's yours?"

"Mayte. We don't use surnames at the Village. I'm the only Mayte there except for my grandmother and no one gets us confused with each other."

"Hmm! Must be a small town. I'll look forward to hearing about it."

Shawn Rawlins left Mayte and ducked into the woods moving up the gulch. Mayte went back to the clear-running river with its smooth boulders and its rattlesnakes. She heard them rattling a warning to her as she approached the shore, but she paid little heed to them as she stripped off her clothes and stepped into the water. First, she washed her jeans in the cold water using the bar of soap she kept in her satchel. She laid them over a large flat stone to dry. Then she stowed her dirty t-shirt, stockings and panties in the satchel in a small ditty bag and pulled out the fresh set. She would wash the dirty ones later. Then she used the soap to bathe herself. The cold of the water was refreshing, and she enjoyed the idea of being clean and fresh again, the way she was when she left her uncle's camp. When she was finished, she stepped back onto the shore to a trio of snake rattles.

"Silly snakes!" she said. "Don't you know that you'd be safer if you stayed quiet?"

She sat naked for a while on a large boulder by the shore to dry in the sun and let her jeans dry a bit more as well. Then she dressed and headed for Shawn's cabin. Shawn's directions had been easy to follow. It was clear from the well-worn path that Shawn was not an occasional visitor, but a resident here. When she saw the cabin, she knew, also, that Shawn (or someone) was a master cabin builder. The cabin was about 15 feet by 30, made of native hand-hewn logs, cleanly barked and perfectly notched and fitted so that no visible sealant had been necessary in the building. The pitched roof was covered with hand split shakes, again, perfectly fitted and lapped. An eight-by-12-foot covered porch surrounded the front door and it, in turn, was surrounded by climbing vines covered with multicolored blossoms.

Shawn was sitting in a rocking chair on the porch with an on-the-rocks glass half filled with golden-brown liquor in his hand.

"Welcome to my parlor . . ." he began.

". . . said the spider to the fly," she finished.

They both laughed.

"May I offer you whiskey or a mixed drink?"

"Yes, you may, but I won't drink it. I don't like the taste of hard liquor."

"Then, how about a nice root beer?"

"I don't know what root beer is. Is it alcoholic?"

Shawn smiled at her naiveté.

"No. No alcohol. Just roots! Really, it tastes good. Sweet, bubbly, cold, brown. You'll like it."

"O.K. I'll try it."

He went into the house and returned almost immediately with a can labeled "Umm! Good! Root Beer." He handed it to her and offered her the rocking chair he had been sitting in. He chose the other chair on the porch, a canvas folding chair with a stump in front of it for a foot rest. They both sat down.

He noticed that she had not opened her root beer. Rather, she was turning it around and around in her hands and looking at it carefully.

"It isn't a bomb," he said. "Just open it."

"How?"

"Just pull up on the tab, the little round thing on the top."

"Oh!"

She stuck her first finger under the tab and lifted. It hissed. Nearly dropping the can, she gasped.

"What was that?!" She asked.

"You've never had a carbonated drink?"

"I guess not. At least, I never had a drink that hissed at me like a snake."

He laughed out loud this time.

"Fresh pasture!" he thought to himself.

"Did you say something?"

"No," he replied. "I was just thinking."

"And what were you thinking?"

"Just that I must hear all about where you came from and what you are doing here."

"I'll be glad to tell you all about it just as soon as I figure out how to drink this stuff that hisses at me."

She took a timid sip, swallowed, and smiled.

"That's good!"

She drank more.

"That's really good. What kind of roots is it made of?"

"I really don't know," laughed Shawn. "You'll have to ask the company that made it.

"You have company? Will I meet them?"

"Not that kind of company, a bottling company—people who put hissing drinks in cans."

"Oh!"

She drank the rest of the can.

"Do you have more? That was too good to be true!"

"Yup! Plenty!"

And he got her another can, and then sat down to listen to her story.

August 18: Fourth Movement—Cain.

Were this a full novel, I would allow Mayte, at this point, to tell her story of the trip down the mountain and across the abysmal swamps in her own voice. But this is a short story, in which the focus needs tightness. Know, then, that Mayte told her story to the apparently amazed Shawn, amazed more by her primitive quality and naiveté than by the story itself.

When she had finished, she and he both heaved a sigh of relief. In the meantime, while he had listened, he had provided a dinner for the two of them on the porch of halved pheasant and potato slices and skewered vegetables, all deliciously prepared over a portable charcoal grill. Mayte licked her fingers after she finished both the story and the pheasant and complimented her host on the repast. She suddenly realized just how tired she had become. Leaning back against the high back of the rocking chair, she closed her eyes. Shawn thought to himself that she was, by far, the loveliest woman he had seen for a very long time.

"Do you know, Mayte, just how beautiful you are?"

Mayte opened her eyes and smiled.

"It isn't true! I am plain Jane from the Village. Not a beauty. My hands and feet are covered with calluses and my face has great freckles blotched across it from too much sun. And my hair looks like a tumbleweed."

"You are beautiful," he repeated. "But you are tired, too. You can hardly keep your eyes open. You must sleep in my bed tonight. I'll sleep on the couch in the living room."

"I'll accept your offer of a place to sleep," replied Mayte with a thankful smile, "but not in your bed. I'll take the couch. I am used to sleeping on the ground. I'll feel like a princess, sleeping on the couch."

"If you insist. But, since you are tired now, I will restrict my movements to the kitchen and the bedroom. You have the living room to yourself. There are fresh towels in the bathroom. For water, just pump the handle over the basin. The outhouse is 50 yards down the path behind the house. If you need anything, just ask. Sleep well, Princess Mayte."

And he disappeared into the kitchen.

Mayte roused herself from the rocking chair and, after exploring for and utilizing the outhouse, she went into the house, passed Shawn in the kitchen where she bade him good night and went to the living room, closing the door behind her for privacy. The living room looked comfortable with a large soft couch of the Victorian style and an over-stuffed easy chair to match, a huge fireplace which looked as if it had not been used for a while, a roll-top desk with the top down and fronted by a wooden swivel office chair. Otherwise, the décor was sparse. Just an ornament here and there on small tables and shelves, a few books and a set of fireplace tools. She looked over a short shelf of books: *Paradise Lost, Robinson Crusoe, the Scarlet Letter, Beowulf, Pamela, Lolita.*

"Such old books for a young man!" she thought. "I must remember to read *Pamela* and *Lolita*. If he likes these others, they must be worth reading as well."

In the bathroom, she found a similar Spartan quality. Just a washstand with a basin and a pump handle beside it. She pumped the handle three times. Water gushed out. It was cold and pure.

"He must have a running spring right under the cabin," she thought. "How nice!"

She washed her face and hands and dumped the basin out of the open window behind the washstand. Then she returned to the living room. She took off her boots and socks and stretched out on the couch which had room to spare, covered herself with the blanket she found folded over the back of the couch and rested her head on the pillow at one end. This was, indeed, the most comfortable bed she had rested in since she left the village. She thought for a few minutes about life in the village, about her great uncle, the teacher-at-the-Frontier, and her trek through the swamp. She thought of Shawn, just for a moment, and then fell fast asleep.

She awoke with a start to find herself weighted down by another human body. The room was entirely dark, but she could smell strong liquor on the breath of the man who was astride her body, struggling to unbuckle her belt.

"Why do you wear your clothes to bed!?" grunted the familiar voice.

"Shawn! What are you doing?"

"Isn't it obvious?" came the reply. "You know you want it. I could tell by the way you smiled at me. Now, cooperate!"

"No, Shawn! I don't want it! I don't want to! Get off of me! Let go of my belt! You're hurting me!"

The only reply was more heavy breathing and grunting as her jeans slid down and off one of her legs. Her panties were ripped from her, and she felt her legs being yanked apart and Shawn's body forcing his erect organ against her groin. Her right hand felt for her boots and reached into the shaft of the right one. She pulled out the thin stiletto that she kept there. She felt for the left side of his rib cage and deftly ran the stiletto between the ribs into his heart and twisted the blade downward toward her own chest. His body arched suddenly upward. He groaned. Then he collapsed forward, his naked body completely covering hers, his bare and flaccid genitalia resting against hers. No breathing. All was still in the dark.

She shuddered, pulled the stiletto out of his heart; she felt his blood running across her right hand and arm. She put the knife down beside her boots, raised her right index finger to her lips, and touched it with her tongue. It was sweet, Shawn's blood.

August 19: Fourth Movement—Cain (Cont.)

Shawn's dead weight was oppressive. She placed her hands under his chest and pushed. His congealing blood split away from her skin with a ripping sound. She pushed again hard, rolling him over and off her body. She heard the thud as his body hit the floor. Breathing deeply, Mayte felt the breeze from the open window across her body, wet with blood and perspiration. She wondered if the perspiration was his or hers. "A silly notion!" she thought. She sat up on the sofa and pivoted her feet toward the floor, but they landed instead on Shawn's naked body. She lifted them quickly as if she had stepped on a snake and found a place on the floor where she could stand up. With her first step, her feet became entangled with her jeans and she fell headlong to the floor. Fortunately for her, Shawn was a man of little furniture. Nothing to fall against. She stood up, rubbing what felt like a skinned elbow, put her jeans on properly, and buttoned them up to the waist. She felt more secure. In the darkness she could make out the dim outline of a kerosene lantern on the roll-top desk. She moved carefully toward it, trying to remember the positions of all of the furniture. She remembered that there was a box of wood matches beside the lamp. She removed the chimney, lighted a match, and touched it to the wick and watched the flame skitter across the top of it until it formed a smoky pyramid. Then she blew out the match, dropped it into a nearby metal cup and replaced the chimney. The flame was high and smoky, so she adjusted it down until it burned clean, mostly blue with an orange fringe at the top of the flame, and it dimly illuminated the room. Turning to survey the room, she saw Shawn's body on its back beside the couch, arms spread like a martyr, naked, darkly streaked with blood—especially on his right side.

"I have killed him," she said forthrightly to herself. Then, "I have killed a *man!*" she said again more loudly for whatever part of the world was listening to hear. She wanted to run away as quickly as possible and was suddenly at the door, turning the knob and swinging it fully open. Her right foot was across the threshold when she heard in her mind the words of the Teacher-at-the-frontier:

Whole to parts analysis, then parts to whole synthesis. Finally, you must synthesize the whole of the specific situation to the whole of the general situation. Then you should be ready for the evaluation which leads to the solution of the problem you started out to solve.

"The whole of it is that I have just killed a man in his own home," she began aloud as she stepped to the porch and sat down in the rocking chair. "The problem to solve is how to deal with what I have just done."

She felt a little calmer.

"I feel guilty because I have killed this man. But he was trying to rape me. He would have done so if I had not prevented it. I could not have prevented it without killing him or, at least, severely wounding him. It would be difficult for me to wound him in a way that would make him too weak to hurt me without killing him. Thus, the sensible conclusion is that I could not have done better than to kill him.

She ceased feeling guilty. But she was still afraid.

"I am afraid because I don't know what the consequences of my action will be. I am a stranger in a strange land. I don't know what friends this man had or what they will do to me if they find out I have killed him. Therefore, since I have an important mission to carry out, and I am not guilty of a crime, at least in a moral sense, the most important thing for me to do is to prevent anyone from discovering that I have killed him. I must get rid of all evidence and leave as quickly as possible. It is not a problem that I will be breaking the law of the locality because I cannot determine what that law is. If I were in the village, it would be my responsibility to report the killing to the legal authorities; but in this place, I don't know who the legal authorities are or even if there are any legal authorities. I am not sure that I have yet come close to where the New World is being developed. This might be a place where there is no law except the law of nature.

"I will assume that this place abides only by natural law. Natural law would require that I treat this man's body with dignity. I will provide a funeral and either burn the body or bury it. To burn it would cause a great deal of smoke which might bring down other persons upon me. Thus, I will bury it.

"Then I will clean the cabin of all blood and wash myself and my clothes in the river. I will take everything I brought with me, and I will leave by the most promising route possible and try to find some sort of civilization as quickly as I can. Not too quickly, however, since I don't want to arouse suspicion that I had anything to do with Shawn's death if he is discovered soon."

She began immediately to carry out her chores. First, she dragged Shawn's body (no easy feat for he weighed at least 225 pounds, she only about 100) outdoors and around to the back of the cabin where she knew there was a large clearing which looked as if it had been a garden in former years. She found a shovel, fortunately quite sharp. She saw this as a good side of Shawn that he kept his tools in good order. She dug a grave. The soil was unusually soft and deep here. Whoever chose this spot for the cabin knew a lot about such choices. In an hour she had a hole four feet deep and large enough to accommodate Shawn's body. She rolled him in, said a prayer over him (lest there be God), and backfilled the hole, mounding it up at the top and stomping the dirt, then adding more dirt to accommodate for the compression that would happen naturally over the next few days. Then she gathered large weeds and grass from the immediate vicinity and scattered them as naturally as possible over the grave. In the lantern light, except for a slight mound, it looked as if nothing had happened there. She would check it again at daylight to be sure it looked natural.

Next, she cleaned up the inside of the cabin, scrubbing up the blood from the floor and from the upholstery of the couch. Again, the lamplight might not tell all, so she vowed that she would check it again at daylight. She cleaned the bathroom, wiping away any fingerprints she might have left on the pump handle and the basin, even the walls and window sill.

This thorough cleaning took more time than she had anticipated. By the time she was finished, dawn was breaking over the eastern horizon. She went to the river, listened for a moment to the familiar rattlesnake sounds and then commenced the same kind of ablution she had accomplished the previous day. She took special care to remove all the blood from her jeans and her boots and the T-shirt she was wearing. The panties Shawn had ripped, she decided, would be evidence of the rape, if she were called upon to produce it. They could be repaired later. Thus, she didn't wash the blood from them, but folded them into the little ditty bag where her other dirty clothes resided. She washed the other panties and rung them out as dry as possible and put them on. When she had finished she went back to the cabin porch to finish dressing. Her clothes were wet and chilly, but she liked that better than bloody, so they were something of a relief to her. She knew that they would dry quickly when the sun rose.

227

Finally, she went to Shawn's kitchen and, being careful not to leave fingerprints, took advantage of his well-stocked larder: several hard rolls, canned beans, fruits, and vegetables, dried venison and fish. She packed them all neatly into her satchel. It was quite puffy and round when she buttoned it up. Then she ate a breakfast of fresh bread and a bowl of blackberries from Shawn's cooler, an innovative device built below the kitchen floor which kept food cool by immersing a metal box in the cold spring water below.

By then, it was full daylight and the sun had risen. "Time for the final check of the place," she thought. She first inspected the cabin. No sign that she had ever been there. She paid special care to the path she had made by dragging Shawn's body, brushing it natural with a leafy bough from a nearby tree. She went out back to inspect the grave. It looked like very little had happened there. Then she saw that she was not the first grave-digger. In a little nook surrounded by a white picket fence were four white wooden crosses. On each cross was carved vertically the traditional acronym: RIP. On the cross piece were the following respectively: Mom, Dad, Willy, Sheila. These could be Shawn's parents and siblings. On the other hand, Willy and Sheila could be previous victims. She shuddered to think that her name might have been carved on a fifth cross. Sheila's cross looked fresher than the rest and the thought entered her mind that a year ago, the village had sent a girl named Sheila, Mayte's friend, on the mission Mayte now was committed to fulfill. It was just a thought, but it unsettled her as she picked up her satchel from the front porch and started down the trail toward the other trail which seemed to lead somewhere.

August 20: Fifth Movement—Interlude from Country to Town.

The trail leading away from the river was easy to follow and downhill. Mayte followed it all day, passing by lesser trails that she guessed led to other hermit abodes like that of the late Shawn. All day, she kept thinking, "Sheila! Could it be Sheila under that cross? From the village there had been three before Mayte: Sheila, David (her brother), and Uilaria (the first to leave the village more than three years ago). If the grave belonged to Sheila, that was one explorer accounted for who would not be returning to the village with Mayte.

When it was almost sunset, Mayte noticed a change in the trail. It had now become two tracks as if wagons had traveled there. That meant civilization was near at hand. She estimated that Shawn's cabin was 30 miles behind. She was a fast walker and had covered a lot of territory during the last 10 hours. That was a significant distance, but she was probably the only person to walk this trail all day today which would make her a legitimate suspect in Shawn's death if he were to be discovered right away. Yet, she reasoned, if the discovery were not made for a couple of days, any delay in her entry into civilization might just converge with the time of that discovery. She would still be suspect. She decided not to delay. However, she was tired and dusty from her walk through the humid warmth of the foothills. She did not want to show up looking like a hobo.

The terrain was still wooded. The path crossed a small stream and she followed it away from the road, downhill, until she came to a modest-sized clearing where she could rest for the night. The clearing was at a bend in the stream where the current had washed out a hole deep enough for her to bathe in and rinse out the sweaty T-shirt, socks, and underwear she had been wearing all day.

"This will make me smell less like a ripe armpit to the next person I meet," she joked to herself. She was in a better mood, having convinced herself that she had committed no evil in killing Shawn, especially, since it was probable that she was not his first victim and she might have saved others from a similar fate. The water was cold and invigorating. The evening was becoming cool and that, along with the cold water, made her teeth chatter. She let her teeth chatter for a few moments while the breeze dried her body. Then she pulled on her clean panties, T-shirt, and socks and buttoned on her jeans.

Still a little chilly, she retrieved the tiny silver bundle from her leather satchel which was her emergency blanket. It was made of a substance that looked like tinfoil but felt more like cloth. When she blew air into it through the valve at one end, it became a soft and warm protection from the elements. It was tough material, but she was careful when she sat down with it wrapped around her not to snag it and lose the insulating benefit of the air inside. She remembered that this sort of blanket was the invention of Great-Great-Grandfather. He had seen firefighters with such a blanket, less the pneumatics. He took two of the fireman's blankets sealed them together in a crosshatched design leaving air passages between each mini-compartment that this design produced, and he added the valve to blow it up. Once he had tried it himself several times during overnight fishing trips, he decreed (he was quite the decree-er) that all of his children and grandchildren should have one whenever they traveled. By the time of the northward migration, his emergency blanket, in a refined factory-made form had become a staple of every pack. At the village, Cal, the handyman, set up a room in his house and dedicated it to the production of new blankets for old ones that got snagged. He was, also, good at fixing damaged blankets in case there was a shortage of new ones. He was not a fast worker and he had a lot of other things to do, being the best of the handymen.

Her stomach told her that it was well past her normal supper time. She took advantage of the hard rolls and a can of sweet peas retrieved from Shawn's larder. She opened the peas with the can opener blade on her ancient camping knife. After she ate, she had a momentary moral crisis, what to do with the empty can from the peas. The environment in which she camped was pristine—no human trash, no tin cans. She did not want to be the first to spoil it. Yet, her leather satchel was quite full with the booty from Shawn's cabin. It was a small thing, yet it loomed large morally. She decided that she would keep the can until it could be discarded properly. In the meantime, it would make a good drinking cup, something she had not had since she left the village. Besides, it was empty now and lightweight. She filled it with a wrapped hard roll and stuffed it into her satchel softly whistling a little tune as she worked. She was practicing what she had been taught by her parents and grandparents and in school and by the Teacher-at-the-Frontier, things both great and small. They all seemed to matter here. Mayte wondered if they would matter as much when she reached the civilization of the New World—the part beyond Shawn.

Soon, Mayte, listening to the music of the rushing stream, became sleepy as the night descended, and she lay over with her head on her leather satchel and went to sleep. An old owl and a couple of whip-poor-wills provided soothing company for her peaceful repose and she slept until the new day began to dawn through the crease between the high mountains to her east.

August 21: Fifth Movement—Interlude from Country to Town (Cont.)

In the dawn twilight, a woman, white haired, face and coloring of a Mayan septuagenarian, dignified and straight, dressed rustically in leather shirt and trousers, stood on a hillside boulder overlooking the campground Mayte had chosen. She stood as still as the trees that surrounded her. Two heavy gold chain necklaces with colored pendants, one emerald green, the other ruby red, she wore around her neck. She remained silent, expressionless, on the boulder, looking down at the sleeping Mayte. She touched gently the pendant stones on her chest with the fingers of her left hand. When Mayte stirred, awakening, the woman turned quickly and disappeared, quiet as a hunting cat, into the woods.

August 22: Fifth Movement—Interlude from Country to Town (Cont.)

Mayte arose from her peaceful night's sleep unaware that she had been watched. She had mixed emotions. She liked being alone in the woods. Of course, she really didn't feel alone at all. She had all of nature to keep her company—and she was in charge. She scorned the philosophers who considered humanity to be inferior to nature, to be a helpless naked ape. She saw nature more like the Biblical Garden of Eden where humans were responsible for management. And she liked nature—the rocks, the water, the plants, the animals—even if she, sometimes, had one of them for breakfast.

No killing of animals for breakfast this morning though. As much as she loved camping in the woods and as much as she dreaded coming face to face with the culture of the New World, she knew it was time; and she was anxious to get started. She must find her brother David or, at least, find out what happened to him. She shuddered at the thought that he might be dead, and she thought of her friend Sheila and what must have happened to her. "I guess she just hadn't learned her lessons well enough," Mayte thought. And of course there was Uilaria. Mayte had not known her well. Mostly, she lived in the lowlands in a cabin-tent at the farms. Though beautiful, with long dark curly hair, slender and muscular, creamy dark skin, she seemed cold and sullen to Mayte when she occasionally saw her in one of the stores in the village. They had never spoken. Of course, this was not unusual since Uilaria was three years older than Mayte and considered her to be just a child. It seemed ironic that, now, the child was responsible for rescuing the woman or, at least, responsible for finding her or finding out what happened to her.

She had another of Shawn's biscuits and some of her dried rattlesnake and washed it down with a tin-can cup of water from the stream. Then she packed up and headed back to the main road, for that is what it had now become. It was obvious, now, that civilization was near. There were even some wooden bridges over the streams and a fence here and there confining a few goats. Confined goats are as sure a sign of civilization as are wild goats a sign of the wilderness. Nearly every society on earth has started out by confining and domesticating goats. Mayte enjoyed that part of society; she liked gamboling about the pasture with the goats and pretending to head-butt with them. But she rather wished that society had not gone on to domesticate other animals. They were so much better in the wild. Cow pastures, for instance, were always smelly and fly-ridden. And dogs, as far as she was concerned, had little business in close proximity with humans. They were always the losers. First, they lost their sense of freedom, following the commands of people. Eventually, they seemed to lose their sense of individuality entirely and become, merely, the slaves of the humans. Mayte despised the idea of slavery of any kind, especially for animals. Humans should manage the animals, not turn them into slaves. She could not look at a work-horse without feeling contempt for both the horse and its master. "Let the man pull his own plow," she thought, "or use his fine mind to invent a machine to do it for him." Of course, she realized that such invention had taken time and that, in the interim, it was practical to take advantage of the strong muscles of the horses and oxen and elephants. But, now, they should be released from their bondage.

In no time at all, Mayte was ten miles down the road. The forest had ended, and the farms had begun. She had expected this. Farms were always in the lowlands. These farms were large and were populated with large implements to do the farming—tractors, hay cutters, balers, stackers. Extravagant farm mansions, not cottages and tents like the ones near the village farms, dotted the horizon. Some of the farms had large lots confining dairy cattle in extraordinary numbers, thousands it seemed to Mayte, their tails bobbed stubby so they were no good for shooing flies, covered with manure to their bellies, poking their heads through stanchions to eat the dry hay that they apparently lived upon. Here and there, an adventurous cow had climbed to the top of a gigantic manure pile, playing king of the mountain. And the smell! It was appalling to Mayte's olfactory sense. She held her nose and turned her eyes away in embarrassment for the cows and for her fellow humans.

"Is this why we are on the earth?! To enslave and abuse these beautiful animals?! Let us drink their milk and even eat their flesh, but this is criminal!"

She hurried by these dairy farms, sometimes even running past them to put them behind her and out of her mind.

And then, in the distance, she saw what seemed to be smoke, not rising, just hovering over the roofs of what appeared to be homes and business buildings and multistoried warehouses and factories with tall chimneys each belching out black smoke. And now, the automobile traffic, mostly ancient cars, cars that had been current at the time of the migration, restored as well as possible to be operable, but here and there a new model, sleek and shiny, but, obviously using technology as old as Great-Grandmother. Apparently, although the New World had rediscovered the means of resuming the carbon-based economy of the 20th century, it had not moved past it. Mayte had read in her textbooks about that economy and how it had contributed to the global warming which had, finally, led to conflagration and the mass migration north and south. Great-Great-Grandfather, who had been a college professor, had written some of those textbooks. Some of his textbooks were still being used in the village, because so little had changed there since its founding.

When night began, and Mayte had not yet reached the suburbs of the town, she detoured onto a side road, one not paved with asphalt but with loose gravel from some river's bed, and sought out a convenient grove of trees where no house had been built and none was near at hand. Her neighbors were cattle and horses in a large pasture that surrounded the grove. It looked like a peaceful place to spend the night. She would not be able to build a fire because the smoke would be noticeable, she thought. But she should be able to sleep well. The only deficiency would be the slightly acrid smell of smoke (smog, she remembered that it had been called in the textbooks) and the competing smell of the CAFO (confined animal feeding operation) dairy farms. She had read about those, too.

"I think that this will not be a good place for the people of the Village-in-the-Mountain to live. They must find another place. At least, that much I know that I can tell them when I return, even if I never enter the town."

August 23: Sixth Movement—Mayte's Triumphal Entry.

But she did enter the town early the next morning. On her way to town, she met up with an old she-cat trailed by a litter of three kittens. The old cat was a calico with bright orange and black and white patches. Two of the kittens were of the same hue as their mother. The other was orange. Mayte knew that meant the orange one was a Tom and the other two were she's. That is the way with calicos. The old cat, leading her kittens, decided, I guess, to escort Mayte into the town. Every now and then, she would look over her shoulder and meow as if to say, "Follow me." Mayte obeyed like a dignitary escorted by a marching band; past the sign that said, "Entering New Denver, Population 27,496" (from which some jubilant new parent had struck out the '6' with a black X and replaced it with a '7'); past the rows of boxy little houses with half-dressed and filthy children playing in the yard who stood up and craned their necks to see the passing parade; past the cemetery with its monotonous small white marble markers all in rows no matter what angle you looked at them; past the mansions of the rich, the liquor stores, the notion stores, the boutiques with fancy ladies walking in and out. Right up to the front steps of the New Denver Community Christian Church, a massive building with huge concrete steps and a matching concrete wheel-chair path in a semi-circle leading to the same massive wooden doors. And a similarly massive cross at the top of a tall steeple. Mayte wondered whether there were other houses of worship for Muslims or Jews or Buddhists. It would appear that the Christians thought a great deal of their religion.

She stood there for a moment contemplating the grand structure. The sign on the front lawn said "Welcome!" The she-cat with her kittens following her walked away down the street, her parade marshal's duties complete. Mayte entered the church.

August 24: Seventh Movement—Song of the Priest.

As Mayte pulled open one of the huge double wooden doors, she heard someone moaning. At least she thought it was moaning. Then, she thought again and decided that whoever was making such a noise was not doing so out of pain. There was a tune to it. And words. She could just make out some of the words. They had to do with praising God and Jesus and how awful we are as human beings but how lucky we are to be God's children and how we wish that everyone in the world could be God's children. It went on and on, but it finally stopped. Mayte had, also, stopped—just a couple of feet inside the door. She stood in awe as the great door closed itself behind her. It seemed to her that glowing stained glass was everywhere. And the great hall of the church was enormous, at least 50 feet high and so long that the priest at the front of the church going through all sorts of ceremonial gyrations seemed to be miles away. Between Mayte and the priest was row upon row of pews above which she could see here and there a head sticking up, bowed in an attitude of prayer (or, perhaps, they were all asleep since they didn't seem to be moving). Not very many of them for such a big church! It seemed like an awful waste of space; but it was, indeed, beautiful with all of the colorful stained glass and sunlight streaming through.

The minister, dressed in a floor-length purple robe and a strange pointed hat, was almost through with his activities. He finally went to the side of the rostrum and sat down in a chair that looked like a throne. Then more music started, this time from the pipe organ. Mayte thought that the noise might do harm to her ears, and she put her hands over them. That made the sound more tolerable, even pleasant. She recognized the tune. It was one she had heard some of the older members of the village singing. The words, she remembered when she heard a few voices from the congregation, were, "A mighty fortress is our God." They didn't make a lot of sense to her, not being deeply acquainted with orthodox Christian's military metaphor. But it was a nice tune and the poetry seemed quite effective. "A bulwark never failing" was something she had read about in one of her history textbooks. It was a wall that soldiers stay behind to protect themselves from enemy fire. Mayte wasn't sure what going to church had to do with warfare. She did notice, however, that very few of the communicants sang along with the organ even though the music director was standing on the rostrum urging them on by waving her arms in the air and singing at the top of her lungs, something about "cruel hate." Hmm!

Then the song ended. The priest rose from his throne and, making a sign of the cross over the heads of the congregation, recited a benediction: "May God bless and keep you; may the Lord lift up his countenance upon you; may the Lord make his face to shine down upon you and give you peace; Amen." Mayte had never heard about God's shiny face. It was an interesting idea. She was not even aware that God had a face, let alone a shiny one, but she liked the idea that God could give peace. She could use a little of that, herself. She had been sleeping on the hard ground now for quite a while, except for the one night she spent on Shawn's couch, and that wasn't particularly peaceful. Her idea of peace would be her nice feather bed at grandmother's house in the Village-in-the-Mountain.

Then the church service was over. The priest had walked down the aisle to the door. When Mayte saw him coming, she stepped aside between the rows of pews. He nodded to her as he passed and stationed himself at the door which a deacon had propped open for the exit of the congregation. The people filed out shaking hands with the minister and looking sleepy and relieved. They all squinted as they confronted the bright sunlight shining through the open door. "Indeed," Mayte thought, "they were all sleeping before the final hymn." She would not mind curling up on one of those pews for a long nap herself.

When the last of the congregation had filed out, the priest closed the door and started back down the aisle toward the rostrum. He noticed that Mayte had not left and stopped near to her and said: "Bless you, my child. May I help you with something?"

"You must be mistaken, sir," she said. "I'm not your child. I did see a couple of girls about my age passing the church as I was coming in. Perhaps, one of those is your child."

The priest, taken aback, seemed at a loss for words. Finally, deciding that Mayte was joking with him, laughed quietly and started again. "What can I do for you?"

"I'm not sure you can do anything for me. I was curious about the church building and the sign said, 'Welcome!' so I came inside. Of course, if you can help me find my brother David or my friend Uilaria, that will be good."

"I will do what I can," replied the priest, "but, first, tell me who you are and where you have come from."

"I am Mayte, and I come from the Village-in-the-Mountain."

"And where is this Village-in-the-Mountain, Mayte?"

"Oh! I can't tell you that," replied Mayte quickly and definitively. "The Teacher-at-the-Frontier told me never to tell anyone where the village is."

"Very well, then. Can you tell me anything about your brother David and your friend . . ."

"Uilaria. Yes. She is my friend although I don't know her very well. She left the village three years ago and we have not heard from here since. David left two years ago and we have not heard from him either. We are worried that they have fallen into difficulty. They are young people just a little older than I am. They were sent out from the village to see what sort of New World is being built and to see whether we could come here to live. Their instructions were to come back as quickly as possible, at least within a year, and report what they have found."

Mayte didn't mention Sheila. She thought that she knew where Sheila was. The image of the grave markers at Shawn's place passed through her mind and she frowned.

"And why do you think that they might be in New Denver?"

"Well, this is the first town I have come to and I think, since they were following the same map that I had, the one that helped me find my way across the swamps, that they would have come this way."

"And they would have been walking when they arrived, no car or horse or other mode of transportation?"

"No, they would have been walking."

"Hmm!? I can say almost assuredly that Uilaria has not stopped here. It is likely, since I am given the names of all the new residents that I would be aware of a single young lady named Uilaria arriving from a place called the Village-in-the-Mountain—unless she was using a false name?"

"No, she wouldn't do that. We are very proud of our names and we never tell lies about such things."

"David, though, is quite a common name. I might have forgotten. What is his last name?"

"We don't have last names. We don't need them. I remember that Great-Great-Grandfather had a last name, but I don't even remember what it was. No one since him has had one as far as I know."

"Hmm! That would have been an oddity. Let me look in my records."

The priest led Mayte into a little study and opened a file cabinet. He went through until he came to the D's. "No use looking here. We would have insisted on some sort of surname. What was your father's name?"

"My father's name was Hunter."

"Hmm! Yes. Here we go. David Hunter. Married October 16, 2074, to Elizabeth Welborne. I remember him—a really handsome and mannerly young fellow. Of course, Elizabeth grew up here in New Denver. She was an orphan. Apparently, she lost her parents on the migration here from northern Idaho. A local family, the Welborne's, very wealthy with no children, took her in as if she were their own. David looks a little like you, come to think of it—same coloring, same kind of face. He's strong-looking like you, too."

"Do you know where he is now?"

"Unless they have moved, he and Elizabeth are living in the house where she grew up. Her adoptive parents live in a larger house they built recently on the other side of town. Neither Elizabeth nor David comes to church, so I haven't kept track, but you'll probably find them there."

He wrote down an address and handed it to Mayte. As an afterthought, he went to another cabinet and retrieved a folded map of New Denver. He unfolded it on a table and marked a spot on it. "This is the place," he said. "And here is where we are. You can have this map. I have dozens of them."

He folded the map with the marked location of David and Elizabeth's house showing and handed it to Mayte.

Although she said little, remembering that her great uncle had said that she should not divulge more information than necessary, she was jubilant. She, hugged the priest, something of a shock to him, and almost skipped out the door carrying her brother's address and the map. She would find him today—she hoped against hope that she would find him today. The church door closed behind her as she ran down the concrete steps to the street looking for a street sign as ground zero for her search.

August 25: Eighth Movement—an Unexpected Encounter.

"Elm Avenue and 8th Street! O.K. Now where is David's address? Here it is: 225 Oak Avenue. Six blocks west to 2nd Street; then four blocks south to Oak. Then it's got to be easy to find the number."

And it was. It was a pretty white house, too large to suit Mayte, two stories with three sets of dormer windows in the upper floor. A big front door with brass hardware including a knocker that looked like a lion with a ring in its mouth. The yard was green and well kept. A white picket fence surrounded the lawn and a concrete walk-way seemed to invite visitors. A country style galvanized mailbox stood by the gate. The name on the side was Hunter.

"This is the place!" she affirmed to herself, making good use of a line she had read somewhere in a school book.

She opened the gate and walked up the concrete sidewalk to the door. She was about to lift the ring of the brass knocker when a familiar voice interrupted her.

"Mayte!" the voice said quietly.

"Tutu?" Mayte answered without turning.

"Yes." said the voice of Mayte's grandmother.

235

Mayte turned. There was her grandmother, dressed all in tanned leather with a satchel exactly like Mayte's slung over her shoulder. Even her head was covered with a broad-brimmed leather hat with a beaded band and a leather string for a chinstrap.

"Tutu! It's so good to see you! But, how did you get here? Why?"

"You and David are all that I have. I wanted to be sure that you are O.K. I've been here many times."

"Then," Mayte enquired, "you have seen him. Is he O.K.?"

"More than O.K.," replied Mayte-the-Elder, for that was both her name and her legal title in the Village-in-the-Mountain. "He is more than O.K. He has multiplied. He has a wife and a child, another on the way. Apparently, he is fertile since he has only been married for something over a year. Besides that, he is rich. His wife is the adopted daughter of one of the wealthiest couples in town, and, since she is his only daughter, and she doesn't want to be a business executive, David stands to inherit the job as chief executive officer of the company within a few years. At present, he is pulling down a huge salary as vice president and chief accounting officer. And he seems as happy as a robin with a worm. I guess he *is* something of a robin with a worm." She grinned and wiggled her second finger near her crotch. Then she laughed that infectious laugh that Mayte had learned to expect and love. Mayte laughed, too.

"What does he say about all of this?" asked Mayte getting serious again.

"I haven't the slightest idea. I haven't talked to him. I have a bad reputation for myself as the old Indian woman who watches his house, but I have never walked up to the door, as you just did, to knock on it. And before you knock on the door, I want to ask you if you really want to do that?"

"Of course I do, Tutu!" replied Mayte, a little shocked even though she knew very well that her grandmother was a little odd at times. "Why shouldn't I want to talk to him? He is my brother and he is the biggest reason I was sent to the New World, according to your brother, my great uncle: to explore the New World and bring back information about it and to find David and the others who were sent and did not return."

Mayte-the-Elder became suddenly serious. She moved her right hand to her chest where her fingers lightly touched the two necklaces that she wore.

"I have some bad news for you, Mayte. I think you suspect part of it. Both Sheila and Uilaria are dead. These are their necklaces. I gave them to them before they left for the New World, birthstones. Sheila was born in May. Hers is emerald. Uilaria was born in July. Hers is ruby."

"Where did you find those?"

"In the cabin where you shivved that fellow a few days ago. What was his name? I can't think of it right now. That was good work you did. Uilaria and Sheila didn't master their self-defense lessons as well as you did. They are both buried in the back yard beside that fellow's parents. The fellow was crazy, a serial killer. You really did this town a favor. He was, apparently, taking about one of them a month. He didn't take them home to his cabin, though. He just strangled them and let them lay where he finished playing with them. The town doesn't know he's dead. Most of them don't even know he exists and none of them care. They don't know he's a killer. But I know."

236

"Sheila and Uilaria are both dead? Of course! Uilaria—Willy. So sad! His name was Shawn. How did you know I was there?"

"Haven't I always said that Tutu always knows what you and David are doing? Things haven't changed. When you left my brother's camp, I was right behind you."

"How. . . how did you get past Great Uncle?"

"Oh, he's easy. I've been there a dozen times. He's blind in one eye and can't see out of the other one. And he's almost as deaf. I just walked by about 30 feet behind you. By the way, you need to get those eyes examined that you are supposed to have in the back of your head. I was walking along in plain sight behind you most of the time. Also, you don't always make the most sensible decisions about how to cross a swamp. When I come by myself, I don't even get my boots dirty. But I should have watched you closer. A while before you got to the river, I got sidetracked trapping a rabbit for supper and cooking it, and I didn't even know that you had crossed the river. About midnight, when I couldn't find you on the north side of the river, I had a hunch you had gone across, and I tracked you to the cabin just in time to see you dragging out old bloody-guts. I taught you right about using that stiletto, didn't I Honey?"

Mayte shuddered. "That was an awful night, but you didn't answer my question. Why haven't you talked to David?"

"I wanted to make sure he is O.K. I didn't want to bother him."

"Oh, Tutu! You are never a bother."

"I'm not so sure. If your father-in-law was a millionaire and your inheritance was on the line, would you want me to come out of the shadows?"

"I see your point, but I would. And what do I care about money?!"

"But you are not David. David has concocted a story about how his parents were lost in a storm, and he had to make it on his own until he came to New Denver. In a way, he isn't lying about losing his parents in a storm, if you count a storm of passion. Your mother *blew* off a lot of steam at your father, and your father *blew* out the door and was never seen again. Then your mother *blew* her own brains out with a shotgun, and I raised you and your brother. But that was a pleasure. Do you still want to talk with David?"

Mayte, having long been aware of her mother's suicide and accustomed to her grandmother's lack of verbal restraint, held back her tears and answered, "Yes, I do. And I think that you should, too."

"No! But you can give him my greetings. And I won't give you any advice. I've never been half as smart as you anyway. Just remember that I'll be watching you."

Grandmother and granddaughter met at the middle of the walkway and embraced. Then, the old woman turned and left. Mayte watched her out of sight. A tear made its way down her cheek, and she brushed it away. Then she turned and went to the door. She raised the knocker and dropped it. Its brassy resonance echoed up and down the street.

August 26: Ninth Movement—Mayte and David.

When the knocker fell, the door opened wide almost instantly. David, Mayte's only brother, stood before her with arms outstretched.

"Mayte, so good to see you! It has been far too long."

"Yes. It has," replied Mayte. She stepped forward and returned the hug that David offered. "Why haven't you contacted us? We were all worried."

Mayte saw David looking over her shoulder and down the street. "She's gone," was her reply to the question that she knew his eyes were asking.

"It isn't that I don't want to see her. It's just that it isn't convenient now."

"And why is that, David? You don't want to see the woman who reared you because you are ashamed of her?"

"Not exactly, but Elizabeth's father just wouldn't understand. And I couldn't tell him about the Village-in-the-Mountain. I can't tell anyone that, although I have told Elizabeth. I couldn't keep it from her."

"How do you know he wouldn't understand? Have you asked him?"

"Well, no. But I don't know how to explain it to him."

"Just tell him. Tell him that the strange woman who keeps watch on your house is your grandmother, the woman who raised you to manhood. Is it such a terrible thing that she wears leather clothes and doesn't talk much to any of the people in New Denver? You don't have to tell him about the Village. Just tell him that she (and you) came from a place far to the north in the mountains. If he is the decent man that you seem to think he is, he will not demand more information than you can give. And if he is any kind of a businessman, he will want you to run his business because you are the best, not because of who raised you."

"Come in. I want you to meet my family."

"No. I will not come in. If you do not accept Tutu, you cannot accept me. When I know that you have fully accepted Tutu, I will accept you and your wife and your child and any other children you have by then. Goodbye, David. It is good to see you. I think you are happy, at least as happy as you can be while living a lie. When you have stopped living that lie, I am sure you will be happier."

David hung his head, silent and sad for a moment. Then he straightened up and looked directly into Mayte's eyes.

"If you see Tutu, please tell her to come to the door next time she visits. I want to introduce her to my family."

"I will do so, but that might not be enough. I fear that you will have to go to her. Are you ready to do that?"

"Yes, I'm ready. You have made me feel ashamed. I will be the man that Mayte-the-Elder reared me to be, and I will regain your respect as my sister." Tears were pouring down his cheeks. "I love you, Mayte."

"I love you, too, David." Tears were, also, pouring down Mayte's cheeks. "I will know when you are ready to accept me." She turned and walked away from her brother down the concrete walkway, through the white picket gate, away from the big white house where he lived with his family. She trusted David and expected to return. She looked forward to the reunion with excited anticipation. But now, she had a mission to complete.

August 27: Tenth Movement—Mission's End.

Mayte, returned to the Teacher-at-the-Frontier, reported to him all that she had learned, and suggested that it would not be wise to move the people of the Village to New Denver. She did not tell him that Mayte-the-Elder had followed her

238

to New Denver. Nor did she tell him that Mayte-the-Elder, at that moment, was watching them from the edge of the forest just to the south. Instead, Mayte surprised her great uncle with a very tight hug and a kiss right on his wrinkled lips. Then she bade him goodbye and surprised him again by turning back to the south and disappearing into the forest in the direction of the swamp.

August 28: Coda.

It had been a year since Mayte returned to the cabin formerly occupied by Shawn Rawlins. She rarely had visitors. On this day she would have two.

First, in the forenoon, a young man would come down the trail from the river. Since Mayte's report of her journey had provided hope for such journeys, the village elders had decided to send another explorer before deciding the future of the village. He was the Village's next emissary to the New World. His name was Ernest. He had been a good friend to Mayte in their childhood. They had played together often in the forests near the Village. Ernest was happy to see Mayte, but not at all surprised. They talked for a few moments on the front porch. Then Mayte invited him in and they both entered the cabin and the door swung closed behind them.

Mayte-the-Elder, who had been watching from the edge of the forest nodded in satisfaction. Almost a year earlier, she had read the note David had left for her tacked on the gate of the white picket fence in front of his house inviting her to come in. She had left a note in reply that she would meet him in the woods by the Rattlesnake River, but not until a year had passed. She had business at the village to finish first. Today they had met by the river, and he had returned joyously to his family in New Denver. Later today, she would knock on Mayte's cabin door. She smiled, and it seemed the sun shone brighter.

August 29: Postlude—Two Old Men Talking.

Scribe here! Sam is sleeping. He told me that he was taking a day off and that I should write the entry today. So that I shall.

I read the "short story," the one that doesn't fit with Poe's prescription for the short story unless you can read very fast or for a long time. Anyway, if you have been doing what is appropriate for the reader of an almanac, you will have been reading one entry per day. Thus, it will have taken you twenty-three days to work yourself though this behemoth: too short even for a novella, too long for a short story, unnamable.

But I suppose that Sam has a right to be creative enough to write a story that is too long and too short at the same time. I am more troubled by his perfunctory tossing off of Movement Ten and the Coda. They contain a large part of the action of the story and very few of the words. I brought this up with Sam, and he asked me if there was anything in the presumed action of the last two entries which any dunce would not have known would be there unless he told them. I said that I didn't think so. He said, mimicking my oldest grandchild: "Well, Duh!" Then he invited me to the Silver Spur Bar in Wendell for a beer.

While we were drinking beer, he said: "I could have written forty or fifty pages telling how it all worked out, but this is not a novel. Thus, what we are interested in is not a long detailed resolution, just a brief dénouement and coda. It needed those because it is an artistic piece hovering between orchestration and fiction. But the two entries don't need much content. If they were longer, some readers would enjoy them for the wrong reason. They would get all dewy-eyed and emotional and say, 'What a sweet ending.'

"It isn't a happy ending at all. It is an ending that says we are all frail and incompetent, and we don't really know much of anything. First of all, Mayte fails utterly in her mission. Instead of remaining incognito, she makes a giant splash by killing her sex-crazed assailant. Any good secret agent would know that she blew her cover and should head for home immediately. She pressed on like a naive teen-ager, which she was. Her great uncle, the teacher-at-the-frontier, knows absolutely nothing about what he is teaching Mayte for her entry into the New World although he is a pretty good ethical philosopher. But he turns out to be a lousy gate-keeper being both optically and aurally challenged. His sister, Mayte-the-Elder, is insane, stalking her grandson and failing to warn or protect her granddaughter. Remember that just at the moment Mayte is in the greatest danger, grandma (who is fully aware of the danger) gets sidetracked trapping a rabbit for supper. She's just plain nuts. Mayte's brother, David, chooses to be a leader in all of the evils that destroyed the Old World, and, on top of that, drives wedges between himself and his grandmother and his sister by his choices. He doesn't change this in his reconciliation. He, simply, allows his in-laws to be aware of his roots. Mayte was right. He won't be fired by his father-in-law for this. His father-in-law will, probably, hire some poor literary drudge to write a folktale lauding David's conquering of the giant (his past) with only a sharpened lead pencil.

"Mayte is quite the junior philosopher, though. I like her. I like her a lot. I, also, like her grandmother and her grandmother's brother with all of their shortcomings. They are thinkers, and they are strong and they persevere even when the odds are stacked against them. I have a special affinity for old guys who like to give advice (I'm one of those), for old women who laugh at such old guys (I'm married to one), and for a naïve but well-intentioned teenaged girl who speaks softly but carries a stiletto in her boot.

"There is a little more that I should add just as a matter of form. Mayte and Ernest set up housekeeping in the cabin by the river as proprietors of a new and more practical way-station for a growing stream of emigrants from the Village-in-the-Mountain, helping them along (sort of like the Buddha as ferryman) as they were forced to leave their village which was slowly being smothered by the returning polar ice; if the folks in New Denver ever found out about Shawn's untimely death, they never mentioned it—not their territory, I suppose; and Grandma Mayte, in the later stages of Alzheimer's, spent more and more time with Mayte and Ernest, providing them with abundant supplies of venison, rabbit, rattlesnake and endless tales about the old days; and they all lived happily, usefully, and semiwisely ever after."

Song of the Mountain Maiden
The End

August 30: A Sensitive Issue.

This week a U.S. senator pled guilty and then recanted his plea to a charge of disorderly conduct, a step down from the initial charge of soliciting for sex in a men's public restroom. Whether he was telling the truth when he pled guilty or when he recanted or not at all remains a mystery, one which, I am sure, will be hashed and rehashed in the press *ad nauseam*. Whatever the outcome, the mere suggestion that this Republican U.S. Senator, who made a name for himself as an anti-gay-rights advocate, is homosexual has permanently destroyed his political career. It would, probably, be fair for his career to be destroyed if, indeed, it is discovered that he is homosexual and has been lying about his sexual preference up to this time.

But, no, it would not be fair! It would be no more fair than for a person's career to be spoiled because he or she lied consistently about being left handed, or right handed for that matter. In any case, it might be harder to trust a person who dissembles about such matters (homosexuality or whichever handedness); but since when could anyone trust a politician in the first place. Nothing would have changed. Re-elect the blighter and be done with it.

Earlier today, to continue my *socially sensitive* saga, I was killing a little time before an appointment and discovered a little shop featuring "green" electronic devices (solar panels, batteries, scooters, etc.). The proprietor was one of those people (and I understand the perplexity if I am wrong in my assessment) who simply looks and talks as if he is gay. This fellow was a real gem, in the very best sense. I, as a "green" advocate living my summers with only solar electricity and interested in finding other ways (an electric scooter, perhaps) of becoming greener, found his expertise in the discipline wonderful. I talked with him for over an hour and haven't spent a better hour (other than my phone conversations with Yasmin) all summer. It was a pleasure, and I came away refreshed. This fellow probably will not have his career ruined by allegations of homosexuality. He is not a politician. I don't know whether he is Republican or Democrat. He is just a fine fellow with whom to while away an hour.

These two items convince me (although I was convinced long ago) that it is high time we stopped placing such negative value on homosexuality. The abusive priest scandal, for instance, has nothing to do with homosexuality and everything to do with pedophilia (which I abhor). Our disempowered U.S. senator, if he is of the great value to our country that many citizens have considered him to be, should be re-elected and continue in that valuable role (though I would not vote for him because I disagree with him politically on a number of issues). Except as a matter of casual interest, my friend the "green" proprietor's sexual preference should be no bigger deal to me than whether he is left or right handed unless, of course, I am seeking a unisex tryst—*which I am not.*

I am not here to argue whether homosexuality is a product of nature or nurture. I suspect it is, largely, nature; but I am neither a biologist nor a geneticist, so I am not able to argue for such a judgment on firm ground. Neither am I here to condemn or praise persons with homosexual tendencies for either acting upon those tendencies or resisting them. I suspect, however, that resisting such temptations can lead to uncomfortable situations like the one in which our U.S. senator found himself. Following our own natures, as long as it doesn't lead to harming others, is usually the best policy.

Let me play the political philosopher (not the politician—I'll never be the politician—too many public restrooms to avoid) and make a judgment in a situation which has been newsworthy for too many years, the concept of gay marriage. Let it be! It harms no one. But . . .(and there is a "but"—of course, there is a "but"), since the term "marriage" belongs and has belonged for so many generations to the institution which joined a *man and a woman* in matrimony, it is and will continue to be a kick in the teeth of the many socially conservative persons to call gay marriage "marriage." I believe that in attempting to reach our goals, it is best to kick no tooth that it is not necessary to kick. Thus, while I support the right of gay persons to join in a fully marriage-like partnership (except, of course, for the man/woman thing), I would urge them to call it something else. There is already a copyright on the word marriage, and, like it or not, it includes the man/woman thing.

I even have a suggestion as to what it should be called, something better than "marriage" which has lost its original epistemological/linguistic meaning anyway. Call it "felizamony." Translation (if there can be a translation of such a word): "Joyous Union."

This is my recommendation for the day. May God, if God exists, add his/her/its blessing to it and to all else that is meant to be good as well as light-hearted.

August 31: Last Night I Dreamed a Dream.

I hope that doesn't make me one of those mystics! I'm not into much mysticism—unless you count that I usually avoid walking under ladders. That was a tough one for me. My outdoor summer shower requires a ladder leaning against it for purposes of getting the hose to the top of the water tank for filling. When it is leaning against the shower wall, I have to walk under it to take a shower. For a couple of days, I refused to succumb to the urge to remove it, but the mythology was too powerful. On day three, before my shower, I removed the ladder. Now I put it up and take it down whenever I need to fill the tank. I don't know if everyone has at least a pint of superstition, but I suppose I have to admit to it.

But back to the dream. I dreamed that I was in a church. Apparently, the congregation was in the habit of hanging around in the foyer chatting instead of coming in and sitting down on time. It was shortly before the start of services. The preacher made the announcement that, starting today, the last one to sit down before the service started would be kicked out. As it happened, the fellow right beside me was the last to sit down. The preacher turned to him sporting his saddest countenance and said: "Well, Tim, I guess you are it. I have to ask you to leave."

The deacon hurried up to the preacher and whispered in his ear. The preacher again turned to the congregation with the following amendment: "I guess, Lucy and Timmy [Tim's wife and son] have to go, too. They're the same family and all."

Tim and his family left obediently, heads hanging. I rose instantly to my feet, took my most fearsome rhetorical stance (right foot slightly forward, left eyebrow raised regally), and declared: "If Tim and his family must leave, then I must leave, too. And I won't be coming back."

As I marched down the aisle toward the door, I noticed that the entire congregation was leaving as well. They, however, stopped in the foyer to hold a prayer meeting condemning the preacher's action and supporting Tim and family. This completed, they left, too.

Silly dream! I don't know whether to think of it as cause or effect. Most likely, though, it is the effect of my reading David E. Cooper's *World Philosophies: an Historical Introduction.* In spite of their psychological hazards, I read one such book every once in a while to see if I am missing anything I should be reaping from primary texts. Cooper's thesis (which he claims is more of a tendency than a thesis) is that "alienation" is an important connecting theme throughout philosophy all the way back to Socrates and Lao Tzu before him. Sure enough, once in a while Cooper takes a page or two to talk about alienation as he goes along with his historical summary.

My dream, though the content was much more interesting than alienation, presented at least three versions of it. First, Tim and his family were alienated from the church for a seemingly minor infraction—not surprising when one considers that churches prefer to deal with trivia rather than important issues. Next, the preacher himself was alienated, except from the deacon, and deacons rank too low to be fit company for preachers. Finally, though, and most interesting, I felt alienated. First, I alienated myself from the preacher by challenging him on his own turf. More devastating, however, was my alienation from the congregation when they held their prayer meeting without inviting me. You see, for a moment, I thought I had become the leader of the congregation, revolting against the tyranny of the preacher. But I discovered that I was no one to the congregation. A woman who reminded me a bit of Madame De Farge led the prayer meeting (I seem to recall that she was knitting—I vaguely remember the clicking of her needles), and her severe glances at me from the corner of her eye told me that I was not welcome there. No one spoke to me or even acknowledged my existence. That is when I woke up feeling alone. That is when I realized that, although I doubt that he had any thoughts about *A Tale of Two Cities* or even Charles Dickens, Cooper was right about the important place of alienation. I would place it more squarely in psychology, but from there it is but a doleful stare away from philosophy. I will see what affect such mystical stuff as this foolish dream has on the rest of my life. In the meantime, I could really use a hug.

243

September 1: Cease to Change? Cease to Live!—Why I am Grudgingly Willing to Accept the Label of Liberal?

In my every-day life, I don't always look much like a liberal. Of course, a bushy white unkempt beard looks liberal. I have that. Also, liberals are likely to live a "green" life. Except for flatulence, Yasmin and I contribute comparatively little to global warming. I guess, overall, I do look like a liberal. I just don't feel very much like one. I live quietly. I don't join liberal organizations for the preservation of the planet. I tend to do the same things over and over again. I'm not very fond of change, and change is the heart of liberalism. But I am in favor of change, not change for the sake of change, just change that actually makes something better. For instance, in one particular liberal cause, I think that scientists should be allowed a slack rein in stem cell research. Of course, that is all mixed up with the ideas of abortion and cloning; so, first, in terms of abortion, I am a confusing person. I don't like abortion. It is not a good thing in general. However, I don't believe that I have a right to condemn it outright for other people. Thus, I would like to force people to be reasonable about abortion with laws that require special conditions (serious health danger to the mother, for instance) for abortions that occur after the first trimester. Some insist, in keeping with the idea of an immortal soul, that abortion should be banned any time after conception. That, however, is driven by religious belief and laws driven by religious belief, unless they also have powerful nonreligious sociological reasons for being, should not be passed. In reality, a fetus cannot be rational in any significantly human way (an important benchmark for being human) until well after the first trimester. Thus, limiting (not banning) abortions after the first trimester would seem to be an excellent compromise among the various parties involved in the discussion. What circumstances would make abortions legal after that time would be a matter for serious consideration.

As to cloning, I have to admit that the idea appeals to me. It would be interesting to see if I could prevent a little Me from making the same mistakes I have made during my life. But we need to delay attempts at human cloning until we are much better at cloning procedures and know a lot more about the life prospects for cloned individuals (using animals as subjects). In the meantime, I'd like to see significant progress in the cloning of human parts: livers, hearts, noses (avoiding, of course, uninvited noses that get into other persons' business).

But I was about to discuss the idea of change. It is not only a major principle of liberalism. It is the central principle of material existence in the cosmos. As far as we can know, change never began. In the infinite cosmos, it always was. In order to consider change in the context of our own finite world, we have to pretend that there was a beginning and an initial unconditioned state for every material thing that exists or has ever existed. Each generation of each thing is caused by the previous generation but with conditioning which makes its present manifold existence differ from its previous manifold existence. In addition, each manifold thing changes from moment to moment in its form and function. This is change.

Everything material changes. Thus, if everything we can possibly experience changes with every generation and every member of every generation changes within its own time of existence, what can possibly be our objection to change? Those "people of the Book," who object to change, should read Genesis. In that segment of "the Book," newly created humanity is commanded to nurture nature. What is nurture but the supervision of change? A newborn child changes to an adult. A primitive family-based society changes to a complex politically governed city or nation. A new nation changes to an established nation and, inevitably, a declining nation. A log becomes a wheel, then a set of wheels, and, eventually, a car for an Andretti to drive at Daytona. And the wheels lift off the ground to fly between cities and nations and, finally, away from the planet to other worlds which are changing. How, indeed, can we object to change? Certainly, it is our place, as the only rational creature on earth, to manage and use change, but how and why would we want to curtail it? Without it, we are nothing. Geez! I guess I am a liberal!

September 2: This is Not the Last Day of Summer.

For some reason I have come to think of September 2nd as the last day of summer. Perhaps, that is because of its closeness to Labor Day in America and the closeness of Labor Day to the first day of school (although schools have demanded earlier and earlier openings apparently in order to waste more money on air conditioners which would not be needed in temperate zones if schools were to open a little later in the fall and to close a little earlier in the spring. In fact, students would be better off, too. They would have more access to the best campus for learning (nature) during the two times in the earth's temperate zones when the temperature is, actually, temperate. I recall trying to concentrate on studies in a stuffy classroom with desks in straight rows and a teacher wearing a scowl. (I presume that the teacher was as out of sorts about having to stay inside as I was.)

"Let freedom ring!" Release all those captive students and teachers from their bondage until the first Tuesday after Labor Day and after April 14. Study books during the long cold days of winter. During our long period of liberation (April 15 through Labor Day) let us all study in that brilliant classroom that has no scowling teacher, no chalky blackboards (or smeary whiteboards). Leave the computers behind and the smart boards smarting indignantly on the schoolroom walls.

But wait! Listen to Siddhartha Gotama, the Buddha, for a moment. He had an idea for a new philosophy, a new religion, fine learning. He said that, while you are whiling away the long summer hours in the meadow or the baseball diamond or sitting on a park bench, keep your mind awake. (Actually, I added in the stuff about meadows and baseball and park benches.) Watch out for those actions and thoughts and objects that are harmful to you and to others spiritually or materially and eliminate them. Watch out for those actions and thoughts and objects that are beneficial to you and to others and incorporate them into your life. If you do this with your summer, you will be learning the good.

Of course, I am aware that you will probably be spending most of the next nine months cooped up in a stuffy classroom with a scowling teacher or in some other negative compartment such as your living room in front of a scowling television or in your bedroom in front of a scowling computer screen or a screeching video-game or reading mindless romance novels. But, even in such unpleasant circumstances, you can open your mind to change: *Discover that which is evil and dispel it. Discover the good and go into it*—even if it is only in your imagination—in your plans for next summer.

September 3: Cleaning the Camper.

The old pickup camper that Yasmin and I now call "the cook-shack" has quite a history. Much of it, I know little about. Someone purchased it in Utah from Bountiful Trailer and Camper Sales probably in 1970. I don't have the paperwork, just the faded stickers near the door. According to those stickers, it moved to Idaho in 1982. My family acquired it in 1990 when my youngest brother broke his back and needed better than a tent for camping during his rehabilitation. He sold it to my second youngest brother when he (the youngest) and his wife bought a pull-behind camper that was more luxurious. Small simple things never appealed to my youngest brother's (now) ex-wife. That is part of the reason he now lives in a small simple house. I like to think that it is mainly, though, that he has good sense. I bought the camper from my second youngest brother for $300 in 1996 at the same time I bought three acres of my mother's farm so I could spend my summers in Idaho. That was, also, the time that I acquired Mom's old granary, built when I was three years old, mainly by my mother's father who was legally blind. It had no square corners. My summer migrations to Idaho lasted two years until my heart went south and had to have its arteries bypassed. I thought at the time that I would never be in any condition to live in a primitive campsite in the camper. I closed out the campground, sold it back to Mom and parked the camper near her house where I could hook up to her electricity and spent a week or two there from time to time until about 2003 when I realized that I was in pretty good shape again and decided I needed a new campground. This time I bought four acres (the original three and an additional one as a border, all with irrigation water rights. The camper and the granary were the central focus, this time with solar panels on the roof of the porch I built over the front of the granary so I could proudly proclaim Walden-San (as Yasmin and I jointly dubbed it) "green." Our daughters went together that first summer and remodeled the inside of the camper with shiny black tile around the sink and black indoor-outdoor carpeting on the floor. It looked snazzy. And so it is, expanded now with a 36-foot used travel (but firmly rooted where it is) trailer to make Yasmin more comfortable when she lives here with me, along with a well and septic tank, lots of trees and shrubs and more green lawn than I can mow comfortably with my push mower. I do, however, mow it with a push mower. My plan is to turn most of the lawn back into desert once I figure out how to grow sage brush.

Yesterday, a particularly hot day for September in Idaho (105 degrees), I cleaned the old camper. It was, largely, a symbolic gesture. Over the past couple of years I allowed it to become quite dirty and encrusted with burnt cooking grease. I was depressed because I had been here for quite a while with only a brief (and hectic) Greyhound trip to Missouri to get acquainted with newborn grandchild #8. Depression makes me do symbolic things, like cleaning an old camper with a significant past. Now it shines like it did just after the girls remodeled it.

It is more than symbolic. Symbols are not, simply, material things. They refer to spiritual or other material things. Their special ability is to refer to such things in many different ways at once. Thus, not only does this symbol represent the material remodeling, but the spiritual feelings of appreciation and love I have for the girls (not just for remodeling but for being such good daughters in general). Also, I think of Yasmin who, along with grandson #1, had a difficult summer a couple of years back being stuffed into the old camper late at night to avoid mosquitoes while I worked in the granary with my online students. Since I had no internet service except what was available with my cell phone attached to my laptop computer, I had to work from 9 p.m. to midnight or later every night to take advantage of the free minutes (hours?) of online service. Daytime work would have been prohibitively expensive. And, of course, all of that is why, at the end of that summer, we bought the larger trailer. Yasmin is much happier there. Grandson #1 still sleeps in the old camper when he visits. Of course, now he is older and not nearly so much afraid of the odd night-time noises that go on in there. And he, usually, has grandson #2 there to keep him company.

Finally, this symbol refers to my human freedom which, over the past few years, that old camper has played such a role in drawing my attention to. I have, of course, always been free, but free only in the midst of all that I seemed to be compelled to do, all of which seemed necessary. Through all of those difficult (though happy) years, the old camper became a symbol of my innate human freedom which is a product of rational thought which comes so freely with the old camper and the old granary and the green grass and pasture surrounding us all in the remoteness of southern Idaho. My cleaning of the camper was a symbol, too, of my thanks to it as a staunch material ally in my quest for the good.

September 4: Language as the Heart of Philosophy.

As I read the philosophy survey by Cooper that I mentioned above, the closer I come to the end, the more I sense the approach of that twentieth-century thesis I dread, that philosophy's only useful purpose is to purify language for the sciences. In essence, it claims that philosophy is a discipline without content, that it must, in order to be of value, provide a linguistic service for the sciences. Such an appalling thesis!

It is born out of reactions to conclusions of both rationalism and empiricism. It came to full fruition with the approach of the age of absurdity, when it became both reasonably and empirically obvious that we humans cannot know anything for sure (except that we exist—*cogito ergo sum*). Our senses, the only connection we have with the cosmos outside of ourselves (meaning our rational minds or will or soul), cannot provide anything but sensual phenomena which are somehow connected to that outside cosmos (including every cell in our own bodies). Our minds (souls, wills) can provide nothing which is not already present in the mind and that is limited to those ambiguous phenomena presented by the senses. We can *think* that we know things, but we cannot *know* that we know things. Thus, philosophy is empty. For content, it must go to science which has faith in the phenomena processed by the senses to the extent that they remain consistent with the phenomena already studied by science. Essentially, this is inductive reasoning. Science is pragmatic. If a conclusion works, it is applied until additional phenomena (provided, usually, by advancing technology) prove that adjustment must be made in the conclusion to make it more accurate.

247

The problem that science has, according to linguistic philosophers, is that it does not have the appropriate language for examining scientific problems. Thus, its conclusions are always biased by the flaws in the language. Language is like that, according to these philosophers. Each form of language has a context within which it is the perfect language for the task. However, any language attempting to discuss a task which it is not intended to discuss will misstate the parameters of the task as well as its details. There is the argument, touched upon by Cooper, for instance, that ethnographers from, say, America, attempting to explore an African ethnicity, will get it all wrong because they will have to study it using English. Even if they learn the language of the ethnic group they are studying, they will not fully understand that language and that language will not have the tools for studying its own ethnicity and presenting it to the English speaking world. Thus, although a complete description of the ethnicity is available conceptually, the only people fully cognizant of it are the members of that ethnicity speaking their own language, and they cannot explain it to members of an English-speaking ethnicity. Thus, the ethnographers go home unsatisfied, or worse, go home thinking they understand that which they have not the capacity for full understanding.

And the linguistic philosophers think that their job is to provide solutions to this problem. Unfortunately, after more than 100 years of applied linguistic philosophy, not a single scientific problem like the one above has been solved by linguistic philosophy. Indeed, philosophers have become so enmeshed in their own linguistic net that not one philosopher can understand what the other is saying; and, even if there are two who think that they understand one another, they will surely disagree in terms of a conclusion. A veritable Tower of Babel has been erected on the battle-plain of contemporary philosophy.

It is almost as if, in order to get a fresh start, we need to go back to the time of Kant, examine again his three critiques, sort the wheat from the chaff (there is plenty of both in Kant's critiques), and re-establish the purposes of philosophy.

In metaphysics, Kant proved, essentially by claiming that he proved the existence of God, that such existence, at least in the sense of the God of Abraham, is possible but cannot be proven or disproven. Indeed, what he proved about God is that, if we consider the infinite power of the cosmos to be God, then there is a God, largely ineffable.

As to knowledge, Kant showed us that, *a priori*, there is space and time. *That* we can know. He spills a lot of ink trying to prove other matters. Mainly, he fails. He doesn't challenge Descartes' *cogito ergo sum* conclusion (where Descartes probably should have stopped), and that, too, along with space and time, seem to be knowledge held by each rational human being.

Indeed, these are slim pickings for philosophers to live on for the ages to follow Kant—if they were, indeed, the only pickings. Consider, however, that there is much more to philosophy than metaphysics and epistemology. There are history, politics, ethics, aesthetics, and, indeed, language (including logic, for logic is language and little else).

The mistake of the linguistic philosophers and a number of other 20th century philosophers is that they have come to think of logic as all of philosophy. Indeed, it is not philosophy at all unless it is coupled with other aspects of philosophy. Logic, not philosophy, is the empty (contentless) discipline. This is no

Eureka moment for anyone. It was always known that logic, just like mathematics, is abstract. Without material context, it is of no value.

We philosophers have a task, not to complete, but to continue. Like what used to be inappropriately called "women's work," our work is never done. All that Socrates tried to explain to Plato and a few other young men of Athens must be explained over and over again in context after context, and where Socrates was wrong, his wrongs must be righted. And every context, though each context is an independent discipline on its own, becomes part and parcel of philosophy in philosophy's continuing debate. Now, for instance, we are aware of the negative side of pedophilia; and, armed with that vision, we, the current philosophers, can make sure that flawed part of Socrates' vision has no part in our own cultures. That pedophilia of the ancient Greeks was much more than what it seemed. It was part of a larger philosophy which minimized and marginalized the greater part of the Greek society: women, children, slaves, anyone who was not a citizen in that early democracy along with any citizen who did not happen to be well-endowed financially or politically. Actually, a small percentage of immature male Greeks were *privileged* to be the prodigies of wealthy upper-class male citizens. These boys were the beautiful *lovers* of which Socrates speaks so positively.

And we still have entire societies who insist upon interpreting the *possibility* of God as justification for *absolute* wrath against anyone who disagrees with their interpretation. We still have a tremendous struggle with society to accept changes (advances?) which can lead to a better life for us all if we can, also, convince those in politics to abandon their quests to unnecessarily restrict the freedom of the human will.

In short, the philosophic purpose is to seek and advocate **THE GOOD**— nothing more, nothing less. It matters little whether we interpret the good as ideal forms or as empirical phenomena. It matters little whether we accept or reject the concept of a personal, benevolent God. Personal benevolence can emanate from the ordinary human without reference to God. It matters little whether we find aesthetic uplift in Beethoven or Paul Simon. What matters is that we find philosophic *uplift* and pass it on to others.

And, finally, we have the new philosophic problem of a shrinking world. Problems are no longer confined to a privileged few men on a politically exclusive street in Athens. They are universal. Indeed, in our day, the breeze from the wings of a butterfly in Calcutta stirs up a hurricane in Miami. We, even more than Cain, are keepers not just of our brothers but of *all* living beings with which we share the earth. And this is a consideration with which the rich minds of philosophers must occupy themselves.

I am thankful that many philosophers are now moving away from the nonsense that philosophy turned to in response to that inevitable recognition of absurdity that struck us so harshly during the trials of the 20th century. I am happy that so many philosophers have condemned the absurd behavior of their colleagues and seek, now, instead, to understand and to be understood in a newly pragmatic and, potentially, a far more rewarding existence than was possible for humanity in the recently deceased ignorance of exquisite absurdity.

September 5: Kant's Subtle Contribution.

One of Kant's most valuable contributions to philosophy, I am reminded by my discussion yesterday, is related to one of his greatest philosophical failures, the obvious weaknesses in his arguments for the existence of an immortal human soul. Although his failure to prove the soul's existence conclusively is a disappointment for those whose religious beliefs would be supported by such proof, his inability to do so is important to all of us who recognize that not everything can be approached with pure abstract logic. Some of the most important elements of human existence must be, simply, enjoyed (or despised) without logical proof.

This is the point where Kant enters the romantic vein of philosophy which was evident in Germany during the late 18th century and so popular in America during the earlier half of the 19th century. Thoreau, for instance, speaks of his occasional urge to run with the wild predatory animals in the forest, killing and eating his prey, fresh hot animal blood running from the corners of his ravenous mouth. (He doesn't use these words, only the ideas. The words are mine.) The philosophical impact of passages such as this defies logical analysis. Yet, I find this page of *Walden* to be one of the most memorable and inspiring in all of philosophical literature. It reminds me that, but for the rational quality which has evolved in my brain, I would be both predator and prey in the same forest which I now enter and sit on a stump to think or read—the same forest in which I wait for the dark of late evening so that I can lie on my back and contemplate the stars—and what lies beyond them.

It has been over thirty years now since I spent significant time with Thoreau. Yet my "soul" chases his through primeval forests at least once a week, sometimes in my daydreams, sometimes in nightmares.

September 6: The New Phenomenology.
Not to be confused with the Kantian phenomena, 20th century phenomenology is a confusing mess in its various explanations. It is, however, arguably, the most important adjustment in philosophy since Kant's critiques. That is the fluid, rather than particulate nature of substance. I'll not try to define substance except to say that substance is immaterial and comprises all phenomena (Kantian and Husserlian).

The most confusing thing about substance is that it comprises both phenomena representing material things as they are and immaterial *a priori* existences (if I may refer to immaterial possibilities as existences) such as space, time, God, and immortal human souls. In addition, substance comprises all other existences which enter through or are already contained within the human imagination. These, of course, are immaterial.

A second consideration of the phenomena of the new phenomenology is that, by the time they are phenomena, we are no longer considering things as they are, but things as they appear in the human mind, as the mind composes them. Thus, although they are the means through which we relate to things as they are, they are, more or less, far from things as they are, farther from them than Kant's phenomena claim to be.

I will illustrate.

This morning I learned of the death of Pavarotti. Thus, my mind, though I have never seen Pavarotti in person, formed an image of Pavarotti as I have seen and heard him on television, videos, in movies, interviews, sound recordings, etc., over the years of my life. To that image, I now had to add the concept of his death. Thus, he no longer continues (i.e., flows) in my mind as he did before this morning. That, of course, is obvious. There is a great difference between the living Pavarotti and the dead Pavarotti. However, what I realize is that, thanks to my rational memory, the living Pavarotti still flows alongside the dead Pavarotti. That makes two. With further thought, I realize that, as a young man, I listened to and saw Pavarotti as a young tenor. Thus, there are now three Pavarottis. Finally, I realized that Pavarotti existed during every moment of my life (and a little more) and that at each moment of my life (although I didn't witness every moment of his life) he was a different Pavarotti than he was at every other moment of his life. Indeed, those moments, themselves, do not really exist and thus, those momentary Pavarottis do not exist separately. Instead, they are a flowing of the existence of Pavarotti in my mind from the time of his entrance into my consciousness until today when he died and moved on to another phase of my phenomenal representation of him. Indeed, although Pavarotti did not enter my consciousness until I was well into adulthood, I can imagine him at younger and younger stages of his life and even imagine him being born. These, of course, begin and end based upon immaterial existences because they are fed through my imagination. All of those moments in his life wherein I did not see him are, also, imaginary to me. I do have, however, material evidence in the form of all other human beings I have known and have witnessed moving through life, so my imagination is able to fill in my gaps in Pavarotti's life quite adequately. And now, beyond Pavarotti's death, he continues to exist and will continue to exist in that liquid fashion until I die, at least.

As all of this is flowing, my mind, in order to preserve my sanity, is slicing Pavarotti's life up thin so that I can know him as if he actually existed for a finite period of time in the form of each of these slices, which, of course, he did not. This slicing causes a disjunction between the real existence of Pavarotti, represented by phenomena as flowing substance which is an unquestionable *a priori* principle of existence, and the Pavarotti that is required by a mind which works on finite principles of axons and dendrites and electricity and bodily fluids, hormones, etc. In other words, our natural mental state is a kind of dualism, fed by both the finite and the infinite, and both the material and the immaterial.

Greek Philosopher Heraclitus tells us that he "cannot put [his] foot in the same river twice." American Philosopher Henry David Thoreau adds that "Time is but the stream [he goes] a-fishing in." My mother's old round oak dining room table is a different table each time I eat my dinner on it. Indeed, at some point in the past, it was not a table at all and in the future it will return to a state of being "not-table." The only reason that I perceive it as a solid unchanging object is that its flow is slow relative to the flow of a river or the maturation of a pumpkin or the smile on a baby's face.

Music, ah, music! It is the closest thing to perfect new phenomenal representation. It flows without slices. One note means nothing except in the context of the composition of the whole, or, at least, in the context of that particular phrase. Hard luck, again! Even music has its pretence to being unchanging. And we listen to Tchaikovsky's violin concerto and think we are hearing the same music we heard yesterday, but the context is different (static on the radio, I just had a spat with my cat, my nose itches, a different orchestra, soloist, etc.). Thus, it is a different concerto, and why do we call it a concerto at all when the definition of a concerto is ambiguous and could, conceivably include an extended session of 1000 monkeys beating on bongos as long as they did it in three movements and there was a lead performing monkey taking solo parts from time to time. This is where language enters the picture. As humans, we mislead language into expressing what is not true. In turn, this misleading language prevents us from learning the truth.

I have heard that the Big Bang happened long ago and was a unique event. But I know it is not so. I was there at the Big Bang; and, although it was loud, it was accompanied by an infinity of distant bangs and was preceded by an infinite chorus of the same which I, also, attended and succeeded by an infinite reprise of bangs which I have attended (carrying popcorn and soda pop) and they continue to this day—to this moment.

I know this is true because you were there with me and can verify every word of it.

Also Sprak Sam Clear Water.

September 7: College Libraries.

Today, I am taking advantage of the wireless internet connection in the library of the College of Southern Idaho. In many ways, this library is like other college and university libraries: quiet, full of books, young students, mostly 18-25, sitting around tables and in semi-uncomfortable stuffed furniture.

And that is the key. Those students, working diligently to increase their understanding of, at least, some little part of the universe (although most of them would tell you they are just the victims of unreasonable professors' demands), are the hope of the world for tomorrow—because they are thinking!

Here in Idaho, I can be quite sure that most of them will turn out to be Republicans of moderate to radical right-wing persuasions. That is because most of their parents are Republicans of moderate to radical right-wing persuasions. That, although it is something of a handicap to clear thinking, is not a deadly sin. Many Republicans go on to become relatively fine thinkers and fine leaders in our American democracy and in the ever shrinking world. Beyond that, Republicans are necessary for a healthy democracy. Without them, Democrats would, more than likely, lead us toward some untoward experiment in left-wing socialism which would surely fail like all such experiments have failed in the past. Let us continue, I say, to follow the path of socialist endeavors in the environment of a well-managed capitalism.

Some of these 18-25-year-old Republican students would like to eliminate my Social Security check and Yasmin and I would have to go back to work. I would be a true curmudgeon and Yasmin, by now, has probably forgotten which medicines go with which diseases. Although she would once again be a delightfully attentive nurse, she would have to go back to school to learn modern techniques— and old folks are not always the quickest learners. It is better that she continue caring for her grandchildren while her children care for the world outside.

But why should I worry. These Republican students will not be able to outvote the majority of folks who want to keep getting Social Security checks and those who want one in the near (or sort-of-near) future. They will, however,

252

prevent the Democrats, those liberal souls, from leading us into neo-Marxism or postmodernist absurdity.

I hope that these young people (clean, neat, huddled quietly over their books and notepads and laptop computers, both Republicans and Democrats, will emerge from this best-of-all-possible-times of their lives and lead us to the best-of-all-possible worlds by preventing each other from doing more stupid things than their parents and grandparents are doing now.

Although I expect the best-of-all-possible worlds will be far from perfect, if it continues having peaceful, semi-uncomfortable, quiet, book-filled college libraries, I will be satisfied, at least, with that aspect of it. There has been some talk of the books disappearing, replaced by electronic reading materials. I hope not. Those stacks create interior walls that make the place almost private. One must feel free to scratch what itches in the best-of-all-possible libraries.

September 8: West Wind.
Whirling, chasing mountain fervor,
Whisking fall leaves with its tail,
The West Wind howls past my cabin door.

Its song—a largo of moans and sobs,
A sigh of eloquent fellowship
With hill-spirits, severed from life—
Chants relief to summer-droughted souls,
Whispers frosty sensuality
To high-born children of snow.

My scholar's soul greets you, wind of autumn:
Many-colored oracle of change,
Somber-browed frolicker,
Ice merchant,
Murderer of a million warm melodies.

September 9: Strobe Pictures.
Decay-dark wood at the root of a black oak
On the sky-clouded meadow portends dying.
As a striped skunk thumps under a car tire
Scenting midnight's silent umbrella.

Prancing stallions paw at dead trees
Whose gangling limbs rake an impenetrable canopy of cloud,
And all but the whinny of a worried mare for her colt
Is silence in the warm death watch of Fall.

Beneath the haystack, mold and mice run;
Sensing quiet through the tangled stems,
Inquisitive eyes peer from under a straw porch,
Blink at jagged bone-white lightning strokes

Illuming stallions' tossing manes.

I watch car lights describe a curve of highway
Flashing against the white of summer-stacked alfalfa,
Glancing from a barricado of mouse eyes.

I inspire the caustic sweetness of the skunk's epitaph
As stallions' flying hooves make windmills of white lightning,
And I take uneasy comfort under the palm of a close sky,
Shuddering as the first large drops
Splat against the shoulders of my summer shirt,
And the black oak's dying root grows glossy with rain-water.

September 10: The Deacon.
A wizened wizard of smiles,
The deacon commands his corner
In the foyer of the Sunday morning church;
Passing out programs
And nimble affectionate salutations
With crisp handshakes
And crackling, whispered laughter.

Silky white hair, thin on top,
Lies smooth where he brushed it;
And every sharp wrinkle beams energy
At the sleepy congregation wiping its feet on the entrance-way carpet.

At offering, every row is attended just so;
He shuffles nervous feet, hiding anguish with a smile,
When a neophyte colleague fumbles, nearly spills, a tray.

For Holy Communion, he stands
At stiff attention
Until he is served Eucharist
By a young minister half his dignity:
God's butler, dignified, attendant, quick.
Each Sunday I watch his adroit stepping.

But last week on Tuesday, I saw him alone
On a paint-pealed park bench
(Feeding popcorn to squirrels.)
I hadn't known he was old
Until I saw how his broken body
And the tired bench
Were a pair.
I passed by quickly out of the range of his dim sight.
Now, I know why he and I like Sundays best.

254

September 11: Work Ethic.

The American Puritans were right. Regular physical labor is a good thing. I think that most people hold that opinion tacitly, but too many do not live it out, so it is to be doubted that they actually believe it to be good. It was Socrates that said that people do what they truly believe to be good. Socrates was wrong. Otherwise, nearly everyone would be slender and muscular and far healthier than they are. They would not smoke tobacco. Only a teen-ager believes that smoking is good. I have not yet met an adult smoker who didn't want to quit, who didn't think smoking was a bad thing, especially now when society in general goes out of its way to make smokers uncomfortable. I see them lined up day after day each winter on a "smoke break" in whatever little outdoor ghetto they are afforded for fueling their tobacco habit, shivering in the cold and wind because they are not allowed to smoke inside. These are intelligent people. They know that smoking is not good for them and that to smoke is to be alienated. Yet they still do it. They are addicted. Addiction can be more powerful than the will for good. Of course, food and drink are other addictions that overpower the good. Yes, Socrates was wrong.

One negative addiction is the aversion to labor. I call it an addiction because, like the addiction to alcohol or cocaine or tobacco or marijuana, or food, the aversion to work is an impulse stronger than the will to good. The good of physical work is obvious and multiple. I know, because I break my work aversion addiction for six months each year, returning to it during the winter months. While I spend April to October at my Idaho campground, I work hard. I mow a quarter acre of grass once a week with a push mower. I irrigate 6 acres (sometimes more) with a shovel—no sprinklers for me, just digging ditches by hand. My calluses thicken to a quarter inch. I build fences. I clean house and wash dishes. I fill water tanks. I repair what breaks down. I shop for groceries. I do it all. I expect no assistance and seldom get any. And I lose about 20 pounds of unneeded flesh each summer. Also, my muscles get hard and flexible. My tolerance for 100+ degree heat and other forms of bad weather becomes enormous. I work right through it. When I return to Kansas City each fall, I take pride in letting my grandchildren line up to punch me in the gut to see the pain in their eyes as their little fists hit the solid wall that makes up my abs. I have to admit that makes me vain, not good.

But a few weeks after I return to Kansas City, I am back in the old recliner, avoiding all physical labor until spring. I convince myself that there is really nothing to do in the winter to keep myself in shape. No irrigating, no lawn to mow. This is just my addiction talking. The basement floor needs retiling. The living room and kitchen need painting. Even if there were no work, there is always the nature trail with its marvelous hilly settings and privacy. I would enjoy them no end—if I could just get myself out of my easy chair or my high-backed executive office chair where I spend six or seven hours a day, several of them sound asleep. By spring, I am fat, my belly has gone spongy, I live for my next trip to the refrigerator. (Yes, addiction to food goes right along with the addiction against work.)

Then, in April, it's back to Idaho and back to work and back to the work-centered life that makes me well again. It's Jekyll and Hyde, I know; and I should fix it. But one good does come of it. I can tell you as an undoubted authority on the issue that the working summer Sam is better than the non-working winter Sam. The work ethic is, truly, ethical. It is, like the end of each of the seven days of creation, God having worked up something of an ambrosial sweat from his labors and declaring it "Good!"

September 12: "Mind" Work Ethic.

The mind is not a muscle. It is living tissue, but of a different stripe than that red stringy stuff we so proudly strut as teen-aged boys (or girls?) but only realize how minimal it was when we look at the skinny kid in the high school basketball picture some years later. Beside the point! I'd rather not think of that today.

Although the mind is not a muscle, it wants exercise. Lots of it! But, just like the red stuff, it resists. In fact, the mind and the rest of the body seem to have gone into league against exercise. When I know I need to exercise my muscles, my mind leads me as quickly as possible to a situation comedy on TV or a nap on the couch. When I know the time has come to read a good philosophical text or prepare taxes, my body decides it wants to take a long walk in the forest—or a nap on the couch. This is another proof of the existence of God—one with a sense of humor.

However, if we have the will to do it, the mind needs exercise. I have an example of how we can exercise the mind while still occupying the body to keep it from getting bored. This morning, I baked bread. Not the way I normally do when I'm at the campground, by going to Mom's house and popping the ingredients into her bread machine, choosing the 1½ pound whole wheat loaf setting, pressing "on"; then I'm off to the couch to watch an episode of *The Price is Right.* No, today, when I went to Mom's house, the electricity was off—something about the power company replacing wires. It doesn't happen often. The last time I remember a power outage was two or three years ago when a storm blew all the wires together into a fireworks display and executed Mom's previous bread machine. Since then, she has always unplugged the new one when it is not in use.

But at my house, I do not depend upon Idaho Power Company. I have resisted paying the $7000+ it would cost to install rural electricity at Walden-San and continue to use only solar power. "Aha!" I exclaimed joyously to myself. "Since the last time I tried to use a bread machine at Walden-San (and failed), I have installed a more powerful DC to AC power inverter. Let us try out the new inverter today. So I did.

First I mixed up a batch of dough in the machine. Then I took it to my outdoor counter just over the battery box on the granary porch. I noticed that the bread machine had a setting for "Bread in One Hour." "I'll try it!" I exclaimed to myself. And I did. This is proof that my mind really needs the exercise. I know that my wheat bread prefers the four-hour setting. Even when I mix one-third whole wheat flour with two thirds white flour, it takes nearly three hours. What made me think that I could make it in one hour? I remembered the old saw, too late, after I had irretrievably pushed all the buttons for "Bread in One Hour": "If it sounds too good to be true, it is." An hour later, I dumped the small, heavy lump of uncooked dough encased in a burnt shell of crust over the fence hoping the cows would like it. It is wheat, after all. Don't they like wheat?!

I could have taken a nap then. It was nearly noon. But I resisted the temptation and started over. I went back to Mom's house toting the little bucket from the bread machine, reloaded, returned, pushed the buttons for the four-hour setting and turned it on. This time, I had to hook up the generator-operated battery charger because my first experiment had used up quite a lot of available amperage, and I didn't want to wait for the sun to recharge the system. The battery charger had me and the system pumped back up in half an hour. Deadly global warming was drawn a few moments closer by the emissions from my gasoline generator. I felt a twinge of guilt. I got over it. The bread machine is now in operation, and it looks as if I might have a success on my hands. The most important result, however, was mental exercise. While the machine worked, I didn't dare go far from it for fear that there would be some kind of explosion, so I re-read Locke's "Essay on Human Understanding," the essay where he gives us *tabula rasa*. Also, I learned a little about how the bread machine works on solar power, this time with a little gasoline generator assist; but, next time, I'll wait until afternoon when the batteries are fully charged by the sun. My mind is a little tired. I think I will take a nap. I'll have to let you know how the bread turns out. There is still about an hour on the timer.

September 13: Beauty and the Senses.

One who has read a little 19th Century British poetry can hardly consider beauty without thinking of the line from Keats:

> *'Beauty is truth, truth beauty,' –that is all*
> *Ye know on earth, and all ye need to know.*

That is, perhaps, all we need to know for sure. But it is interesting to consider the role of the senses in beauty. All five of them count: taste, touch, smell, sight, and hearing. The loss of any one of these would have made my experience on the front porch this morning less beautiful.

It was fresh coffee that I tasted. I bought the new bag Monday. I don't buy the can. It seems so un-green to buy that tin can which would last through a dozen years of refills. Some of the cans are made mostly of cardboard, but that just means I can't dispose of them properly because the top and bottom are still metal. In what bin does one put something that is part metal, part paper? Easy answer, the landfill bin. Not green at all.

I, also, smelled the coffee. I must have smelled it in my dreams first because I wanted it as soon as I woke up. I went right in and put on the pot. So I had both taste and smell from one cup. Good economy!

I, also, had smell (or lack thereof) from another source, nature herself. The lack of smell came (rather, did not come) from the mega dairy CAFOs (Confined Animal Feeding Operations) located about a mile to my east. They did not stink in my direction this morning due to the gentle breeze coming in from the west. And there begins the sense of feel. It was chilly early in the morning. My toes were a bit pained from the chill of the kitchen floor as I put on the coffee and the rest of breakfast. By the time I finished breakfast and took my cup of coffee to the porch and my canvas easy chair and elm-stump ottoman, the sun was shining brightly. It would have been hot had it not been for the cool breeze. The combination made me mimic Goldilocks as I leaned back in my comfortable porch chair: "Just right!"

In the distance, I heard cars and trucks hurrying down the Wendell-Hagerman road half a mile south. I was glad I have nowhere to go today. "I will mow the northeast third of the lawn," I thought. "But not now!" The traffic was distant and unobtrusive, the way traffic should be. More than the traffic, I heard the gurgle of the little stream of water which I constructed from the irrigation water for Yasmin's pleasure with waterfalls representing each of the five surnames in our extended family. It seemed as if the falls had been tuning up all night and, this morning, they stuck a perfect chord. There were, also, the birds who always sing quietly to each other while they look for worms and opportunities to steal strawberries from my patch. I don't shoo them away from the strawberries. There are plenty for me and for them, and I don't mind eating the ones they take a small bite of. I wash the partly eaten ones. The whole ones, I eat just as they are, bugs and all. And the other sounds. There are many of them if I listen closely—all of them harmonious if my soul happens to be in harmony with them. It is more my soul, not theirs, that lacks harmony if they seem out of tune.

Notice that I have not mentioned the sense of sight so far. That is not because I am blind. I see quite well compared to the rest of my brothers. Most of them have (or once had) serious "seeing" problems. Thanks to the miracles of modern ophthalmic surgery, two of them have improved vision. #1, as I have said before, is still in bad shape for vision. My youngest brother still has good vision. He has bad lungs instead—not a good bargain. Sis has great lungs and eyes. She can spot an ant on her crocus from 100 yards.

As I said, I see quite well.

This morning, I saw the panorama of my newly mowed southeast lawn, the little stream of water with its waterfalls, my Rose of Sharon bushes blooming profusely in shades of purple, pink, and white, young elm and cottonwood trees pushing their limbs toward the sky, the elms with delicate tendrils of limbs hanging back toward earth. And, in the distance, the high snow-peaked (yes, snow-capped again after a couple of bare months) mountains of northern Nevada 100 miles to the south—all of this crowned with pale blue Idaho sky and a faint haze of smoke drifting across the horizon from dying desert wildfires.

The five senses are limited, but what they sent to my soul this morning (I call it my soul when it is good to me; otherwise, it is just my mind) was pleasant beyond the measure of language to express. In this sense, the twentieth-century linguistic philosophers are right. Language needs fixing if it is to express philosophic/logical concepts perfectly; but they will never fix it if they have their minds upon language, logic, and philosophical concepts. Instead, they must arise on a cool, clear Idaho morning, perk a cup of fresh coffee and drink it on my front porch. (I am not inviting them, mind you. I don't need a bunch of shade-bleached twentieth-century philosophers on my front porch.) They will not be able to express it with language anyway, but they will *experience* it in the spectacular multimedia cinematic phenomena provided free of charge by their senses.

September 14: Confession.

258

The previous entry claimed to be a product of the senses. I admit, here, that the snow-capped mountains were imaginary. I read that some of the Colorado mountains are now snow-capped, so I extrapolated that the Sierra Nevadas are now snow-capped as well. I could not tell for sure. The smoke haze which I painted so beautifully from imagination was, actually, so thick that I could not see the mountains in Nevada. Sorry! But a point is made. Even the best of sensual experience can be made better through the power of the imagination. Score one for reason.

September 15: Hope for the Perfection of Humanity.

> *We observe that the labors of recent ages have done much for the progress of the human mind, but little for the perfection of the human race; that they have done much for the honor of man, something for his liberty, but so far almost nothing for his happiness. At a few points our eyes are dazzled with a brilliant light; but thick darkness still covers an immense stretch of the horizon. There are a few circumstances from which the philosopher can take consolation, but he is still afflicted by the spectacle of the stupidity, slavery, barbarism, and extravagance of mankind; and the friend of humanity can find unmixed pleasure only in tasting the sweet delights of hope for the future.*

This could have been written yesterday. If such were the case, it would not smack in the least of anachronism. I'll not analyze it for you. You know too well of the horrors of the last century which are, obviously, stretching into the present and, interminably, into the future. It was not, however, written yesterday. It was written in 1793 by Antoine Nicolas de Condorcet (translated here by June Barraclough for *Classics of Western Thought: The Modern World.* Charles Hirschfeld and Edgar E. Knoebel, Eds. Harcourt Brace Jovanovich: New York, 1980), a Frenchman, at the conclusion of the French Revolution.

Condorcet's book, *The Progress of the Human Mind,* stands even today as one of the most respected works in support of the perfectibility of humanity. Condorcet did not say that the human mind was entirely perfectible. He recognized the slow and endless march of infinity. He felt, however, that he stood at the opening door of the greatest movement toward that perfection that the world had ever known. France was free of tyranny. America was free from Britain, and Condorcet was sure that, very soon, she would free her slaves and would, quickly, free the Indians from the slavery of their lack of European-style civilization. And the rest of the world, seeing the brilliance of the light shining in the western sky would follow suit. For the first time, the world would be governed by enlightened politics, and progress in that world would be in the hands of enlightened scientists seeking to make it a better place for everyone in equal measure: no war, no slaves, equal rights for all including all races and both genders.

The following year, 1794, Condorcet died in a French jail, apparently by suicide.

259

September 16: Speaking of Naiveté in the Age of Enlightenment...

Considering Condorcet, I must conclude that there was, at least, a smattering of naiveté in the age of enlightenment. Perhaps, it was not so enlightened after all. Consider, for instance, the philosophy of Edmund Burke who opposed the French Revolution. One could find plenty to oppose in that little spat, especially in its bloody aftermath. But Burke did not oppose it for that reason. He opposed it because he favored King Louis and all the Louises and Henrys and Edwards, etc. who reigned throughout the centuries along with all the dukes and earls and nobles of every stripe who had come to their fortunes and castles and parcels of land and positions in the government and their right to sever heads of lesser persons from their bodies through their hereditary nobility or royalty. Such a stance seems odd considering that Burke was neither noble nor royal. He was, however, rich, and that made all the difference. You see, he not only favored the inheritance by blood of titles of nobility and privileges of royalty, but the inheritance of anything any man's family had gained (through whatever good or evil it had been gained) by the man. This, he liked.

He makes quite an argument for the whole inheritance game. Most important to his argument is that the system of inheritance lends stability to the social contract. In short, it retains the essence of the ancient feudal system: each tier of society scratching the itchy behind of the tier of society just above them in the proper scratching order. This insured that everyone (everyone who counted, at least), got their behinds scratched. Consider that this was an age before regular ablution was in vogue if your name was not Ben Franklin. It was not an easy matter to get someone to scratch a behind which had not been washed for a few months. I have a friendly yearling steer here on the farm which is, constantly, urging me to scratch his, and I always manage to find some other territory to scratch. The steer accepts the substitute gracefully since he is not entitled to either nobility or royalty—nor is he wealthy.

But the hereditary royalty and nobility and the rest of the wealthy (hereditary or not) are in such a position. Indeed, they have been known to lop off heads just because the fingers on the bodies below the heads to be lopped refused to scratch as they had been ordered to scratch. Such is life in the feudal order—and in many ways it is still the same today. I've spent many an evening metaphorically scrubbing my fingernails, tainted by my attempts to remain employed under a contract that paid far too little and required far too much scratching for its fulfillment.

Condorcet?—indeed, naïve! Why else would he trust the post-revolutionary French political hierarchy not to continue the traditions of the royals and nobles and wealthy even as they methodically lopped off the heads of all three classes (assuming, I assume, that none of those would be much good at scratching). But Burke was not naïve. Fortunately for him, he was, also, not French.

September 17: It Is Finished!

At 3:00 o'clock this morning, I awoke to intense darkness and to the realization that my pilgrimage to the mountaintop, except for closing out the record, packing up and traveling back to Kansas City is finished for this year. It was good! I have discovered the universal solvent and have nothing to store it in. Not really, but I experienced an epiphany upon awakening at that ungodly hour on a night without moonlight. Indeed, my task is complete. And I was not even entirely aware that I had a task. And, in further ambiguity, I am still not sure how to state the task or exactly how to explain its completion. That means you will have the joy of watching me process those ideas over the next few entries. Look out! It might be confusing—not because I want it to be confusing. In fact, part of my task is to state the task and the solution clearly so that anyone who is mature enough and intellectually capable will be able to understand.

That is one of my primary objectives as a philosopher. The greatest difficulty for today's readers of philosophy is that philosophers seem to have a language all their own which no one else is privy to. In addition, they do not seem to have a common language with the common folk who really need to understand philosophical treatises in order to gain from them. That is not to say that reading philosophy should be easy. However, the difficulty should not be in the rhetoric but in the concepts. Some concepts are complex, so complex that one needs a great deal of background in philosophical thought to understand them. Thus, at times, understanding one philosophical treatise requires the understanding of several others as preparatory reading.

However, my hope is in this particular treatise, this book, that no one will be required to have great expertise covering the nearly 3000 years of the development of world philosophies. I have tried to provide some of the basics in the previous hundreds of pages which will help you to understand what will emerge beyond this point. But don't hesitate to study more on your own. The more you bring to this text, the more you will take from it. If you bring the minimum, you will take away the minimum.

Second and a bright illumination in my 3:00 a.m. epiphany: The chief discipline of philosophy is not "language" as has been claimed by many recent philosophers, and not "metaphysics" as was claimed by a large number of earlier philosophers. Neither is it "politics" as a large class of 17th and 18th century philosophers would have us believe, although politics comes a little closer to the truth. It is "ethics."

Third, and critical to judging ethics above politics and above every other discipline of philosophical discourse, philosophers (among whom are some excellent poets) must become as Shelley claimed for poets "the unacknowledged legislators of the world" for, beginning in the present generation, philosophy, which has always been ethnocentric (confined by particular nationalities, cultures, races, religions, a single gender, etc.), must be free from such prejudices. The world has suddenly become too small for them. I'll say no more about this today. There is much to be said about it, *all* of it, and it is too much to digest at once.

Hear clearly, and do not fall asleep at this critical moment in time and space. How we humans (the only rational beings on earth) respond ethically to the needs of every human, animal, plant, and inanimate object on the earth will not, merely, make a difference. It will make *all* of the difference.

I cannot say whether I was awakened at 3 a.m. by the warning spirit of a loving God or by an electrical impulse in my cerebral cortex—a power surge stimulated by that can of cheap beer I drank yesterday; but, I assure you, I am fully awake.

261

September 18: Ethics 101.

At the heart of ethics is the continuum of good and evil. Before I go further, let me put a good deal of separation between the good and evil I am speaking of and the good and evil touted by the religions of the world. Certainly, there is a relationship, but the second aspect of philosophical ethics makes the difference. Religious "good and evil" nearly always has something to do with revealed ethics, that is, what God has revealed as good and evil. Of course, it is impossible to say who is right and who is wrong about what God has or has not revealed. It depends to a great extent upon whether God is that benevolent old greybeard whose kingdom favors little children above all others or the beast who drowned the Egyptian army and sacked Canaan. Philosophical ethics has little to do with that sort of good and evil. The bar between philosophical ethics and religious ethics is, to a large extent, that philosophical ethics is a finite rather than infinite study. Ethical action gauged by philosophy is limited by human boundaries. It is empirical. Religion is not. This, also, means that philosophical ethics is entirely bound up in the pragmatics of action. It is not merely an activity of the mind. We can have all of the evil thoughts we care to have. As long as our actions are ethical, we have done no evil. Thus, Jimmy Carter's lament that he had committed adultery in his mind and had, therefore, sinned, does not receive the attention of the philosophical ethicist. His only evil was in reducing his political strength as President of the United States with such foolish statements, a finite problem. I am pleased to note that he has gone on to become the finest ex-President the U.S. has ever known. Although he is not usually considered a philosopher at all, *I* count him among the foremost living political/ethical philosophers.

Indeed, he and others of his ilk are the very philosophers, with the reduction in the impact of poets, who must now become the world's "unacknowledged legislators." I was pleased to hear that he and some others of the world's elder statesmen have decided to come together from time to time to discuss the affairs of the world and to offer their combined wisdom. The world's "acknowledged" legislators should listen carefully.

I said that ethics is a continuum. Good is at one end, evil at the other. Does this leave an excluded middle? No, it does not. That is one factor that makes ethics such a complex subject. No action, as far as we know is totally good, and no action is totally evil. Every action falls somewhere on that continuum between absolute good and absolute evil. That is one finite quality of ethics. In addition, we must consider another dimension of ethics. Each ethical dilemma has its continuum. However, no problem exists in a vacuum. Crossing the continuum of the original problem in astronomical numbers are the continua of a multitude of other ethical dilemmas. Each crossing point is a hurdle which must be overcome. Indeed, it is impossible to reach a final deductive conclusion for any problem. Every answer will be reached inductively and will be conditioned by literally millions of other ethical problems.

Let us take for example one of Kant's most memorable statements which would fall under the categorical imperative: "There must be no war." It stands as a truth for me, but it is conditioned. First, in the case that one country attacks another country, must the other country refuse to participate in the war and be slaughtered.

Of course not! Another case. What if a religious or ethnic group has been constantly abused by the rest of the world for many centuries? Finally, they develop a league of nations capable of conducting war against some of their persecuting neighbors. Is the war justified? A final scenario. What if one nation is certain in its mind that another nation intends to attack them, but they have little empirical evidence to prove it? Is pre-emptive attack allowed? What if one tribe in a country is systematically exterminating another tribe in that country? Is war allowed to stop the extermination?

Of course, an important backdrop of Kant's imperative against war is that we must look carefully down the corridors of time to consider the actions of today to be sure that, in the future, today's actions do not lead to the wars of tomorrow. For instance, if the Christian world had not carried out the Crusades against the Turks (Muslims) many centuries ago, would we be fighting the war in Iraq today?

Even the most astute minds of today could not possibly foresee all of the problems that decisions of today will lead to; but, with careful thought by the wisest of our people, and heed paid to them, we could avoid many future wars. Had the world firmly condemned Hitler earlier instead of making his Nazi army wealthy beyond measure in preparation for such things as the extermination of the Jews, could we have saved the Jews, their homes in Europe, millions of lives in WWII, and the devastation of the current fighting between Palestinians and Israelis? It was easy to see that Hitler was up to no good. Why did we not say "No!" to him in the 1930s?

Class dismissed!

September 19: Now That You Know . . .

. . . the nature of the study of ethics, I can begin to tell you what I set out to say after my September 18th 3 a.m. epiphany. The world is now so small, made that way by modern science, that it must come together as a single larger ethical community. Note that I did not say "political" community. The world as a single political community could lead to nothing but tyranny and misery. Nor did I say that we must be a single "ethnic" community. Such a world would be tedious beyond measure. No! I said "a single larger ethical community." I did not even say that all nations, ethnic groups, racial groups, communities of any sort would have to live under a single detailed ethical code.

What we must have is a broad set of ethical parameters in a code for the entire world within which all of the world's smaller communities must fit their specific codes of ethics. Moses gave us a good start with the Ten Commandments. I whacked that a bit earlier in the book so it is bruised. But, still, it has promise. For instance, it says that we should not kill. We should alter that to say, "Don't kill people, even in war or at the gallows, except as mercy when they are deathly ill or in horrible pain (and with their permission); kill animals only as mercy when they are sick or in pain—or humanely and sparingly for food." I suppose we would not escape our argument about abortion with this edict. We can't solve it all immediately. That is why we need a world council of elders to take on those thorny problems that the world in general can't seem to solve. At any rate, I am not, in this entry, intending to solve such problems.

263

We could, however, since the internet has all but erased many of the social boundaries between nations and all other communities of the world that do not reject the internet, decide upon some over-arching rules of ethical conduct that fit everyone who leaps over these boundaries in cyberspace every day as they telecommute to work.

Of course, the physical boundaries have become almost as porous. It is no longer, it seems, possible to keep people in or out of neighboring countries. With the advance of democracy as the major political system in much of the world comes a sort of humaneness that does not allow us to capture and enslave illegal aliens for the rest of their lives. Instead, we employ them, usually at a lower rate of pay than citizens, and come to depend upon them so much that, no matter what laws we pass against their entry and continued residency, those laws are just so much waste paper in the enforcement. And no matter how high we build the fences intended to keep out the aliens, someone always has wire cutters and no one, seemingly, has a kit to repair cut wire.

Even in those countries which do not have democratic systems (e.g., the Islamic nations which have theocracies and various other oligarchies, kingdoms and tyrannies) such nations find it extremely useful to hire floods of engineers, English language teachers, etc. and to keep them happy with large salaries from those countries' oil revenues. Interaction in huge numbers among communities of the world is inevitable. Such interactions seem to call for a world-wide system of ethics which covers basics of human interactions wherever humans encounter one another.

But these are simple matters compared to the much more tragic and intolerable situations which are occurring around the world which we seem to have no ethic to manage. Just to name four: 1) the isolation and near starvation of the North Koreans and (the other side of the coin) their threat of nuclear attack on other nations; 2) the continuing strife between the Israelis and the Palestinians; 3) the continuing ethnic cleansing in Darfur, 4) the seemingly endless wars in Iraq and Afghanistan. There are many more such situations that could be mentioned. These are just the ones that appear in the media most often.

We can make one rule for each of these problems. 1) There must be no starvation or lack of shelter, clothing, or medical care anywhere in this world of plenty. 2) A world court will settle border disputes which cannot be settled by the communities which have the disputes, and world police will enforce the decisions. 3) There must be no ethnic cleansing or genocide. 4) There must be no war. And a fifth for good measure: 5) Political leaders with weapons of mass destruction who threaten or attack communities (their own or others') will be neutralized. (Note that I did not say, nor did I mean "executed.")

I'm sure there are a few more "imperatives" which could be added to this short list, but they should be added only as they are obviously needed. In general, communities with social contracts of their own should be left to manage their own affairs as long as, in keeping with the theory of John Stuart Mill, people are not allowed to do things that interfere with the reasonable rights of other people or fail to do things that must be done in the defense of reasonable human rights.

And that unacknowledged legislative world board of elders? It must be. And we must listen to what it has to say.

September 20: Listen, if You Will, to Georg Wilhelm Friedrich Hegel.
In one of his rare moments of absolute clarity Hegel said the following:

> *The laws of ethics are not accidental, but are rationality itself. It is the end of the State to make the substantial prevail and maintain itself in the actual doings of men and in their convictions. It is the absolute interest of Reason that this moral whole exist; and herein lies the justification and merit of heroes who have founded states, no matter how crude . . .*

> (from *Classics of Western Thought: the Modern World*, Charles Hirschfeld and Edgar E. Knoebel, editors, New York: Harcourt Brace Jovanovich, 1980.)

Hegel goes further than I would go in attempting to prove a divine purpose in everything which makes everything a single fabric. On the other hand, he doesn't go far enough with his dialectic. He considers the dialectic of the State to have reached nearly its final stage of rejoining with pure spirit (freedom) at his time in the 19th Century Prussian state. What he failed to understand is that, in keeping with his own doctrine of unity, his dialectic could not be complete until all of the people of the world were unified under a single general ethical code.

I would not go along with his assessment of the potential of the dialectical struggle either. But I will give Hegel credit. Whether there is divine purpose behind every staggering step forward or not, many states have moved toward greater and greater freedom in many of the ways Hegel indicated that they had moved at his day. I do not expect that the world will ever be an entire unity, and I do not expect that poverty and misery and war will ever be entirely erased. Even cruel tyranny is bound to raise its head at times as far into the future as we can predict. It appears to me, however, that all of these can be reduced and freedom of humanity will be increased by a worldwide effort on the part of political leaders in cooperation with philosophers (in the broadest sense of the title of philosopher—those who first seek the "good" through wisdom and truth—not at all the narrowest sense).

September 21: Colors Hot and Slow.
It's chilly this morning
sitting on my porch at Walden-San
(named to honor wisdom from East and West)
about 40 degrees Fahrenheit
while I eat my breakfast of fried eggs and raison bran
with blackberries I grew when Idaho's summer was over 100 degrees
almost every day for two months.
The weatherman on the radio morning show says it will be
85 degrees tomorrow.

I remember when I was a boy, like a kid goat,
gamboling through the canyons over the Snake River.

I didn't think it was hot then.
Maybe it was.
But the river was blue
(not green with long streams of water weed defining the slow current),
and swift with ripples everywhere and whitecaps when the wind blew
sandy dunes down the bluffs on the west bank.

From the west bank I could see Thousand Springs
which were a thousand then, it seems,
maybe only a few hundred,
but many
until Idaho Power captured them in a big pipe
and made electricity
and dumped the water without its electricity
into the river at the bottom of the cliff.
They left a few springs shining in the afternoon sun
lonely harbingers of a time
when their mates will escape the pipe
and, once again, flow free,
long in the future.

I caught fish in the river then, big rainbow trout with snowy white flesh.
The water was blue—
except for small streams of water spilling over the black cliff—
looking like springs, only brown:
Used irrigation water from the farms on the hill.

A century ago
the old pioneers like Edmond (Hagerman's oldest cowboy when I was a boy)
and Julius (the pastor of the Church and a farmer
like most every man from Hagerman)
and a lot of their fellow pioneers took mules and ditchers and scrapers
and dug out long canals from above dams across the Snake River
hundreds of miles east of Hagerman
and up in the mountains
all the way to Hagerman and the hundred other towns
that wanted to turn more of the desert into farms—
and did.

Back then the hilltop farm lands glistened green:
oases in the silver sagebrush desert;
and southern Idaho's farmers were rich,
Not in money, but in green grass
and all the animals green grass could grow
and milk cows and sheep and horses;
and jackrabbits were thick and coyotes loved that;
and the farmers loved the coyotes for killing the rabbits

that ate the beans before they were ripe for harvest;
but they killed the coyotes for killing chickens
and for a long time there were no coyotes or jackrabbits,
and not many chickens because it was easier and cheaper to buy
them in stores, dead, cleaned, even cooked.

They say the river is green, not blue, and streams with water weeds
because fish farms fed fish for sale to the whole world.
The fish food and fish feces flowed with the river
and made it green and it was rich—
not in fish, but in green and brown water weeds.
(The governor's boat got stuck in the water weeds once,
as a stunt most people think.) The river is still green.
I recently caught a trout from the river—yellow flesh—
I fed it to the cats.

I do not think we will clean up the river soon.
China is to blame.
They have turned the Yellow River blood red with poison
and Chinese farmers are dying
because they drink the water
and they breathe the air which is almost as poison as the water.
And the Yangtze is just about as red.
These rivers, the Yellow and the Yangtze,
are worse than the Snake.
If the Snake were the worst,
we might clean it and turn the water blue again
and the trout flesh white again.
That is how China is to blame.

Usually, by mid-September, we have had a killing frost,
and the lawn-grass is limp and the garden shrinks to little bumps
of frosted cantaloupes and cucumbers and green tomatoes.
Not this year!
Until October, the irrigation water flows
from the reservoirs behind the dams in the mountains
to the farms and the grass stays green
and the farm waste water is brown
and the river is green with water weeds streaming.

And I enjoy my breakfast of fried eggs
and raison bran and berries on my front porch.

Coda:
I imagine a time many years hence
when a young boy gambols across canyon meadows above
a blue Snake River, the son of a hermit

and his wife who is a hermit,
both of whom together survived
by living deep in the mountains on berries
and the tough flesh of jackrabbits and chipmunks.

There are not many people here living and farming in the canyons
of the rivers that flow blue and clear.
No brown waste water flows over the cliffs
because there are no farms on the hilltop anymore.
The Chinese died first because they drank and breathed
too much poison from the Yangtze and the Yellow.
Then the big cities on the coasts joined Atlantis—
cities in the sea.
Dead politicians' lips burble
warnings of what has already occurred
while fish swim in and out of the yawning maws
of drowned executives.

The boy does not remember
because he was born here by the blue Snake
but his parents remember that it was hot—
too hot.
And that is why they went deep into the mountains
and lived
and why the boy
gambols across green canyon meadows
beside a thousand springs,
maybe only a few hundred springs
but looking like a thousand,
spreading white veils like pretty brides,
above the blue river.

September 22: "You Can't Marry Ten Pretty Girls," or Things the World Must Ignore.

> *You can marry one,*
> *But you can't marry ten;*
> *No, you can't marry ten pretty girls.*

Burl Ives sang that little ditty nearly half a century ago, and he was right—unless you happen to be a wealthy Muslim living in a predominantly Islamic republic or you are a traditionalist Mormon elder with a lot of chutzpa and more semen than brains. For most of the rest of us, such behavior is not only illegal, it is considered immoral. However, that is the sticking point: "considered." Polygamy cannot be denounced as a categorical imperative. If the plural spouse is adult and does not object to the arrangement, there is no absolute human moral which condemns it. There are plenty of religious doctrines against it, and there is a good deal of evidence that it leads to social trouble, but there is nothing absolute about it. Indeed, America, at the present moment, is inching closer and closer to the removal

268

of its prohibition. Plural marriage is hanging tenaciously to the coat tails of the homosexual marriage movement. If that movement succeeds, acceptance of plural marriage might not be far behind. The arguments for each are similar.

This exemplifies the many concepts which certain parts of the world think are absolute sins while other parts of the world consider them the norm for appropriate behavior. That traditionalist Mormon, for instance, not only considers polygamy a right. He considers it to be a God-ordained duty. He might not even like it. According to Mormon doctrine (considered by Mormons to be revelation from God), a woman cannot go to heaven unless she is married to a Mormon elder. Thus, the elder is not a sex addict; he is saving female souls. He does not want those ten pretty girls to burn in Hell.

The idea that polygamy is commanded by God is absurd, but then, this is an absurd world in which we live, and it is difficult to justify passing laws against concepts simply because they are absurd. If that were the case, we would have to immediately outlaw the entire human race. We are all absurd in some way or other. Even if 98% of us believe that polygamy is not good, we must not interfere with the 2% who consider it to be good as long as their polygamy does nothing to physically or mentally harm others. Of course, we might argue that it harms the children. That, simply, cannot be proven. Through all the ages of the world and in most places in the world, some of the finest offspring have emerged from polygamous marriages. Beyond that, even in our own country at the present day, about 50% of the population is involved in serial polygamy as they divorce and remarry almost as regularly as they change their shoe styles. Still many of their children grow up to be successful adults.

What other concepts are like this? Public nudity? Drinking of alcoholic beverages? America tried to outlaw "Demon Rum" and failed. Much of the Islamic world successfully outlaws it. Every nation will have to decide for itself. How about riding a motorcycle without a helmet? That is more absurd than polygamy, but many folks line up in loud protest against laws requiring a helmet. How about the death penalty? Abortion? How about a global prohibition of war?

September 23: Employer vs. Labor.

It is of interest that most philosophers when confronted with the dilemma of employer vs. labor are most likely to come down firmly on the side of the employer. Exceptions to this are limited. Marx of course, centers his dialectical materialism upon the crushing by the laboring class of the employing class. Also, anarchists generally favor the working person. We must note, however, that Marx has been, largely, discredited because of the failure of badly conceived and failing national and international experiments. Yet, there is a great deal of truth, especially, in the argument of Marx that the employer class (the wealthy owners of property and the economic machines of the nations) is guilty of exploiting the worker. For a while, it seemed that powerful labor unions would overcome that exploitation, but it was not to be. The unions, themselves, became too much like the exploiting owners, gaining too much for some workers and leaving a major percentage of workers on the outside to be exploited even more, so that employers could make up for their inability to exploit the unionized workers. And, of course, in the final analysis, those workers who had been helped too much lost their jobs and their

269

lucrative pensions largely because of inexpensive foreign goods trumping their good (but expensive) working conditions. Now we are back nearly where we stood in the 19th century just before labor unions stepped in. Contemporary American workers are thankful for FDR's New Deal. At least, even though the wage they work for forces them into slavish poverty, perhaps worse, because the slave owner has an interest in keeping his slaves well-fed and healthy whereas the wage-earner's employer cares nothing for the welfare of his employees, with Social Security and Medicare they can look forward to a retirement without utter starvation or lack of reasonable healthcare.

The most common defense by philosophers of the exploitive upper class is the natural right to personal property. Somehow the owner has *earned* title to much more property and money than he can possibly manage with only his own work, so he hires the laborer (who, most likely, he cheated out of his property) to do the work necessary for the owner to collect even more property. Rousseau's version of "personal property" is fairer. His version is that the owner of property may hold claim to only that amount of property which he can manage without hiring workers. In contemporary society, that is unrealistic because modern enterprise requires various combinations of labor skills in order to produce its complex goods. Still, it seems a shame to defend anyone who exploits other persons.

Personally, I like the concept of the graduated income tax whereby those who make more profit are required to pay a larger percentage of it in support of the government. Administered properly, this works as redistribution of wealth which is necessary in order to ensure some degree of equality among the members of a society and, by extension, the chance that some others might improve their financial status if they are not held down so solidly by the weight of the upper classes.

Beyond this, we should stop immediately this chatter instigated by the wealthy about eliminating the inheritance tax. Indeed, I would eliminate inheritance itself except for a modest estate (say the equivalent of the value of a 160-acre farm with machinery and livestock and other operational necessities)—the $600,000 non-taxed inheritance now in place in the U.S. is about right, except that no inheritance at all above that rate should be allowed, taxed or tax-free. America cannot be free of the stigma of inherited nobility until it is entirely rid of excessive inheritance.

Along with all this, must come a war on tax loopholes. Loopholes, it should be remembered, were the death-knell of America's progressive income tax. Once all of the taxes of the wealthy were siphoned back to the wealthy (remember Ross Perot's "great sucking sound" in a different context) through loopholes, it was necessary to revise the tax code to be sure that poor and middle class workers/taxpayers made up the difference. It seems that many members of the congress and senate and even some Presidents have an interest in keeping rich people (not unlike themselves) rich and poor people in their humble places.

I am one philosopher who believes firmly that rich persons should stay in their place on the far side of the "eye of the needle" barred by their bloated wallets and their economic gluttony from further excessive profits and unearned inheritance. If I lose a couple of pounds and grease my belly, I think I can slip through that orifice.

September 24: Cell Phone Etiquette.

I am sitting in the College of Southern Idaho Library, beginning my entry for today. Behind me, perhaps 10 feet behind me, a cell phone bleats out a terrible ring-tone loosely based upon Beethoven's "Für Elise." A loud female voice sings out: "Hello!!" and even more loudly, "I'm in the library. I can't talk loud now." Pause. Then continuing with uproarious laughter: "Yeh! I have to talk quiet. If you call me Wednesday or Friday at lunch-time; I can talk then. Yeh!" More laughter. "Yeh! Just call me Wednesday or Friday, and I'll be sure to have lunch with you. Yeh! O.K.! Bye now. Love ya!"

I am thankful to the young lady for reminding me that the fact that we have rational minds is no guarantee we will use them.

September 25: Countdown Week to Coming Down from the Mountains.

Although the mythology would not support it, the philosophy of Socrates would firmly support careful planning. His most famous line in support of planning is the one regarding the necessity of a well-examined life. That well-examined life would include examination of the minute parts of that life and the life as it might extend forward in time. Thus, although it could seem that his life was one of carefree accidental encounters and discussions, it was, largely, a life planned and decided in advance.

As far as I can tell, none of us, including Socrates, is a prophet, so deciding in advance requires a great deal of rational and empirical thinking: rational because nothing in the future has happened before, and empirical because what has happened in the past has positive relations with what will happen in the future. We might as well say that inductive and deductive reasoning are combined in proportions appropriate to the situation. For instance, if I am about to teach a class and know that 25 students are enrolled, my inductive reasoning can input the data that, in this sort of class in the past, an average of 22 students actually show up. However, reason considers possibility. Thus, I reason that if 25 students are enrolled, there is a possibility that three or four more might show up as late enrollees. Also, it is possible that all 25 of the original enrollees will appear. Of course, Reason could announce that there is a possibility that at as many as the entire student population of the university could show up in my class. Empiricism chuckles, loudly clears its throat, and replies, "Fat chance!" Empiricism and Reason trundle off to the pub for a beer. I bring 29 copies of the syllabus to the class.

The same planning began yesterday for my departure from Walden-San for the winter in Kansas City. I will leave next Wednesday, eight days from today. Yesterday, I restarted the irrigation water so that I could water the lawn one more time before my departure, one last drink before the long cold winter for all those little trees I planted this summer. Of course, that restart was planned a week ago when I shut down the irrigation water just short of my lawn in order to wait for the appropriate restart day. Yesterday was that day because it takes two days to water the lawn. Thus, on Thursday, I will be able to proceed with other preparations without slogging through standing water. I, also, need to mow the grass one more time before leaving. It takes me three days to mow all the grass with my push mower (an hour a day). Those days are Thursday, Friday, and Saturday. I would do it later but fall weather is unpredictable. I might be delayed and this planned calendar allows for delays. (Nature was kind, by the way. Last night it delivered the first killing frost of the fall which will slow the growth of the grass significantly.)

Also, on Thursday, I will be able to close down my outdoor shower and toilet—not a pleasant duty, but one that must be done in order to keep my water barrel and portable potty from bursting with winter ice or filling with vermin.

Today, I started moving files from my desk to my portable file cases. All of my business and academic materials must be transported, and it takes time to be sure that I have everything I will need. Nothing is much more frustrating than to find that I need a particular document in Kansas City which I overlooked and left in my files at Walden-San. Also, as the week progresses, I'll decide which books to pack for the trip. I'm neither wealthy enough nor wasteful enough to buy duplicate copies of all the books I need regularly. (I look forward to the time when most such books will be readily available online. Many of them are there now.)

Yesterday, by the way, I started buying the few provisions I will need for the trip. I bought a roll of cheap paper towels and a bag of pretzels. I'll be in town again soon because I visit my mother in the rehab center twice a week which takes me right past the Walmart in Jerome. Yes! I shop Walmart! Yes! I recognize that Walmart's management is made up of greedy capitalists who import cheap Chinese goods made by poor people in unhealthy conditions. But the fact is that Sam's family is more honest about it than most American capitalists. I have to buy my stuff somewhere, and I'm not made of money. Besides, Walmart's participation in the Chinese economy will help to make China wealthy and, eventually, the poor people of China will not be any poorer than the poor people of America. (Hmm! I'm not sure that came out just right. Something to consider on another day?)

The last two days will be dedicated, mainly, to packing and sorting into the back of my truck with the camper shell on it. With any luck, Wednesday morning I will have only a few items to complete: bedding to store, water shutoff and pipe winterization, electrical shut-off (I have to put the solar power in winter mode just keeping the batteries charged), and gas shut-off (a mere turning of a valve and a twisted wire on the tank in use so I will know which tank is partially used when I return in the spring—more advanced planning). Then I say goodbye to my Idaho family and head out for Rock Springs, Wyoming—Rock Springs because it is six hours drive from Walden-San. If my departure is a little slow, I still have time to make it to the Motel 6 where I have a reservation before dark. I turn into a zucchini if I drive after dark.

This is just a general outline. There are thousands of details that must be considered as the week progresses. The first time I departed, I thought that, surely, a day of preparation would do the trick. I ended up nearly killing myself trying to get ready. Now I know that the deductive/inductive procedure, both reason and empiricism must be applied for a good long time in advance if I am to have a pleasant trip and a successful winter in Missouri. Yasmin is waiting for me, and I am anxious to see her!

I must plan next year to install gates. That fall I took crossing the fence last night which ended up with me lying on my back in a ditch full of irrigation water was the last of those I want to take. I could, like my mother, break a hip. As it is, my left shoulder hurts like Hell. A little better planning would have prevented that. The previous similar fall happened about a month ago when my friendly backyard garter snake startled me in mid-crossing by appearing under my nose as I crossed the same fence. I am not a swift learner.

September 26: A Tree Blown Down.
I thought it was a perfect day:
Sunshine
Blue skies
Green pastures
Red and black and white and brindled, all shades of cows
Eating grass in the pastures
Water tumbling over irrigation dams
In ditches brimming clear with satin water plants
Gentle breeze combing what's left of my hair.

Then I saw the downed Russian Olive tree in the pasture
Rolled over by last night's windstorm
Dying with one root in the ground and a few gray leaves
Choking on top of the pile.

I remembered an old cow expiring by our kitchen window
The rest of the herd keening funeral bellows
As Yasmin and I ate Cheerios and milk and drank orange juice.

I recalled a gopher running in mad circles
Seeking sanctuary
Until I cut it in half with my shovel
And how its exposed heart kept beating
Until it stopped.

"This—all of it—is Nature," I whispered to myself.
Then, "This is Nature," I repeated aloud
Though there was no one to hear me
Except Nature
Who was jabbering insanely,
Not listening to anything
I had to say.

September 27: I'll Tell You *My* Dreams.
You might guess from my topic (dreams) that I have been reading Freud and Jung—and you'd be right. It is an interesting, though enigmatic topic. Although both Freud and Jung seemed to think they had discovered important psychological foundations in dreams, shades of the unconscious; perhaps, in Jung's case, shades of mysticism; but since the time they were researching, little progress on dream therapy or the philosophy of dreams (science or myth) has emerged.

But dreaming is still an important philosophical topic in that dreaming bridges the gap between the material world and whatever it is that lies beyond it, whether that is God or, merely, electronically housed thoughts in a material mind. I am particularly interested in dreaming because I have such interesting and disturbing dreams, and they are so repetitive and apparently symbolic in nature. I don't pretend to know exactly what causes them or in what way they are connected to truth or nature or God or psychic capacities of my mind. But I *think* that I gain some understanding of my *self* through analyzing them. I'll present the dreams (the first one today and others to follow) in detail with some limited cogitations about their material and metaphysical referents.

Dream #1: "Anchors Aweigh!"

This is the most persistent and, probably, the most frequent and most simply analyzed dream. It arrives in several variants, but the crux of it is that, through some terrible error, I have re-enlisted in the U.S. Navy and find myself in boot camp all over again. I am miserable. I wonder to myself how it could have happened and wish with all my heart that it had not, but I am bound by contract and the laws of the United States to serve out my term.

Further details are unnecessary. I had a miserable hitch in the Navy. I went in with great hopes and an almost assured appointment to the U.S. Naval Academy. I hated boot camp. I found it, not difficult, but demeaning to obey without question the orders of an idiot alcoholic company commander who was, obviously, not a *superior*. Indeed, I was responsible before the end of my boot camp tour for his dismissal from his position as company commander. Shortly after boot camp, I was assigned to the Naval Preparatory Academy (preparatory for Annapolis). I discovered there that I was self-deluded about what it meant to be a naval officer. First, it dawned upon me that I did not want a degree in engineering. I had always been far more interested in the humanities. Second, and more important, it dawned upon me that I was not a natural military man. My experience in boot camp should have been a warning to me. I do not like doing what I am told to do. Embarrassingly, truth about myself had been hidden from me by my immature fixation on that brilliant white naval officer's uniform. Instead, I ended up spending my four years in bell bottoms and a silly little round hat. I spent one of the two required semesters at the preparatory academy, then checked out, after which I spent a miserable two years assigned (as punishment, I think) to frigid Argentia, Newfoundland, then another year of what I considered slavery aboard an ammunition escort. I appreciated the trip to the Mediterranean, but I spent most of my time chain smoking in the ship's office, hiding from human contact. This, too, all of it, was a demeaning and disheartening experience. It is little wonder that the specter of being, somehow, transported back to that four-year Hell haunts me. Some analysts would suggest that the dream is a symptom of post-traumatic stress disorder. In other words, I'm nuts—but I've always known that!

September 28: Dream #2—My Atheist Existentialist Dreams.

It would appear that I am an atheist existentialist—that is, if I judge by the content of my dreams. I rebel at this because I feel that I have a good relationship with God, the one that I assume to exist on the flawed basis of limited logic and to whom my imagination has supplied material godly attributes. The reason that I say this is that my dreams are a spitting image of the description of atheist existentialism provided by Jean Paul Sartre including anguish, forlornness, and despair.

Let me explain. In terms of anguish, I am aware in my dreams of my responsibility to act and I act in accordance with that responsibility. I somehow know that my action is the only action that counts and out of that action will come my essence and the essence of all other persons (at least, those persons represented in my dreams). I experience the anguish caused by this responsibility since my dreams are always of a nature that no action I take is ideal. Every action leads only to more need for action with no apparent conclusion. Consider, for instance, a recurring dream wherein I (along with unidentified others) enter a large city and am lost. I seem to be solely responsible for finding whatever it is that I am supposed to find (a commodity which changes from dream to dream) and I continue endlessly to take action which I judge should lead to success in the hunt—but which never does. It merely leads to more blind alleys and hallways and continuing alienation from whatever it is that I am seeking.

Sartre defines forlornness as the quality of being the highest authority in existence for the making of decisions about actions to be taken. In other words, there is no god to provide the pattern for human essence or to come riding to the rescue when we fail to create or follow our own pattern. We must act upon our own best judgment and accept the outcomes as the best that could have happened because no other outcome exists except as fantasy. In my dreams, there is no god. Never do I remember God taking any part whatsoever nor do I remember seeking the help of God or even thinking about the possibility of there being a God or of seeking help from such a being. This is disturbing to me. If I believe in my *imagined* God, and I think I do, why is that God not some sort of presence in my dreams? I cannot lie to my dreams. They reflect the absolute nature of what is there in my dream consciousness, whatever that is. It would appear—indeed, it seems almost a sure thing—that there is a disjunction between my waking self and my sleeping self. My sleeping self is atheistic. This is a step beyond alienation. It is forlornness. Alienation occurs when there is something from which to be alienated. There is always hope of ending the alienation. Forlornness is permanent—as durable as rational life.

Finally, with anguish and forlornness, comes the inevitable despair. There is, of course, no hope. In my dreams, I will always be enslaved in the Navy or whatever "Big Brother" wraps its tentacles about me. I will never find the commodities from which I am alienated in that impossibly complex labyrinth of a city. At least, I am confident that I will meet up with no Minotaur. That would be an end and there is no end—except when I awaken to a new day beyond the world of dreams—a day wherein I can manage my imagination to include the pleasant fantasies that make up such an important part of my *real* world.

Or is it my real world? The dream world demands absolute truth as it appears in my psyche. The waking world misinforms in the form of my self-managed imagination. Or is the truth in the dream world actually just more imagination which I am incapable of suppressing in the dream state?

Whatever the case, I seem to be at least two: the waking I and the sleeping I. Both are equally subject to "*cogito ergo sum*." Yet the two are starkly different.

September 29: Dream #3—*the Ruined Mansion*.

Two versions occur frequently. One is, specifically, a ruined mansion. The other is more like an incomplete mansion.

The ruined mansion is an extremely large two story frame house, looking like an abandoned Victorian-style small-town hotel. It is located in a suburban district of an ordinary town, and it is in bad shape. If it is not condemned, it should be. It is falling apart at every joint. In fact, in several of the dreams, it actually collapses into total ruin as part of the action, with me on the second floor. It is not so much what takes place as the desire I have to live on the second floor of that mansion. I am so intent upon doing so that I move in even though it is in danger every moment of collapsing, and often does. This dream is sometimes peopled by me alone. Others are sometimes present but play little active role.

The incomplete mansion is somewhat different. It is, by appearance, a southern American plantation mansion, extraordinarily large, more than three stories. This dream has progressed over the years in that, gradually, the upper floors, my main reason for loving the house, have disappeared. Several years ago, when I first began to have the dream, I was free to wander through the entire house. It was a marvelous escape from other people since everyone else stayed on the first floor carrying out their ordinary commerce. I, alone, traversed the upper floors. Exception! Occasionally, a security guard would walk through the upper floors. I would hide from him until he was out of sight then go on with my explorations. Each room was decorated richly and completely. I don't remember the details of that decoration, but each room was vastly different from any of the others. Then, a room or two at a time simply disappeared. Recently, only one room remains above the main floor. It is a small room just at the head of the right hand grand staircase which curves gracefully up from the great hall on the first floor. The room is furnished simply, just a desk and a chair and a single bed, much like a monk's cell. Still, it is my favorite place to go. Unfortunately, each time I go there, the security guard chases me out. Even this one little room at the top of the stairs is off limits to me. It is not so much that the rest of the rooms are not there. I have a real sense that they are still there. I simply cannot see them— and I cannot go there.

I can't help thinking that the two dreams (lost in the city and the ruined or incomplete mansion) are related symbolically. I have a model that seems to be the source of all of the mansions. Especially, for the incomplete mansion I have one, a nearly exact replica for the first and second floors, complete even with a pipe organ and a large variety of rooms furnished as offices and classrooms. No monk's quarters, however. It is an antebellum mansion on the grounds of the Naval Preparatory Academy at Bainbridge, Maryland, used as the headquarters for the school. Perhaps, another connection to my *ruined* naval career. Certainly, both dreams place me in a position of being alienated from the fulfillment of my desires. Indeed, the incomplete mansion presents an image of desires that are not only alienated but imaginary.

The odd thing about most of my dreams is that they seem to represent me as willingly and persistently acting to attempt fulfillment of higher goals but always failing to do so. There is one divergence from atheistic existentialism. Action in atheistic existentialism should end in some sort of accomplishment, however unsatisfying it is, which could be considered positive, at least, in the sense that it is an attainment whether the one aimed at or not. My dreams present no attainment at all. I always wake from my dreams frustrated that *nothing* has been accomplished. This, of course, would be in keeping with the realities of the modern world in which most existentialists live: a meaningless world of the absurd. My dream-goals themselves are absurd and the outcomes are just as absurd. No progress occurs—no material or spiritual dialectic—simply endless seeking with no finding.

I do have pleasant dreams as well. Unfortunately, their content escapes me instantly as I awaken. Too bad! I simply wake up thinking, what a pleasant dream that was. I wonder what it was.

September 30: More Wind Damage.

Idaho is telling me goodbye in violent fashion. Yesterday, a west wind blew the top out of my favorite elm tree, and it was a cold wind. That was depressing. It froze what was left of the garden, a sort of "I'm-tired-of-you-taking-fresh-produce-out-of-my-soil" notice. The west wind blew hard all day and bent two more of my young elms (for which I have great hopes as eventual shade trees) into permanent eastward leaning. That is not unusual for Idaho elm trees. Any of them without windbreak protection from the west end up with an eastward lean. The upper branches will make up for it by growing westward to balance out the total weight of the tree. This morning, it was even colder (27 degrees F.) and the wind was coming in from the east. The good news is that the sun came out and charged up my batteries so I have a good supply of electricity for watching football on television today.

The sun and the warmer temperatures have, also, charged up my psychological batteries, so I don't feel depressed anymore. The ten-foot elm which was a twenty-foot elm before yesterday is, actually, pretty. It looks like a frilly cone with no ice cream, just a circle of leafy branches all around the outside edges and flat on top. Besides that, it now matches the other little elm next to it on the lawn in height and width.

So I called Yasmin and suggested that we should try to sell our Kansas City home and build a nice house out here just north of the tree that lost its top so that, eventually, that tree will shade the south lawn of our nice new house. Of course, Yasmin knows that I will not make her live year around away from her three daughters and eight grandchildren, but a nice house in the country is a pleasant fantasy.

I am listening to your voice, Idaho, in today's east wind which is busily standing up my eastward leaning elms. They are looking good, just about vertical. They will lean to the east again tomorrow when the east wind stops, just enough to remind me that it is time to go back east to Kansas City. I hear you. I emptied out the little pond by the cook-shack and put graphite in all the locks and loaded the bamboo chairs that Yasmin wants returned to Kansas City into the back of the truck. I'll be leaving in three days if the snow doesn't get too deep on the Wyoming high plains.

A couple of evenings ago, the rising full moon, big and orange like a pumpkin, stared across Walden-San at the setting sun, bright and orange but not so much like a pumpkin, just as it did at the start of this quarter of my book. There is nothing too surprising about that since that was almost exactly three months ago and

277

the rising moon takes a nearly direct look at the setting sun once a month. The calendar months, after all, are related to the lunar cycles. Still, I can imagine it as symbolic and spiritual that I began recording this part of my philosophical almanac near the time that the moon was staring at the sun and will end it at a similar part of the lunar cycle. Imagination is, after all, as important as science in seeking what is Good.

I'll see you in *The Last Quarter Moon*. That is what my imagination has told me to call the final quarter of this almanac. So it has been decreed! So it shall be!

End of Volume 3
The Harvest Moon

The True Book of Sam Clear Water
Wisdom from Walden-San
Volume 4: *The Last Quarter Moon*

A Last Note from Yasmin's Auntie:

Dis one long buggah book! I tink I no gonna finish today. But I like da mountain pa't. Remin' me of Kilauea summit by dat army base. Moke drive me dere to pick Ohelo Berry. I sleepy! Pau read! Mo' read tomorrow.

October 1: Where Are You Going from Here?

This volume, the last volume in the set, could easily become anticlimactic and redundant. Redundant, I will accept. It is a natural part of existence. Indeed, everything that we have done and said has, very likely, been done and said before. Repetition in an evolving context is an important part of understanding. Anticlimactic must be conditioned.

Notice that I have not entirely rejected "anticlimactic." In the usually intended negative sense where "everything is downhill" toward the final conclusion from here, I reject anticlimax. But there is another more positive sense in which I accept it. In that sense, a rather romantic sense, every well-developed thought is an epiphany, a sudden and exciting discovery of truth; and, since I try to have a well-developed thought every day, I expect an epiphany every day. Thus, every day is an intellectual climax, and the following day is "anticlimactic." In that sense, anticlimax is a normal part of my day. It is not only the aftermath of climax; it is the predecessor of epiphany. That is what I expect of myself, and that is what I hope for you.

Where are we going from here? First of all, I will visit my mother in the rehabilitation center in Twin Falls. That is repetitive. I do it twice a week and the rehab center is not exactly Philosophy Central. At least once during each of my visits, my mother, hearing a strange noise coming from a patient somewhere in the building, nods toward the general totality of the Center and spins her right index finger around her right temple as if to say, "Everyone is screwy here!" Except for being a tad forgetful at almost 88 years old, she is anything but screwy. I expect, today, to ask her, again, about Thoreau's *Walden* which I left with her a couple of weeks ago and which she had read about the first quarter last Friday when I visited. Her response was intelligent and in keeping with her life experience which included the great depression, early family poverty, escape from the dustbowl of Montana, no college, but, still, intelligent in its relationship to that existence, and I will gain insights from what she tells me. One insight is that Granddad Butts was a better man than Henry David Thoreau. They were equally creative about making something out of next to nothing. For instance, Thoreau built his cabin in the woods for a pittance; and Granddad, heading his family on a remote Montana farm, developed an effective electrical system: a windmill, the blades of which he carved by hand out of scavenged wood, turning a used automobile electric generator, charging a bank of used 6-volt car batteries, likewise, scavenged from junkyards and rebuilt, and a variety of scavenged DC appliances (radio, lights, etc.). Of course, I have heard this family legend before, but never before in a comparison/contrast with Thoreau. You see, Granddad was a dedicated public servant as well as a creative and inventive mind. Thoreau seems rather selfish. As I listened to her, I had a feeling that Mom's assessment was exactly right. I remember, for instance, reading about Thoreau's failed attempt at teaching school wherein he ended up paddling every student in the class and quitting after his first day. On Friday last, Mom's comments were an epiphany to me that had to do with the truth about human worth.

Where will we go from here? I don't know about you, but in two days, I'll start my three-day trip back to Yasmin in Kansas City, and we'll see what happens after that.

October 2: Flexibility.

I have learned in my old age to make up for my inflexibility of joints and body with mental flexibility. At least, I think that is what it might be called. On the six o'clock news last night I saw that a storm—a veritable blizzard—will be moving into southern Wyoming on Thursday. My plans, including Motel 6 reservations, called for me to wake up on Thursday in Rock Springs, Wyoming. This called for heroic flexible action on my part. I decided to move up my date for departure from Idaho from tomorrow to today so that on Thursday, when the blizzard strikes Rock Springs, I will wake up in North Platte, Nebraska, where the forecast for Thursday is wall-to-wall sunshine. So far it has worked. It is Tuesday night and I am in Rock Springs. The weather is fine. I hope the forecaster was right.

I just watched the first installment of *Cavemen* on ABC TV. As I predicted (silently since there was no one to predict it to along the highway), it was awful. Thus, today has been productive: one positive, one negative. In philosophy (for your information and education), both positives and negatives are counters. So I am up, 2 and 0. That is better than the San Diego Chargers. Thanks to the KC Chiefs coming out of semi-hibernation this Sunday, the Chargers are down 1 and 3. In football, negatives count against you. Football players might be paid better than I am, but they can never match my win/loss record.

By the way, Yasmin is overjoyed that I will arrive a day early. That means that I am 3 and 0.

October 3: Why I Don't Object to Being Called a Conservative.

Although, when I look in a mirror, I don't see a conservative, I don't mind the label because:
1) My first love and my most important commitment is to my family, Yasmin first, then my children and grandchildren, then my extended family.
2) I am a proud Walmart shopper. All of those badly paid Walmart employees should be glad that they have a job at all. Although, I don't approve of the Chinese attitude toward the wages of the lower class, I can see that shades of capitalism are beginning to have a positive impact even on the lowest classes of China. Of course, the Chinese make us proud because they are worse environmental polluters than we are.

3) I value human life, even unborn human life. I believe that a woman should consider other alternatives before considering an abortion; and, certainly, she should not have an abortion after the first trimester of pregnancy except to protect her own life or to prevent some other catastrophe, and someone much closer to the situation than I am must define "catastrophe" for the individual case—perhaps the woman herself with the advice and prescription of her physician.

4) I have spent my entire life struggling with the concept of morality so that I could be the most ethical person that I can be and so that I could teach others to seek the highest ground and strive for the "Good."

5) I believe that God loves me and all of the rest of his creation, and I pray, not often, but well.

6) I believe (although I don't always follow my belief) that I should not judge other people except in the sense of trying to help them to find a higher road to the good.

Note: I could add other stuff, and for each of the above and the other stuff I would add, I should, in all good conscience, add conditioning footnotes. Read the rest of the book and you will understand why. I do not believe that any conservative should be a conservative on the model of any other human being or book or organization. The task of the conservative should be to *conserve truth* as he or she has discovered it, tested it, and proven it, not as he or she has *received* it in its raw form from someone else or from a book.

October 4: Back in Kansas City.
And neck-deep in family! Whether I am neck-deep with my feet down or my head down will remain a mystery.

October 5: Being Organized.
There is a great deal of satisfaction to be derived from a neat, well-organized work-space. I am now experiencing such satisfaction for the first time in six months—my office, the cave within a cave within a cave.

Here at the beginning of the end of this book, it is satisfying to know that I will have all that I need for research, for quiet contemplation, for "vision and revision" as Prufrock puts it. In short, I have in this little office space with one limestone wall (painted off-white) and three human-fabricated walls of glass, wood, and sheetrock, everything I need to complete a masterpiece. I am convinced that even my addled and limited brain is enough, given the excellence of my context.

I miss my Idaho sanctuary, Walden-San. But it is good to be back again in the university underground. Wordsworth said that poetry is "experience recollected in tranquility." I have had the experiences, and I now have the tranquility. Let me proceed to recollect.

October 6: My Learning Disability.
I watched a television movie last night wherein an old man of immense intelligence had managed to hide his learning disability (dyslexia) all of his life because he was so ashamed that he had such a disability. The crisis: his grandson, who inherited the same disability, became upset with him for lying about his ability to read. Outcome: the old man admitted to the town (in which he was about to be

elected to the board of aldermen) that he was dyslexic, he was elected by a landslide, the grandson's wrath was appeased, and they all lived happily in a growing puddle of emotional slobber ever after.

This has prompted me to admit my long hidden learning disability, not so I can live in slobber, but so others might get some good out of what I have done to get past it. When I was 13 years old, I caught what was called Asiatic flu. The resulting long-term fever did some minor damage to my brain which 1) wiped out much of my memory of matters up to that point and 2) has made it difficult for me to process mental experience from short-term into long-term memory. Essentially, what happens is that the information gets side-tracked and, often, lost in some dimly-lighted gray-matter recess where it resides comfortably and can be retrieved only with the greatest of difficulty, often not at all. I struggled with this disability for years. I even managed to go through my doctoral hoops to a PhD using, almost entirely, short-term memory. It was a comedy of errors whereby, to write a research paper, I had to pile up hundreds of books that had every possible reference marked so that I could return to it over and over as the short term memories disappeared into dendrite and axon limbo.

My extended dilemma is easy to illustrate. Once, as I was teaching a British literature course to university students, I suddenly could not recall the name of the author of *Hamlet*. I was desperate enough that I had to ask the class to tell me so that I could continue the lecture (I seldom use notes). Of course, the class took it well because they knew about my disability. I had been teaching them (only about 15 people) three times a week for most of a semester, and I had taught many of them (because it is a small university) in other courses, and I still had to have them raise their hands for role call each time we met. They simply considered me the typical absent-minded professor. I knew that it was more.

An immediate example: at this very moment, I cannot recall the name of that renowned quadriplegic physicist who can talk only through the means of a computer voice. I have been trying to think of that name since yesterday afternoon. I know a great deal about him; I even disagree with him on a couple of philosophical/scientific points having to do with the Big Bang theory.

This leads to my solution (or, at least, a patch) for the problem. I will now break away, save my work, and consult Google with key words: "physicist," "quadriplegic," "computer voice." . . . . And I'm back, tugging Stephen Hawking by the sleeve in less than 30 seconds. The information technology revolution has provided access to that seemingly boundless store of information in my long-term memory which I cannot retrieve through normal biological processes because my biological processes are flawed.

True, it is a little awkward to carry my laptop wherever I go and to be, constantly, consulting Google for the right words as if I were following a roadmap to navigate roads I had traveled many times before. But it is necessary if I am to maximize my own mental powers. I have been doing this frequently for the past couple of years. But I only recently realized that it is not cheating, no more than Stephen Hawking is cheating by using a computer voice. Of course, I would not be able to take my laptop into an I.Q. test. But I.Q. tests mean next to nothing anyway. What a relief to me to discover that I can, through the magic of key words, access the information in my brain that I need for clear analysis, synthesis, and evaluation of problems and situations whether from every-day life experience or in the midst of philosophical/political/ethical/scientific discussions with my professional peers. I might even try my hand at quantum physics over the next year or two.

And you, too, no matter what your disability, if it is reducing your ability to maximize your production, whatever production you value, material or immaterial, mediate or immediate, find the solution to the disability. It will change your life. Don't wait like the old man in the TV movie and I did until there is not much left of us but a few dendrites and axons. Do it now while there *might be* lots of time left for you to self-actualize.

October 7: Desire.

I think I mentioned someplace before that I once kept a sign on my desk that said, "Annihilate desire!" I seem to recall that I put it there after reading something from Bertrand Russell, but those were my "salad days." Although this fits well with some Eastern philosophies, I fear that it is not quite right. Without desire, we simply have no way to progress. If we come to a place wherein we have all knowledge and all power including total control of space and time, desire will, presumably, be annihilated. Of course, then we would be God which would be impossible because there can be only one absolute power in the universe and we will never be it. We might share in it (i.e., be part of *it*), but we can never be *it* inclusively. Thus, desire, in its ideal sense, gives us purpose in our lives, even in an absurd world where, as far as we know, everything is without meaning or purpose.

Thus, I must condition my sign, ruining its neatly aesthetic aphoristic value. I could get away with a conditioning that would turn it into another aphorism, a trite one which might be attributable to Socrates: "Annihilate desire but for the Good." Then I would have to go to work and decide whether or not each desire is, indeed, for the Good.

Right now, for instance, I harbor a desire to join Nelson Mandela's "Global Elders." I'm sure he would not choose me as one of the core group of elders because I have no credentials for such an office. I have never been a president or prime minister or even a catholic archbishop. Although I would like to be in that core group (an unlikely-to-be-fulfilled desire), what I really desire as an alternative is something less auspicious such as serving on the traveling retinue to be of direct assistance to some member or members of the core. I am quite sure that my input would, eventually, lead to the total cessation of war and human misery in the world. "In a pig's eye!" I must quickly add. But I might be of some small value in such a role.

The question is whether this is a true "desire for the Good." On the one hand, it has a purity to it that is a companion of Good. I assure you that my desire is not for self-aggrandizement or power or any other evil design. It is, purely, that I want the best for my fellow humans. I have to admit that I would, undoubtedly, gain wisdom from rubbing shoulders with that core of persons who are truly the Global Elders. But I think that the desire to gain personal wisdom is, also, Good. On the other hand, if I went off like a superhero to save the world, what local responsibilities would I be shirking? I'll not enumerate them here since this note is intended to stimulate your thinking as well as my own toward appropriate analysis of every situation in search of the Good.

283

It is entirely possible that the best thing I could do is to stay right where I am and serve Good purposes in Kansas City in the winter and in Idaho in the summer. But I have been missing something. In gaining retirement and personal security and comfort, I seem to have become largely extraneous, a figure to be loved by grandchildren and former students, admired and envied by former colleagues, but of little practical use to anyone except Yasmin, who needs me to take out the trash. It would be wrong, however, to make a decision too hastily. Some of the greatest Good is done locally and is only felt more broadly over a greater period of time. On the other hand, like Grey's buried and forgotten peasants in the country churchyard, "the good is oft interred with their bones." (Do you suppose Grey had been reading Shakespeare when he wrote his elegy?)

October 8: Pause.

I am pausing for a moment to think—about nothing.

I told grandson #1 last evening that the world is absurd, meaningless, unless we provide the day-to-day meaning that it lacks. He had been having some difficulty with another boy in school who insists upon pestering him about various matters including his race (my grandson's) and other human characteristics which he might or might not display. I was telling him that the fellow who retaliates against such inappropriate behavior is nearly always the one who gets in trouble. Thus, it is better to build one's own structure of meaning which places such stuff, when it is aimed at us personally, at a low level of importance. I hope he understands. If I had understood this concept—that we create for ourselves the only meaning that exists—at an early age, I could have avoided a lot of misery. I'm not sure that I have entirely mastered the concept yet—or that anyone has.

October 9: Ramadan and Laylat al-Qadr.

We are nearing the end of the Islamic holy month of Ramadan. In places where Islam is not a major social factor, one does not hear much about Ramadan. This is unfortunate since such a large part of humanity considers it a holy month and, especially, since the Muslims have managed to keep their holy days and months quite pure in their celebration, not like Christendom which has so intermingled its holidays (Christmas, Easter, etc.) with commerce and recreational activities and non-Christian mythology that it is hard to think of them as *holy* days. One must respect Islam for keeping its holy days *holy*.

The holiest of holy days (in this case, a holy night) in Islam is (according to some Islamic calendars for this year) tonight: Laylat al-Qadr—the night of power—celebrating the night upon which Mohammad was endowed in his soul with the Holy Quran. On this night, the act of worshipping God is said to be empowered exponentially. Indeed, the worshipper hopes that, eventually, through keeping the Islamic faith in a single God and in utter obedience to that God, on some Laylet al-Qadr he/she will enter into the actual presence of Allah. For what more could one ask?

May I answer that? I will—with or without permission.

The *more* that one could ask for would be the actual presence of God at all times and in all places. In fact, one doesn't have to ask. How could the absolute power and intelligence of the cosmos not be present in every place and time in the

284

cosmos? Keep in mind that I am speaking of what *I* understand to be God; but in essence, without the ritualistic hullabaloo attached to religion, mine is the definition of God which is given by all of the "people of the book" (Jews, Christians, and Muslims) that is, the absolute power and intelligence of the cosmos.

I respect the worship of God in whatever forms it takes as long as it remains decent and humane. It is good that people should recognize and adore that power. What I do not respect, indeed, what I consider ludicrous, is the claim of the various religions that they have a corner on the God market. Absolute absurdity! How can any human being or group of human beings *know* anything more than the very minimum about God (i.e., the absolute power and intelligence of the cosmos)? The answer: they cannot.

People of the book and others who are interested in meeting with God: I invite you to my chapel, the whole of the cosmos. Services begin—well, they don't begin—and run constantly until—well, forever, and they take place everywhere. I'll see you there. BYOB! We won't be drinking any human blood or eating any human flesh or slaughtering lambs or examining bullock livers. Nor will we slaughter one another. We can feast on tasty discussion, but a glass of chilled Sangria and a chunk of extra sharp cheddar cheese would be a welcome repast.

October 10: Navaratri and Vijayadasami.

Yesterday, I spoke of my respect for Islam in its devotion and utter submission to a single, omniscient, omnipresent, omnipotent God. Today, on the other hand, I can speak with equal if not similar respect for a religion which has remained largely unevolved since days coeval with the ancient mythologies of the Greeks and the Germanic and Native American tribes. That is Hinduism. Two days from now marks the beginning of Navaratri, nine days and nights of worship of Hindu gods and goddesses who are special to women of the Hindu faith. I won't go into the details, but it would appear that Hindu women have a great deal more fun in giving and receiving gifts with their worship of many gods and goddesses than do Muslims with their concentrated worship of Allah.

The most important day in this Hindu holy period, though, is the day after Navaratri, called Vijayadasami (victory day) when the Hindu goddess Chaamundeshwari is said to have killed the demon Mahishaasura. This day of victory, as well as the preceding days commemorating the nine-day war between the goddess and the demon, is celebrated by the ladies with candy and other sweet treats. This brings me a step closer to the conclusion that we should consider having women arrange for all of our battles and, especially, their commemorations.

October 11: Grading Writing Competency Tests.

I decided, when I was invited to do so, that, since "The Global Elders" seem to be ignoring my offer to become one of them, I would return to an old Wednesday afternoon Park University tradition which I helped to found: the grading of student Writing Competency Tests. This is a test that all Park students must pass in order to progress from the required lower division writing program to the required upper division writing program. It is, also, one of those absolute benchmarks which must be met before a student can be granted a baccalaureate degree from Park. Thus, we take it seriously.

But in all of that seriousness, it was a good excuse for me to get together with some of my old colleagues whom I seldom see since my retirement. It is one of the few environments where just about everyone knows who I am, and the new people who have joined the team since I retired are interested in getting to know me. That is a good feeling in a world where anonymity seems to be the byword.

Three persons need mention here, and that is the heart of this entry.

First, is the colleague with whom I was closest during the last decade of my career, the fellow with whom I traded off positions (department chair, division chair, etc.) during that long and difficult period. He was happy to see me, and I was happy to see him and, as the person most knowledgeable about the WCT system (since he was a co-founder), he normed me (i.e., assessed the first five papers with me to prove that I still knew my stuff). He was, again, pleased when our scores matched (his a tad lower than mine) just as they have always matched.

Next was a former student, now an adjunct instructor in English, a fellow who retired from a previous successful occupation to become a teacher. He had been a fine student in my classes a decade ago, and he is a fine teacher today. He has never gotten over his attitude of respect for me which he developed in his student days. He is still not comfortable referring to me by my first name. I'm still "Dr. . . ." to him. I like that respect. There is far too little of it in society today. It is something which cannot and should not be required, but which is a wonderful social asset when it arises as a result of normal human interaction.

The third colleague takes us to the other side of that respect continuum. He is a gentleman who spent his entire career as a Park professor. He was here for many years before I arrived and retired just a couple of years before I did. I presume he assesses WCTs for some of the same reasons that I do. He is a man for whom I hold profound respect, but who, I have reason to believe, for many years did not approve of my appointment to faculty. I'll not argue the validity of his objections. That is water under the bridge. I had a sense, however, yesterday, for the first time the water was completely down-river from the bridge for him as well. Indeed, I felt for that two hours, with few words spoken between the two of us, a sense of collegiality that I had never sensed before with him and, perhaps, stronger than with any other person in the room. I think it had something to do with our shared depth of experience at the university. He was the senior professor present, I was second senior. Together, our presence was an anchor symbolizing the stability of the greater institution, not a legislated rule but an *a priori* truth. And it was good!

October 12: Peace!
My soul cries peace to the winds of hate that howl through a tattered land.
There's never been a time before so in need a master's hand.

October 13: Gore, Paul, and Peace.
Sam is talking with Patrick Sherman, a former student, in the cave within a cave within a cave.
Sam: So Al Gore won the Nobel Prize for his work of global warming.
Pat: It's all a hoax.
Sam: No. It's a real Nobel Prize.

Pat: I don't mean the prize. I mean the idea of global warming. There is no man-made global warming.

Sam: Hmm.

Pat: Nope! It's all just a way to rob us, to get extra money. Here. I'll write down a couple of web sites where you can read all about it.

Sam: Now, Pat, you know that the web is full of lies and half-truths. I read them all the time just for a laugh.

Pat *(bristling)*: There's a lot more truth on the internet than there is in the public media. All of the public newscasters are communists and criminals. So are all of the politicians and so is Al Gore. He's just a liar. He said that the melting of the ice caps would cause a 20-foot rise in the ocean tides. He knew that there was an error in the calculation and that the rise would only be four inches and he just stuck to his lie. There isn't any global warming. It's just a natural cycling of world temperatures. You know the government is already charging a surcharge for global warming. They're just communists and criminals. All of them!

Sam: But Gore isn't part of the government any more. He lost the election and he's now a private citizen.

Pat *(again bristling)*: He didn't lose. He won. Bush stole the election, and the Supreme Court gave it to him. They are, as I've said, all communists and criminals.

Sam *(his tongue in his cheek)*: I'm not sure that it's necessarily a bad thing to be a communist, but don't you mean "socialist" instead of "communist? And, certainly, Bush is not a socialist. He is a true capitalist. He's one of the leaders of the Republican Party.

Pat: Socialist! Communist! No difference! They're all criminals. They're all trampling on the constitution.

Sam: Who would you suggest as an alternative?

Pat: Senator Ron Paul.

Sam: Good fellow, *Representative* Paul! A fine physician! I kind of like his stance on the Iraq war, though it is a little too radical, but he wants to do away with just about all of our national infrastructure to save money, and I'm not sure that is such a good idea. But that is almost beside the point. He can't even get the Republican nomination, let alone win the general election. Some Republicans will vote for him because he wants to end the war, but not a majority of them. The Democrats won't vote for him because he wants to do away with Social Security. He doesn't stand a chance.

Pat: When more people hear what he stands for they will get behind him and elect him. What do you bet *(holding out his hand for a shake)*?

Sam *(rejecting the handshake)*: I don't do much betting, but he doesn't stand a chance.

Pat: Just wait and see.

Sam: Yes, I will. I don't suppose I have a choice.

Librarian *(peering through the open door)*: Shhh!

Sam: Sorry! We'll close the door.

Pat: Oops! I guess I was Yelling.

Sam: Yup! You were. Rethink this global warming thing. Gore might be wrong about some of the details, but there's a lot of scientific evidence for global warming and a lot of evidence that we are causing part of it with our carbon pollution and that it can lead to some drastic situations in the world.

Pat *(loudly)*: Nope! They're all communists and criminals. Read it for yourself *(handing Sam a professionally printed card with a number of websites listed on it)*.

Sam *(taking the card and sticking it in his denim shirt pocket)*: O.K. But I have an appointment right now.

Pat *(quickly preparing to depart)*: Oh, sorry! I didn't mean to take up so much time.

Sam: No problem. It was good talking to you.

Pat *(leaving)*: See ya soon.

Sam: O.K. I'll look forward to it.

    Sam leaned back in his chair and took a long sip of tepid green tea from the cup at his elbow. He picked up the copy of Hemingway's A Farewell to Arms *which he was re-reading in preparation for a seminar he planned to attend in November and opened it to the bookmark, and he smiled and chuckled as he settled into his appointed reading.*

October 14: A Communist and a Criminal?!

    I suppose, now, that I will have to accept, along with the labels of both conservative and liberal, the labels of communist and criminal, although these latter I accept more reluctantly than the former. The reason I must accept them is simple. I must trust Pat's judgment without question! Is there not a philosophy somewhere which says that everything we can say must be true? That sounds a little like Wittgenstein turned on its head, doesn't it?

    But here is my confession:

Sam *(in the Catholic Church confessional)*: Forgive me, Father, for I have sinned.

Voice *(from the other side)*: When was your last confession, Sam?

Sam: Well, I'm not a Catholic (although I might have to admit to that label someday, too); but, let's see, I confessed about a traffic ticket I got that I was going 50 in a 25 MPH zone. That was about 20 years ago. Does that count?

Voice: Hmm. I suppose it will have to do. And what do you have to confess today?

Sam: According to Pat's Libertarian political analysis, I'm a communist and a criminal. After thinking it over, I have to admit it. So I confess.

Voice: This could be serious if it's true. I might have to consult Homeland Security.

Sam: I'd rather you wouldn't. Yasmin does a good job with *our* homeland security already. She'd be offended if some Washington politician came in and told her how to do it.

Voice: O.K. I won't, then. What makes you think you are, according to Pat (I suppose that would be short for Patrick), a communist and a criminal?

Sam: Let's take 'em one at a time. First, I am a communist, according to Patrick, because I don't take offence at illegal alien Mexicans. In fact, I kind of like them, at least the ones I've met in Walmart. They are always helpful about giving me directions. Sometimes I don't understand their directions because my mastery of Spanish is limited, but that's my fault, not theirs. And it would, really, make me feel bad if we shipped them all back to Mexico. They're such nice, courteous folks!

288

But that makes me a criminal, according to Patrick, because these Mexicans are criminals because they entered America illegally, and by being nice to them, I'm aiding and abetting criminals which makes me a criminal myself. But it, also, makes me a communist because I can't see any reason not to take good care of them while they're visiting us here in the United States. If they get sick, they should be able to get medical care. If they want time off to write a novel or something, someone should offer them a room with a table and paper for writing and a cot with a couple of blankets and a pillow for sleeping and some food and water and other stuff they need to get by while they write it. If they have a novel in them, I'd sure like to have the chance to see it before we send them back home. That's socialist thinking, and I fear that, according to Patrick, all socialists are communists as well as criminals.

Voice: It all seems confusing to me. But I suggest that you say a couple of "Hail Marys" every day for a week and . . .

Sam: Wait! We haven't gotten into all of my sins.

Voice: That's O.K. It doesn't make a lot of difference what the rest are. I'd still recommend a few "Hail Marys." The line's getting long outside the confessional and I have to get through with them before mass.

Sam: O.K. Thanks. I'll think about the "Hail Marys." But it all seems a little silly to me.

Voice: Forget the "Hail Marys"! They would be an offense to God coming from your heretical mouth. Meet me at the Power Plant about 7:00 tonight, and we can have a couple of Stouts. Maybe Siebert can make it, too. But he likes the Pale Ale.

Sam: Yeah! He never had much of a stomach. O.K. See ya there.

Voice: Next?

October 15: Accelerated Wisdom.

I will share something with you. One who wishes to gain wisdom must pursue it vigorously and constantly. Any cessation in vigor or constancy in the pursuit results almost immediately in a rapid loss of wisdom. On the other hand, continued constancy and vigor result in an exponential acceleration in growth of wisdom, far more than we could imagine from the vantage point of every-day mundane lives. It would appear that such exponential growth would lead us nearer and nearer to perfect wisdom. Of course, since wisdom is infinite and our minds are limited, we cannot attain perfect wisdom, but it seems possible that we could, with near-perfect diligence in both vigor and constancy, live just behind the growing edge of perfect cosmic wisdom.

Lewis Carroll said through Alice, "We must run as fast as we can just to stay in the same place." Alice goes on to say that, if we wish to get ahead, we must run faster than that. This would seem to be impossible if it were not for "exponential acceleration." Indeed, it has been my experience that to accelerate beyond the possible through vigor and constancy takes less effort than to "run as fast as we can just to stay in the same place." And it is less frustrating.

October 16: The Big Read—*A Farewell to Arms.*

It's called "The Big Read," and Park University is participating, and some of my English Department colleagues will be on the panel, and the chosen book is

Hemingway's *A Farewell to Arms*. This book conveniently falls into line with my thoughts about existentialism, an alternative view of existentialism to that of Sartre. I want to sound as if I know something when I attend the panel discussion in November, so I am reading the book again for both reasons.

I have found the most important line in the book. It isn't important to identify the context because it is in the book, and that is enough of a context, but I will tell you that it is in Chapter III.

> *"I had drunk much wine and afterward coffee and Stega and I explained, winefully, how we did not do the things we wanted to do; we never did such things."*

This could be called Hemingway's "passive" existentialism in contrast to Sartre's "ideologic" existentialism. We could not expect Hemingway to support Marxism. Indeed, Hemingway could be classed loosely with the Taoists: "Just go with the flow!" Hemingway was in Italy. It struck his fancy that war would be interesting and, perhaps, rewarding in some way. So he joined the Italian army and drove an ambulance in WWI. With a little political maneuvering, he might have succeeded in joining the English army which would be in the campaign shortly. There, he would be more in his element socially and linguistically. But the Italian army was convenient. So he joined it.

Sartre, on the other hand, seems to have struggled for years before deciding, late in his life, that the right thing to do would be to join militantly in the cause of Marxist communism. It seemed to him that it was a cause worth espousing. It was the logical extension of Hegel's dialectical perfection of humanity. It is difficult from our 21st century perspective to see how Sartre, who was so intelligent, could have been so wrong in his assessment, but that is how he saw it. He joined the cause, not because it was there, but because he considered it to be the right thing to do.

So which is the true existentialist? Both! The key is in the credo of existentialism: existence precedes essence. Both Hemingway and Sartre stood upon the foundation of existence to create their own essence—worlds apart, both hopeless except in the essential hope born of absurdity—which leads to another important exchange in *A Farewell to Arms* (from Chapter XI):

> *"Then it's hopeless?"*
> *"It is never hopeless. But sometimes I cannot hope. I try always to hope but sometimes I cannot."*
> *"Maybe the war will be over."*
> *"I hope so."*
> *"What will you do then?"*

The conversation continues, but it is existentially important for us to break away on this question. "What will you do then?" For Hemingway, it is a matter of context. For Sartre, ideology. Both will create essence for themselves and—godlike—for the world that forms the context of their existence—even if essence must be strained through a "wineful" haze.

October 17: Slowly! Slowly! Slowly!
Slowly, slowly, slowly,
Let the voice of freedom
Echo from the mountains,
Shout it to the mountains,
"Let there be Joy!"

Let the hills hear the word!
Let the mountains reply
Let my heart overflow
With Joy!

. . . And yet, the irony is, the truth is,
That freedom is the most profound servitude:
Hallowed slavery in Wisdom's
Velvet shackles!
Ah, what freedom in slavery!

. . . Let the hills hear the word!
Let the mountains reply
Let my heart overflow
With Joy!
Let there be joy!

October 18: Carved in Granite Ten Steps from the Summit.
Ten steps up, I saw the sunshine, and assumed it was God.
A quarter mile up, I saw the moon and worshipped.
Half a mile high, I noticed stars in the sky and thought them
To be my own children.
On a ridge a mile above the valley, I rested a moment,
Breathing the kind thin air.
When I reached the next ridge (Who knows how high?)
The sun was gone, and so was the moon, and darkness owned me.
I continued on spidery legs,
Never reaching the summit.
The climb was exhilarating.
Stay, traveler, and talk awhile!
You have tales to tell.

**October 19: "Philosophy Aims at the Logical Clarification of Thoughts"
(Wittgenstein, *Tractatus Logico-Philosophicus* 4.111).**
 With this statement, Wittgenstein narrows philosophy to a mere servant status to the natural sciences and proves that he does not (at the young age when he first makes this statement) have a comprehensive understanding of philosophy.
 I will not deny philosophy's goal of clarification of thought. That, indeed, is one of its most important designs. Anyone who reads Kant's *Critiques* or (their

291

alter-ego) Nietzsche's *Also Sprach Zarathustra* cannot deny that. And, certainly, both Kant and Zarathustra say things in their attempted clarifications that are both nonsensical and illogical. Modern and contemporary philosophers have made marble dust of both of these iconic iconoclasts. And this is as it should be. But even marble dust from icons contains the essence of truth which later philosophers can sweep up and restate in equally flawed (and equally useful) critiques and rants.

Wittgenstein is correct when he insists that philosophy has made little or no progress toward any goals, even those narrow linguistic servant goals to which he insists philosophy should be limited. But that is where he, along with many philosophers, errs most egregiously. The twin goals of philosophy are to explain and *to guide*, not to invent. Invention is the goal of the artist or the scientist, not the philosopher.

Wittgenstein does not entirely deny this, but he insists that the explanation be perfectly logical to be acceptable. Otherwise, it is meaningless nonsense. But what has the last 150 years of philosophy taught us if it has not taught us that reality is nonsensical and illogical. Wittgenstein said it himself when he said in the *Tractatus* (2.062) "from the existence or non-existence of one state of affairs it is impossible to infer the existence or non-existence of another." States of affairs are, indeed, unpredictable except by the very flawed means of induction which leaves out of the equation everything that is unknown to us—all of the rest of infinity which has not been experienced.

Natural science pushes back the boundaries of what is known to us and the technologies associated with natural science rearrange what is discovered into useful (sometimes deadly) states of affairs. Philosophy, with each new revelation of the natural sciences and with each newly discovered or newly organized state of affairs, must start from the very beginning (Socrates, Lao Tzu and earlier) of philosophy and re-explain it in keeping with the new state of affairs while consumers of philosophy in any age are guided by what they consume. In neither the discoveries of the natural sciences nor the explanations by the philosophers is the full "truth" about anything revealed. That part of infinity which lies beyond scientific exploration continues to be the unknown. Thus, although we are aware of (and have arranged) additional states of affairs which change our lives and our thoughts, we are still just as ignorant of the *whole* of the cosmos as we were in the first place—because it is, indeed, infinite. Who has the knowledge to say that, just over the next scientific/philosophic horizon, a discovery lies which will turn much of what we think we know about the cosmos on its head, and who's to say that new discovery won't be turned on its head shortly afterward? No Body! That is who. And just as it was treacherous in the ancient cave of Polyphemus, the name Ulysses called himself, "No Body," is treacherous for both scientists and philosophers today and will remain so forever. Lacking the body, murder (or resurrection) cannot be absolutely proven. *Habeas corpus!*

So let me change my statement about reality. Reality is not necessarily nonsense—not the total reality of the cosmos—at least, as far as we know. What is nonsense certain is the assumption that the little bits and pieces of reality of which science has made us aware and which philosophers have done their best to explain are the same as the total reality of the cosmos. Those little bits and pieces are, however, all we have to work with in our existence. They are *part* of the reality of the *part* of the cosmos wherein we must delineate our essence. Thus, no matter how far the explanation is from the truth of the entire cosmos, it is absolutely essential truth for us; and the philosopher's explanation and guidance, no matter how nonsensical they may appear in the light of new scientific discoveries, are the best we have. It is not nonsense today even though we are quite sure it will be nonsense tomorrow.

Einstein and other scientists have managed to stretch and bend and distort our scientific analyses of time and space until Galileo would no longer recognize the formulae. Philosophers, Wittgenstein included, are having a devil of a time re-explaining the outcomes (as evidenced by the gibberish they regularly present as wisdom), and the consumer is left, equally, in a state of confusion. A straight line is no longer a straight line. A mile is no longer a mile. A cubic foot is no longer cubic. A minute is no longer a minute. Darwin shows us scientifically that the Garden of Eden story was more legend than truth at the same time Nietzsche turned over God's responsibilities to the *ubermensch*; and, why not, since science was turning God into an anachronistic corpse. But *Habeas corpus!*

And it is *all* Good! Especially, it is good if an *ubermensch* can resurrect that corpse of God as a brand new *imaginary* God—a warm and loving one like mine.

October 20: A Wittgensteinian Linguistically Logical Essay.
Sam Clear Water opposes immediately deporting all persons who are now in the nation known now as the United States of America and who do not have the legal right (referring to laws enacted by the elected legislative representatives of the nation known now as the United States of America) to be in the nation now known as the United States of America. Sam Clear Water has been proven by standardized testing approved by academic authorities in the nation known as the United States of America to be an intelligent human being according to officially approved (by the elected legislative representatives of the nation known as the United States of America or human beings legally appointed by said representatives) standards for intelligent human beings living in the nation now known as the United States of America in the year 2007 C.E. Intelligent human beings (as defined in the previous sentence) are always right about matters of persons who are now in the nation now known as the United States of America and who do not have the legal right (as defined in the first sentence of this essay) to be in said nation. Thus, persons who are now in the nation known now as the United States of America and who do not have the legal right (referring to laws enacted by the elected legislative representatives of the nation known now as the United States of America) to be in the nation now known as the United States of America should not be immediately deported unless they are engaged in activities which prove them to be hostile to the security and basic civil rights and privileges of the people of the United States.* **

*Any human being who disagrees with Sam Clear Water on the above issues is a dumb ass.
**The total inanity of this essay is proof that Wittgenstein's idea of a pure logical language is nonsensical.

October 21: Deportation of Illegal Aliens.

In contrast to the entry for October 20, the following essay takes chances by using language which might be misconstrued and reinterpreted by various readers.

I have never seen an issue which has American opinion so spread along a continuum as does the issue of illegal immigration today. It goes all the way from "give them all nearly instant citizenship and elect them to congress" to "deport every blessed one of them (after taking away all of their money and personal possessions, including such items as perfume and hemorrhoidal ointment and administering 200 stripes with a cat of nine tails, especially to the small children) before sunset." And every inch of the continuum between these two poles is heavily populated.

"Come, let us reason together!" Speaking practically, let's eliminate the cat of nine tails. It is not allowed even for cattle or goats.

Then, let us speak of those who are born in America of illegal alien parents. The law states that they are citizens automatically as long as they renounce citizenship in any other country when they reach majority. Ron Paul would have us change the law so that we could deport the little renegades along with their parents and older siblings. I disagree, Congressman Paul. Keep in mind, sir, that these are some of the residents of America who will be most likely to grow up poor and Democrat. Although you are not a Democrat, I would suppose that you are not really a Republican either. You are, indeed, a Libertarian. As an aside, you might consider, when you lose the Republican primary, continuing your run as a Libertarian. You won't win there either, but you might raise some havoc with your two or three percent of the vote. We need someone to stand up for Libertarian principles and what principle is more firmly established than the idea (coming from medieval English law) that the person born in a country is a citizen of that country? Think of that, Dr. Paul, when you help to bring one of our new Hispanic-Texan citizens into the world.

Next, let us speak of their elder siblings, those who as tender children braved the dangers of an illegal border crossing with their parents, not of their own free will, but by mandate of their parents and the desperate poverty or lawlessness which chased them across the border in the first place. And when they grow up, speaking perfect English and with not even faded memories of their mother country, they are told to go back to where they came from. Some of them, those whose parents were most demanding that the children become well-integrated American children, cannot even communicate fluently in the language of their parents. To what are they returned? Surely, it would be inhumane to deport such "aliens" to be aliens in their own country. The U.S. is surely not that inhumane, is it?

Let us leave the middle here and go on to those illegal aliens who have lived peacefully, obeying the laws of the land except for their illegal presence along with odds and ends of misdemeanors associated with that (even though in relative poverty) for several decades. Perhaps, they are retired in the various stages of old age and decline. Surely, we should not evict such gentle tenants. I would not ask that they be granted citizenship, just the respect of legal resident alienship and the right to basic needs for minimal comfort and sustenance in their old age.

Ahh! But then there are the many of the middle, those recently arrived illegal adult aliens who continue to be mostly like the people of their native land. Many of them are doing important work that few American citizens will dirty their hands or bend their backs to do. Without them, much agricultural and other hard manual labor would, simply, not be done. And these are jobs that cannot be exported. To milk the cows or pick the fruit or pour the concrete, you must have people, people who are willing to get their hands and, often, the rest of their bodies dirty to earn a meager living. We must have these people in America. As it stands, a large part of the American establishment turns its eyes away from the steady stream of illegals crossing our borders and going to work here. What else can they do? Many of them depend upon those illegals to do the work required for their American enterprises. Yet, if they wait for the immigration authorities to approve visas for immigrant workers, they will have to harvest their crops in the dead of winter after they have rotted away. They will have to build that factory in a year or two, after other entrepreneurs have already exported the jobs.

The reason this huge category of illegal aliens, the ones we would have most justification to deport and the ones who would be least damaged by deportation, is that we have failed as a nation to develop a reasonable immigration system which puts foreign workers at their American jobs at the times and places where the jobs (jobs that Americans reject) exist. This calls for a system of seasonal visas for seasonal jobs and a system of longer-term work visas (which can lead naturally to naturalization) for immigrants who will occupy permanent jobs. In addition, these more permanent immigrants should be able to move their families to American on permanent visas as quickly as the original immigrants prove by their diligence and honesty that they have promise of being good citizens or resident aliens.

This reasonable immigration system must be put in place before any wholesale deportation of illegal aliens begins. In addition, when this system is in place, the borders must be carefully monitored, temporarily, until those who want to immigrate begin to trust the new system, and permanently, because we must always be on guard against the immigration (legal or illegal) of terrorists bent upon destroying America. Massive deportations should never become an issue. Most of those who are here illegally came here because America was sending not-so-subtle signals that they would be welcomed here, legally or not. Thus, only those illegal aliens who have not been as law-abiding as they could have been under their illegal status should be deported and placed at the back of a line in their own countries for re-immigration. This might all seem a little unfair for those who have been waiting patiently in line for legal immigration, some of them for years, but life is not often fair.

It will take time for the immigration lines to diminish, but it will happen sooner than we might think. Even if we do nothing about illegal immigration, it will wane as other countries (especially Mexico) gain in wealth and in their willingness to share it with the natives of those countries; and that is already happening in some developing nations. All you have to do to prove that to yourself is to call for an online technician to help you sort out difficulties with your new computer software. Where do you suppose that technician resides? Not likely in the U.S.A.!

October 22: Wild Strawberries.
I didn't tell her she had red on her chin
—That Levi-clad strawberry blond teenager—
She looked so contented scrambling down the steep bank
Of Camp Manitou's gravel pit
Where she had been eating wild strawberries
And thinking about who knows what:
But something told her it was there,
And she wiped at it with the back of her hand,
Grinning self-consciously,
But it stayed put
Like a lump in your throat at a wedding
Or a tear in your eye at a birthday,
Or the sweetest Sangria
You've ever tasted.

October 23: A Sloppily Sentimental Poem without End.

A Town Apart
There was a town apart
From others of its kind,
A lovely town with trees and hills
And rocky walls and pines,
And the people loved their town.

A bristle-bearded beggar,
Blind and broken,
Daily grinned the sun up with his yellow toothy smile;
His rusty old tin cup
(Which he jangled now and then)
Was always full by noon
Because they loved him.

The cross old widow sat for hours
And screeched at kids
That tramped her flowers
And gave them cookies, milk, and bread, and hugs
Because she loved them.

Within this town, when people met,
They smiled, shook hands, and went their ways.
They worked, they played, they cried, they raved,
But most of all they loved.

October 24: Failure!

296

One might think that, after all of the introspection, after all of the study and analysis of facts and theories, I could find the means of living without these moments and days. I am speaking of awakening this morning with the wish that I had not awakened. Would it not have been better to pass away quietly in my sleep?

If you are not one of us who suffer from depression, you probably do not fully understand. You cannot understand why I cannot, merely, "cheer up." Why could I not analyze my life to find out what makes me sad and eliminate those elements. Unfortunately, it is not as simple as that. When I examine my life for such factors, they do not exist—or, perhaps, they play hide-and-seek so well that I end up, like a frustrated child, weeping and begging them to come out in the open to be eradicated. But they do not. Be assured that I do not understand it myself; whatever the epistemology, it is a fact of my life and, as I have heard, in the lives of many. And I have heard that many have acted upon the death wish to end the problem—if it can be ended with death.

I call it failure because, as an existentialist, if I can justifiably refer to myself in that fashion, I should be able to create my own essence, an essence free of depression—at least, an essence that foresees and overcomes depressive episodes before they become death-wishes. It is one of an infinity of absurdities which inhabit (I was going to say "infect") the cosmos.

But

> *Out of the night that covers me,*
> *Black as the pit from pole to pole,*
> *I thank whatever gods may be*
> *For my unconquerable soul.*

I remember this poem which Eleanor M__ recited for us in high school and told us was about blindness. I know, now, that she was wrong. Yet it was right for her to introduce us to Henley's poem for there seems to be no defense against these episodes which come to me, as Matthew Arnold says,

> *. . . here as on a darkling plain*
> *Swept with confused alarms of struggle and flight,*
> *Where ignorant armies clash by night.*

But, eventually, I think of Henley's lines and cower in shadow awaiting the light of day which will all but surely come.

October 25: Comes the Dawning!

And here it is, a new morning, as near to frost as is possible without killing tomato vines: sunny, bright, and beautiful. Yesterday, I assessed student writing competency tests and quietly enjoyed joshing with faculty members new and older. I took a double walk around the campus on a pair of errands. I indulged myself last evening with a big bowl of vanilla ice cream with chocolate shell, strawberry syrup, and "star" candy sprinkles. Then I popped a big batch of popcorn and watched a mindless movie about incompetent ghosts. When, at midnight, I finally retired to bed with Yasmin at my side, I became aware that I had reached the other end of my

297

depressive episode, the side where I am a little too gregarious. I had a one-way chat about this and that and the other thing with Yasmin until I noticed she was snoring in my ear. Then I shut up and just lay there listening to the sounds of her snoring and of the night for an hour while I waited for sleep—which eventually arrived.

And here I am. I am reminded of the supposed source of the name of Idaho, an old Indian legend that the Shoshone Indians had a worshipful respect for the sunrise and that, as the rays of the invisible sun behind the eastern mountains began to shine each morning on the peaks of the western mountains, a leading Indian, perhaps, the one who couldn't sleep late because of his arthritis, would cry out: Eeee-Daaaa-Haaaaaaoooowww! (supposed translation: "Behold the sun coming down the mountain!") making damned sure that no one else would be able to sleep late either. This entire epistemology of the word "Idaho" has, by the way, been debunked. It appears that the debunking is something along the line of northern Idaho Indians not wanting the Shoshones to get credit for the state name. But I don't know. I guess nobody does.

I have slept overnight in the tops of the Rocky Mountains where the temperature drops from a daytime high of 80 degrees F. to 20 degrees during the night, and I know the morning joy of the sun coming down the mountain. It is, truly, Godlike. It is much like the day after a depressive episode which ends successfully.

October 26: Contemporary Philosophical Issues.

If there is a thesis to this meandering year of philosophizing, it is that philosophy continues to have issues which cannot be dealt with so well in any other discipline or combination of disciplines. Montaigne in his essay entitled "On the Education of Children" says "it is philosophy that teaches us to live." Adding emphasis to this is his immediately previous statement that, if the tutor should discover that his young charge lacks an interest in philosophical topics, the tutor should "strangle him early, if there are no witnesses." During the 20th century, English philosophers and some others were arguing that philosophy has no use except as a mere linguistic clerk and proofreader to the natural sciences. What this indicates is that those philosophers failed to note, in the hustle and bustle of burying God and all stinking corpses metaphysical, that not only was metaphysics (sensuous, rational, or not) alive and necessary in the minds of the bulk of human beings, but that metaphysics is but a small part of the responsibility of philosophers. *Philosophy teaches us to live.*

Religion, that good old mistress of the occult and drill instructor for Arnold's "ignorant armies clash[ing] by night," does its best to help us live with its false doctrines and authoritarian priests and inquisitors, but it is philosophy which, in the end, must be the "voice crying in the wilderness" where the souls of humanity may hear it if they can hear the cry over the clash of ecumenical swords. Ecumenicism has come to include economics and politics along with ethics, metaphysics, epistemology, and other classical disciplines claimed by philosophy. Religion has conquered and claimed them all and has, thus, become the dragon, the enemy of truth, comprising one army in the contemporary war for the human spirit. The other army, an army of pacifists, is philosophy. The two harnessed together have become something of a metaphysical conceit, a "yoking together of opposites" an ass and an albatross drawing blunt weapons from the same cache to attack each other: the albatross helpless and awkward on the ground, beautiful soaring through the heavens; the ass recalcitrant, lacking a trigger finger, but braying its winged harness-mate to death by reading aloud repeatedly and incessantly its supposedly "revelatory" quack-yop.

Currently, the albatross, philosophy, has been all but silenced by its own retreat into linguistics with indecipherable hieroglyphics for its language of communication. Yet there are many of us who see the rest of philosophy, that formula for the "art" of living—more a paradigm than a formula, for it is necessarily different for each human being. That, indeed, is the real miracle of rational human life—we are each individual and different—that is the nature of genetics. Even identical twins with identical DNA strands differ. That is the nature of existence, the nature of essence, the nature of human life, at least of human life on this planet which is all we know of human life and infinitely less than we think we know.

I propose, as my time and inclinations permit over the next few entries, to present some essential elements of contemporary philosophy, elements of successful (i.e., satisfyingly "Good") living in today's world.

October 27: Contemporary Philosophic Topics.

I want to prove that philosophers still have things to talk about (if there was ever any question about that), so I made a list of contemporarily appropriate philosophical topics for discussion just off the top of my head. I make no claim that this list is complete, and the most negative comment that could be made of it other than its incompleteness is that it is redundant. The topics bleed into each other to the level of deadly hemorrhage. For instance, some philosophers consider metaphysics and epistemology to be synonymous. I disagree, but there is significant overlap between the two. Also, topics such as ethics are broad and could subsume such topics as kindness and ecology. I keep them separate so that I can consider them apart, especially since I wish to discuss ethics on its own as a major branch of philosophy.

The purpose of philosophy: It teaches us how to live. Various topics follow in no particular order.

1) War and peace
2) Politics
3) Religion
4) Psychological health
5) Physical health
6) Ethics
7) Metaphysics
8) Epistemology
9) History
10) Language
11) Gender
12) Race and ethnicity

13) Action vs. nonaction
14) Diet
15) Economics
16) Vanity
17) Family
18) Technology
19) Globalism
20) Ecology
21) Employment
22) Retirement
23) Travel
24) Freedom
25) Aesthetics
26) Personal responsibility
27) Kindness
28) The "Good"
29) Personal satisfaction
30) Honesty
31) Crime and punishment
32) Abortion
33) Sexual preference
34) Evolution
35) Genetics
36) Cultures

October 28: Beginning at the Top with Ethics.

With the withering of metaphysics during the century following Kant's Critiques, ethics stepped forward to be the chief topic for philosophy, at least the topic most suited to philosophers who wanted to do something useful for humanity and the world.

The pulse of God was taken, and he was declared (by Nietzsche and others) *tot.* As is the wont of so many philosophers, the baby was thrown out with the bath and, instead of picking up the baby, wiping the mud off, and patting it on the back, the baby was *buried alive* with the wash—"no more philosophy!" was the hue and cry.

Yet with philosophers so plentiful and swelling to the bursting point with desire to philosophize, it was necessary to continue the tradition to prevent the unsanitary condition of philosophical guts being spewed over everything. Thus, we continued blathering. In nearly 200 years, we have gone about, mouths moving, pens scribbling, computers clicking, saying little, refuting all. It has been "pharmaceutical" (to quote John McCain on another topic) but not enlightening.

Pop philosophers (culminating with Dr. Phil and a host of other daytime talk-show hosts) kept the Socratic light burning (although the smoke stank) awaiting an awakening which would bring forth more intellectually nutritious fare. Also replicating their kind prolifically are the pseudo-philosophical theologians. But these always ride vainly into the arena on some mangy sectarian faith agenda which summarily bucks them off not far from the gate.

Always, the topic, whatever the manifestation, often barely recognizable under its monk's-hood of self-aggrandizement, greed, and utter stupidity, is ethics.

It is not a beautiful scene, and yet it is needful that we get our hands muddy by cleaning up the ethics sewer and move forward to a real ethical philosophy which will serve the needs of humanity and our environment. Indeed, environmentalism seems to be setting the tempo for the many other subtopics under ethics, and the most coherent voice, although his environmentally insensitive lifestyle belies the voice, seems to be that of Al Gore. He has captured the ear of the world with his argument regarding global warming. Perhaps, he is more the prophet, a new John the Baptist, a voice crying in the wilderness, foreshadowing greater philosophers to come. His message is compelling, especially, to one like me who spent the last couple of summers in the high altitudes of Idaho being blistered by a sun the intensity of which has recently become greater. This summer, for instance, during July and August, the daytime high temperature seldom dropped to 100 degrees Fahrenheit and the dry air became even drier promoting constant wildfires to smoke up the sky, turning the sun blood red, and pumping even more excess carbon dioxide into the atmosphere. Perhaps, as some current nay-sayers insist, it is just the final receding of the most recent ice age; but, if there is anything that we humans are doing to make it worse, may we please stop? I'm burning up!

I'll not try to encapsulate the entire discipline of philosophical ethics. That would be nearly impossible since every topic and subtopic of philosophy involves ethics in one form or another. That is the way I will leave it. In later entries, I will deal with some of the more intriguing and practical subtopics.

October 29: War and Peace.

War and Peace is one of those topics which always entail ethics. First, it is a materialization of Kant's categorical imperative stated thus: "There must be no war." On the other hand, many philosophers argue that war is a political necessity. As firmly as I am convinced that there must be no war, I know that there will be war. Not deductively do I know this. I know it inductively, which is, I suppose, not knowing at all, but is nearly as convincing as pure knowledge would be if we had any of that. Until humanity has evolved past the points of greed, jealousy, lust for power, etc., there will be war; but, even knowing the present futility of our practice, we must practice for the time when humanity is ready for the imperative. We must continue to hope.

In the meantime, we must continue to condemn those who incite war, including not only the tyrants and warmongers who conduct the wars, but those whose greed causes them to provide armaments and other tools of war. And we must constantly seek the least warlike solutions (e.g., negotiations, internationally enforced borders, no-fly zones, *truly* precise air strikes, special-forces maneuvers, trade sanctions) to conflicts which burst forth.

And what are the philosophers to say? They must cry: Peace! Peace! Peace! And they must seek out the causes of war and denounce them.

At this point, the finger of blame must, often, be pointed toward organized religion. It is not enough for the three major Western religions (Judaism, Christianity, and Islam) to call themselves peace-loving. They must prove it by shunning and otherwise squelching their members who advocate violence in the

301

name of peace. For instance, Israel must embrace Palestine's right to a *fairly* delineated homeland even though Palestine will not embrace Israel's right to exist; and America and Europe and the Islamic world must stand ready to *equally* enforce the security of both nations, especially considering the inane decisions made by America and Europe about a Jewish homeland in Palestine after WWII. Islamic Jihad must be condemned unconditionally by the leaders of Islam when it includes any form of violence. Christianity, the dominant religion in America, must condemn America's recently adopted default policy of preemptive strikes.

Finally, the United Nations must be strengthened and reorganized to make it an effective catalyst for and instrument of world peace.

Of these things, philosophers must talk *constantly, coherently, and publicly*, even when no one listens.

October 30: Politics and Language and Commerce.

Politics is a perennial top favorite topic of philosophers, and it is now, if anything, more important than it has ever been. The reason for this is that we are moving rapidly into an age where much that we thought we knew about politics is crumbling. Central to this decay is the shrinking and flattening world. A major factor in that shrinkage is language, especially, the English language. A common world language has long been a dream of humanity and is fast becoming a reality. All airline pilots worldwide, for instance, must speak and understand English. Most countries require English competence of their students before they can graduate from secondary school. And the internet, the new worldwide book and newspaper in English is the standard worldwide. That does not eliminate national or regional or cultural languages (even on the internet). It merely adds a universal language without which persons all over the world will be at a great disadvantage.

Beyond a universal language (or as an extension of it) comes, inevitably, more and more movement toward universal world government. It is unfettered international commerce that has sparked both. No longer must we wait for autumn in America to have fresh apples. We import them. At Christmas, toys need not come from the North Pole. They can come from that great Santa Claus, China, lead paint and all. Of course, that is, also, where more and more of our cars will come from as China produces cheap vehicles, high fuel-efficiency models to match our high gasoline prices from oil (and ethanol) imported from sources around the world.

But the most critical change, the one that no one seems to welcome but which is inevitable is that national politics will be gradually eroded by more and more influences across national borders. It is already happening between the United States and Canada. Although both countries have a host of laws to prevent it, commerce flows both ways at an astounding rate, largely ignoring the laws, by virtue of internet connections which make legal oversight impossible. I, a legitimate American citizen, can, with a few key-clicks, order my pharmaceuticals from legitimate pharmacies in Canada, pay with a legitimate credit card, have the drugs delivered by U.S. Mail, and no government agency can possibly stand in the way. I don't do that because Walmart is doing it for me for a smaller price (not just with Canada, but with the whole world) than I can do it for myself. Notice that the American government with its senior citizen prescription plan bans itself from negotiating prices with drug companies. The result is that American seniors can buy the great majority of prescription drugs cheaper from Walmart than they can buy them through the government's prescription drug plan. Further, many senior Americans are required to pay the monthly premiums for a government-operated drug plan which they seldom use. If seniors opt out of the plan now, they are threatened by the government with high financial penalties if they must opt into it later. Odd!? It seems like a formula for financial failure of the government-operated plan. But what about an international plan which takes advantage of negotiated prices, a plan like that which Walmart already has in place? That seems quite sensible. Perhaps, too sensible! But it will happen (and is happening) unofficially by default.

The solution to the U.S./Mexican border crisis is as inevitable. Mexico will become as wealthy as the United States. That will cause Mexico to redistribute its wealth so that it reduces its poor classes and increases its middle classes. With the availability of the internet to all classes and the increasing universality of the English language, it will not be long before the poor Mexicans learn from America how to become middle class and will make that adjustment. Mexico is, after all, a democratic country. All it will take is an informed electorate to make it politically, economically, and socially more like the U.S. With political change will come the economic changes (and the redistribution of wealth). That process is already well underway in emerging countries like India and Indonesia. With outsourcing of jobs from the developed nations, it will become universal across most of the third world.

And here is the inductive leap. With the universalization of language and education and commerce will come the universalization of politics. Certainly, national governments will continue to exist and continue to be healthy and strong. But international law will gradually overshadow them to the extent that their constitutions will be almost (an essential *almost*) interchangeable.

Perhaps, however, I am too optimistic. Perhaps, instead, we will irritate one another with political and religious and economic squabbles to the extent that we turn to nuclear power and reduce the whole world to a cinder. That, indeed, seems to be the only viable alternative (or not so viable since "viable" denotes continuation of life).

October 31: Samhain.

You probably know it better as Halloween; and Halloween, the way American kids celebrate it, is more similar to the original Samhain than anything the big people have been able to come up with to sterilize it.

Samhain was, to the Celts (pronounced /kɛlts/) of ancient Britain, like New Year's Eve which happened twice a year (once at the end of winter—Beltane—and once at the end of summer—Samhain). Samhain was a time when the spirits of dead loved ones could join the family for one evening to celebrate family ties. And a joyful time it was, eating and drinking and dancing and playing.

Leave it to the Christians to turn it sour. "Yes!" they said, "All Hallows Eve is a time when the spirits of the dead come forth, but a goodly number of them are evil and have nothing but ill will for the folks they visit on that night. But there were the good spirits as well." These, the early Christian church commemorated on All Saints Day (following the evening when evil walked about). That way they were able to condemn to Hell, as was their wont, the pagan spirits and bless the

303

dead that the Christian religion chose to bless. The Christians have always been a creative lot when it comes to cursing and blessing.

November 1: A Two-Season Year.

We can gain important insights from ancient mythology. For instance, I have always had the feeling that, instead of four, there are really only two seasons in temperate zone climates: summer and winter. Spring and autumn have always seemed to be mere transitions between summer and winter. Of course, they have certain characteristics which set them apart, but each of these characteristics is transitional in itself and, thus, reinforces my two-season theory. For instance, the first hard frost is a transition to the deep freeze of winter and the rains of March and April merely announce the coming of summer verdure. After yesterday's Halloween entry, I am reminded that the ancient Celts felt the same way. They understood that, in their part of the world, November first was the most common time of the year which can truly be understood as winter. Usually, the first killing frost comes about then or a little earlier. Also, that is a time when snowfall could become an actuality. Farming is finished. Unharvested crops are in danger of spoilage and freezing. It is time to build that woodpile for winter heat.

On the contrary, the calendar which includes four seasons delays the onset of winter until the winter solstice in mid-December, far too late to start a woodpile—long after the last pumpkin is harvested—winter is at near full force, not merely beginning. Certainly, the winter solstice has meaning, but that meaning is out of synchronization with our instincts and our actualities about the seasons of the year. And waiting until the middle of June to declare the advent of summer is just as "out of joint." We can keep our calendar. It helps us to understand the cycles of the moon in relation to the various movements of the earth in relation to the sun. But for plain old everyday living, the ancient Celts had the right calendar idea. Beltane (May 1), the Celtic first day of summer, is not quite so convincing. I think I would put Beltane at April 15 instead. But the argument could be made that May Day is the time when we can plant in most areas of the temperate zones without serious concern of killing frost. So to make summer the yang of the winter yin, of equal mass and size, I'll go along with May 1 as the beginning of summer. Anyway, what choice do I have other than waiting for June 20 (the summer solstice) when the radishes I plant would surely die of heatstroke?

November 2: Abortion.

I'll not say much here about abortion because its very mention is proof that it is a viable philosophical topic. It must not be left to the irrational claims of religion to decide its fate if that fate can, indeed, be decided by public decree at all. Abortion has become a simple and not particularly dangerous operation for the mother when it is conducted in the proper medical context. Therefore, the harm of it, other than the psychological harm it might do to the mother or to others involved in the situation, is to the unborn child. Although the unborn child might suffer some or even a great deal of pain during the operation, the pain is brief (truncated by unconsciousness). The fetus has little understanding of life and, except for a natural instinct toward survival, no objection to death. Thus, the physical harm that is actually experienced by the fetus is no more punishing than many of us experience as a product of every-day living, less, if we consider that the fetus is not rationally cognizant of its danger of dying. The remaining question, then: Are we doing harm to a human spirit through abortion? The answer (which I have given before): None

305

whatsoever! Only God (if God exists) can harm a human spirit. All we can do is prevent that spirit, if it exists, from continuing its occupancy of a particular human fetus. By the Christian definition, a human spirit is infinite and, thus, safe from any physical harm we can do to it. Certainly, it seems a rogue's trick to short-circuit a spirit's trek through mortality before it sees the light of finite day, but I see no reason to believe that such a spirit, for which time and space are mere constructs, not material realities, would be the least bit disappointed since the possibilities of incarnation in another body, probably one offering a more congenial welcome to mortality, are large if not infinite. More likely, the spirit would be back at the knee of God, thanking him for its redemption from birth to a mother so antagonistic toward it that she would kill its antepartum human body.

November 3: Metaphysics.

Over and over during the past couple of centuries, metaphysics as a philosophical topic has been declared dead (along with God and a host of other *a priori* entities). One of the four definitions given by the American Heritage Dictionary provides what is generally the most accepted version of what metaphysics comprises: *"A priori* speculation upon questions that are unanswerable to scientific observation, analysis, or experiment."

In the entire realm of philosophical metaphysics, this definition, like nearly any brief definition of any philosophical topic is critically simplistic. Yet it is about as good as it can get; and, over the past couple of centuries, many philosophers have ignored the claim of their fellows that metaphysics is dead and continue to beat it unmercifully as if it were among the quick.

I have good news for both parties: Metaphysics is neither alive nor dead. It, merely, *is*. Whether a god is anthropomorphized to whatever extent it is necessary to provide a security blanket (or a moral whip); or, at the other pole, a god is seen as an imaginary corpse of a being which never actually existed physically or spiritually as atheists believe, the *Idea* of God (along with the rest of infinite metaphysics) is real and has a profound impact upon the entire philosophical endeavor. Wise Western philosophers, especially starting with Socrates, realized that philosophy's purpose is not to answer questions, but to raise and study them. Surely, any reader of Plato eventually realizes that satisfactory conclusions in the dialectics are absent about as often as they are present. They are relatively unimportant. Even Socrates' conclusion that he is the wisest of all men (because he recognizes that he knows nothing) raises more questions than it answers. How does he deal with his oxymoronic *knowledge* that he knows nothing? Does he still know nothing in the context of knowing something even if the something that he knows is nothing? The question cannot be answered, just as no legitimate philosophical question can be definitively answered. Just as our opening definition of metaphysics is simplistic and just as a simplistic definition is often better than a complex and convoluted one. Just as I am I and you are you and God is God and the three of us cannot, it seems, come to final terms.

All of this proves metaphysics not dead or alive, but infinite. This must make a difference. Do you have endless infinity to hang around with me to discuss it?

November 4: Ecology.

I just saw on television this morning that there is a "Draft Al Gore" site on the internet. I'm going there shortly, more as a symbolic gesture than as a hope that Gore could ever become President. The voters are not likely to elect a President who is fat and makes odd claims. As far as I'm concerned, ecology (especially global warming) has suddenly become the most important political and ethical, and, thus, philosophical topic for the beginning of the 21st century.

November 5: Globalism.

I notice that globalism is such a new term that it is not included in the dictionary of my word processor.... (There! I fixed that. It is now included.) But the fact that the term was not included might indicate that it is not getting nearly as much play in public as it gets in the universities and colleges of America. Perhaps, the dated term, internationalism, is still holding a place for it. Internationalism will no longer work. Internationalism implies an understanding and acceptance of cultures and customs and politics across national boundaries. Globalism implies much more than that. Globalism implies that we all live in a single world. Everything else comes second to that. For instance, my brief mention of global warming in the previous entry is entirely hollow as anything but an all-world concern. America, with its puny acknowledgement of global warming, could not solve it even if it did its fair part of the work or even if it tried to force its solution on the rest of the world. It is a problem which must be approached globally. The wood-stove fires of Siberia must be considered along with the smoke-belching factory chimneys of China, the shrinking rain forests of Brazil, and the SUVs of America. At present, we citizens of the world have no inclination to discuss it seriously, let alone do anything about it. In the meantime, it is killing our living world.

Globalism is what should have preempted the preemptive strike which initiated the Iraq war. Globalism should end the horrors and the killing in Darfur. Globalism must come to grips with the ethically bankrupt practices of the businesses of the world in regard to off-shoring: the sweatshops, the lost jobs, the lead-laden toys, and on and on and on. Globalism will continue as a major topic in philosophy. It has hardly yet begun as such a topic. I have initiated it by adding it to my cyber dictionary.

November 6: Family.

According to Rousseau and most political philosophers, the first human government was the extended family, headed, ordinarily, by the most powerful or influential male. It was not an ideal system for rational human beings. It favored, as it does in most animal species, brawn over brain, brawn being the most important factor before rational thinking came to a point in human evolution where it could compete with brawn. At that point, when the previous instinct-driven humanoid became the thinking human, a more enlightened government became appropriate.

Still lingering, however, is that primeval brawn which was, in early humanity, the necessary center of family living, both to protect the family from external threats and to maintain order within it. And still remaining within the context of the enlightened social contract of nations are the nuclear and extended families of pre-enlightenment humanity. Although there is movement in the direction of enlightened family management, little has changed in this part of society. Husbands, often, rule wives through some sort of assumed superiority largely based upon their larger skeletal frames and stronger muscles. And husbands and wives, together, rule their children by virtue of the same superior physical power.

The family is primitive, yet it is far from anachronistic. It is a necessary part of human culture, but not for physical continuation of the species. That can go on without the family. Rather, the family is a buffer *against* "enlightened" culture. For instance, although religion *seems* to reside in the cathedrals and churches, its actual home is in the dwelling of the family where all of its primeval application originates. In essence, religion begins in the bedroom of the family home and flows from there to the nursery and kitchen out the front door where it encounters other families and joins together with them in contracts to build cathedrals to what has been demonstrated in the privacy of homes and in the encounters among families outside the homes. Not just cathedrals, but all of the artifacts of the social contract emerge in much the same way from that nuptial bower.

This, by the way, is a major reason for the conservative opposition to homosexual marriage. It challenges the dominance of masculine brawn over feminine weakness as a necessary part of the family. And notice that conservative women fight to retain their subordination as valiantly as conservative men fight to retain their dominance, arguing that God (totally masculine) declares this to be His law. It's right there in Genesis!

Enlightened social contract is a necessity for the future of humanity. The family is its necessary foundation. But we must remember that the family is a primitive establishment. It has little place in enlightened governance which must squelch the primitive instinct toward brawn that is so recalcitrant in the family. Consider, for instance, that the death penalty (a shadow of the alpha male's primeval brute dominance over the clan in the family cave) still exists. And note that, occasionally, an alpha male tries, convicts, and executes a member of his family or even his entire family in the primitive style.

November 7: History.

And that brings us to history. The key is to realize that history is not, merely historical. It is the creator of the present and the harbinger of the future. In a very real sense, this is what Socrates meant when he said that the unexamined life is not worth living. What can we know of a life except its history? What can we examine except what has gone before? And we cannot examine our own history without examining that of the world as it has been up to the present. We look back on the past which only continues to exist in our imagination as the fleeting present bows out of the back door and the future enters the front. If we know enough about what has gone and is going out through the back door, there is a slender thread of hope that we can draw a fine line of difference in the future as it enters the front. That, like Frost's choice of the path in need of wear, can make all of the difference.

November 8: Crime and Punishment.

Just this morning a newscast revealed that three boys (now men) who, over a decade ago, were tried and convicted for the satanic cult murders of three 8-year-old boys might be innocent. DNA evidence newly applied has shown no connection between the murder scene and the three convicted men. Instead, two hairs linked the father of one of the murdered boys and a close friend of the father to the scene. Of course, this is slender evidence and the prosecutors of the original case intend to fight to save their conviction.

This last sentence is the one that becomes our philosophical topic. I have not yet seen an instance wherein new DNA evidence which, no matter how counter it is to the original evidence for conviction, has elicited a response from the prosecutors of the original case of something like: "Maybe we were wrong." This points to an all-too-human trait which makes people believe a previously established falsehood no matter how insupportable it proves to be. It was the large-minded Emerson who said, "A foolish consistency is the hobgoblin of small minds."

Human minds are small—not much heavier than a hand grenade—and many of them accept foolishness more readily than wisdom, often with deadly consequences.

November 9: Aesthetics.
Armageddon ECE: A Poetic Primer
7 is for the seven Roman hills
Made famous by Hannibal astride an elephant
With his best officers astride lesser elephants
Attacking Rome via elephant
While Rome sacked Carthage;
Or why start so late;
Why not the sack of Troy by 7 (or more) Greek kings;
Or 7 big wars across 7 big oceans.
At least 7 big wars, I think.
We humans learned to hate (or envy) what lies
Across big oceans and rivers—
Like Jordan and such—
A long time ago, at least seventy times 7 years.
Or a lucky number in Vegas.

6 is for 666
On a forehead
Or on a box or a book
Or on someone's nightgown;
Someone devilish or Satan's kin herself wears it.
Or the 6 holy points on the Star of David
Which stands for keeping the Book—
The really big Book—
From Adam to just before Jesus.
Or that half-sized box of eggs
For small families
That need only 6 eggs instead of a dozen.

5 is a lesser star, short one point of being Hebrew,
Or a pentagon for Devil worship,
Or a light atop a Christmas tree
Or a good time to start kindergarten.

4 is a triangle with too many sides.
Who really cares about 4
Except claustrophobic perfectionists
With a fear of acute angles?

3—Ahhhh!
The triangle, with the perfect number of sides,
Vaunted as the strongest, the most majestic,
The shape to be emulated
Pyramids along the Nile with their 4 triangles
(Built upon a square?!)
A priori design . . .
Or a wedge of pumpkin pie
With whipped cream
Served on a round saucer
On a holiday,
Either
Christmas
Or
Thanksgiving
Or
Chanukah
Or
Lincoln's birthday if you are politically inclined.

2 is for the number of opposing armies
In a fight between 2 nations on opposing sides
Of a big ocean.
I am sure they are fighting *for* something,
But that isn't the important thing.
They are fighting *against* each other.
Or the number of a baby's feet,
Inked for footprints on a birth certificate,
Kissed by a doting mother
Until her mouth is black.

1 is for
God,
Jehovah,
Allah:
(That's three—two too many for 1 Big Book).

Or for a snowflake that just now landed on my outstretched fingernail
And melted instantly,
Gone but for a tiny puddle.

November 10: Epistemology.

How do we know what we think we know, and do we actually know anything? That is epistemology. Is it important to contemporary philosophy? Some philosophers say it is a moot subject since we already know and understand everything that can currently be known and understood about this. In their way of thinking, it is simple. In order to know something, we have to have evidence in support of it. Our only dependably proven method of receiving evidence is through the senses (five of them). Anything beyond this is empty speculation. This does not disallow scientific progress in making the five senses work better. Such progress is what the perfectly logical language some philosophers are attempting to construct for the sciences is intended to facilitate. Unfortunately, after nearly a century of trying, the linguistic philosophers haven't agreed upon even a phoneme, a morpheme, a grapheme for this perfectly logical language, let alone an entire language.

But is there something to this rejection of anything which does not arrive through the senses. Is there, really, anything new to say about this? I'll leave the question with you. I will, however, suggest that the human race, in general, does not appear to let the question lie. Just one piece of information should serve as evidence. No one who does not claim to believe in God has ever been or is likely to be elected President of the United States. Belief in God opens the whole panorama of metaphysical possibility for the reception of knowledge.

Thus, it would appear that the epistemological labors of the philosophers are not completed. At the very least, if epistemology is dead, the philosophers have a great deal of convincing of the public to do. If it is alive by virtue of the opinion of this vast majority of persons in the most powerful nation on earth, there seems to be more to talk about around the epistemological grape and cheese plate.

Can we, indeed, know by virtue of the senses, or are what the senses deliver mere second-hand phenomena which tell us nothing for sure? Can we know some things *a priori* (e.g., from God through revelation), and how in the name of Heaven could we ever prove them too be knowledge?

But we have it all wrong. Epistemology is not *knowing* itself but *the study of knowing*. To explore and to discover are two entirely different things, neither requiring the other for their fulfillment. Epistemology is exploration, not discovery. Yasmin and I have explored one another physically and spiritually for over 40 years. Many years ago, we knew that further exploration of one another would be highly unlikely to produce any new continents or oceans. Yet we continue our exploration with each passing year. With all that we learn about sensory experience and how it contributes to what we imagine that we know, with all that we feel has been spiritually impressed upon us by *a priori* connection to that which is unconditioned (God or whatever), we still must talk about it all and consider it all in the highest schools of human existence. Philosophy, if it is to be of any use whatsoever, must not only *dwell* in those schools but must be headmaster over them.

311

November 11: Gender; especially Hillary's Gender.

Many people might insist that Hillary Clinton in her political persona is neither male nor female; rather, she is gender neutral; but the fact that I refer to her with feminine personal pronouns must mean something. The something that this means is that Hillary (no matter her personality, no matter her strength of character, her powers of persuasion or her methods of employing them) is a woman. She is running for President of the United States in a field of eight other democratic candidates, all men; and no woman has ever been elected President; none has even been nominated by either major political party for President. Indeed, persons still live today who were around when women could not vote for a Presidential candidate (or for or against anything else on a national scale).

So, does it make a difference that Hillary is a woman. There, I did it again. It would be odd for me to refer to any of the other candidates, especially those with titles like "Senator" or "Congressman," by their first names. I have told students, time after time, that they should not, in their formal essays, refer to authors by their first names, so what happens? They refer to male authors by their last names, but they continue to refer to female authors by their first names. And, of course, I do it, too, to ~~Hillary~~ Senator Clinton. Should I stop that? Or maybe I shouldn't. Perhaps, even a female *President* is best called by her first name. Would that reduce our respect for her?

So here we stand. Even on a simple issue like what to call a woman in politics, we have a philosophical topic which is important enough that it is coming up in the newspapers on a daily basis. Gender is an issue in the Presidential campaign. Certainly, it is a political issue. But as Senator Clinton has proven by bringing it up (even briefly and tangentially), it is impossible for us to approach it reasonably as a political issue during a Presidential campaign. However, we can approach it in philosophy because philosophy is the one discipline (if I can call it that) which cannot be bound by political correctness or any other form of the suppression of truth. Why not? Because philosophy is the study of truth—not the source of it. Truth flows from other springs, but philosophy is the fountain for truth, bubbling it forth from all of truth's springs in combination with all manner of partial-truth and outright falsehood.

November 12: Complaints Department, Please!

This book is called *The True Book of Sam Clear Water.* I am Sam. Thus, I have a right, from time to time, to enter herein my complaints about the world in general. Today, I have several.

1) The trash man, today, opened my trash can, pulled out the small bag of mulched fall leaves I had discretely put in there, and dropped it in my driveway. He loaded the rest of the trash (not much of a bundle) and drove off. I know that they have a rule about not hauling fall leaves, but it was a small bag that fit neatly into my trashcan with the rest of the trash. He went to a great deal more trouble rejecting it than if he had just dumped the trash can into the truck. We have absolutely no way to get rid of fall leaves in Parkville except to sneak them into the trash truck. Yasmin, being less idealistic than I, said it was my own damned fault for not hiding them better. I did use a bright-orange leaf bag with a black Jack-o-

312

Lantern printed on it instead of a plain black bag, so she has a point. Chicanery is not my best suit. I hate city life!

2) On Friday, I got a prescription filled at Walmart. I discovered shortly thereafter that they had given me only a one-month supply and that my mail-order drug store would have given me a three-month supply for the same price. I went to Walmart yesterday and asked for the prescription back so I could send it to the mail order drug store for use there starting next month.

They said, "No dice. Once we've given you one prescription on it, it's ours. You can't have it."

Irritated but still civil, I asked, "Then can I get a three-month supply next month?"

"No," they said. "Your insurance won't allow it."

Less civilly, I said, "But the mail order pharmacy can give me a three-month supply for the same insurance company."

"That's because the mail order pharmacy *belongs* to your insurance company," they replied.

"That is idiotic," I said. And walked away defiant but defeated.

Later I called the mail order pharmacy to ask if they would contact the Walmart Pharmacy to transfer my prescription from Walmart to them.

"No," they said. "We don't do that. You'll have to have your doctor fax a new prescription to us."

So I did. Rather, I had Yasmin do the calling while I fumed in the corner since she has more tolerance for such stuff than I do. I boiled fervently as I watched the master at work arguing with the receptionist through each objection to reality. Finally, after an extended and extraordinarily civil conversation, Yasmin hung up and announced that they had agreed to submit the new prescription.

"And without my driving forty miles and approaching them crawling on my knees?"

"Sam, you are so negative!"

"Grnnnfff!"

3) Also, I feel lousy. I went with Yasmin on Friday to K.U. Medical Center to get our annual flu shots. We waited in line for an hour an a half. The following morning, I woke up with the flu and have been sick ever since. Yasmin feels fine.

"Grnnnfff!"

November 13: Retirement.

I just got a note from a faculty member of an east coast college. He is working with a retired faculty member from another east coast college on a campaign to get college students to pledge to consider the social and environmental impact of jobs they choose after graduation. Some time ago, I told them that I have a little free time on my hands since retiring. They said that they could probably fill it. And so they have.

Since I retired, I have noticed that retired people are treated more like dead people than retired people. I keep expecting passersby to make the sign of the cross in order to fend me off. But I didn't retire to die. I retired because I needed a change. I get the feeling that this graduation pledge movement could be just the thing for me, at least, to fulfill my need to go on *ad nauseam* about ecological and social environments.

Retirement, at least in America, is becoming a larger and larger factor in society. First, with the baby-boomer retirement wave coming up right away, we will have a much larger sector of our population retired. We need to keep them busy and out of mischief. I, certainly, don't want all of them fishing in my Idaho streams. But, also, there will be a smaller proportion of the population left to do the work of society. That seems to call for a volunteer or, perhaps, a part-time paid force of retired persons to fill the gap.

Yesterday, I saw a report on the segment of the population called "the millennials" (born between 1980 and 1995) who never learned how to work and were always told that they are special. This group might be a fine match for the retiring baby boomers who no longer want to be told what to do after rising through the ranks and being dumped on the compost heap at retirement. The two groups working together could make the office a living Hell for generation X.

November 14: Race and Ethnicity.

In America, when we think of minority race, most often, we think black. When we think of ethnicity, we generally think Latino. But both of these notions have become less appropriate since both the Black race and the Latino ethnicity have grown so dramatically in number that one or the other (or both combined) could well become the majority voting block of the United States. Another ethnicity (sometimes considered a race) has taken the least favored minority status, the Middle Easterner.

Middle Easterners in America and Europe have always been treated badly. Think back (if you are old enough) to the movies during the second one-third of the 20th century which featured Middle Easterners. One story stands out: *Aladdin and the Lamp.* Aladdin, a Middle Eastern boy, is supposed to be the hero of the story. Notice, however, that even his name is anglicized in its pronunciation. And what sort of actor portrayed him? A pale white boy of obvious European extraction. Apparently, this was no accident. In the animated version, the same anomaly occurs. And who are the villains? Mostly northern Europeans darkened to look Middle Eastern with huge black brows, sinister sneers, and dark and dirty fake suntans. And, except for a few clowns, who were fat and stupid, they had that Cassian "lean and hungry" look, a sure sign of misanthropy. They were the image which was impressed upon my young mind as the evil A(pronounced as in hay)rab.

Things have not improved for the Middle Easterner, especially, since the 9-11 attack. Now the Middle Easterners are not only evil conspirators, they are the most dangerous terrorists in the world. At least, that seems to be the dominant attitude. And the Islamic religion is included in the prejudicial mix.

Certainly, there are dangerous radical Middle Eastern Muslims, and some of them have every intention of doing harm to America. In the individual cases of these particular villains, it is right to be on our guard and even to take physical action against them when they prove through individual actions that they are dangerous. But (and I feel like I am saying something here that is so obvious that it goes without saying) the bulk of Middle Eastern Muslims in the United states are peace-loving persons who want nothing more than to be good Americans. There has never been a time when it was good to be an American of Middle Eastern extraction. The present time is probably the worst of their bad times.

This is a problem American religion refuses to face squarely. It is a problem that the federal government cannot solve because of its primary mandate for homeland security. Local governments are busy with water and energy and education problems. It is a problem that the general population of the U.S. does not care a whit about. It is one of those dilemmas which calls for the "voice crying in the wilderness," the philosopher's voice. That voice is a long way from solution, but its continued wailing is essential to any eventual progress with such a sticky problem.

November 15: Speaking of "Sticky," I Eat My Peas with Honey.

I eat my peas with honey;
I've done it all my life.
It makes the peas taste funny,
But it keeps them on the knife.

I learned this little poem way back at Junior Camp when I was six years old, the same camp where, while climbing Little Smokey Mountain with the other campers, I leaned over to pick up a stick and tumbled head-over-butt-dimples down the mountain side over logs and rocks and, finally, came to rest against a fallen pine tree, bloody and bruised, but wiser.

Both the poem and the tumble were learning experiences. I have spent the rest of my life remembering not to lean downhill but, otherwise, insisting upon doing things my own way. Coincidentally, I've switched from honey to mayonnaise with my peas, something Yasmin taught me. Mighty fine flavor—and nearly as adhesive to the knife!

November 16: Physical Health.

Since I continue for the fifth day to be sick with whatever this scourge is that afflicts me, this would be a good day for approaching the concept of physical health as a philosophical topic. Of course, the obvious is that no one can feel happy when the body seems to be at war with itself in every pore and organ, but there is a great deal more to physical health than "flu or not flu." I know that this minor sickness will pass in a week or two or three and I'll, once again, be able to go about my business unhindered. But the happiness requirement which Aristotle seems to embed in "the Good" is heavily involved with the physical health of the body and of the mind.

Ancient and medieval physiology blamed melancholy (the lack of happiness) on black bile, one of the four humors, supposedly fluids. They had not yet heard about clinical depression and the impact of serotonin levels upon it. But they seem to have had it about right. If something physical in the body is out of balance, mental balance is also disturbed. The bottom line is that, if your body is sick, your mind wants to follow suit. It is possible, to a certain extent, to wriggle around this paradox. I grew up in the neighborhood of a fellow who was struck down by polio during the 1950s and spent the rest of his short life in an iron lung.

315

This was long before the advent of the portable computer; so, since he could neither speak nor move, his communication with those around him was limited. I remember, however, how pleased he was when his friends came to visit him. He could read. He did it with mirrors. His mother would hold a book and turn the pages in front of a series of mirrors which, eventually, put the text in front of his eyes in the right direction for reading. And he relished it. Although it is hard for me to imagine, he seems to have had a happy life. As I recall, he died in his early twenties.

I have spoken in earlier documents about my own bouts with depression. Sometimes it outflanks me, and I spend a miserable day or two hating my life and everything associated with it. Most often, however, I recognize the symptoms coming on, step outside myself, and get a darkly comic kick out of watching the progress of the disease. I, too, can have a happy life. I have from time to time medicated my depression; but, in retirement, I prefer to ride it out in other ways that don't involve dulling my senses with medication. I'm dull enough in my normal incarnation. I am fortunate that mine is a *mild* chronic depression, one that *can* be dealt with through psychological legerdemain.

Aristotle didn't really say that the "Good" and happiness are one and the same. The term happiness is one potential translation of what he said. It could, just as honestly, be translated as contentment or satisfaction. It is quite possible to be satisfied in a life that is more limited or more painful than the run-of-the-mill life.

I have to stop now because "satisfaction" is dripping from my nose. I fear that it might contain a share of black bile which would not be good for the inner workings of my computer keyboard.

November 17: Enough! Enough! Enough!

Descending a list of potential contemporary philosophical topics and striking them off as I go has become hum-drum—*taedium*! I have offered sufficient proof that a place exists in the contemporary context for philosophical discussion. Indeed, if human existence is to be examined in an impartial way, philosophy is the only medium for that examination. All other disciplines have agendas which slant the discussion. Science has theses to prove. Religion has doctrines to support. Politics consists of bias. Only philosophy has no prejudice. Of course, that cannot be said of particular philosophers. Indeed, here's the rub. The philosopher's quest is for the nearest thing to the unprejudiced truth, but each philosopher is the product of his or her own exposure to prejudice. In fact, every sensual contact (and there is no other verifiable contact) with the cosmos is prejudicial. That is, it favors (or disfavors if the sensual contact has negative impact) singular miniscule aspects of the cosmos over all others. Thus, the philosopher's prejudice is exactly proportional to his contact with the cosmos as it is. The more sensual contact the philosopher encounters, the greater his prejudice. How does the true philosopher overcome this immense obstacle to nonprejudice? Through the recognition that anything the philosopher believes to be true has a much more than equal chance of being false. That is, the true philosopher is not seeking the absolute truth at all. What the true philosopher is seeking is the possibility of truth. In this sense, each sensual experience of the philosopher is fitted into the infinite space/time continuum providing another possibility of truth, not denying other possibility, but tightening the warp and woof of the entire fabric of existence.

This might seem like small consolation for the human mind which would only be fully satisfied with the full truth, but consider this. Those details of cosmos which are experienced and placed by human reason into the space/time continuum are the ones most directly involved with human life. Thus, although, there is an infinity of time ahead still remaining to explore and a similar infinity behind us, overlooked and unexplored along with unexplored infinity of space in every direction and from infinitely great to infinitely small, that finite place and time in infinity which seems to be reserved for our particular human existence can be examined in some detail. The true philosopher need only stand as far away from the web of life as possible to see the general patterning which begins to appear in order to exercise closure upon the vague patterns of truth which would be perfectly evident if all the pieces were in place in the human sector of the continuum. This is far from a perfect view, but it is better than no view at all, and only the mind that can reduce the impact of prejudice by standing at some distance from it can exercise closure in the patterns to a degree sufficient to be of value. It is the philosopher who must develop this capacity to view experience from a distance. All others must keep their hands upon the grindstone, their noses to the tiller, their feet on the pot, their palms on the ground. They cannot see for seeing, hear for hearing, feel for feeling, taste for tasting, smell for smelling. Only, the philosopher, deaf, blind, and senseless, can return, like blind justice, a just verdict. And who in his right senses obeys the senseless? Ah, the irony of it!

November 18: A Siebert Song.

Siebert Wilson wrote this for the church choir. He had great hopes for it, but the choir never got around to singing it. I thought it was truly inspired work on his part, so I'm reproducing it here.

Send the Lamb to the Ruler
Chorus:
> Send the lamb to the ruler;
> Make me the lamb that is sent to the ruler;
> As a gift for the altar;
> Make me the lamb for the ruler.

Old times, new times, always full of cryin';
Send the lamb to the ruler.
Folks keep hurtin', and Folks keep a-dyin';
Send the lamb to the ruler.

Chorus:
> Send the lamb to the ruler;
> Make me the lamb that is sent to the ruler;
> As a gift for the altar;
> Make me the lamb for the ruler.

Trouble is trouble ain't on account of tryin';
Send the lamb to the ruler.
Most folks stan' around watchin' souls a-sighin';
Don' wanna be the lamb for the ruler.

Chorus:
>Send the lamb to the ruler;
>Make me the lamb that is sent to the ruler;
>As a gift for the altar;
>Make me the lamb for the ruler.

Ol' Isaiah didn't wait for his orders
When God asked "Who will go for me?"
Stood up straight and threw back his shoulders;
Answered the Lord, "Here am I; send me!"

Chorus:
>Send the lamb to the ruler;
>Make me the lamb that is sent to the ruler;
>As a gift for the altar;
>Make me the lamb for the ruler.

Wanna be jus' like ol' man Isaiah;
Wanna be the lamb for the ruler.
Give my life for goodness every day, a
Sacrifice to God for the ruler.

Chorus:
>Send the lamb to the ruler;
>Make me the lamb that is sent to the ruler;
>As a gift for the altar;
>Make me the lamb for the ruler.

Note: This song loses a lot on paper. You really need to hear it. It's a rip-roaring spiritual.

November 19: Take a Day Off from Work.

I'm not going to the office today. The primary reason is that I have this blumin' cold and I hope another day of rest beyond Sunday will work toward its remission. Sunday wasn't all that restful because Manning and the Colts wore me out beating the Chiefs and their new quarterback Brody Croyle. Brody did a fine job, but he wasn't quite up to facing Manning. But the real entertainment didn't happen until Sunday evening when the Pats provided their 56-10 walloping of the Bills. My, oh my! What a drubbing that was! I watch professional football because professional football players are an example to me of what I should be as a philosopher. A real football star is not just talented. When he needs to do it, he can reach deep into his soul to get that last bit of potential in order to do what has to be

318

done. Of course, the Pats didn't really have to do that last night. They just walked over the Bills on almost every play. But I watched Peyton Manning do it near the end of the Colts' game with the Chiefs. When he needed that last yard, he pulled himself together and got it and won the game. I saw a little of that kind of spirit in Brody Croyle, too. That gives me hope for my ne'er-do-well Chiefs in the future.

I always hope that I can learn to dig that hidden talent out of myself when I need it. So far, I've dug up a lot of dirt and rocks, a couple of pop bottle lids, and a rusty cork screw, not much hidden talent; but I know that digging for it is the key.

An old friend of mine from the university told me something similar many years ago when I was struggling to get my doctorate. He said, "It isn't how smart you are but your persistence that will get you to the goal. Just keep working at it as hard as you can."

So I did. And it worked.

Now, I have another piece of advice. Take a day off once in a while. Sometimes, it's the only way to get the old body to take charge and kill off whatever virus is plugging up your sinuses. But when you get into the groove of working all the time, taking a day off can be one of the hardest jobs you can do. I'll just have to dig in and figure out how to handle that. Is it lunch time yet!?

November 20: Well, That Didn't Work! Maybe, Prayer!

I still feel as lousy as I did yesterday, so I went to work anyway. Here I am, tapping on the keys, sweating profusely, head like a balloon, breathing through my mouth, lips chapped, coughing up [shall I call it black bile] every now and then. What I really need here is a televangelist: "Heal! Damn it, Heal!!! Throw away your pitiful crutches and WALK!!!" But I'm neither halt nor lame. I just have this cold that won't go away. Somehow, this does not rise to the majesty of the healing powers of the Lord of the Universe. Shouldn't a few Sudafed do the trick? Or, at least, a combination of Nyquil and Dayquil!? But the Nyquil just gives me nightmares. Last night I dreamed that the whole world had become cannibalistic. The only question was the etiquette of who could be eaten by whom. Is it O.K. to eat a close relative or should one stick to members of other families. That crowned rack of Uncle Henry looks delicious. How about the roast rump of Betty? A lot of saturated fat there! The Chuck steak would, probably, be tough. He, after all, was a longshoreman. All night long, on and on and on! I decided I should suspend the Nyquil.

What question should be asked about all this? Is it possible to be both "Good" and have a persistent upper respiratory infection? Any answer I could give at this moment to that question would be suspect at best.

November 21: Passion Fruit and Snow.

I watched an old movie on TV last night. It was set in Cuba in the late 19th century. As I watched it, snow was falling on the streets in Parkville which had been liberally wetted down with cold rain. Since it was a rather commonplace movie that required little attentiveness to follow the plot, it was a good opportunity to think about the relative merits of tropical vs. temperate zone living. I'm not an entire stranger to tropical living having spent five years in Hawaii during the 1980s and 90s. And the temperate zone is well-known to me from the windy banks of

Newfoundland to the craggy heights of the Rocky Mountains and both the Pacific and Atlantic coastlines. I have information to be processed about both the tropics and the temperate zones.

But a wealth of information is not necessary in the comparison. Vague impressions carry more value. The aroma of flowering trees is a constant in Hawaii. My memory of that aroma is equal to my memory of the smell of new-mown hay in Idaho—both are vague but no less cogent than the Hawaiian hurricane that bankrupted nearly every insurance company doing business there or the tornado that ripped a new beltway around Parkville last year. In last night's movie, I saw outdoor Cuban pavilions always open to archways into hotels and mansions, and it reminded me of the same phenomena in Hawaii; and not just for hotels and mansions. Our house in Hawaii had no screen doors to slam behind us and the front door was not always closed. In the tropics, people have learned to cohabit with flies, cockroaches, and geckoes. Perhaps, there are fewer of them. I don't remember them being a problem in the tropical places I have inhabited. Only in the temperate zones. Life is delightful in the tropics.

Yet, when I peered through the Venetian blinds of our living room window in Parkville last night, I was awestruck by the sight of snowflakes slanting past the streetlight near our house. I wondered how one could stand a year without winter.

I am still wondering. And what a wonder this world is! With all of my degrees and book-learning, my greatest education has come from the mild aromas of flowering trees, the vague chill of sea mist on my cheek—the quiet chirrup of a pasture cricket and the croaking of choral bullfrogs in irrigation ditches—thin mist over a frigid mountain lake—distant evening stars appearing over a rope hammock, silent snow at midnight. And what have they taught me? That is even more vague, more fuzzy, the best part of the greatest education.

November 22: Thanksgiving Day!

Thanksgiving Day is the holiday that is the gift of America to the world. It is, without doubt, the greatest holiday ever, anywhere. That is, largely, because of its beneficial timing just a month before Christmas, which has left it almost entirely unscathed by market forces. We can thank Christmas and, to a lesser extent, Halloween, for draining the accounts of the American middle class so that they can enjoy Thanksgiving without commercial interruptions except, of course, for those endless reminders that every merchant on the planet will be opening at 4 a.m. tomorrow to receive all of the money you can possibly scrape together and bring to the shopping center. The merchants will give you some small penitential particle of material glitz for your financial contribution to a better world economy.

But most of us can ignore such commercials. We are busy cooking the turkey or getting the family into the van to be on our way to grandmother's house ("Hi ho! Hi ho!"). Of course, the worst of us, those of us who could not resist the temptation to put ourselves in frustration's way, are trapped in grounded or delayed aircraft on tarmacs or in holding patterns in the skies.

Not me! I outgrew such nonsense long ago. Yasmin and I will navigate the 7½ miles to the home of #2 daughter where we will share a turkey and all the trimmings with daughters #2 and #3 and their families. #1 and her family are off fishing in the South Dakota badlands. Hmmm! We'll eat ourselves sick and silly and, lying belly-up-on-the-floor, watch a couple of football games. Belly-up-on-the-floor is the holiest of all possible body positions on such a day.

November 23: The Will of God.

This morning in the K.C. Star's Letters to the Editor there appeared a letter from a devout Catholic explaining why Catholicism could have no female priests. She said that it is the same reason why men cannot give birth to babies: because God said so.

This is the very heart of why organized religion is one of the most divisive and destructive forces on earth. The vast majority of "saved" people claim to have some sort of absolute knowledge of the will of God. Yet there is not a single soul on earth who can produce a scrap of evidence that God has ever revealed anything to anyone about his/her/its will, if God, as I or any other human being or any human institution imagines God to exist, actually exists at all (for which there is no empirical and scant rational evidence).

If we as the human race could concentrate on being good stewards over the things that we are suited to manage (the material domain within the actual and potential scope of our physical senses), enjoying those things which lie beyond our ken as *a priori* conceptions decorating and illuminating our rational minds (e.g., infinity and its twin continua of time and space), perhaps, we could begin to take baby steps toward human actualization, not becoming Nietzsche's *Übermensch*, the powerfully evolved tyrant-lords parented by arrogant fools such as mythical Zarathustra, but strong, gentle souls, green souls, nurturing souls, souls that know the difference between joyous sustenance and avaricious greed, preferring the former for the world—and for themselves.

Do I fantasize? Tell me, God, if I am wrong! What is that I hear?! Dead silence?! Ah, Me!

November 24: Martyrdom of Tegh Bahadur.

Guru Tegh Bahadur refused to convert to Islam in 1675, was transported to Delhi, and beheaded on a site that later sported a Sikh temple. He, according to Sikh teaching, died for the religious freedom of all peoples. His death is commemorated on November 24th this year, two days after American Thanksgiving and a month before Christmas Eve. Few non-Sikhs have any knowledge of this fellow, which is unfortunate given that he and Jesus along with several other martyred prophets, philosophers, and saints have much in common regarding religious freedom and other really excellent stuff that most people place small value upon.

November 25: My Brother's Keeper.

In the hearts of Judaism, Christianity, and Islam, the big question, "Am I my brother's keeper?" has burned since the beginning. But that is stripling youth in comparison to the origin of the larger question which encompasses it, "What is the measure of a thing?" The origin of this second question is infinity. Ever-existent space and time have contained it. Even eternal space and time themselves are inextricably wound into one another. How much more devotedly are my brother and I bound together?! And my sister and I?! And a centenarian rain-forest tree burning in Brazil to make way for my brethren stalks of sugar cane? And the gasoline that powers my pickup truck, and the carbon dioxide that warms the air a little too much? And the melting polar ice? And my dear old mother in assisted living? And the romance novel she prefers to *Walden*?

Siebert told me yesterday that he will not see me until after New Year. He is going to Rupert, Idaho, to the farm where he grew up to be with his older sister during her last days. I was sorry for his sister's circumstances, but I was sorrier that he won't be able to share the load of finishing this book with me. I could have used his wisdom.

And the Scribe seems angrier than usual. Of course, he always seems a bit put off by the world in general, as if he doesn't really want to be so bound up in its affairs. His problem is clear to me. He spends too much energy spooning reality about in its bowl to check it for maggots, and not enough time eating it with plenty of sugar and cream and a mug of stout. At any rate, he'll help me with my editing because he always does his "duty," but he'll grumble about my bad spelling and sour the atmosphere with his acid reflux breath.

I'll miss the sweetness of Siebert, but I know that, as long as I'm here, he'll come back—eventually; and I'll get a good chuckle watching the Scribe mutter his way through my entries for July and August.

Yasmin's arthritis is giving her fits, so I have to be careful not to shake the bed too much when I climb into it after sleeping through Letterman. I've started rubbing left-over Proctosol hydrocortisone cream (prescribed for hemorrhoids) on my arthritic index-finger joints. As I said above, everything is connected—nothing exists in isolation. Thus, at least, we might find the measure of one small thing. We might find whether my arthritic knuckles have something in common with hemorrhoids.

November 26: Philosopher Clinton.

Not Hillary, Bill. Although, I suppose Hillary might be something of a philosopher, too. After all, she wrote *It Takes a Village*. In 1997, Bill Clinton said the following:

> The real differences around the world today are not between Jews and Arabs; Protestants and Catholics; Muslims, Croats, and Serbs. The real differences are between those who embrace peace and those who would destroy it; between those who look to the future and those who cling to the past; between those who open their arms and those who are determined to clench their fists.

I don't think I can improve on that statement. As a fellow human, I am happy that another fellow human said it. I will leave it as it stands.

November 27: *It Takes a Village?*

It continues to intrigue me, the idea of having a philosopher President in the United States. Could Hillary be the one? She did write that book (*It Takes a Village)* which seems to be largely a focused philosophy. The premise of the book is that we are all the fellow keepers of other members of our human family and the "village" is the symbol for that human family in its first extension into Social Contract (beyond the contract of *Father Knows Best and You'd Better Accept It or Father will Beat the Hell out of You*).

A couple of images spring to mind when we think of the responsibility of the village. For WASP baby boomers it might be those delightful Donna Reed years including a highly competent mother along with a somewhat clownish Father (who knows best, but only in a neutered, Gentle Ben sense, not in a dragging the woman off by the hair sense). The village here is represented by the stay-at-home mother's coffee klatsch of suburban housewives, a small group of neighborhood children of various mentalities and personalities, an occasional trip through the halls and classrooms of the local school, a stop-off at the local Christian church, and a mythical (never really located) white-collar high-pay executive office job for Father.

Another image, equally stereotypical and false, is that of the African village where few can read or write, but there is always a center of wisdom, usually a woman, and a semi-wise war chief, always a man, and hoards of small mostly naked children, and semi-naked adults who act like small children bouncing about the clearing as if they were anxious to find a place to pee—all this demeaning to the African village culture.

Not much fodder here for Hillary's philosophical treatise! Yet, there is the possibility of important philosophical statement. The message, again, returns to "Am I my brother's keeper?" And the answer continually rings back: "Yes!" Even to the extent of the grandest of all villages, the entire earth where, at the moment, the greatest emerging enterprise (China) is pointing its myriad smokestacks skyward to belch pollution into the air and its myriad factory sewers earthward squirting endless poisons into rivers and the earth; and the greatest of previously emerged nations (the U.S.A.) out-Heroding Herod with its myriad factories and fossil-fuel-guzzling engines blasting the land and the atmosphere with gasified carbon wastes; while France and Japan pile stacks upon stacks of nuclear waste which the world has no way of eliminating, all the while claiming to have solved the problem of nuclear waste. And the wheels on the bus go round and round, and the children on the bus go off to school, and some children not on the bus starve to death while their parents kill one another for the sake of pleasing God, and where the remaining Donna Reed wanna-be's hold their coffee klatches, and Eddie Haskell is still trying futilely to prove he is the coolest, but where the Beaver's mother is, obviously, the coolest, and if we modernize all this just a bit, there is the natural ascendancy of that skinny black kid "Di-no-mite!"

And, yet, Hillary is right: *It Takes a Village* to raise a child. Somehow, all of this insanity and human shortcoming can, if it is applied humanely and as fairly as possible, emerge as human success. At the moment, things look mightily bleak, but continual meeting of the minds of village elders with village idiots will lead once again to that profound democratic mediocrity which all of us who are older grew to know and love.

November 28: Speaking of Village Elders . . .

Somehow, I can't visualize Hillary Clinton as a village elder. She shows a lot of promise, but she is almost as old as I am and, like me, she is still not quite mature. Nor can I picture Barack Obama as a village elder. Although he is a fine young man, he could not yet be an "elder," unless he were, like Mitt Romney, a Mormon, in which case he could have been an "elder" at 18 years old. But that is another story, an epic about ecclesiastical sins against lexicography. Here, I am speaking of the leadership of the free world—so to speak.

Last night Joe Biden was interviewed on CNN because he is running for President, and I beheld in him a village elder. I haven't seen that in him before. He was always, like Hillary Clinton, too much in the thick of the fray to rise above it, and only in rising above the fray can a person become a village elder.

I suppose that the question is whether the President should rise above the fray or be busily involved with it—in other words, should the President be a village elder? I have the answer, and it came to me only last night as I was watching the Biden interview. The President not only *can* be above the fray, but *must* be above it in order to be a first rate President. Bill Clinton, as President, managed for part of his term to rise above the fray. But the fray rose up to meet him, ironically, in the form of his sexual passions. These should not have become a factor in his Presidential task. Other Presidents (e.g., John Kennedy) had what appears to be uncontrollable sexual drive. But they did not let it interfere with their Presidential missions. For Bill Clinton, sex drive, with the help of the Republican neocon-controlled House of Representatives, nearly smothered an otherwise excellent Presidential effort. Thus, the latter part of the Clinton era was clouded and limited. The ships of state arrived and departed on a terribly delayed schedule.

When I looked at Joe Biden last night, what I saw was an equal to John Kennedy in his ability to rise above the fray, and he doesn't have the sexual baggage (or any other excess baggage for that matter). He is a modestly older gentleman, about my age, who has spent most of his adult life as a U.S. Senator. During that time, he has not raised his personal profile to the level where the general population would look at him and say, "Here is a great statesman who should be President." Yet, when things needed doing, he did them. He was smart about dealing with members of both parties and, in a reasonable way, became a solid leader in the senate. Now, he is ready to accept the responsibility of being President.

When I looked at Joe Biden last night, I thought I saw Bill Clinton on his best day (with no albatross dangling from his neck). That is an image that impressed me. It was a vague image, but I have said before that vague images are, often, more important than solid facts in decision-making. Not that the facts are not important, and the facts about Biden's ability to stand the heat of the kitchen are solid. He has endured the trials, both personal and professional, of time and service and come up strong and smiling, and the world is better for his having served in it. But vague and important images tell me that this, now, is a Joe Biden who has become a village elder, one with little to distract him from the essential mission of, *finally*, moving America (for seven years, pawing and panting like a spooked horse at the edge of a precipice) across the divide and into the new millennium.

I doubt that the American electorate will see these images the way I see them. Probably, next November, America, tired of the war in Iraq and out of sorts with the Republicans, will vote for the Democratic choice of candidates for President, and it will not be Joe Biden. He is too calm, too far above the fray. They will not see him as "Presidential" because he is *not* carrying the baggage which is so often an unfortunate appendage to that office.

November 29: A Reason Not to be an Atheist.

George Santayana said, "My atheism . . . is true piety towards the universe and denies only gods fashioned by men in their own image to be servants of their human interests." In following this creed, he sucked all the fun and much of the value out of the *a priori* cosmos. Of course, God is imaginary. Of course, I create God in the forms and for the functions that serve my interests. The problem with "religious true believers" is that they fail to *realize* that they create their own gods in their own images, then build idols to represent them instead of looking in the mirror. The problem with atheists is that they can't enjoy *a priori* what they see in the mirror. In support of my thesis, Santayana also said, "Perhaps the only true dignity of man is his capacity to despise himself."

November 30: Fear God! Know God!

> *"The fear of God is the beginning of wisdom."*
> Proverbs 1:7
> *"Nothing is perfect except your words."*
> Psalms 119:96-100

I was exploring web sites about wisdom and found one that talked about the wisdom of God. It was a meditation that started out well, saying that our human wisdom is severely restricted by our severely limited human context and that God's wisdom is infinite. Then, however, it turned to a discussion of how to increase our human wisdom. According to this Christian author, the two Bible quotes above are the heart of the method for doing this. Let's look at each of them.

It is true that the Bible gives the first instruction in Proverbs. Therefore, whoever insists that every word in the Bible is the pure and perfect word of God, might as well stop reading this entry and move on to something more fulfilling— perhaps the slaughter of every man, woman, and child in an enemy state whose land we feel we have the God-decreed destiny to occupy. To that person, whatever is in the Bible is pure wisdom. But for the rest of us who demand at least some test of the validity of Biblical statement, those of us who do not consider *thinking* a cardinal sin, it is important to consider exactly what this quote says: "Being afraid of God is the starting point for being wise." Fear, I would argue, is a means of controlling us, not a way of making us wise. Indeed, it is a means of keeping us ignorant, therefore, anything but wise. The supreme power of the universe is, indeed, an awesome thing. Yet, fear is not a wholesome or wise approach to it. We should approach that supreme power as a child approaching a bowl of ice cream, happily, with our mouths watering for its content.

Second, it is only the most naïve of the naïve who believe that the Bible (of which not a single word can be confirmed to be a pure and perfect word of God) is the pure and perfect word of God in its every word. It would be true that, if the

Bible reflected the pure and perfect mind of God, it would be a tremendous store of wisdom. What more could we desire? All we, as philosophers, seekers of wisdom, would need to do to answer any question would be to open the Book. It would tell us the answer immediately. Indeed, the philosopher (or the minister, for that matter) would no longer have a job. In our age of the Google search, we could find our answers with simple key words. Unfortunately, as valuable as the Bible is as a resource for the philosophic mind, it cannot be proven to be "the word of God," pure and perfect *or* adulterated. And, since no other book, either, can be proven to be the word of God, there seems to be no verifiable pure and perfect word of God for us to turn to, no matter how afraid we are.

Thus, the author of the meditation is, like all other such authors, merely blowing smoke. This simplistic view advocated by Christianity about how to attain wisdom is nothing more than a means of keeping Christians ignorant and afraid. There is no shortcut to wisdom.

December 1: A Most Important Day.

The first of December is an important day to our family because it is grandchild #7's birthday. He is four years old today. Last night, he required that his parents and brother stay up until midnight to wish him a happy birthday. This morning, he was quite disappointed when he hurried to the mirror only to find, to his horror, that he looked the same as he did the night before when he was a mere three-year-old. He has learned something about aging through this disappointing experience. In less than an hour now, Yasmin and I (along with grandchildren #3 and #6 who are spending time with us today after I spent time singing with #3 in her second and third grade intergenerational choir at a Christmas craft fair at Winnitonka High School), will join the rest of the family for a party at the Riverside Athletic club for #7. We have a busy life, Yasmin and I.

December first would still be an important day even if it were not #7s birthday. It is important to all of us who abide by the Gregorian calendar. For us, it is pragmatically (though unofficially) regarded as the first day of winter. Although winter does not officially begin until the winter solstice (December 21st this year), everyone knows that today is the day when we can no longer deny that winter has begun and autumn has passed. It can't be helped that the calendar is immutable in its flawed opinion. None of us will wait until December 21st to consider it wintertime. Even if we have no significant snow until sometime in January, which sometimes happens in Missouri, winter began this morning with the turning of a calendar page. And, as I woke up beside Yasmin in our cozy bed, I gave a little shudder acknowledging that fact; and, at this very moment, I am wearing the gray winter stocking cap I put on before I brushed my teeth. My Stetson XXXX Beaver Silver Belly is retired until the first of March when winter is over—unofficially.

December 2: World-Wide Winter.

Of course, there is no such thing as world-wide winter (without the intrusion of nuclear explosives). The world provides a perfect meteorological continuum of weather with a central point (the equator) of *no* winter and two terminals (the poles) of *all* winter. These are finite, not infinite measures, bounded by the earth itself. However, they seem to be something like microcosms of some infinite meteorological continuum which has no terminal points and, thus, no center. Temperate zones on the earth have been good for human innovation. Perhaps, it has been the manageable necessities that made it so.

I am thankful for winter. Once I have gathered in the necessities for surviving it, the cold arrives and freezes down the dross of the warm season's production and polishes the land with ice. It forces me into a house warmed by the wood I gathered in the fall or by the fuels that temperate zone humanity has captured and delivered to my furnace. When, in the rare instance that I want human company beyond that of my immediate family and neighbors, I get into my truck, with its mechanical heater and wind-tight cab and snow tires and drive on the paved highways which were built during the warm season so I could use them in any weather, especially because we have invented such machines as snow plows and that little propeller on the back end of snow-plow trucks which flings salt and sand across the icy highway surface, melting it to navigable slush which eats away the paint on my truck.

And, while I long for spring and green grass and flowers and the sight of small children playing in swimming pools, I find the winter a time when the frost peels away the distractions of summer from my mind leaving it a keen instrument for the winnowing of good from evil and arranging the results neatly in lines typed on my laptop computer screen, another invention which would never have been developed except for the desires of temperate zone civilization.

Were I a child of an equatorial tribe, and my tribe had not been disturbed by invaders from temperate zones seeking wealth from my jungle, what need would I have felt for writing books of philosophy or for saving whatever ideas happen to course through my sleepy mind? I would feed on wild plants and slow animals and, occasionally, less docile animals would feed on members of my tribe. I would live in the open air with a primitive hut to shield me from the rain. I wouldn't care much how long the rain lasted because I would have little to do when it went away, although I would like it when it ceases because the air outside the hut smells better than the air inside. I would be comfortable unless I was seriously injured or developed a terminal disease (in which case I would, *probably*, die before I suffered for long) or a tiger decided to eat me (in which case I would *surely* die before suffering for long). What need would I have to write a novel since my life is a novel with no reading required? What need for a pencil or word processor or computer?

It is in the temperate zones that we think we need such things, and they have made our lives more meaningful. Or have they? We are born, we grow to adulthood, we creep into old age, and we die, unless, earlier on, we contract a terminal disease (in which case we die with managed suffering) or a tree falls on us (in which case, if we are lucky, we die quickly with little suffering).

Still, I am thankful for winter. I have lived in a languid tropical culture, and I have lived in a harried temperate zone. I was bored by too many rope hammocks and by tides that swished against jungle shores as regularly as clockwork where there were few clocks. I came back to winter, and that has made a positive difference.

December 3: Live for the Future!

What I am about to say is revolutionary. Conventional wisdom has it that we should live for the present moment, but that is absurd because there is no present moment, only a past and a future. Since the past is dead except as thought, the only living place is the future-about-to-exist. Thus, if we are to live productively, we must concentrate our life force there.

I have been soundly berated many times for this attitude, especially by Yasmin. When I start planning my next trip to Idaho a few hours after I return to Missouri, she considers it an insult to Missouri. Not so! Although I store up many insults that I could and sometimes do aim at Missouri, what she doesn't realize is that I start planning my return to Missouri within a few hours after my arrival in Idaho. On the other hand, I do spend significant time in the past. I enjoy thinking of the long ago times when I could stroll across the south 40 without all the aching in my body. Occasionally, I relive moments of glory on the hardwood while I watch Shaq slam-dunk a basketball. But I don't spend excessive time in the past. I spend it mostly in the future. If I am delinquent about any time period (and I am), it is the immediate future. I suppose that is why sometimes, after a grocery shopping trip, I walk right by my truck in the parking lot while, in my mind, I'm sorting out the details of my next camping expedition.

The immediate future, the moment right after the moment of future that is slipping into past as I type—*that* is the moment most important. That is when I decide what the rest of my life will be. And I must do it time after time, sliced infinitely, and I, ordinarily, don't even know I'm doing it. Go figure: the only time that we are actively living, and we simply let it slip by without any reasonable thought about it.

Yet there is another dimension to that: the moment of future that just disappeared into the past. That was an important moment as well. But it is gone. I should have taken better care of it. For instance, when the instant passes during which I trip while ascending the stairs, it is important that I be prepared to catch myself before my nose makes contact with wood, but I leave that decision to instinct. Reason has no time to respond. I'm thankful for those traces of primitive animal instincts which I still retain. Without them, I would have a nose like a twenty-year veteran boxer.

Unfortunately for our noses, we can't always do enough about that most immediate moment in the future. But what of our next hour? How can we make it more profitable by concentrating our powers of reason upon it? The answer is manifold, and it is the most important answer we have for ourselves. My next hour and the next and the next and the next in perpetuity are (in the order in which they occur) the most important hours. In the opening minutes of each of these hours (while the instinct for what we erroneously call "the present moment" rises and subsides), I must decide to plan out my life for the rest of that hour in keeping with a reasonable plan for the rest of my life, and reason tells me that I must use that next hour to plan a reasonable attack on the hour after that and the hour after that and the hour after that. Of course, as Burns tells us, "The best laid plans o' mice an' men gang aft agley"; but that is why we have the next hour and the next and the next to adjust our plans rationally. In fact, what we worship as spontaneity is most successful when it is properly planned, even if we plan it only a millisecond before it happens. For instance, consider that commercial where a cell-phone conversation is dropped at a key moment, right after we deliver what will appear to be a stinging insult to the person on the phone with us. With just a second's rational delay, that insult which has left us in serious social trouble might have been reasoned out of existence.

Often, we can tell which people use this window of opportunity to change the future. They are the ones who always seem to be momentarily on "pause" before they speak or act. After that pause, their speech or action seems wiser than that of most of us. They are, also, considered to be a little odd since our human conversation, like nature, abhors a vacuum. We get nervous as we wait for them to collect their thoughts, and we often interject something irrational into the empty conversation balloon. Then, both we and our delayed-reasoning friend appear less than socially competent.

Be that as it may; my earth-shaking pronouncement stands (a few minutes after it sank into the necrophilian abyss of the past) as the best wisdom for today. Use each moment and hour of the immediate future to plan reasonably your future from the next hour to that grand moment when you, like Shaq, deliver a slam dunk winning the game, saving the world, at the final buzzer as the crowd goes wild!

December 4: Suppose.

Suppose that you had everything that you could imagine ever wanting. What would you hope for? Nothing, it would seem. Suppose that, except for your life, you lost it all. What would you gain? Hope?! Perhaps, but not inevitably. Can hope exist if wisdom is gone with all else that you had?

Suppose that you had only wisdom. To what would you apply it? Suppose that you lost wisdom and gained the entire world. Where is the gain without wisdom?

Suppose you have a bucket for wisdom. How much wisdom could you place in the bucket before it became too heavy to carry? And suppose you decided to carry lead instead of wisdom in your bucket. How much lead could you transport from place to place in a bucket? More or less lead than wisdom?

Am I comparing apples to dreams? Let us dream our dreams and eat our apples and be glad to have them both. Perhaps, they are all we need—along with a little wisdom.

December 5: What is "Progressive"?

I have been receiving email recently from a group advocating that the next President of the United States be "progressive." I'm not sure how they are defining that word, "progressive." I know that this email is coming from a liberal website because all of the candidates that they name as progressive are Democrats and they say that any of the Democratic candidates would be better than any of the Republican candidates.

The term, progressive, is problematic for me because every candidate that I have seen wants to make some sort of progress, with the exception of Ron Paul, who wants to regress to the gold standard and to the elimination of Social Security and nearly everything else managed by the federal government except national security. I think that the email authors mean by progressive that the candidate favors the acceptance of the theory of evolution and all that it entails (embryonic stem cell research, etc.). Also, it would seem that such a candidate would favor the quick ending of the war in Iraq. I suppose that would be progress, though the Republican candidates are saying that we are now making progress in that war.

It is confusing to me. I think that I need the people at the progressive website from which I am receiving email to define more carefully what they mean by progressive. I rather like the candidates they are supporting, but if I discover that "progressive" means something that I don't support, I might have to change my mind and vote for someone else, someone who is not progressive. I'm all for ending the war in Iraq, but it isn't particularly because that would be a "progressive" step in the contemporary world. It is just because I am opposed to the nations and non-nations of the world lining up their children and barely-adults to be shot or disintegrated in the name of some outrageous religious belief or lack thereof.

The biggest news headline of this week is about an elementary school teacher, an English woman somewhere in the Islamic world, whose execution has been called for because she allowed her students to name the class Teddy bear

"Mohammed." I fully agree that Mohammed, as a name, is far too heavy for a Teddy bear. Freddy or Ike, even Moe, would have been better, not so difficult for elementary students to spell when they write home about how their teacher was hanged in the schoolyard in the peaceable name of Allah.

I wonder how all of this fits into the doctrine of progress. They didn't end up hanging the teacher, by the way. She wasn't even whipped for her indiscretion. She, merely, lost her job and spent a few days in prison. Perhaps, she should mount a campaign for Member of Parliament. She might have progressed in her road toward wisdom. At the very least, she could get rich by writing a book about her ordeal.

December 6: Fascinating People.

I saw, this morning, a preview of Barbara Walters' most fascinating people of the year list. I agree with two of the preview list: Bill Clinton and Hugo Chavez. Bill Clinton is multifaceted and extraordinarily influential even though he is out of office; and, also, he stands a good chance in being the next Presidential spouse, an incredibly fascinating possibility. Even though Hugo Chavez is a tinhorn dictator running a pseudo-democracy, he is revolutionizing South America and has been one of only a few who back George W. Bush into corners he can't get out of. We should take his threat to turn South America socialist seriously. At the moment, it all turns on how thoroughly he has the Venezuelan electorate wrapped around his finger. He would probably be better off if they don't let him change the constitution. That way, he wouldn't have to bear the eventual indignity of being voted out of office or executed by firing squad when the social tide turns against him. At any rate, his invention of the "smell of brimstone" calculator for detecting George Bush is a masterstroke. If nothing else, he's a fine stand-up comic.

But the other preview choices are plain, not fascinating. Not intellectuals, but paparazzi bait. We will have to wait to find out who the rest of the Walters choices are. Perhaps, she is saving her better choices for the show. I would, certainly, pick Al Gore. What is fascinating about him is that he chooses to continue in his important nonpolitical roles instead of making another run for President. I would have liked to see him as President, but I am proud of him for abstaining.

December 7: Dietary Health and Me.

I have no credibility in the area of dietary health even though I have a great deal of experience with it—nearly all negative. I have had two heart surgeries, one of them a quintuple coronary bypass, both of them associated with my inability to avoid foods containing large amounts of saturated fat and cholesterol. My belly looks ever so much like a globe of the world and it "shakes when I laugh like a bowl full of jelly." My four-year-old grandson has fun poking it and poking fun at it.

However, even my negative experience gives me a certain amount of expertise. Each day I set out on the right path to right eating, and each evening I curse myself for not following it. But I know the right path, so "pay no attention to that fat man in the booth." Just listen to what I say over *der Lautsprecher*.

This morning I woke up at 3 a.m. suffering from Excess-Spicy-Beef-at-7-p.m. Syndrome. It is well-known to me. It entails severe gastric cramps and a great deal of running back and forth to the bathroom. I am still in pain. It is similar to, with slight differentiation in color from, Excess-Spicy-Chicken-and-Cauliflower-at-7 p.m. Syndrome which struck me down at 3 a.m. a couple of mornings ago. I had barely recovered from that when the Beef version hit me this morning.

I bill myself as someone who is capable of choosing between good and evil. Surely, health is good and illness is evil. At least, I thought so as I ran multiply back and forth from bed to bathroom and bathroom to bed this morning. If I know better, why don't I act better? I think the answer is simple and clear. I really am as stupid as I look.

December 8: The Hurricane Carter Model.

We look for models of personal morality to follow, means of coping with the "slings and arrows of outrageous fortune" and ways of being of value to the world in which we live. Reuben "Hurricane" Carter's book, *The Sixteenth Round*, and the movie (*The Hurricane)* which was inspired by it provide helpful models both for what works and what does not.

Hurricane Carter was a black prizefighter in the 1960s who, for whatever reason, drew the ire of a Patterson, New Jersey, police detective. The detective eventually found means of bringing Carter to trial and conviction on murder charges for crimes he did not commit. Carter spent 30 years in prison before his conviction was overturned and he was released. He remains a strong advocate for those who are wrongfully convicted.

After Carter's incarceration, his means of survival took the form of refusing to "wear the clothing of a guilty man" in prison. Fortunately for him, the leading prison guard, after Carter spent 90 days in "the hole" protesting the clothing rule, permitted him to wear clothing other than the standard stripes and numbers. In addition, he was permitted to remain constantly in his cell so that he did not have to participate in prison life. In his isolation, he wrote the book mentioned above, and it was published.

Life was difficult for him; and, for that reason, he adopted a philosophy of the annihilation of all desires. Indeed, he told his wife to divorce him and not to communicate with him, and he refused any sort of friendship. This seemed to work for him for a number of years; but, finally, the ascetic life would sustain him no longer. Life without desire, he discovered, was not life at all. He, then, permitted himself to have relationships with persons who loved and supported him. Through these new relationships, friends came to his aid, some of them white (which was important because he had not previously learned anything but contempt for white people), and, eventually, the enormity of the crime against him was recognized in the court of a federal judge who ordered him released.

At one time, after reading Bertrand Russell, I, like Carter, came to the conclusion that desire was a contemptible thing that should be annihilated. I discovered quickly, though not as forcefully as Carter did, that I was wrong. What we must do instead is to filter our desire through wisdom. We must desire, today, the things which are good and possible for today; and, tomorrow, we must desire the things which are good and possible for tomorrow. Other desire, that which is not good or which is not possible for a particular day, we should annihilate, or, at least, suppress—permanently if the desire is not for the good (e.g., a desire to see a personal enemy painfully obliterated) or temporarily if a desire is good but impossible for the time being. That is the balance which should be the basis for all human morality if we add right action to right desire at the right time.

December 9: The Four Sundays of Christian Advent.

The four Sundays of the Christian Advent provide a slope for gaining momentum for Christmas. It is a shame that Christendom concentrates more on the mercantile aspects of the advent season than on the moral. The advent of Christ, his incarnation, "the Word made flesh," represents one of the most positively significant myths in all of world history. We peoples of the world have several incarnations of gods, but that of Jesus is the most poignant because Jesus represents all that is good about a Jehovah who is not particularly warm and fuzzy. Consider, for instance that this is the same Jehovah who ordered the slaughter of every man, woman, and child in Canaan in order to make secure and comfortable room for his "chosen people," the Hebrews, who he had just abandoned for no good reason that we know of (although they did sell their brother into slavery) for several hundred years in abject slavery to the Egyptians. He, also, drowned the entire human race like unwanted puppies, saving only a remnant in Noah's family, a branch of which he cursed with slavery through all succeeding generations to the rest of the family because Ham saw his father (Noah) drunk and naked in his tent shortly after the flood receded. It was good to see Jesus coming forth as a good side of this harsh dictator God. Jesus represents love—first, last, and always. We can't forget all of the other commandments, but love is the catalyst for them all. He, also, represents unselfish sacrifice, giving his entire (though short) adult life to the good—in the Socratic model, permitting and staging his own execution for the sake of a good cause. Even in this, Jesus out-Socrateses Socrates, by doing it at a young age when he had much to live for while Socrates waited until he was an old man and would have died soon anyway.

Four Sundays of Advent! Except for the controversy over the divinity of Christ which need not be controversial at all if we just accept him as a child of the supreme power of the cosmos (that power being represented by God) and full-blood brother to the rest of us, all of us can share in the wealth of this advent. Even atheists get a lot of good from his message.

December 10: Happy Chanukah!

And here we have Chanukah! A minor Jewish holiday celebrating a minor miracle (i.e., having a one-night supply of consecrated oil last for eight days). Yet this is the most famous Jewish holiday of them all. That is because it happens during the same season as the Christians' Advent and has similar means of celebration (gift giving and feasting). So let it be! Such intercultural accommodations are the best things we can do. Bring on the dreidels and latkes and let's have a party. Then, right after Christmas, we can celebrate Kwanzaa with the African-Americans and finish up just in time to celebrate New Year's Eve. Wow! If you throw in Halloween and Thanksgiving, we have one hell of a two-month holiday season in America. I would call for a cessation of all unnecessary work during that period; but I think that, *de facto*, all unnecessary work ceases anyway, without a declaration.

December 11: The Big Ice-Water Storm.

The one-and-one-fourth inches of frozen rain predicted for last night didn't happen. Instead, it rained hard and steadily for about fourteen hours and the temperature gradually rose from 29 to 34 degrees Fahrenheit, melting, except for a thin glaze of ice, what snow was left from a previous storm, and leaving the streets merely wet with an icy patch here and there. The trees got the worst of it, but only a few branches were broken including a couple of big elm branches that plopped down in our back yard from trees in our up-hill neighbor's yard. We lost electric power for quite a while this morning, probably because of such tree mishaps. The schools had all cancelled classes the evening before which was probably a good idea since the children were in favor of it even if nothing went wrong with the weather. They are always in favor of a snow day. I didn't go to the office either. I didn't have much of an excuse. I was ready for a snow day, too, I suppose.

The meteorologists had a hey-day. They were not fazed by the lack of a frozen product. They spent most of the night and half of the day, preempting Yasmin's favorite soap operas, contacting every conceivable potential victim of the storm and receiving the same report: "No problems here." One reporter spent at least ten minutes explaining the difference between ice and water, showing us chunks of ice he pealed from a walkway with his ball-point pen and puddles of water in case his explanation of the difference was insufficient to our inferior nonmeteorologist minds. He concluded his report with a confirmation that a survey of hospitals revealed that no one had been injured today by slipping and falling on the ice. What a relief!

I am convinced that, as a society, we are hard up for disasters. We are compelled to make up a disaster where none exists to fill the void. We do this so frequently that I doubt we would know a disaster when it happened. I still remember the look of utter confusion that nailed itself to the face of George W. Bush when an aid reported in a whisper to him in an elementary classroom he was visiting that the World Trade Center had been attacked. Had someone not led him away, he might still have been sitting there in stunned silence. This is not a pretty image, but I fear we have all been so benumbed by noncatastrophic catastrophes that, should a real one occur, we would be as frozen as was our President. The government's response to Hurricane Katrina was much the same, frozen silence, in that case lasting permanently—along with those immortal words: "Brownie, you're doin' a heck of a job!"

December 12: An Apology to Those Who Suffered from the Storm.

Yesterday, I spoke too hastily. Although the freezing rain became nothing but an inconvenience to us in Parkville and most of Kansas City, neighboring towns which didn't get much media attention during the storm suffered sore. St. Joseph, 35 miles from us and historic home of the Pony Express, lost a host of beautiful trees; and the storm froze and iced and crackled throughout the central USA, doing billions of dollars of damage to property and taking 34 lives. I am amazed that the Kansas City meteorologists didn't report more fully those disastrous storms, some within a few miles of Kansas City, but I apologize for my flippant comments yesterday. I do not erase them. That would be dishonest. When I prove myself to

334

be ignorant and insensitive, it is important that I fess up and willingly suffer the consequences of my ignorance and insensitivity, never to seek escape from them. They serve a necessary negative role in my total character and to my rational contribution to society.

Socrates, even though he had really done nothing evil, submitted to the consequences of his freely accepted subjugation to the Athenian democracy—drinking hemlock with a smile on his face. I am not being offered hemlock. I'll suffer nothing but a little embarrassment at being wrong in my assessment. How silly it would be to try to talk my way around my silliness—or to erase it. We must not erase what is our nature. Perhaps, we could hide it temporarily, but it will rise again to the surface. What then? Do we keep batting it down like we bat down the little gophers in the arcade machine? Not a good solution. No matter how many times we bat them down, they keep popping up—until we run out of coins to feed into the slot. Why waste our precious capital of reasoning upon such mundane employment as swatting ever-reappearing gophers. Forget the gophers. Leave the arcade to the children for whom it was intended. "Let us reason together." Let us clean and polish the dark glass through which we view reality so that we are less likely to see mountains as mole hills or ice storms as ice-water storms.

December 13: Thursday the 13th.

Whew! We missed the "bad-luck" day (Friday the 13th) by one weekday. But our luck won't last. Friday the 13th will surely arrive "as the night follows the day." I, like many others, are not particularly concerned about such myths. The key words here are "not particularly." I doubt that anyone who is reasonable and coherent can entirely escape these primitive feelings of unease in the presence of myth. It is easy to point to the greatest collection of these myths: religion. Most of us have some kind of religion which is literally stuffed with such unlikely stuff. But even those of us who do not ascribe to a particular religion, even hard-core atheists cannot avoid a certain "zero at the bone" when we unexpectedly encounter that "narrow fellow in the grass" who carries such a burden of negative myth upon his spine. And most of us, I think, are just a little nervous when we awake to find that it is Friday the 13th. The feeling goes away with the first spoonful of raison bran, but we cannot deny that it was there.

So, what do we do about it? Nothing at all! Why mess with natural inclinations which provide so much entertainment. Yasmin loves her monster movies even though she knows they have no material basis in anything. I have to admit that I enjoy watching a good old Boris Karloff flick. I see no harm in a little bit of supernatural or psycho fright. Where I draw the line is in fearing God. What a silly notion that is!

December 14: Suffer the Children to Come to Me.

"Suffer the little ones to come to me and forbid them not, for of such is the kingdom of Heaven."

Wise words from Jesus; perhaps, a bit naïve! It is obvious that he has never run a day-care center or taught a class of third graders. Heaven goes out of mind quite quickly and Hell comes rushing in. For those who didn't know, children can be little demons as well as little angels. Last evening, however, I caught a group of them at their best, and it was a good experience. I participated in a holiday season concert at a local elementary school.

My oldest granddaughter, a second grader, recruited me this fall to sing in her second and third grade intergenerational choir. The intergenerational part, I discovered, is a handful of elderly ladies and I who sing from the back row of the choir as *continuo* under the children's voices. The ladies' voices, of course, are not bass. Therefore, mine is the only voice available to add *basso-continuo* to the "Ho! Ho! Ho!s" of "Up on the Housetop." The ladies are better with the "Click! Click! Click!s." And the choir gains something, I think, from my round belly and white beard. They, also, have me play my classic guitar for "Silent Night." All in all, with Ho! Ho! Ho!s and arpeggiated G, D, and C chords, I had a busy evening though brief. Primary school choirs cannot sustain long holiday season concerts without the "Hell" beginning to leak out.

I have to thank my granddaughter for recruiting me. In doing so, she provided me the opportunity to be adored by not only my granddaughter but by the rest of the choir members and the intergenerational ladies as well. You have not seen love until you have seen it exuded from the eyes of a second grade girl or boy (red or yellow, black or white—and in this choir we have them all). I can't help loving them back. During the performance, many of them could not help casting furtive glances with smiles to match in my direction in the back row, not a happy situation for the director who was trying to keep them all on the same musical phrase, but delightful for me, smiling and winking back. And by one of the intergenerational ladies, I was even honored to be invited to entertain at the February meeting of her senior citizen's club. I accepted the invitation gracefully. I hope the winter weather cooperates. The seniors have regained, in their maturity, some of that "Heaven" that children have.

December 15: Half-Past December.

It is a Saturday near the halfway point of December. Snow is falling steadily. We have about two inches of the soft, fluffy stuff now. Probably, we won't get much more, but that is enough to make Yasmin jubilant. She loves nothing better than a clean white snowfall in the middle of December. The temperature is only 23 degrees F., so it won't melt for awhile. I suppose, if it stops later in the afternoon, I will have some shoveling to do in the morning. I make it a habit not to shovel until it stops falling. I'd just have to shovel it again tomorrow. Today, I will watch it fall. Snowfall must happen naturally. Try as they might, the computer techies have not found a way to make a screen-saver that matches a real big-flake snowfall. It is because of the nature of real snow flakes: no two are alike. Screen-savers depend upon repetition, and even if *one* flake were to be exactly like another, it would break the magic spell of the whole storm. Thus, no perfect big-flake snowstorm screen-saver!

There is, also, a unique magic in the 15th of December. It is a minor miracle, sort of like the Chanukah miracle with the oil—except better. The magic of the oil can be explained in non-miraculous ways (e.g., a sneaky rabbi and a hidden jug of impure oil). The magic of December 15th has no material explanation.

It is not a holy day. It has no particular official significance. It is not even, exactly, the middle of December. Yet, to those of us who are true nonsectarian romantics, it is a magic date, something like the beginning of the end of a year, a moment when we can be fairly certain that we will get to New Year. A life insurance company would, surely, not feel threatened by insuring me cheap for the next 16 days. They should consider it almost a sure bet. A day longer (including that dangerous New Year's Eve) would be a day too long and would make them nervous. It is magic, December 15th, and it only happens once a year, and when we are very lucky, on that one day a big-flake snowfall occurs with a magic of its own. If, in addition, you are lucky enough to be married to someone who still sticks his/her tongue out to catch snowflakes, you have triple magic today, and that is about as magic as you can get.

December 16: Graduation Pledge Alliance.
It's official! Starting February first, I will be building and maintaining the textual content of Bentley College's Graduation Pledge Alliance e-xplore.org website.

> I _____ pledge to explore and take into account the social and environmental consequences of any job I consider and will try to improve these aspects of any organizations for which I work.

I like this pledge. It looks like something that I could sign my name to. I have to admit that, had I signed it as soon as I graduated with a bachelor's degree, I probably would have broken it quite frequently between then and now. Still, my failure to do what I thought was right is no reason to quit trying to do what is right. From what I can see, the Alliance is expanding and strengthening through involvement with more and more colleges and universities nationwide. It will be my job to provide and discuss resources on the interactive e-xplore website for college graduates who take the pledge to do the "exploring" and "improving." The site is not yet posted except in a primitive form.

Between now and February first, I am committed to bringing myself up to speed as a knowledgeable leader in the Alliance so that I am ready to finish building the website, posting it on the web, and maintaining it in the most useful way (with the help of a website technician).

The whole thing makes me a little nervous, but it is just the thing for me. Every day now, I hear or read something else that convinces me that our world ecology is collapsing at a rate even faster than most scientists believe it to be. Just today, for instance, I read that a new discovery regarding global warming is that the seas will become more and more acidic as the process continues. Consider the potential death of many or all living things in the oceans of the world because they cannot adapt to that acidity—and what it will mean to human life. And last night, I watched on CNN two segments by Christiane Amanpour, one on radical Islam, one on fundamentalist Christianity. After those four hours of balanced reporting, I was thoroughly depressed. It seems impossible that these two worlds can come together in any sort of peaceful coexistence, and that is without yet counting significantly the other member of the triad of Western religion, the Jews. A particularly alarming statement, alarming because it seems true, arose from one interview (and I paraphrase for want of the exact words): "It is impossible for fundamentalists (Islamic or Christian) to change their minds because that would require them to proclaim that God has been mistaken." At present, the most fundamental, both Islamic and Christian, see the answer to the problem as either total enslavement or annihilation of all persons of the opposing viewpoint. Fortunately, that is not the current viewpoint of the majority of most of the world's populations. It does, however, seem to be the majority opinion in some politically and militarily powerful nations.

I hope that, through encouragement and services the Alliance provides, more persons will turn away from environmental irresponsibility, hatred, violence, greed, and vengeance—toward *peace on earth, good will toward its inhabitants.*

December 17: Something Old from #3 Daughter.

I found this in an old file that I thought I had lost. It was written by #3 daughter when she was in grade school. I can't reclaim my childhood, and neither can she, but this little poem is a snapshot of hers.

Going to School
On the way to my bus stop
all I can hear is the birds chirping,
and the slush under my feet.
The orange-ball of sunlight reflects
off the brown-muddy snow
which hasn't been melted by now.

As I sit down on a bench to take a breath
I take a big exhale
with clouds floating out of my mouth.

I hear the joyful cry of a friend
sending me a cheerful hello
with a kind wave of a hand.
As we chat in the silent air
we hear the screech of the Bus's tires
coming to a full stop.

We walk up the stairs
into the loudness of the happy children;
we sit down
and are on our way with the door slamming shut!

December 18: Goldilocks and Moderation.

Should we practice moderation in all things? It is tempting to say, "Yes!" but more rational to say, "No!" Let us use the story of "Goldilocks and the Three Bears" as a representative narrative. Goldilocks comes to the cottage of the three bears and enters without any sort of invitation. This could be considered immoderate "breaking and entering" although she, apparently, did not break anything in the process of entering which makes this the more modest crime of trespass. So far, so good!

But wait! She, immediately, begins her criminal saga, first, by tasting and eating the porridge. She, merely, tastes the porridge of Momma and Poppa Bear—a modest crime, though she should have washed the tasting spoons to prevent the spread of germs. Then, however, she commits obvious larceny by eating all of Baby Bear's porridge. Still, this is petty larceny. A moderate trespass. She then tries out the chairs. No harm done to Momma and Poppa. But Baby Bear's chair crumbles under Goldilocks's apparent obesity (perhaps, she has been tasting a lot of porridge lately). If Baby Bear's chair is valued highly, this could be major destruction of personal property. We must assume this to be the case since the bear family is obviously of a more advanced class (living in a house, eating porridge from bowls, sleeping in beds, etc.) than that of the average bear. No moderation here!

Finally, she causes havoc by trying out all of the beds (probably, leaving them in disarray) and falling asleep in Baby Bear's bed. The Bear family returns to find their domicile ransacked and the intruder sleeping. Before they have time to offer her a gift certificate for Holiday Inn, she leaps out through the window (probably causing more property damage to the window and the flower bed outside) and leaving the scene of the crime (not a petty crime in certain situations).

So Goldie's record of moderation vs. excess is mixed. Let us analyze. First, Goldie goes into the woods alone—obviously, not a moderate action for a child. For the rest of us, this might represent, as it does for Hester in Hawthorne's *The Scarlet Letter* a challenge to the forces of evil. This is not moderation, but it is something all of us must do if we are to accomplish anything of value. Score one for excess.

Second, Goldie openly violates property rights. Some philosophers (e.g., Hobbes, Locke, Rousseau) would count this as one of the highest crimes. On the other hand, philosophers of the socialist ilk (e.g., Marx), have little respect for property. Hmm! How is this resolved? My father always left the doors of our house unlocked when we went out so that, if a hobo came by, he or she could go inside without the necessity of breaking a lock. Dad said that he, also, would expect the hobo to eat anything in the house that he was hungry for and feel free to listen to the radio or even sleep in one of the beds if we were not returning for the night. After all, Dad (an unpaid Christian minister and a farmer of limited financial means) concluded that all of this wealth he had acquired still belonged entirely to God. On the surface, Christianity seems a lot like socialism and, perhaps, that's how Jesus intended it; but it takes only slight association with most Christians to discover that, in terms of property rights, they are not socialists. I once went through a Christian lady's living room window while she was out so I could borrow a book she had offered to loan me. I thought nothing of the unauthorized entry since she seemed, in church, like such a charitable soul. However, when she discovered what I had done, she was ready to call the full force of the law down upon me, and would have if it had not been for the intercession of my father who was pastor of her church. I guess we have to be pretty moderate about property rights, but I still have a lot of sympathy for my father's point of view.

Finally, Goldie's retreat without even saying goodbye is the most audacious of her crimes, the least moderate. At the very least, she could have complimented Momma on the taste of the porridge. But Goldie was afraid. Fear or, rather, inappropriate response to fear is one of the greatest causes of evil. If Goldie is the smart girl that I suspect she is, she knew the danger involved in abusing the hospitality of bears. They are strong, and they have been known to rip humans limb from limb. Thus, good sense would have told her to raid the home of rabbits or domestic cows, beings less dangerous. Thus, her real crime was in not responding appropriately to her rational fear of bears. In this, she should have been more moderate.

December 19: The Real Estate Salesman.

I should explain what brought Goldilocks to my attention yesterday. It was the real estate agent who is helping us to buy a new home. Yes, indeed! After 28 years (less five which we spent in Hawaii) of living in Parkville, we are selling our present house and attempting to buy another house in cooperation with daughter #2, a house with old-folks quarters over the garage. But I won't go into that decision today.

Our real estate agent is the nearest human thing to a perpetual motion machine. Largely, this is a product of the cell phone that he carries with him. He not only answers it from 6 a.m. to 10 p.m., but responds to it professionally during those hours and more. He simply does not quit working until he has done everything that he can possible do during a day. I remember when I used to do that. I credit my much-diminished physical and neurological prowess to that lifestyle. I don't recommend it to anyone.

The real estate man and I (before my awakening) are examples of persons who do not exercise proper moderation. I realize, however, that proper moderation is not as simple as just quitting at 5 p.m. It is like the old military credo: "Decide which hill you are going to defend and defend it." That was, essentially, my wake-up call regarding moderation. I decided that, whenever something was asked of me which was not "my hill to defend," I would reply, "Not my department!" and go on my way. It works . . . usually. When my hill seems too big to defend, I subdivide and defend only a defensible segment of it. The rest I assume to be someone else's responsibility (or God's if he hasn't had the foresight to train up someone for its defense).

Goldilocks is an interesting study because she seems not to have sought out the hill she should defend. Certainly, snooping in the home of three bears, eating their porridge, breaking their chair, sleeping in their bed, cannot be her "department."

December 20: Eid Al-Adha

"ALLAH, GREATEST ALLAH, ACCEPT THIS WHICH IS ALREADY YOURS AS MY SACRIFICE!"

Eid Al-Adha: Festival of the Sacrifice. To the Muslim, this is one of the chief religious festivals. It takes place at the end of the Hajj (pilgrimage). Most important is the event which it celebrates: the story of the willingness of Abraham (Ibrihim) to slaughter his son Isma'il (Ishmael) at the behest of God. It seems simple enough to the devout Muslim. If God commands something, it must be done.

Here is the problem. How do we know for sure that God has commanded something? We know that the audible voice of God in our day seems to be missing. When we hear of someone who has been personally and vocally instructed by God, we have a name, indeed, several possible names for it, all of them having to do with insanity. Why then, are modern persons so quick to accept totally unverifiable accounts of God's audible conversations with ancient persons found in books of mythology of unverifiable origins or in books said, unverifiably, to have been written by prophets of God (who cannot be verified to be true prophets of God) as the pure and perfect word of God? I speak not just of Muslims but of persons of all faiths which depend upon such documents for their belief systems. Each of the three major Western faiths (Judaism, Christianity, and Islam) claim that God is unchangeable. Thus, if he spoke to the ancients, he must speak to the moderns.

Even more important is the fact that human beings of any era who feel that they are hearing the voice of God, cannot be sure that the voice they hear is that of God. Our finite minds are, simply, unable to separate revelation from fantasy. Nor could we, if Satan truly exists, reliably tell the voice of that being from the voice of God. And if the cosmos is populated by various angels and devils as Western religions report, how do we know, in this montage of possible spirit voices, which voice is God's? Certainly, we humans who have not been able to explore the cosmos in person beyond the moon of our little earth and the rest of the infinite cosmos only "through a glass darkly" cannot say with assurance that the anomalous voices in our heads are God speaking—and commanding. Persons, today, who murder their children (or anyone else) claiming that God commanded the murders must be confined in prisons or hospitals where they cannot present further threats to civilized society. Certainly, they should not be revered as prophets. Stories of ancients who murder or are willing to murder their offspring claiming that God commanded it must be read with some level of skepticism.

December 21: The First Day (Officially) of Winter.

Missouri has given us a frosty greeting at winter's official advent. We awoke to rain which changed to sleet and then to snow within a couple of hours, and we now have a two-inch blanket of pure white surrounding us on the weekend before Christmas.

Saturday, December 21, has been a banner day. On this day it snowed. On this day, we received word that Park University would buy our present house. On this day, Yasmin received a long letter and a package from her sister in Hawaii detailing a trip she and her husband along with their oldest son and daughter took to Japan wherein they visited the Temple of the Golden Pavilion. On this day we received confirmation that the owner (the bank that repossessed it from the previous owners) of the house we will buy has agreed to our offer and we will sign a contract to confirm that agreement on the day after Christmas. On this day, I spoke with the husband of daughter #2. They and their children are spending Christmas in Guatemala with his family. They will sign the contract and Fax it to the real estate agent. On this day, I ate saimen for lunch. On this day I awoke after a full night's sleep, surprising because my nasty cold has been keeping me awake at night. Last night I took a dose of Nyquil and slept like a baby. On this day, I am alive, and life is good.

Today has been an especially eventful day, but that is not the reason life is good. It is good for simple reasons. I can breathe in the fresh cold air of winter. I can move my arms and legs and walk in the snow. I can taste food (although my old taste buds and poor sense of smell have difficulty differentiating a chicken salad sandwich from a tuna salad sandwich). I can hear Yasmin's wind chimes and feel the wind. I can eat peanuts and drink chocolate. I can smell coffee brewing. I can see rocks cemented one upon another into a wall, all capped with snow.

And I can reason with my mind.

And I can imagine!

Life is good!

December 22: Another Siebert Poem.

We just got a card from Siebert Wilson and his wife. They're visiting their oldest son and his wife in Alabama where the boy works. They are all fine and eating well. He sent me this poem. I guess it's close enough to Christmas for a Christmas poem.

Grandpa's Christmas

It's Christmas time, says Grandpa Jones,
As sure as God drops hail stones;
I can smell it in my bones
And in my nose: it's Christmas.

All year long my den's been mine,
My workshop too, and that was fine;
I'm neck-deep now in auld lang syne:
Ten grandkids say, "it's Christmas."

They yell and scream and set my nerves
On edge; a whop's what they deserve
From Ma, but they don't get it;
She just grins and says,
"Aw, Gramps, relax! It's Christmas!"

That bowl yon ankle-biter broke
I carved myself from solid oak;
I'd like to take that brat and soak
His head—but, no: it's Christmas!

Yes, I can smell it, and it's rank,
The baby's diaper, dark and dank,
Molds on my desk-top; and its content
Shouts aloud, "It's Christmas!"

342

Deliver me from "Silent Night,"
And, holy cow, give me a mite
Of privacy before I shout,
"Be gone with merry Christmas!"

But, suddenly, it's mousey quiet;
All is calm; there's no more riot;
The kids in bed, their moms asleep,
Refrigerator humming.

From room to room, I wend my way;
Kids like angel sardines lie
In beds where moms and dads once stayed;
I smile: "Thank God for Christmas!"

December 23: The Value of the Subrational.

I speak here, not of the irrational but the subrational. The term, irrational, implies that which *cannot* be proven logically. The subrational, a term that I coined and use without authority, implies that which is assumed to be but has not been proven to be rational. Yet, a faith in the subrational is an important component of everyday existence.

At this moment, as I said above, I am involved in the sale of our present home and the purchase of another home with the additional confusing element that we will be co-owners of the newly acquired (not new) home with daughter #2 and her husband. This process is exceedingly complex for persons like us who have only the financial expertise to manage the day to day expenses of life. Thus, as we sell our house, the money from that sale, which does not exist as yet except as equity, is in part being promised as down payment for the house we will soon be living in. Another part is being promised as financing for finishing our loft over the garage in the soon-to-be-acquired house. After the down payment and the loft building, about two-thirds of the total new value (another subrational concept) of that house will be unpaid, and that liability will be managed by an unnamed finance company which will require insurance companies to guarantee that, should the whole lot of us leap off a bridge in total frustration, they will still receive their money. And the chain of subrationals goes on. I have a degree of faith in all of these things which, at present, are subrational. Thus, I move through the process guided by professional persons (real estate agents, bankers, etc.) who *seem* to know more about it than I do.

In addition, another special circumstance, Park University has indicated (though there is not yet a contract) that they will buy our Parkville house immediately after the holiday season. We have nothing in writing regarding this informal agreement, yet I trust it, too, to become rational and dependable, not because of any legal binding, but because we are long-standing members of the Park family, and I trust its leaders not to, intentionally, do us harm. Some people would tell us we are fools to exhibit this trust in the entire enterprise; we are like Shakespeare's Lear, pulling down our trousers to be spanked; and this could well be true; but the image of two wrinkle-butted oldsters with pants down being spanked by younger folk with willow switches and frowns is ludicrous enough to give me a terrific belly laugh—a laugh long and sincere enough to be worth any losses I might sustain in this transaction. If we should lose all that we have in financial worth, we would not be losing much.

So much of life must be subrational in order to be lived well! So often we must trust in the weak arm of flesh to deal with all that is stronger than it (the arm) is!

December 24: A Christmas Eve Song.

A Western Farm Christmas
Silver frost makes a jewel of the farm;
The white moon makes it sparkle rare;
And the tree row shades the coming of dawn
On the eve of Christmas,
A western farm Christmas,
When Joy sings on crystal air.

Happy is the year that ends with Christmas
Spread in a feast back on the farm;
I would spend all year in the harness
If it leads me through to that charm.

I can feel the sharp wind cutting through me,
Through my fancy Eastern clothes,
So I wrap up in ragged coats from Dad's tree,
And through the rocks and sagebrush I roam.

From a rocky knoll overlooking that place,
I see fields with corn that will grow;
But for now, all the ice has a grace
That only God and I can know.

See the kids, so excited to be
By a pine cut for Christmas from the hills;
Eyes that sparkle at the sights that they see;
Our whole family knows the joy that thrills.

Silver frost makes a jewel of the farm;
The white moon makes it sparkle rare
And the tree row shades the coming of dawn
On the eve of Christmas,
Many years ago at Christmas
When joy sang on crystal air.

December 25: Christmas.

It is Christmas day and, on this chief day of Christian celebration and endless commercialism, I present another of Siebert's innocent little songs, one that he wrote for children to sing in a Christmas pageant about a child born in a manger who grew up to make a profound difference in the world.

Take my Sins Away
Refrain:
> Jesus, born on a bed of hay,
> Take my sins away, Lord;
> I'll be a child like you if I may;
> Take my sins away.

On a day like this was Jesus born
In the cold, cold night just before the morn;
He was sent from God as Mary's son
So that our great struggle could be won.

Refrain

Yes, he's my good teacher and he's my good friend,
And I hope to live like him to the end;
If I follow him in every way
We'll be happy together every day.

Refrain

The very reason why I do
What Jesus wants me always to
Is that he loves me, and I love him, too;
Don't you know that we, also, love you?

Refrain

December 26: Zarathosht Diso (Death of Zoroastrian Zarathustra).

My first extensive contact with the name, Zarathustra, was not with the original Zoroastrian philosopher, but with Nietzsche's prophet of the *Ubermench* in *Also Sprach Zarathustra*. Since I owe a debt of gratitude to Nietzsche's portrayal (i.e., I remind myself of that crusty old prophet on mornings preceded by evenings wherein excessive gastronomical indulgence "hath murdered sleep"), it would be appropriate for me to provide a place here, on the anniversary of the original Zarathustra's death, to introduce you to the original and his contributions to philosophy and that is, largely, what it is, not religion, but philosophy.

I get a good feeling when I consider interpretations by students of Zarathustra's original philosophy. Zarathustra, according to Bahram Varza and other such students of *the Gatha* (a book of Zarathustra's hymns), was not a prophet, not a person with direct contact with God, but a philosopher dividing good (*sepanta minu*) from evil (*ankera minu*). The way to the good is through "good

345

reflection, good words, good deeds." The way to evil the opposite. Further, God, the creator of the cosmos has no need of human clergy or worshippers. Zarathustra condemned the building of houses of worship as idolatry along with all other forms of attempting to represent God in material form. Also, since there is no sectarianism involved in early Zoroastrianism, there is no evangelism. No one is pressured to believe as a Zoroastrian believes. Proponents of all religious beliefs are tolerated as long as they do not attempt to force their beliefs on or cause grief to others.

Truthfulness was one of the highest ideals. Along with truth come 1) equality of women with men, 2) cleanliness of water, land, air, and fire, 3) absence of slavery, 4) denunciation of laziness, 5) absence of clergy, houses of worship, and idolatry, and 6) denunciation of cruelty to animals.

The human spirit, according to Zarathustra, is immortal. The Good that persons do in this life elevates them to a better life in the world beyond (a world which is delineated sparingly).

Loyalty and faithfulness are the twin bases of Zarathustra's philosophy.

A study of modern Zoroastrianism reveals significant and important adjustments to Zarathustra's original philosophy. Those students who cleave to the original blame the clergy for this change. Original Zoroastrianism denied them both power and wealth in their spiritual vocation. They desired both. That changed the entire basis of the philosophy after Zarathustra's death (perhaps 1000 or more years before the birth of Jesus).

December 27: Benazir Bhutto: She Has Been Martyred!

I awoke this morning to the news that Benazir Bhutto, a "once and future" political leader of Pakistan was assassinated. I wept at the news, and I weep now at the thought of it. It is not that Bhutto was a perfect person. She failed more than once in attempting to lead Pakistan to democracy and an open humane society. It is that she was willing to sacrifice her life (apparently, the last member of her family line likely to have such an opportunity) in another attempt. And now she is dead. Who is left to lift up the banner of hope for the Pakistani people? *Oh, Pakistan! Oh, Humanity!*

December 28: In Answer to Calamity, a Jubilant Song.

I said once that when truth overcomes rational thought, poetry can partially bridge the chasm between truth and our expression of it. Here at the end of this tome, I sense the need, as you might have already noted, for positive poetic expression.

Bells Hailed My Heart
Bells hailed my heart:
They were singing out wild songs of passion—
A child in a manger and love in my soul;
Bells hailed my heart
With a soft dulcet melody playing
A life that will always be whole.

346

I rambled through cities of life and I heard
Clamoring discordant notes strike the ground.
I thought there could never be peace in that land
'Til I heard a jubilant sound.

Bells hailed my heart:
They were singing out wild songs of passion—
A small infant stranger and joy in my soul;
Bells hailed my heart
With a soft dulcet melody playing
A peace that will always be whole.

I roamed through the deserts of unwatered passions
And heard not a sound but the moan of the sad.
Silence hung heavy—great mountains of sorrow—
Till heavenly songs made me glad.

Bells hailed my heart:
They were singing out wild songs of passion—
Of hope for tomorrow, of light for us all;
Bells hailed my heart
With a soft dulcet melody playing
A love that will always be whole.

Tenderly, tenderly, rising and falling;
Joyfully, joyfully, singing their song;
Chapel bells ring out the joy ever after
And drive out the shadows of wrong.

Bells hailed my heart:
They were singing out wild songs of passion—
Of tender young children and love in my soul
Bells hailed my heart
With a soft dulcet melody playing
A life that will always be whole.

And may we, all of humanity, continue to believe in the eventuality of peace on earth, good will toward all persons.

December 29: Kwanzaa.

One of our newest celebrations in America is Kwanzaa. It starts on December 26 and ends on New Year's Eve. African Americans deserve a celebration of their own. They and their ancestors, for hundreds of years, have experienced a hard, uphill climb from defeated members of African tribes to slaves on Southern plantations to residents of America's poorest ghettos, and now, to the possibility that one who is black could become the President of the United States a little over a year from now. I have not decided whether I will or will not vote for him; my vote will have nothing to do with his race; but, if Obama is elected in 2008, I will celebrate with him, with America, and for the triumph of the African American community. This year's Kwanzaa celebration is especially positive because of the hope that Obama's candidacy has inspired. Next year's celebration should be even brighter, whether or not he actually wins.

December 30: A Winter Love Song for Yasmin.

In Your Eyes
The gale through the trees
Will cradle stark winter branches in its arms.
We'll rest at our ease
Before the fire with its red charms.

The winter snows turn summer to dust
To sleep through icy blasts of storm;
But here safe and warm,
Love's flames dance heavenward in your eyes.

Our love's known them all—
It's seen the snow and the rain and summer sun.
We've made us a bower
Of ice and fire as our course is run.

The summer's heat could not melt our bond;
The dying fall has caused no sighs;
To us, cold is kind;
Loves flames dance heavenward in your eyes.

December 31: New Years Eve and a Final Anthem.

Now Comes Another Joyous Year
Now comes another joyous year
To do with as we will;
Before us lie the hopes and fears,
A promise to fulfill.

We do not ask for gaudy wealth
Nor painless hours each day;
Just for the common sense and health
To guide us on our way.

The year just past was full and free;
We've known the best of love—
We've cried, we've laughed, what jubilee
To make a season of!

God, grant us a tender touch
For every human soul,
That we may know each fragile heart
To make its spirit glow

Now comes another joyous year—
A promise to fulfill.

End of Volume 4
The Last Quarter Moon

* * * * * * * * * *

One final note: "There must be no war!—in our hearts, in our families, in our communities, in our nations, in our world."

* * * * * * * * * *

The End of
The True Book of Sam Clear Water
Wisdom from Walden-San

Made in the USA
Coppell, TX
20 April 2022